The
Analysis of Behavior
in
Planning
Instruction

James G. Holland · Carol Solomon · Judith Doran · Daniel A. Frezza
University of Pittsburgh, Learning Research and Development Center

The
Analysis of Behavior
in
Planning
Instruction

Addison-Wesley Publishing Company

Reading, Massachusetts
Menlo Park, California · London · Amsterdam · Don Mills, Ontario · Sydney

LB
1570
A63

Copyright © 1976 by Addison-Wesley Publishing Company, Inc. Philippines copyright 1976 by Addison-Wesley Publishing Company, Inc.

All rights reserved. No part of this publication may be reproduced, stored in a retrieval system, or transmitted, in any form or by any means, electronic, mechanical, photocopying, recording, or otherwise, without the prior written permission of the publisher. Printed in the United States of America. Published simultaneously in Canada. Library of Congress Catalog Card No. 75-28722.

ISBN 0-201-02912-X
ABCDEFGHIJ-HA-79876

Preface

Skinner has compared the creative act of writing a poem with that of a hen laying an egg (see *Saturday Review,* 15 July 1972). His point is that behavior, whether traditionally considered noble or ignoble, is the result of environmental and biological variables. In this sense, the author of a poem or a book has originated nothing. Authoring a manuscript is like "having" a baby. The author, like the mother, is the place where a process occurs. This implication of Skinner's radical behaviorism is shocking because it rejects the basis for blaming or giving credit to individuals. The hen's egg is neither good nor bad; it is simply a result.

The experimental analysis of behavior provides the means for using the basic behavioral processes to shape desired outcomes, such as better teaching, improved skills in reading or math, and even the increased production of creative works. This book is designed to expose would-be curriculum developers to a set of experiences that will result in their "having" better curricula.

Although we have followed the tradition of listing authors, the text is the result of a process, and only a small part of the contributing history is known to us. Very early precursors to this work were the intensive workshops on programmed instruction taught by the first author when directing the staff of the *Harvard Committee on Programmed Instruction.* This organization cooperated with Harvard faculty members in developing curriculum materials for their areas of expertise. The special workshops were attended by professional people, principally college faculty members from Harvard and elsewhere, committed to using the new technology to improve education in their field. Although there is little actual direct overlap of the present book with the original workshops, contact with workshop participants, discussions with my colleague William Holz, and exposure to the materials written in the workshops all influenced the developing embryo that became this book. A particularly significant early contribution occurred in the summer of 1965 when the first author was asked by Professor Norman Balabanian to instruct a three-week institute for professors of engineering who were to spend part of the following year programming course material in that subject.

Shortly after, Holland and Doran, and later the other authors, became involved in the work of the University of Pittsburgh's Learning Research and Development Center. Here the individualizing aspects of the new educational technology were emphasized in the work of Robert Glaser, Mauritz Lindvall, and others. The exposure to interesting and innovative curriculum materials developed at the Center shaped our general research project and greatly influenced this book.

At this time Jackie Liebergott made a critical input to the text. She and the first author developed a set of pre-reading curriculum materials and assembled from available programs a full set of curriculum materials for use in a community-based learning center. Jackie's insightful analyses of widely divergent materials had an important impact on this book. Later, as a faculty member of Emerson College, she and her colleague Susanne Swope provided valuable data in a field-test of an earlier version of this text.

This basic material went through several versions before assuming its present shape. Jane Hayes (then Jane Reynolds) helped extensively in the preparation and organization of these earlier versions. Each version was revised based on student input. This "final" version has, in many senses, been "written" by these students. Christine Frezza, Dennis Hanko, Carolyn Peel, and Kathy Pikula provided the technical help vital to the production of the final manuscript. Pam Meadowcroft and Debbie Cochrane produced the index.

Midwife at the birth of this book was the National Institute of Education, which made possible the several evaluations and revisions through a grant (No. OEG0711176) ably directed and administered by John Yeager, Glenn Heathers, and John Ebner. But although NIE made the book-birth painless and our many colleagues and students made the process interesting, the reader is reminded that the product is the result of our own folly.

Pittsburgh, Pennsylvania   J.G.H.
February 1976

Contents

Introduction

WHAT THIS BOOK IS ABOUT

Our objective is to present methods of designing and evaluating effective curriculum materials—*not* to set forth any particular model of curriculum design. While a specific instructional model may be useful in teaching one kind of skill or a particular subject-matter area, designers who have learned simply to follow that model will have limited success in developing materials outside the model's domain.

The authors believe that specific instructional models are merely particular codifications of underlying learning principles, principles exemplified in the analysis of operant behavior. Since curriculum design is a practical application of the science of behavior, designers who learn the fundamentals of the science will be better able to create effective curriculum materials for a wide range of learning tasks. Therefore, basic learning principles are emphasized in the text.

However, this emphasis does not mean that details of curriculum design are ignored. Indeed, experience with a variety of real lesson materials in a variety of contexts is necessary for designers to abstract useful principles. More than fifteen widely different teaching "programs" are described or sampled in this book, including a poet's description of teaching poetry writing to grade-school children, an early nineteenth-century doctor's attempts to teach a feral child, and numerous, more conventional lesson materials on subjects ranging from handwriting to music theory.

The book is organized into six parts. Behavior Theory and the Technology of Teaching (five units) provides a general overview of behavior theory and illustrates its application with some of the original writings on programmed instruction, Individually Prescribed Instruction, Keller's personalized system of instruction, and contingency management. This overview introduces the critical principles reflected in all good curriculum materials and provides a rationale for looking at basic learning principles in detail.

1

The second major part, Behavior Theory in Practice (five units), teaches the fundamental principles of the experimental analysis of behavior. For these units, students select a supplemental text such as *The Analysis of Behavior* by Holland and Skinner, *Behavior Principles* by Ferster, Culbertson, and Perrott Boren, *Elementary Principles of Behavior* by Whaley and Malott, or *A Primer of Operant Conditioning* by Reynolds. (More information on each of these texts is presented later in this introduction.) Each unit directs the student to certain readings on the basic principles in the selected supplemental text and illustrates an educational application of those principles.

Preparation for Teaching: Analysis of the To-Be-Learned Behavior (seven units) focuses on writing behavioral objectives, analyzing a subject matter, and devising appropriate instructional strategies and learning hierarchies. Each of these tasks is based on the behavior-theory principles presented in Parts I and II.

In the last unit of Part III, students begin work on their curriculum design projects. Since one goal of this course of studies is to equip students to write effective instructional materials, three production or project units occur at particular points in the course (Units 17, 24, 29). In Unit 17 students are asked to select a topic they feel capable of teaching and to devise behavioral objectives and an appropriate instructional strategy. In later units students will be asked to write the instructional material and, if possible, submit it to a tryout.

Part IV, Teaching—Selecting and Writing Instructional Materials, consists of Units 18–26. In these units, students learn methods of evaluating lessons, practice evaluating a wide range of instructional materials, and write instructional materials for their curriculum project.

The fifth part (Units 27–29) is concerned with the uses of tests in developing instructional materials. Students learn methods of evaluating the testing used in materials that adapt to individual differences in the learner's entering knowledge of the subject matter. They also examine the tryout and revision cycle, used to develop effective instructional materials, and are asked to submit their own instructional materials to this kind of evaluative testing.

Part VI, People to People, presents examples of behavior analysis in relatively open instructional situations. Both articles describe teachers who devise instructional strategies on the spot to achieve their goals.

This book is designed to be self-instructional. In most units, after students read the source material (usually either an article or a lesson sample) and answer related questions, they can then check their answers with the answer key at the back of the book. When the text is used by an instructor as the basis for a college or graduate course, we suggest that students review each unit's work in a personal interview in addition to using the answer key. Students evaluate their own work in the project units, having previously developed the pertinent critical skills.

WHO MIGHT USE THIS BOOK?

The present course material is reasonably ambitious and has been used by professionals actually engaged in applying behavioral principles to curriculum writing. On the other hand, stringent prerequisites are not assumed—students need not have specialized in psychology or educational research to find this book useful. The reading and intellectual abilities one can expect of an advanced undergraduate are sufficient for successful use of this text in a college course.

Students who work through the units in the suggested manner will learn to:

1. describe the principles derived from the experimental analysis of behavior;
2. state learning tasks in behavioral terms;
3. describe the extent to which instructional materials reflect the principles of the science;
4. design and produce curriculum materials that achieve a given learning task and are in accord with scientific principles.

Thus, the book speaks directly to the needs of people attempting to write educational or training materials and to those who are responsible for selecting educational materials. Its format facilitates its use as a self-instructional text by interested professionals, including university faculty members, industrial-training-division staff members, writers on curriculum-development projects, school administrators, classroom teachers, and educational policymakers.

HOW TO USE THIS BOOK

The text may be used in a number of ways: as the basis for an individualized college or graduate course in curriculum design, by an interested professional working alone, or by a cooperative training group without a designated instructor. When the book is selected for a regular course, the teacher may add specific instructions on its use. However, the text is basically self-instructional and the following directions are pertinent to every application.

Each unit begins with an introduction in which the unit's source materials, instructions, and objectives are described. The objectives should be used to direct the reading of the unit's source material. A set of questions follows the source material. *Each question should be answered completely and in writing.* Then, the answers may be checked against the answer key at the back of the book.

Although the units are of unequal length, average unit completion time for graduate students is three hours, with some units requiring as little as one and one-half hours and others as much as five hours. We recommend that the units be done in the numbered sequence since later units involve skills and knowledge established in earlier units. Skipping units or doing them out of sequence will cause particular difficulty in Parts II and III. After Unit 19 the order is less critical. An instructor may wish to have students apply their new skills on analysis of some different curriculum materials and, therefore, may choose to make a few substitutions in Part IV.

While skipping units is not recommended, you may, if you wish, attempt to answer the unit questions before working through the source material. If your answers are satisfactory, you may go on to the next unit. However, we have some reason to expect that working through the source material is necessary for developing the skills requisite to answer unit questions adequately. While diagnosing student needs through pretests in order to prescribe only the necessary instructional materials is an important feature of many new curriculum materials, such an approach is not suitable for all objectives. In Unit 27 you will learn methods of evaluating the adaptive features of such curricula and some ways of estimating the useful parameters of adapting. Suffice it to say that, in the authors' experience, unit pretests for this course material simply waste student time.

Using the Answer Key

It is very important that you completely formulate an answer to each question before referring to the answer key. Since answers are usually fairly extensive, writing each one is a time-consuming process. The temptation to skip this vital step may be especially strong when the answer to a question appears to be very simple or very difficult. However, those who skip or skimp on writing an answer may not develop a high level of skill in curriculum production or discrimination.

The answer key for a few units consists of several student answers with critical comments. To evaluate your work in those units, you should select the answer most like your own and read the relevant comments carefully.

However, the answer key for most units does not represent a typical student answer; rather, it represents the most complete answer. Although students have produced answers as complete as those in the answer key, a typical passable answer covers the main points in somewhat less specific or less technical terms. In general, as you progress through the course, your answers should more and more closely resemble those in the answer key. But while you may allow yourself somewhat more latitude at the beginning of your work, you should never be satisfied with extremely brief, general, vague, or nontechnical answers when the answer key indicates that something more was called for.

If you decide that your answers to some questions in a particular unit are not acceptable, do *not* go on to the next unit. Your ability to do the work called for in later units often depends directly on your successful completion of earlier units. If you decide that you need further work in a unit, take a break of at least half an hour. Then go back to the unit objectives and the source material. Reread the source material carefully, use the objectives to guide your reading, and take notes if necessary. Then answer the problem questions again and recheck your responses.

Evaluating Your Own Lesson Materials

At three points in the book you are asked to practice certain curriculum-development skills. In your selected subject area, you will do a task analysis, derive behavioral objectives, and produce and test lesson materials. You will have learned and practiced relevant methods of evaluation in earlier units. However, since it is frequently difficult to be entirely objective about one's own work, it may prove very helpful to discuss your curriculum materials with your peers or instructor, if possible.

Selecting a Supplementary Text

We believe the developer's ability to design effective lessons creatively and flexibly depends to a large extent on an understanding of basic learning principles. Part II is devoted to developing an ability to articulate these learning principles and to recognize their application to curriculum design. Each unit in that section will direct you to readings in a supplemental text. Therefore, you must select *one* of the following four supplemental texts to complete your work in this book.

1. J. G. Holland and B. F. Skinner. *The Analysis of Behavior.* New York: McGraw-Hill, 1961. The unit questions and readings were originally based on this text: the other books were later keyed to the units. *The Analysis of Behavior,* a programmed text, is highly recommended, especially for persons working on their own. No psychology background is necessary. The book emphasizes basic principles and includes detailed examples from everyday life.

2. C. B. Ferster, S. Culbertson, and M. C. Perrott Boren. *Behavior Principles.* Englewood Cliffs, N.J.: Prentice-Hall, 1975; or the 1968 edition published by Appleton-Century-Crofts. This text has a more conventional format than *The Analysis of Behavior,* with chapters followed by "interview" questions. Students working independently should be sure to write answers to these interview questions and then check them by referring back to the text itself. Again, no psychology background is presumed. The concepts of the science are explored in some detail, with ample illustration of the basic principles involved. This book offers a finely detailed analysis of complex human interactions. For the purposes of answering unit questions, the coverage is as complete as Holland-Skinner.

3. D. L. Whaley and R. W. Malott. *Elementary Principles of Behavior.* Englewood Cliffs, N.J.: Prentice-Hall, 1971. This introductory text heavily emphasizes behavior modification. Many detailed, descriptive examples illustrate the basic concepts of the science. Each chapter concludes with questions to which students should write answers. Those using this text will have some difficulty with a few Unit 9 questions that deal with an important concept termed continuous repertoire; otherwise, the coverage is satisfactory.

4. G. S. Reynolds. *A Primer of Operant Conditioning.* Glenview, Ill.: Scott, Foresman, 1975 or 1968. This is a very concise presentation of the basic principles —few descriptive examples or illustrations are provided. It is recommended for students who have some background in psychology and need only a brief review of operant principles. Since chapter questions are not included, a written summary of each chapter is a recommended study aid. Again, coverage is not complete for the concept of continuous repertoire, but students using this text should be equipped to answer all other questions.

A NOTE ON DEVELOPMENT

This book has been through three cycles of test and revision. Results of the tryouts, described below, suggest that undergraduates can best use the material with regular interviewing by an instructor or monitor (after each unit, if possible). Graduate students and professional curriculum writers will, of course, also benefit from regular interviewing with personal feedback. However, as they usually have the skills needed to make effective use of the answer key, interviewing immediately after every unit is not critical. Tryouts have also revealed that completion time varies greatly among individuals. Some students have completed the course in six weeks while others have taken two college semesters. Generally, students who are already familiar with some aspect of the material covered in this course (i.e., operant psychology, or curriculum development) are easily able to complete the course in brief, intensive sessions of six to eight weeks. However, students who are approaching this content for the first time probably require a full semester, that is, eighteen weeks.

The material was first used by a group of ten special students under the developer's direction in an intensive six-week institute. All of these students were concurrently employed in positions involving curriculum-development responsibility. A revision of the material was undertaken based on the data derived from this first trial use. There were three sources of data for this first revision: students' responses to unit questions, student-produced curriculum materials, and pretest-posttest results.

At the completion of the course, student answers to all unit questions were evaluated by two people. Answers were judged as "good," "satisfactory," or "unsatisfactory." When a large percentage of answers to a question was unsatisfactory, the question was revised. This detailed feedback pinpointed ambiguous items, mistaken assumptions regarding the students' previous knowledge, and other sources of student confusion and error.

Curriculum materials produced by the students, the second source of data, were highly imaginative and revealed a grasp of basic principles and an ability to implement them. Materials produced in the course by two of the trainees were later used at workshops for elementary teachers conducted by the Pennsylvania Department of Education.

The third source of data was identical pretest-posttest essay questions designed to test the students' ability to articulate basic learning principles and to evaluate and produce materials. Students averaged 53 percent (range 5–79%) on the pretest and 83 percent (range 71–90%) on the posttest. (This test is available in the Teacher's Manual.)

The revised text was then used as the basis for a graduate course in curriculum design in the Educational Psychology Department of the University of Pittsburgh. Sixteen students participated. Again, pretest-posttest differences, individual answers, and student-produced curriculum materials were evaluated. There was a sizable pretest-posttest gain. In addition, student attitudes, as measured by a questionnaire administered at the end of the course, indicated that they had increased their competence, had little trouble with the units, and enjoyed the course.

The text was again revised in preparation for an undergraduate tryout at Emerson College in Boston during a brief interim term. Enrollment was much larger than expected (forty-six) and time was limited, so the instructors omitted the three project units and did not regularly interview students to provide critical monitoring and feedback. In this tryout, the median pretest score was only 6 percent, and the posttest median was 52 percent. Although the gain is sizable, we would expect better undergraduate performance with a full semester and with regular interviews. This relatively severe test was particularly useful in guiding the authors through an extensive revision to simplify the course and to eliminate troublesome areas. This book comprises the final revised version.

SUMMARY

The aim of this text is to prepare learners to be authors of curriculum materials. Hence the book attempts to establish all of the technical skills required for writing curriculum materials, to acquaint students with the scientific base necessary for preparing materials that utilize the best of learning and testing principles, to train them in identifying the degree to which materials reflect such principles, and to have them begin to produce some material illustrating these principles. It is beyond the scope of this book to teach English composition or writing skills other than the technical aspects of learning technology. It is also beyond the scope to consider what should be taught in particular subject matters. But given basic writing skills and a set of curriculum objectives, the individual who completes the units as directed should be able to generate curriculum materials that reflect the best in the technology of education.

PART
I

Behavior Theory and the Technology of Teaching: An Overview

Psychologists, working in learning laboratories, have isolated various basic principles of behavior, and many of the instructional materials developed in the past twenty years have been directly influenced by their findings. These first five units introduce basic behavior principles in terms of their application in recent educational technology.

UNIT

1

Basic Principles
of Behavior Control

Content

Holland, J. G. "Teaching Machines: An Application of Principles from the Laboratory." *Journal of the Experimental Analysis of Behavior* 3 (1960): 275–287.

This unit describes the basic principles of behavior control and their application in developing programs for teaching.

Objectives

Students will list the important learning principles and describe an application for each. They will also discuss the effects of active responding in learning, and of a high error rate on a student's behavior. Finally, they will outline the techniques of behavior control used in teaching a complex skill.

Instructions

1. Read the objectives for this unit and use them to guide your reading of the article.
2. Read the article.
3. Write down the answers to the questions following the article, referring back to the reading as necessary.
4. Check your answers with the suggested answers at the back of the book. *Never* look at the suggested answers for any unit before you have completely formu-

lated your own answer to each question. (For the rationale for this procedure, see the introduction and your answer to question 2 of this unit.)

5. Discuss your work in this unit with your instructor (or in your learning group) before beginning work on the next unit.

Teaching Machines: An Application of Principles from the Laboratory

James G. Holland

Much has been said of teaching machines recently—but the emphasis has tended to be on the gadgets rather than on the much more significant development of a new technology of education by B. F. Skinner (1954, 1958). The technology does use a device called a teaching machine, which presents a finely graded series of problems and provides immediate "reward" or reinforcement for the student's correct answers. But emphasis on machines has tended to obscure the more important facets of the new technology based on application of principles from the laboratory. The machines of today are not necessarily better than those of yesterday. Indeed, adequate machines could have been built hundreds of years ago. The movement today is not simply the mechanization of teaching, but instead the development of a new technology—a behavioral engineering of teaching procedures.

The history of unsuccessful teaching machines illustrates the relatively greater importance of the technique as opposed to the gadgets. The first teaching machine was patented 93 years ago. There have since been a series of patents and a promising burst of activity initiated by Sidney Pressey (1926) in the 1920's. None of these early efforts really caught hold. But during this period in which the idea of mechanized teaching has been latent, the science of behavior has developed principles which permit extremely precise control of behavior. This new technology is not only the so-called automation of teaching, but is an attempt to obtain the kind of behavioral control shown possible in the laboratory.

We have, of course, seen other practical applications of scientific psychology. We are all familiar with the development of a technology of testing, which permits placing an individual in situations suited to his abilities. We are also familiar with another technology called human engineering, which fits machines and jobs to the capacities of man. One places a man in a job that suits him; the other alters the job to suit the man; *neither* attempts to alter or control man's behavior.

For years in the laboratory we have controlled the behavior of experimental subjects—both animal and human—by a widening array of principles and techniques. The new technology of education is the application of behavioral laws in

James G. Holland, "Teaching Machines: An Application of Principles from the Laboratory," *Journal of the Experimental Analysis of Behavior* 3 (1960): 275–287. Copyright © 1960 by the Society for the Experimental Analysis of Behavior, Inc. Reprinted by permission.

modifying or controlling behavior. Such a technology became possible with the realization that we are actually referring to a verbal repertoire (Skinner, 1957) controlled by the same laws as other behavior. The old, defunct explanatory concepts of knowledge, meaning, mind, or symbolic processes have never offered the possibility of manipulation or control; but behavior, verbal or otherwise, can be controlled with ease and precision.

While machines are not the essential or defining aspect of this technology, they do play an important role in providing some of this fine control the technology requires. We will now examine several machines and notice the advantages they offer.

At Harvard there is a self-instruction room with ten booths, each containing a machine. . . . The student gets one set of material from the attendant and places it in the machine. He closes the machine and begins his studies.

This machine presents one item of material at a time. The subject reads the statement, which has one or more words missing, and he completes it by writing in the answer space. He then raises the lever and a small shutter opens, revealing the correct answer. Simultaneously, his answer is moved under glass, where it can be read and compared with the now-exposed correct answer. After comparing his answer with the correct answer, the student indicates to the machine, with an appropriate movement of the lever, whether his answer was correct or incorrect, and the next item appears in the window. He repeats all items answered wrong after he completes the set of items. He does not repeat correctly answered items.

A critical feature of the machine is that it provides immediate reinforcement for correct answers. Being correct is known to be a reinforcer for humans. In machine teaching, reinforcement is immediate. We know from laboratory work (Perin, 1943) that a delay between a response and its reinforcement of a few seconds will greatly reduce the effectiveness of the reinforcement. Adult human subjects can sustain at least small delays; nevertheless, any delay makes reinforcement less effective.

Although other techniques such as programmed workbooks (Homme & Glaser, 1959) and flashcards are sometimes used in this new behavioral technology, they offer less control. Teaching machines eliminate undesirable forms of responses which would also be successful in obtaining the right answer. For example, the teaching machine insures that the student answers before peeking at the indicated answer. There is a strong temptation to glance ahead with only a poorly formulated, unwritten answer when programmed workbooks or flashcards are used.

This write-in machine is a prototype of the most common machine. There is another machine used for teaching young children material which consistently has a single possible answer. In the machine the constructed answer is automatically compared with the true answer. The child is presented a problem, perhaps a statement such as $2 + 2 = $ ___, and he must provide the 4. By moving a slider appropriately, he can insert the 4 into the answer space. He then turns the crank, and the next item appears immediately, so that immediate reinforcement is provided.

Both of the machines we have [discussed] thus far require the student to compose the answer. Figure 1.1 shows a machine for a less mature organism who cannot yet compose an answer. This machine can be used for teaching preschool children.[1] There is a large top window and three small windows. In the large window, there is some sort of problem; and in the three smaller windows, there are three alternative choices. For example, in the machine as seen in the picture, the subject chooses one of the three alternatives which has the same form as the sample, independent, in this case, of color or size. When the correct choice is made, the next frame is presented.

A teaching machine for a still lower organism is shown in Fig. 1.2. This pigeon, with the aid of a teaching machine, has learned to hit the name plaque appropriate for a color projected above him. The principal difference between this and the other machines is that food reinforcement is used. With humans, simply being correct is sufficient reinforcement—pigeons will not work for such meager gains.

Enough of machines. They should not be allowed to obscure the truly important feature of the new technology, namely, the application of methods for behavioral control in developing programs for teaching. We need to say no more about

Fig. 1.1. Child working on the preverbal machine. In the upper rectangular window is a sample which is to be matched with a figure in one of the three lower windows. If the child presses the correct lower window, the material advances to the next frame. In this case, the match is in terms of form, with size and color irrelevant.

[1] Hively, W. An exploratory investigation of an apparatus for studying and teaching visual discrimination using preschool children. (In preparation.)

Fig. 1.2. A pigeon "naming colors." The pigeon pecks the color name corresponding to the color of the light projected above him.

the well-known principle of immediate reinforcement. Our second principle is also well known. Behavior is learned only when it is *emitted* and reinforced. But in the classroom, the student performs very little, verbally. However, while working with a machine, the student necessarily emits appropriate behavior, and this behavior is usually reinforced because the material is so designed that the student is usually correct. Not only is reinforcement needed for learning, but a high density of correct items is necessary because material which generates errors is punishing. Laboratory experiments (Azrin, 1956) have shown that punishment lowers the rate of the punished behavior. In our experience with teaching machines, we have also observed that students stop work when the material is so difficult that they make many errors. Furthermore, they become irritated, almost aggressive, when errors are made.

The third important principle is that of gradual progression to establish complex repertoires. A visitor once asked if Skinner had realized that pigeons were so smart before he began using them as subjects. The answer given by a helpful graduate student was that they weren't so smart before Skinner began using them. And indeed they weren't. The behavior developed in many experiments is like that developed in the classroom. Both are complex operants. Both require a careful program of gradual progression. We cannot wait for a student to describe the content of a psychology course before reinforcing the performance; nor can we wait for a pigeon to emit such an improbable bit of behavior as turning a circle, facing a disk on the wall, pecking it if lit, and then bending down to a now-exposed food tray and eating. When developing a complex performance in a pigeon, we may first reinforce simply the behavior of approaching the food tray when it is presented with a loud click. Later, the pigeon learns to peck a key which produces the click and the food tray. Still later, he may learn to peck this key only when it is lit, the peck being followed by the loud click and approach to the food tray. In the next step, he may learn to raise his head or hop from one foot to another, or walk a figure eight, in order to produce the lighted key which he then pecks; the click follows, and he approaches the food tray. This principle of gradual progression runs through many of the teaching-machine techniques. Both human and avian scholars deserve the same careful tutorage. The teaching-machine program moves in very finely graded steps, working from simple to an ever-higher level of complexity. Such a gradual development is illustrated in Table 1.1 by a few items taken from a psychology program.[2]

The principle of gradual progression serves not simply to make the student correct as often as possible, but it is also the fastest way to develop a complex repertoire. In fact, a new complex operant may never appear except through separately reinforcing members of a graded series (Keller and Schoenfeld, 1950). Only this way can we quickly create a *new pattern* of behavior. The pigeon would not have learned the complex sequence necessary to receive the food if it had not learned each step in its proper order. Obviously, a child can't begin with advanced mathematics, but neither can he begin with $2 + 2 = 4$—even this is too complex and requires a gradual progression.

Our fourth principle is, in a sense, another form of gradual progression—one which involves the gradual withdrawal of stimulus support. This we shall call fading. This method will be illustrated with some neuroanatomy material.[3] A fully labelled cross section of the medulla oblongata is placed before the student while he works with a large set of items pertaining to the spatial arrangement of the various structures. For example, "posterior to the cuneate nuclei are the _____." The answer is: "the cuneate fasciluli." After many such items, he begins another set and has another picture but now the structures before him are labelled only with initials. A new set of items again asks a long series of questions pertaining to the spatial position of the various structures. For example, "between the gracile and the trigeminal nuclei are _____." The answer is the "cuneate nuclei." After many more items, he proceeds to a new set and the next picture. This time the picture is unlabelled. Again, he goes through a series of new items, not simple repetitions of the previous ones, but items pertaining to the same problem of the spatial location of the different structures. This set is followed by still another but with no picture at all. He is now able to discuss the spatial position of the structures without any visual representations of the structures before him. In a sense, he has his own private map of the medulla. He may further demonstrate his newly acquired ability by accurately

---

[2] This program, prepared by J. G. Holland and B. F. Skinner, is entitled *A self-tutoring introduction to a science of behavior.*

[3] This material has been prepared by D. M. Brethower in collaboration with the present author, and it is being used at Harvard for research purposes.

TABLE 1.1
Items from the psychology program (11). These items illustrate the gradual development of a new concept.

Item	Correct answer	Percentage of students giving the answer
1. Performing animals are sometimes trained with "rewards." The behavior of a hungry animal can be "rewarded" with _____ .	Food	96
2. A technical term for "reward" is reinforcement. To "reward" an organism with food is to _____ it with food.	Reinforce	100
3. *Technically* speaking, a thirsty organism can be _____ with water.	Reinforced	100
50. A school teacher is likely, whenever possible, to dismiss a class when her students are rowdy because she has been _____ by elimination of the stimuli arising from a rowdy class.	Reinforced	92
51. The teacher who dismisses a class when it is rowdy causes the frequency of future rowdy behavior to (1) _____ , since dismissal from class is probably a(n) (2) _____ for rowdy children.	(1) Increase (2) Reinforcement	86
54. If an airplane spotter never sees the kind of plane he is to spot, his frequency of scanning the sky (1) _____ . In other words his "looking" behavior is (2) _____ .	(1) Decreases (2) Extinguished (or: Not Reinforced)	94

drawing the medulla. The neuroanatomy example is an elaborate example of fading. Fading is also applied in a more simple form in constructing verbal programs without pictorial displays. A single item may in one sentence give a definition or a general law and in a second sentence in that same item, an example in which a key word is omitted. This would be followed by a new example in the next frame, but with the definition or law lacking.

This brings us to our fifth principle: control of the student's observing and echoic behavior. In the classroom the student is often treated as though he were some kind of passive receiver of information, who can sop up information spoken by the teacher, written on the blackboard, or presented by films. But all of these are effective only insofar as the student has some behavior with respect to the material. He must listen carefully, or read carefully, thus engaging in usually covert echoic behavior. Ineffectiveness of classroom techniques is often credited to "inattention" or poor "concentration." It has been shown (Reid, 1953; Wyckoff, 1952) that if a discrimination is to be learned, adequate observing behavior must first be established. We have further found that observing behavior, or speaking loosely, "attention," is subject to the same forms of control as other behavior (Holland, 1958). This control of observing behavior is of prime importance. When the student becomes very "inattentive" in the classroom, the teaching material flows on; but with a machine, he moves ahead only as he finishes an item. Lapses in active participation result in nothing more than the machine sitting idle until the student continues. There is, however, a more subtle aspect to the control of observing behavior than this obvious mechanical one. In many of the examples we have seen, success in answering the problem depends only on the student's careful observation of the material in front of him at the moment. This may be illustrated by more material from the psychology program. A graph showing stimulus-generalization data is in front of the student while he works on the machine. In the program he may complete a statement: "As the wave length changes in either direction from the wave length present during reinforcement, the number of responses _____." The answer is "decreases." The item serves only to control the behavior of observing the data. Of course, many more such items are used to discuss the same data.

This principle of controlled observation extends to the details of writing a single item. For example, "Two events may have a common effect. An operant reinforced with two reinforcers appropriate to different deprivations will vary with _____ deprivations." The answer is "two" or "both." Here, the programmer's choice of the omission serves to insure a careful reading of the item. *Only* those parts of an item which must be read to correctly complete a blank can safely be assumed to be learned.

Our sixth principle deals with discrimination training. In learning spoken languages, for example, it is necessary to be able to identify the speech sounds. A student may listen to a pair of words on a special phonograph which repeats the passage as many times as he desires. The visual write-in machine instructs him to listen to a specific passage. For example, the student may hear two words such as: "sit, set." He listens as many times as he needs and then writes the phonetic symbols in the write-in machine. He then operates the machine, thereby exposing the true answer and providing immediate reinforcement for his correct discrimination.

However, little academic education is *simple* discrimination. More often, it is abstraction or concept formation. An abstraction is a response to a single isolated property of a stimulus. Such a property cannot exist alone. Redness is an abstraction. Anything that is red has other properties as well—size, shape, position in space, to name a few. There are red balls, red cars, red walls. The term red applies

to all of them, but not to green balls, blue cars, or yellow walls. To establish an abstraction (Hovland, 1952, 1953), we must provide many examples. Each must have the common property, but among the various examples there must be a wide range of other properties. This is best illustrated by examples from the preverbal machine shown in Fig. 1.3.

These are from a program[4] which teaches a child to respond to the abstract property of form. In each item, the upper figure is the sample and the lower three are the alternatives. While developing a program for establishing an abstraction, we remember our earlier principles and move through a gradual progression. The first several items would be like the first one; here, there is a sample and a single match, the other two being blank. The sample and its match are exactly alike at this stage. After many such items, we would begin to have others like the next one, in which the sample and its match again correspond in size, color, and form—but an additional incorrect alternative has been added which differs from the sample in all these aspects. Later, we move on to frames with three choices; again, the

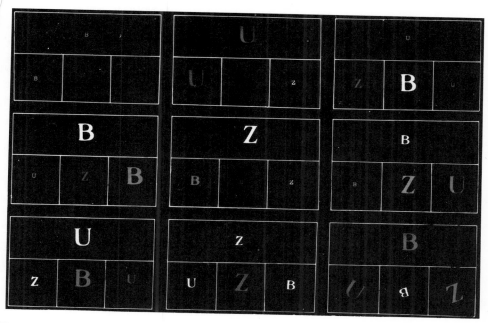

Fig. 1.3. Selected items from a program which teaches young children to respond in terms of the abstract property of form. The upper rectangle in each of the frames is the sample. The child must pick the alternative which corresponds to the sample in form. The color of each letter, as it appeared in the program, is indicated by the various shaded areas.

---

[4] This program was prepared by B. F. Skinner.

sample and its match correspond exactly. Next, the sample and the match may differ in some property such as color, in the case of the next item shown, or size in the next. It is essential that the program contain many items among which the sample and correct match differ in all properties except the one providing the basis for the abstraction. Otherwise, the abstraction will be incomplete because the extraneous property will share some of the control over the abstract response. As we move on with additional examples, the sample and the correct match differ both in color and size, and the incorrect alternatives are beginning to share some of the extraneous properties with the sample. The student continues with many such problems in which the only common property between the sample and the correct match is the shape, regardless of size and color. Even now our abstraction may be incomplete. We have kept the figures in only one orientation. Therefore, we also have a series in which the samples are rotated as in the next item. A great deal of academic education consists of trying to teach abstractions. Concepts such as force, reinforcement, supply and demand, freedom, and many, many other possible examples are all abstractions. Furthermore, in the academic setting, the student seldom adequately forms abstractions. The trigonometry student commonly uses triangles with the right angle as one of the two lower angles. If the triangle is rotated 90°, so that the right angle is upward, the student often does not recognize it as a right triangle. Neither is an abstraction developed simply by learning a definition. The psychology student who learns the definition of reinforcement in formal terms and is acquainted with a laboratory example of food reinforcement may not realize the horrible consequences of sending his girl friend flowers to end an argument. Thus, in the psychology program, we follow the pattern in the preverbal example to develop a new concept. Wide ranges of examples are analyzed which differ in as many aspects as possible, each still having the common property which characterizes the concept.

The last principle I shall discuss is really a question of a methodology which has served so well in the laboratory. This principle is to let the student write the program. A few years ago, a cartoon published in the *Columbia Jester* showed two rats in a Skinner box. One is leaning on the bar and saying to the other rat: "Boy, do we have this guy conditioned. Every time I press the bar down, he drops a pellet in." Although said in jest, it is true that the rat controls the experimenter's behavior. When interesting things are observed about the rat's behavior, the control circuits are rewired to investigate the interesting new facet of behavior. In a sense, that rat is wiring the control circuit. Similarly, the behavioral engineer who prepares good teaching-machine material must be under the control of the student's responses. When the student has trouble with part of a program, the programmer must correct this. The student's answers reveal ambiguities in items; they reveal gaps in the program and erroneous assumptions as to the student's background. The answers will show when the program is progressing too rapidly, when additional prompts are necessary, or when the programmer should try new techniques. When unexpected errors are made, they indicate deficiencies *not* in the student but in the program.

The most extensive experience with this principle of modifying the program

TABLE 1.2
A comparison of the students' errors in using the revised (1959)
and unrevised (1958) program in psychology

	Percent errors	*Percent items improperly scored by students*
1958	20.1	3.6
1959	11.0	1.4

to fit the student has been at Harvard with the psychology program. In 1958, we had a program consisting of 48 disks or lessons of 29 frames each. After using the program and making a detailed, item-by-item analysis of the students' answers, we diagnosed the particular deficiencies in the program and revised it accordingly. The program was also extended to cover a larger amount of subject matter; and in 1959, it consisted of 60 disks. You have already seen a few items from the course. After using the revised material in 1959, we evaluated the extent of its improvement. Table 1.2 shows the percentage of errors on the first 20 disks for each of the 2 years.

The revision eliminated about half the errors. The last column of the table gives percentage of improper self-scoring by the students. Revision also cut these scoring errors approximately in half. Furthermore, the revision decreased the time required to complete the material. Although the second year's material had more disks—60 as opposed to 48—it actually required the average student about 1 hour less to complete the work than the shorter, first version had done.

. . .

Such careful tailoring of material to fit the student is impossible with most teaching techniques. With teaching machines, as in no other teaching technique, the programmer is able to revise his material in view of the students' particular difficulties. The student can write the program; he cannot write the textbook.

We have seen that the principles evolved from the laboratory study of behavior have provided the possibility for the behavioral engineering of teaching. This new technology is thoroughly grounded in some of the better-established facts of behavioral control. The future of education is bright if persons who prepare teaching-machine programs appreciate this, and appropriately educate themselves in a special, but truly *not* esoteric, discipline. But it is vital that we continue to apply these techniques in preparing programs. The ill-advised efforts of some of our friends, who automatize their courses without adopting the new technology, have an extremely good chance of burying the whole movement in an avalanche of teaching-machine tapes.

REFERENCES

Azrin, H. H. "Some Effects of Two Intermittent Schedules of Immediate and Non-Immediate Punishment. *J. Psychol.* 42(1956):3–21.

Holland, J. G. "Human vigilance." *Science* 128(1958):61–67.

Homme, L. E., and R. Glaser. "Relationships between Programmed Textbook and Teaching Machines. In E. Galanter, ed., *Automatic Teaching*. New York: John Wiley, 1959, pp. 103–107.

Hovland, C. I. "A Set of Flower Designs for Experiments in Concept Formation." *Amer. J. Psychol.* 66(1953):140–142.

Hovland, C. I. "A 'Communication Analysis' of Concept Learning." *Psychol. Rev.* 59 (1952):461–472.

Keller, F. S., and W. N. Schoenfeld. *Principles of Psychology*. New York: Appleton-Century-Crofts, 1950.

Perin, C. T. "The Effect of Delayed Reinforcement upon the Differentiation of Bar Responses in White Rats." *J. Exp. Psychol.* 52(1943):95–109.

Pressey, S. L. "Simple Apparatus Which Gives Tests and Scores and Teaches." *Sch. and Soc.* 23(1926):373–376.

Reid, L. S. "The Development of Noncontinuity Behavior through Continuity Learning." *J. Exp. Psychol.* 46(1953):107–112.

Skinner, B. F. "The Science of Learning and the Art of Teaching." *Harvard Educ. Rev.* 29(1954):86–97.

Skinner, B. F. *Verbal Behavior*. New York: Appleton-Century-Crofts, 1957.

Skinner, B. F. "Teaching Machines." *Science* 128(1958):969–977.

Wyckoff, L. B. "The Role of Observing Responses in Discrimination Learning." *Psychol. Rev.* 59(1952):431–442.

QUESTIONS

1. In developing new programs for teaching, which principles from the laboratory can be applied to increase control over the students' learning?

2. Why is it desirable for the student to make active, overt responses when learning?

3. Discuss an application, either one described in the article or a potential application you may have thought of as you read the article, for the following: abstraction, gradual progression, control of observing behavior, immediate reinforcement.

4. Keeping in mind behavioral principles, choose a complex behavior and outline the techniques of behavior control that can be used to establish that behavior in the student (e.g., a good golf swing, proper handwriting, etc.).

5. The advantage of taking small steps in teaching complex behaviors is that you minimize errors. What is the effect on a student's behavior of too many errors?

UNIT

2

Altering the Environment to Control Learning

Content

Keller, F. S. "Goodbye, teacher. . . ." *Journal of Applied Behavior Analysis* 1 (1968): 78–89. (a selection)

This unit presents a report of a classroom application of behavior-control principles. The approach does not employ machines, but alters the class routine to permit a high rate of student responding, frequent interaction with monitors who have previously mastered the course content, and frequent reinforcement.

Objectives

Students will describe the distinctive characteristics of Keller's system of instruction, analyze the classroom situation in terms of the behavioral principles used, note how they are implemented, and consider the advantages of having proctors assist in teaching.

Instructions

1. Read the objectives.
2. Read the article straight through, then write the answers to the questions which follow. Refer back to the article as necessary.
3. When you are satisfied with your answers, look over the suggested answers for this unit.

4. See your instructor for a brief review (or meet with your learning group) before going on to the next unit.

"Good-bye, Teacher . . ."

Fred S. Keller

When I was a boy, and school "let out" for the summer, we used to celebrate our freedom from educational control by chanting:

Good-bye scholars, good-bye school;
Good-bye teacher, darned old fool!

We really didn't think of our teacher as deficient in judgment, or as a clown or jester. We were simply escaping from restraint, dinner pail in one hand and shoes in the other, with all the delights of summer before us. At that moment, we might even have been well-disposed toward our teacher and might have felt a touch of compassion as we completed the rhyme.

"Teacher" was usually a woman, not always young and not always pretty. She was frequently demanding and sometimes sharp of tongue, ever ready to pounce when we got out of line. But, occasionally, if one did especially well in home-work or in recitation, he could detect a flicker of approval or affection that made the hour in class worthwhile. At such times, we loved our teacher and felt that school was fun.

It was not fun enough, however, to keep me there when I grew older. Then I turned to another kind of education, in which the reinforcements were sometimes just as scarce as in the schoolroom. I became a Western Union messenger boy and, between deliveries of telegrams, I learned Morse code by memorizing dots and dashes from a sheet of paper and listening to a relay on the wall. As I look back on those days, I conclude that I am the only living reinforcement theorist who ever learned Morse code in the absence of reinforcement.

It was a long, frustrating job. It taught me that drop-out learning could be just as difficult as in-school learning and it led me to wonder about easier possible ways of mastering a skill. Years later, after returning to school and finishing my formal education, I came back to this classical learning problem, with the aim of making International Morse code less painful for beginners than American Morse had been for me (Keller, 1943).

During World War II, with the aid of a number of students and colleagues, I tried to apply the principle of immediate reinforcement to the early training of Signal Corps personnel in the reception of Morse-code signals. At the same time, I had

---

Fred S. Keller, "Good-bye, Teacher . . . ," *Journal of Applied Behavioral Analysis* 1 (1968): 78–89. Reprinted by permission.

a chance to observe, at close hand and for many months, the operation of a military training center. I learned something from both experiences, but I should have learned more. I should have seen many things that I didn't see at all, or saw very dimly.

I could have noted, for example, that instruction in such a center was highly individualized, in spite of large classes, sometimes permitting students to advance at their own speed throughout a course of study. I could have seen the clear specification of terminal skills for each course, together with the carefully graded steps leading to this end. I could have seen the demand for perfection at every level of training and for every student; the employment of classroom instructors who were little more than the successful graduates of earlier classes; the minimizing of the lecture as a teaching device and the maximizing of student participation. I could have seen, especially, an interesting division of labor in the educational process, wherein the non-commissioned, classroom teacher was restricted to duties of guiding, clarifying, demonstrating, testing, grading, and the like, while the commissioned teacher, the training officer, dealt with matters of course logistics, the interpretation of training manuals, the construction of lesson plans and guides, the evaluation of student progress, the selection of non-commissioned cadre, and the writing of reports for his superiors.

I did see these things, of course, in a sense, but they were embedded deeply within a special context, one of "training" rather than "education." I did not then appreciate that a set of reinforcement contingencies which were useful in building simple skills like those of the radio operator might also be useful in developing the verbal repertories, the conceptual behaviors, and the laboratory techniques of university education. It was not until a long time later, by a very different route, that I came to such a realization.

That story began in 1962, with the attempt on the part of two Brazilian and two North American psychologists, to establish a Department of Psychology at the University of Brasilia. The question of teaching method arose from the very practical problem of getting a first course ready by a certain date for a certain number of students in the new university. We had almost complete freedom of action; we were dissatisfied with the conventional approaches; and we knew something about programmed instruction. We were also of the same theoretical persuasion. It was quite natural, I suppose, that we should look for fresh applications of reinforcement thinking to the teaching process (Keller, 1966).

The method that resulted from this collaborative effort was first used in a short-term laboratory course[1] at Columbia University in the winter of 1963, and the basic procedure of this pilot study was employed at Brasilia during the following year, by Professors Rodolfo Azzi and Carolina Martuscelli Bori, with 50 students in a one-term introductory course.

. . .

---

[1] With the aid of (Dr.) Lanny Fields and the members of a senior seminar at Columbia College, during the fall term of 1963–64.

Concurrently with the early Brazilian development, Professor J. G. Sherman and I, in the spring of 1965, began a series of more or less independent applications of the same general method at Arizona State University. With various minor changes, this work has now been tried through five semesters with an increasing number of students per term (Keller, in press [a], in press [b], 1967; Sherman, 1967). The results have been more gratifying with each successive class, and there has been as yet no thought of a return to more conventional procedures. In addition, we have had the satisfaction of seeing our system used by a few other colleagues, in other courses and at other institutions.[2]

In describing this method to you, I will start with a quotation (Keller, 1967). It is from a hand-out given to all the students enrolled in the first-semester course in General Psychology (one of two introductions offered at Arizona State University) during the past year, and it describes the teaching method to which they will be exposed unless they elect to withdraw from the course.

This is a course through which you may move, from start to finish, at your own pace. You will not be held back by other students or forced to go ahead until you are ready. At best, you may meet all the course requirements in less than one semester; at worst, you may not complete the job within that time. How fast you go is up to you.

The work of this course will be divided into 30 units of content, which correspond roughly to a series of home-work assignments and laboratory exercises. These units will come in a definite numerical order, and you must show your mastery of each unit (by passing a "readiness" test or carrying out an experiment) before moving on to the next.

A good share of your reading for this course may be done in the classroom, at those times when no lectures, demonstrations, or other activities are taking place. Your classroom, that is, will sometimes be a study hall.

The lectures and demonstrations in this course will have a different relation to the rest of your work than is usually the rule. They will be provided only when you have demonstrated your readiness to appreciate them; no examination will be based upon them; and you need not attend them if you do not wish. When a certain percentage of the class has reached a certain point in the course, a lecture or demonstration will be available at a stated time, but it will not be compulsory.

The teaching staff of your course will include proctors, assistants, and an instructor. A proctor is an undergraduate who has been chosen for his mastery of the course content and orientation, for his maturity of judgment, for his understanding of the special problems that confront you as a beginner, and for his willingness to assist. He will provide you with all your study materials except your textbooks. He will pass upon your readiness tests as satisfactory or unsatisfactory. His judgment will ordinarily be law, but if he is ever in serious doubt, he can appeal to the classroom assistant, or even the instructor, for a ruling. Failure to pass a test on the first try,

---

2 For example, by J. L. Michael with high-school juniors on a National Science Foundation project at Grinnell College (Iowa), in 1965; and by J. Farmer and B. Cole at Queens College (New York) in a course similar to the one described here.

the second, the third, or even later, will not be held against you. It is better that you get too much testing than not enough, if your final success in the course is to be assured.

Your work in the laboratory will be carried out under the direct supervision of a graduate laboratory assistant, whose detailed duties cannot be listed here. There will also be a graduate classroom assistant, upon whom your proctor will depend for various course materials (assignments, study questions, special readings, and so on), and who will keep up to date all progress records for course members. The classroom assistant will confer with the instructor daily, aid the proctors on occasion, and act in a variety of ways to further the smooth operation of the course machinery.

The instructor will have as his principal responsibilities: (a) the selection of all study material used in the course; (b) the organization and the mode of presenting this material; (c) the construction of tests and examinations; and (d) the final evaluation of each student's progress. It will be his duty, also, to provide lectures, demonstrations, and discussion opportunities for all students who have earned the privilege; to act as a clearing-house for requests and complaints; and to arbitrate in any case of disagreement between students and proctors or assistants. . . .

All students in the course are expected to take a final examination, in which the entire term's work will be represented. With certain exceptions, this examination will come at the same time for all students, at the end of the term. . . . The examination will consist of questions which, in large part, you have already answered on your readiness tests. Twenty-five percent of your course grade will be based on this examination; the remaining 75% will be based on the number of units of reading and laboratory work that you have successfully completed during the term.

(In my own sections of the course, these percentages were altered, during the last term, to a 30% weighting of the final examination, a 20% weighting of the 10 laboratory exercises, and a 50% weighting of the reading units.)

A picture of the way this method operates can best be obtained, perhaps, by sampling the activities of a hypothetical average student as he moves through the course. John Pilgrim is a freshman, drawn from the upper 75% of his high-school class. He has enrolled in PY 112 for unknown reasons and has been assigned to a section of about 100 students, men and women, most of whom are also in their beginning year. The class is scheduled to meet on Tuesdays and Thursdays, from 9:15 to 10:30 a.m., with a laboratory session to be arranged.

Together with the description from which I quoted a moment ago, John receives a few mimeographed instructions and some words of advice from his professor. He is told that he should cover two units of laboratory work or reading per week in order to be sure of taking an A-grade into his final examination; that he should withdraw from the course if he doesn't pass at least one readiness test within the first two weeks; and that a grade of Incomplete will not be given except in special cases. He is also advised that, in addition to the regular classroom hours on Tuesday and Thursday, readiness tests may be taken on Saturday forenoons and Wednesday afternoons of each week—periods in which he can catch up with, or move ahead of, the rest of the class.

He then receives his first assignment: an introductory chapter from a standard textbook and two "sets" from a programmed version of similar material. With this assignment, he receives a mimeographed list of "study questions," about 30 in number. He is told to seek out the answers to these questions in his reading, so as to prepare himself for the questions he will be asked in his readiness tests. He is free to study wherever he pleases, but he is strongly encouraged to use the study hall for at least part of the time. Conditions for work are optimal there, with other students doing the same thing and with an assistant or proctor on hand to clarify a confusing passage or a difficult concept.

This is on Tuesday. On Thursday, John comes to class again, having gone through the sets of programmed material and having decided to finish his study in the classroom, where he cannot but feel that the instructor really expects him. An assistant is in charge, about half the class is there, and some late registrants are reading the course description. John tries to study his regular text, but finds it difficult to concentrate and ends by deciding to work in his room. The assistant pays no attention when he leaves.

On the following Tuesday, he appears in study hall again, ready for testing, but anxious, since a whole week of the course has passed. He reports to the assistant, who sends him across the hall, without his books and notes, to the testing room, where the proctor in charge gives him a blue-book and one of the test forms for Unit 1. He takes a seat among about 20 other students and starts work. The test is composed of 10 fill-in questions and one short-answer essay question. It doesn't seem particularly difficult and, in about 10 min John returns his question sheet and is sent, with his blue-book, to the proctor's room for grading.

In the proctor's room, in one of 10 small cubicles, John finds his special proctor, Anne Merit. Anne is a psychology major who passed the same course earlier with a grade of A. She receives two points of credit for about 4 hr of proctoring per week, 2 hr of required attendance at a weekly proctors' meeting, and occasional extra duty in the study hall or test room. She has nine other students besides John to look after, so she will not as a rule be able to spend much more than 5 or 10 min of class time with each.

Anne runs through John's answers quickly, checking two of them as incorrect and placing a question mark after his answer to the essay question. Then she asks him why he answered these three as he did. His replies show two misinterpretations of the question and one failure in written expression. A restatement of the fill-in questions and some probing with respect to the essay leads Anne to write an O.K. alongside each challenged answer. She congratulates John upon his performance and warns him that later units may be a little harder to master than the first.

John's success is then recorded on the wall chart in the proctors' room, he is given his next assignment and set of study questions, and sent happily on his way. The blue-book remains with Anne, to be given later to the assistant or the instructor for inspection, and used again when John is ready for testing on Unit 2. As he leaves the room, John notices the announcement of a 20-min lecture by his instructor, for all students who have passed Unit 3 by the following Friday, and he resolves that he will be there.

If John had failed in the defense of one or two of his answers, he would have been sent back for a minimal period of 30 min for further study, with advice as to material most needing attention. If he had made more than four errors on his test, the answers would not have been considered individually; he would simply have been told that he was not ready for examination. And, if he had made no errors at all, he would probably have been asked to explain one or two of his correct answers, as a way of getting acquainted and to make sure that he was the one who had really done the work.

John did fail his first test on Unit 2, and his first two tests on Unit 4 (which gave trouble to nearly everyone). He missed the first lecture, too, but qualified for the second. (There were seven such "shows" during the term, each attended by perhaps half of the students entitled to be there.) After getting through his first five units, he failed on one review test before earning the right to move on to Unit 6. On the average, for the remainder of the course, he required nearly two readiness tests per unit. Failing a test, of course, was not an unmixed evil, since it permitted more discussion with the proctor and often served to sharpen the concepts involved.

In spite of more than a week's absence from school, John was able, by using the Wednesday and Saturday testing sessions, to complete his course units successfully about a week before the final examination. Because of his cramming for other courses during this last week, he did not review for his psychology and received only a B on his final examination. His A for the course was not affected by this, but his pride was hurt.

Sometime before the term ended, John was asked to comment on certain aspects of the course, without revealing his identity. (Remember, John is a mythical figure.) Among other things, he said that, in comparison with courses taught more conventionally, this one demanded a much greater mastery of the work assignments, it required greater memorization of detail and much greater understanding of basic concepts, it generated a greater feeling of achievement, it gave much greater recognition of the student as a person, and it was enjoyed to a much greater extent (Keller, in press).

He mentioned also that his study habits had improved during the term, that his attitude towards testing had become more positive, that his worry about final grades had diminished, and that there had been an increase in his desire to hear lectures (this in spite of the fact that he attended only half of those for which he was qualified). When asked specifically about the use of proctors, he said that the discussions with his proctors had been very helpful, that the proctor's non-academic, personal relation was also important to him, and that the use of proctors generally in grading and discussing tests was highly desirable.

Anne Merit, when asked to comment on her own reactions to the system, had many things to say, mostly positive. She referred especially to the satisfaction of having the respect of her proctees, of seeing them do well, and of cementing the material of the course for herself. She noted that the method was one of "mutual reinforcement" for student, proctor, assistant, and instructor. She suggested that it ought to be used in other courses and at other levels of instruction. She wondered why it would not be possible for a student to enroll in a second course immediately upon completion of the first, if it were taught by the same method. She also listed several changes that might improve the efficiency of the course machinery, especially in the area of testing and grading, where delay may sometimes occur.

In an earlier account of this teaching method (Keller, 1967), I summarized those features which seem to distinguish it most clearly from conventional teaching procedures. They include the following:

(1) *The go-at-your-own-pace feature,* which permits a student to move through the course at a speed commensurate with his ability and other demands upon his time.

(2) *The unit-perfection requirement for advance,* which lets the student go ahead to new material only after demonstrating mastery of that which preceded.

(3) *The use of lectures and demonstrations as vehicles of motivation,* rather than sources of critical information.

(4) The related *stress upon the written word* in teacher-student communication; and, finally:

(5) *The use of proctors,* which permits repeated testing, immediate scoring, almost unavoidable tutoring, and a marked enhancement of the personal-social aspect of the educational process.

The similarity of our learning paradigm to that provided in the field of programmed instruction is obvious. There is the same stress upon analysis of the task, the same concern with terminal performance, the same opportunity for individualized progression, and so on. But the sphere of action here is different. The principal steps of advance are not "frames" in a "set", but are more like the conventional home-work assignment or laboratory exercise. "The 'response' is not simply the completion of a prepared statement through the insertion of a word or phrase. Rather, it may be thought of as the resultant of many such responses, better described as the understanding of a principle, a formula, or a concept, or the ability to use an experimental technique. Advance within the program depends on something more than the appearance of a confirming word or the presentation of a new frame; it involves a personal interaction between a student and his peer, or his better, in what may be a lively verbal interchange, of interest and importance to each participant. The use of a programmed text, a teaching machine, or some sort of computer aid within such a course is entirely possible and may be quite desirable, but it is not to be equated with the course itself." (Keller, 1967.)

Failure to recognize that our teaching units are not as simple as the response words in a programmed text, or the letter reactions to Morse-code signals, or other comparable atoms of behavior, can lead to confusion concerning our procedure. A well-known critic of education in America, after reading an account of our method, sent me a note confessing to "a grave apprehension about the effect of breaking up the subject matter into little packages." "I should suppose," he said, "it would prevent all but the strongest minds from ever possessing a synoptic view of a field, and I imagine that the coaching, and testing, and passing in bits would amount to efficient training rather than effectual teaching."

Our "little packages" or "bits" are no smaller than the basic conceptions of a science of behavior and cannot be delivered all at once in one large synoptic parcel. As for the teaching-training distinction, one needs only to note that it is always the instructor who decides what is to be taught, and to what degree, thus determining whether he will be called a trainer or a teacher. The method he uses, the basic reinforcement contingencies he employs, may be turned to either purpose.

Many things occur, some of them rather strange, when a student is taught by a method such as ours. With respect to everyday student behavior, even a casual visit to a class will provide some novel items. For example, all the students seated in the study hall may be seen studying, undistracted by the presence or movements of others. In the test room, a student will rarely be seen chewing on his pencil, looking at a neighbor's blue-book, or staring out the window. In the crowded proctors' room, 10 pairs of students can be found concurrently engaged in academic interaction, with no couple bothered by the conversation of another, no matter how close by. Upon passing his assistant or instructor, in the corridors or elsewhere, a student will typically be seen to react in a friendly and respectful manner—enough to excite a mild alarm.

More interesting than this is the fact that a student may be tested 40 or 50 times in the course of one semester, often standing in line for the privilege, without a complaint. In one extreme instance, a student required nearly two terms to complete the work of one (after which he applied for, and got, permission to serve as a proctor for the following year).

Another unusual feature of our testing and grading is the opportunity given to defend an "incorrect" answer. This defense, as I noted earlier, may sometimes produce changes in the proctor's evaluation, changes that are regularly checked by the assistant or the instructor. Occasionally, a proctor's O.K. will be rejected, compelling the student to take another test, and sensitizing the proctor to the dangers of leniency; more often, it produces a note of warning, a correction, or a query written by the instructor in the student's blue-book; but always it provides the instructor with feedback on the adequacy of the question he has constructed.

Especially important, in a course taught by such a method, is the fact that any differences in social, economic, cultural, and ethnic background are completely and repeatedly subordinated to a friendly intellectual relationship between two human beings throughout a period of 15 weeks or more. Also, in such a course, a lonesome, ill-favored underprivileged, badly schooled, or otherwise handicapped boy or girl can be assured at least a modicum of individual attention, approval, encouragement, and a chance to succeed. The only prerequisite for such treatment is a well-defined amount and quality of academic achievement.

. . .

Our method has not yet required a grant-in-aid to keep it going. On one occasion we tried to get such help, in order to pay for mimeograph paper, the services of a clerk, and one or two additional assistants. Our request was rejected, quite properly, on the grounds that our project was "purely operational." Almost any member of a present-day fund-granting agency can recognize "research" when he sees it. I do think, however, that one should be freed, as I was, from other university demands while introducing a system like ours. And he should not be asked to teach more than two such courses regularly, each serving 100 students or less, unless he has highly qualified assistants upon whom he can depend.

Neither does the method require equipment and supplies that are not already available to almost every teacher in the country. Teaching machines, tape recorders, and computers could readily be fitted into the picture. Moving pictures and television could also be used in one or two ways without detriment to the basic educational process. But these are luxuries, based on only partial recognition of our problem, and they could divert us from more important considerations. (Proctors, like computers, may go wrong or break down, but they can often be repaired and they are easily replaced, at very little expense.)

The need for individualized instruction is widely recognized, and the most commonly suggested way of filling this need is automation. I think that this solution is incomplete, especially when applied to the young; and I'd like to mention a personal experience that bears upon the matter.

In the summer of 1966, I made numerous visits to a center for the care and treatment of autistic children.[3] One day, as I stood at the door of a classroom, I saw a boy get up from his chair at the end of a class period and give a soft pat to the object on the desk in front of him. At the same time, he said, with a slight smile, "Good-bye, Teaching Machine!"

This pseudo-social behavior in this fundamentally asocial child amused me at the time. It reminded me of Professor Moore's description of the three-year-old who became irritated when his "talking typewriter" made a mistake, called the device a "big bambam", requested its name, and ended by asking, "Who is your mother?" Today, however, I am not so sure that this is funny. It does suggest that affection may be generated within a child for an electromechanical instrument that has been essential to educational reinforcement. Unfortunately, such a machine, in its present form, is unlikely to generalize with human beings in the boy's world, giving to them a highly desirable reinforcing property. In fact, the growth of this type of student-machine relation, if it were the only one, would be a poor substitute for a directly social interaction.

REFERENCES

Keller, F. S. "Studies in International Morse Code: 1. A New Method of Teaching Code Reception," *Journal of Applied Psychology* 27(1943):407–415.

---

[3] At the Linwood Children's Center, Ellicott City, Maryland.

Keller, F. S. "A Personal Course in Psychology." In R. Ulrich, T. Stachnik, and J. Mabry, eds., *The Control of Behavior.* Glenview, Ill.: Scott, Foresman, 1966, pp. 91–93.

Keller, F. S. "Neglected Rewards in the Educational Process." *Proc. 23rd Amer. Conf. Acad. Deans,* Los Angeles, January 1967, pp. 9–22.

Keller, F. S. "New Reinforcement Contingencies in the Classroom." In *Programmiertes lernen,* Wissenschaftliche Buchgesellschaft, Darmstadt, in press.

Keller, F. S. "Engineering Personalized Instruction in the Classroom." *Rev. Interamer de Psicol.* 1(1967):189–197.

Keller, F. S., and W. N. Schoenfeld. "The Psychology Curriculum at Columbia College." *American Psychologist* 4(1949):165–172.

Sherman, J. G. "Application of Reinforcement Principles to a College Course." Paper read at Amer. Educ. Res. Ass., New York, February 1967.

QUESTIONS

1. What are the distinctive features of Keller's system of instruction?
2. What features of Keller's procedure provide reinforcement? Name at least four.
3. How may the student benefit from the use of proctors?

UNIT

3

Individually
Prescribed Instruction

Content

Lindvall, C. M., and J. O. Bolvin. "Programed Instruction in the Schools: An Application of Programing Principles in 'Individually Prescribed Instruction'." In *Programed Instruction: Sixty-Sixth Yearbook of the National Society for the Study of Education, part II*. Chicago: NSSE, 1967, pp. 217–254. (a selection)

This selection presents another example of changing the environment to control learning. An individualized curriculum for elementary school is described.

Objectives

Students will list the assumptions underlying the IPI program, relate them to the general principles of the experimental analysis of behavior, and outline the operating procedures of IPI, including diagnosis and placement procedures.

Instructions

1. Read the objectives and then use them as a guide to your reading of the selection from the article.
2. Answer the questions following the article.
3. When you are satisfied with your answers, check the suggested answers for this unit.
4. See your instructor (or group) for a brief review before going on to Unit 4.

Programed Instruction in the Schools: An Application of Programing Principles in "Individually Prescribed Instruction"

C. M. Lindvall and J. O. Bolvin

AN OVERVIEW OF THE PROGRAM "INDIVIDUALLY PRESCRIBED INSTRUCTION"

Theoretical Bases and Operational Procedures

Since the spring of 1964, the Learning Research and Development Center at the University of Pittsburgh in co-operation with the Baldwin-Whitehall School District has been engaged in a project for the development and demonstration of a program for individualized instruction in the elementary school. For reasons that should become obvious as the program is described, the procedure has been given the name "Individually Prescribed Instruction (IPI)."

One of the basic assumptions underlying the development of Individually Prescribed Instruction is the idea that learning is something that is ultimately personal and individual. Learning may take place within a social context, and many types of instruction are traditionally carried out with groups of students. But it is the individual who learns, not the group. This, in turn, dictates that instructional plans should be prepared for the individual, not for the group. In a conventional classroom, instruction is usually planned as though the classroom group were an organic unit and as though this unit were doing the learning. Obviously, if learning is individual, this type of planning cannot be of maximum effectiveness. Furthermore, ability grouping or other attempts to organize subgroups within the classroom which are more homogeneous than the total group will not really solve the problem. Learning takes place only on an individual basis; consequently, instruction must be individualized.

Teaching machines and programed textbooks have exemplified a useful approach to the individualization of instruction. They have shown that if conditions are arranged so that a pupil can work through a sequence of learning experiences that are carefully graded in terms of increasing difficulty, each pupil can progress at his own individual pace and with little or no outside assistance to acquire relatively complex skills and types of knowledge.

A second assumption of the IPI project is that the same type of planning and "programing" that is employed in a programed textbook can be used to develop a more extensive program which extends over grade lines, covers at least all of the

C. M. Lindvall and J. O. Bolvin, "Programed Instruction in the Schools: An Application of Programing Principles in 'Individually Prescribed Instruction'," in *Sixty-Sixth Yearbook of the National Society for the Study of Education, part II* (Chicago: NSSE, 1967), pp. 217–254. Reprinted by permission.

elementary-school years, and involves a much greater variety of types of learning experiences than can be presented in a textbook.

It is felt that individualization can never be accomplished to any considerable extent unless curriculum plans involve continuous sequences that ignore arbitrary grade-level lines. The use of programed texts has shown that such materials can permit individualization within a grade level. However, the conventional grade-level organization of subject matter has been a major handicap to individualization which does not stop at grade-level boundaries. The idea, represented by material found in traditional textbooks, workbooks, and standardized tests, as well as in the minds of teachers and parents, that certain skills and topics should be covered in the first grade, others in the second grade, and so on, has resulted in a situation such that even if pupils progress at different rates through one grade, they will all start at the same point in the content of the next grade. In developing IPI it has been assumed that if this limitation is to be overcome, curriculum sequences must be developed in such a way that they represent a long-term development process which ignores grade lines.

The application of some of the basic ideas of programed instruction to the development of a total school program results in a new concept of what a school is. In this concept a school is not a place where pupils "attend classes." Instead, it is a place where a pupil works through a sequence of learning activities or experiences at a pace and in a way suited to his interests and abilities. The function of the school is to provide him with this type of opportunity, to identify meaningful and effective sequences, and to arrange for use of materials and for experiences that permit each pupil to progress through such sequences. Such a plan will not impose artificial barriers which force the pupil to keep pace with a class or a group or to confine his study to what is typically covered at a given grade level. Conditions should be such that an extremely bright first-grade pupil, for example, might master all of the skills and content that are traditionally taught during the first three or four years of school. On the other hand, a slow student might take two or three years to acquire the abilities that the "average" child masters in one year. . . .

IPI in the Oakleaf Elementary School since 1964

The project and procedures known as Individually Prescribed Instruction were first put into operation in September, 1964, in the Oakleaf Elementary School of the Baldwin-Whitehall School District, in suburban Pittsburgh, Pennsylvania. This school has one class or section at each grade level, Grades K–VI, and the IPI procedure has been used with instruction in reading, arithmetic, and science. In the other elementary-school subjects, instruction is carried on by rather traditional methods.

. . .

While studying under IPI, students work mainly in a large study area, seating 50 to 80 pupils, formed by opening a folding door between two standard-size classrooms. Student study is largely independent. The visitor to a study area will see pupils working at desks or other student stations, writing on exercise sheets, reading, working problems, listening to recordings, or carrying out simple science experiments under directions provided through a tape play-back device. Teachers will be moving about the room to provide help as it may be needed. This help may be given to the pupil at his desk, or he may be taken to a side room for more extensive individual instruction. Also present in the study area will be one to three teacher-aides who are helping score papers and distribute materials. When a student completes a given exercise, it will be scored either by one of these aides or by the pupil himself so that he will know how well he is doing. At frequent intervals the material with which he is working will include a "curriculum-embedded test," a brief quiz covering the material taught by a limited number of exercises. Scores on these tests are essential aids to the monitoring of pupil progress. As the pupil moves along through the curriculum, his progress is guided by a series of "prescriptions," each of which indicates the materials he is to study next. These prescriptions are developed regularly either outside the classroom or in pupil-teacher conferences. In prescription writing, account is taken of where the student is in the sequence, how well he has done on the lesson exercises, his scores on the curriculum-embedded tests, and any other relevant information that the teacher may have available. Guided by the prescription, the pupil works on lesson materials, primarily of a self-study type, demanding only occasional help from the teacher. He is thus able to proceed through the instructional sequence largely independently, at a pace suited to his abilities, and using materials and modes of instruction selected to meet his needs.

How is this type of instructional situation achieved? What are the essential elements in this type of "programing" for individualized instruction? Having discussed in general terms the nature and operations of Individually Prescribed Instruction, let us examine in some detail the specific elements involved in developing such a program.

STEPS IN THE DEVELOPMENT OF INDIVIDUALLY PRESCRIBED INSTRUCTION

In developing the IPI curriculum and instructional procedures, many of the basic principles of programed instruction were used, and the developmental process has required much of the same painstaking attention that characterizes the planning and production of a teaching-machine program. These principles and the steps entailed in their application are described in some detail in the following sections.

The objectives to be achieved must be spelled out in terms of desired pupil behaviors. In typical classroom situations, the details of what is to be taught are frequently covered by what is included in the textbook, workbook, or similar materials. The teacher merely has to know that "these are the materials that are to be covered this week." Many of the specifics regarding what is to be covered are kept in the mind of the teacher and are presented only as the lesson is actually being taught. This system may be somewhat effective where the method of instruction employed is that of teacher presentation to some total classroom group. However, it is not sufficient if individualized instruction is to be achieved. Individualized instruction requires the extensive use of self-teaching materials—materials with which the student may work quite independently of teacher help. The first prerequisite to the development or identification of materials of this type is to know exactly what it is desired that the pupil should learn. It is not enough that the specifics of what is to be learned are clearly formulated in the mind of the teacher. If IPI is to function effectively, it must be possible to determine whether or not the instructional materials and procedures do, in themselves, enable the pupil to achieve the desired mastery. To determine this it is necessary to know exactly what the pupil is expected to be able to do after he has had this learning experience. Thus, the definition of instructional objectives in terms of specific pupil behaviors is essential.

. . .

To help achieve the essential specificity in objectives, it was impressed upon all persons who played a part in developing the sequences of objectives for the IPI program that a primary purpose which these statements were to serve was to provide a guidance for determining whether or not a pupil had achieved a given specific ability. That is, each objective was to be worded in terms of what the pupil was to be able to *do* after he had had the given learning experience. As one means of assuring this type of specificity, all writers of objectives were asked to accompany each objective with a test item or some suggested evaluation procedure that could be used to assess the pupil's attainment of the given skill. Some examples of specific objectives together with associated evaluation procedures are the following, which are taken from units in counting or numeration and from units in place value.

Objective: Supplies the number which is one more, one less, or in between two given numbers (to 200).

Suggested evaluation: "Circle the number which is one less than 97."

    99   94 ·   96   98

Objective: Completes patterns for skip counting by 3's and 4's from any starting point.

Suggested evaluation: "Complete the Pattern."

    360, 363, _____, _____, _____, 375, _____.

Objective: Identifies the place value of the units, tens, hundreds, and thousands digit in numbers to 1000.

Suggested evaluation: "4625 means _____ thousands, _____ hundreds, _____ tens, and _____ ones."

In the development of the program for Individually Prescribed Instruction, the task of producing the initial version of the sequences of behavioral objectives for all elementary-school grades in reading, arithmetic, and science required approximately four months of sustained effort and involved the work of about twenty persons, including teachers, psychologists, subject experts, and curriculum specialists. In addition, of course, these lists of specific objectives are undergoing continuous scrutiny and revision as the program is being used. The staff of the project feels that these lists of objectives represent the essential framework upon which all of the other aspects of the program are built.

To the extent possible, instructional objectives should be ordered in a sequence which makes for effective pupil progression with a minimum number of gaps or difficult steps and with little overlap or unnecessary repetition. An essential characteristic of an effective instructional program is that it permits pupils to make progress in achieving mastery of the desired skills and content. This progress probably will take place in the most desirable manner if the steps represented by the specific objectives are arranged so that each step helps the pupil approach the subsequent step. The task of sequencing objectives in the IPI program was given intensive and lengthy attention in the development of the program. It has also been given continuing attention as the objectives have been reordered at various points on the basis of pupil performance.

In developing an instructional sequence, supposedly an ideal condition would be achieved if, for example, all of the objectives in elementary-school arithmetic could be ordered in one long chain of prerequisite abilities running from that found in the first grade up to the most complex ability that could conceivably be mastered by the brightest sixth-year pupil. In planning the IPI program, this was quickly recognized as an impossibility. Several types of mathematical abilities were perceived, each of which can be organized in the form of a linear hierarchy of objectives, but each of which is somewhat independent of the other. For example, it appears necessary that skills in addition be learned in some sequential order leading from the simple to the complex. Rather arbitrary decisions, however, may be made as to when the teaching of subtraction skills should be permitted to interrupt the pupil's progress in addition. For this reason, the sequencing of objectives in arithmetic was done separately within each area, such as numeration, place value, addition, subtraction, multiplication, division, combination of processes, measurement, and so on. Furthermore, to provide break points in each of these sequences (points at which a student could move from one area to another), each sequence was divided into units, each unit being made up of a limited number of objectives. These levels were labeled with letters A, B, C, and so on, and each can be thought of as somewhat comparable to a grade level. Some conception of what the resulting organization is like can be seen by an examination of Table 3.1. (The wording of the objectives in this chart is a condensation of the actual wording found in the IPI course outlines.)

In this organizational plan the set of objectives for a given area of study at a given level (such as Level C-Addition or Level D-Numeration) is identified as constituting a "unit." When a pupil begins study on a unit, he typically works on that unit until he can exhibit mastery of all of the objectives contained within it.

TABLE 3.1

*Samples of objectives as organized into levels and units
in the IPI arithmetic sequence*

Level C

Place value

1. Identifies place value of the units, 10's, 100's, to 200. Indicates $>$, $<$.
2. Writes numbers, columns 100's, 10's, units.

Addition

1. Uses associative principle.
2. Adds 2 numbers—sum of 20.
3. Sums 2 or 3 numbers, no carrying.
4. Uses $>$, $<$, $=$. Equation, 2 step, combining addition-subtraction.
5. Works column addition—2 or 3 addends, sums to 20.

Subtraction

1. Subtraction problems—numbers to 18.
2. Subtracts 2 digits—no borrowing.
3. Finds missing addend—2 single digits.

Combination of processes

1. Adds, subtracts, showing inverses.
2. Fill-in frames. Single digit addends.
3. Solves 1-step problems. Greater than 10.
4. Uses $>$, $<$, $=$, $\neq$, sums to 100.

Fractions

1. Divides object. Uses ½, ⅓, ¼.
2. Identifies ½, ⅓, ¼.
3. Divides sets—½, ⅓, ¼.
4. Identifies ½, ⅓, ¼—set of objects.

However, the exact order in which he moves from one unit to another can be varied somewhat from pupil to pupil, depending upon a diagnosis of each pupil's needs and capabilities which he can demonstrate after completing a unit. For example, most pupils might progress from C-Numeration to C-Addition (see Table 3.1), since this is the basic order of progression built into the curriculum sequence.

Place value   *Level D*

---

1. Identifies units, 10's, 100's, 1,000's. Uses $>$, $<$. Writes number before, after to 1,000.
2. Writes numerals expanded notation, to 1,000. Regroups, renames.
3. Uses number families, bridging, to work addition, subtraction problems.

Addition

---

1. Demonstrates mastery, sums through 20.
2. Does column addition—no carrying.
3. Finds missing addends—3 single digits.
4. Uses words: sum, addends—labels parts.
5. Adds, carrying to 10's, using 3 digit numerals, 2 or more addends.
6. Adds, carrying to 10's, 100's, using 3 digit numerals, 2 or more addends.
7. Adds, carrying 10's, 100's, using 3 digit numerals, 2 or more addends.
8. Finds sums, column addition. Using 2 or more addends of 1 digit.

Subtraction

---

1. Mastery subtraction facts, numbers to 20.
2. Subtracts, no borrowing—3 or more digits.
3. Subtracts, borrowing 10's place—2 digits.
4. Subtracts, borrowing 100's—3 digits.
5. Subtracts, borrowing 10's, 100's—3 digits.

Combination of processes

---

1. Supplies missing operational signs.
2. Fill-in $>$, $<$, $=$, to complete problems.
3. Solves 1- or 2-step word problems.

Fractions

---

1. Identifies objects using ⅓, ⅛, ⅔, ¾.
2. Divides set of objects into parts.
3. Adds any 2 fractions with same denominator.
4. Adds 2 fractions, same denominator, which equals a whole number.
5. Identifies an equivalent fraction for a given fraction, using pictures.

However, there may be situations in which an individual student might move from C-Numeration to D-Numeration or from C-Numeration to C-Measurement. The unit organization provides for convenient and meaningful "break points" which enhance opportunities for this type of variation in "prescriptions."

If pupils are to work through a curriculum on an individual basis, it is essential that instructional materials be such that pupils can learn from them without constant help from a teacher and can make steady progress in the mastery of the defined objectives. In conventional teacher-directed instruction, it is possible to use textbook and workbook materials which require the teacher to explain procedures and operations before the pupil is prepared to profit from his own reading or study. However, in a program of individualized instruction, in which each pupil may be at a different point in the lesson materials, this kind of extensive teacher help would require the employment of many additional teachers. For this reason, it is essential that lesson materials be largely self-instructional. The identification and production of materials of this type was the next step in the development of the IPI project, following the defining and sequencing of objectives.

. . .

In individualized instruction care must be taken to find out what skills and knowledge each pupil possesses and to see that each one starts in the learning sequence at the point which is most appropriate for him. From what has been described so far, the program for Individually Prescribed Instruction can be seen to consist of sequences of behavioral objectives together with the materials and activities which enable pupils to achieve these objectives. After these had been developed, the next step in planning the program was to devise procedures for determining where each pupil is to start his study within each sequence. When a student comes to any new instructional situation, whether it is beginning the first day of his first year in school or merely moving on to some new unit of study from the prerequisite unit, he brings to that situation certain knowledge and certain abilities that are not the same as those of his fellow pupils. If instruction is to be efficient and challenging, it must take into account these individual differences in entering behaviors, it must place the pupil at the point in the learning sequence which is appropriate for him, and it must accommodate his program to his needs. For this reason, essential tools in the IPI procedure are the batteries of placement tests that are used in each subject.

It was necessary to develop placement tests within each area of each subject. For example, in arithmetic there are placement tests in numeration, in addition, in subtraction, and so on. A placement test covers a sampling of abilities from each level (A, B, C, D, etc.) and is organized in terms of levels, so that for each pupil a decision can be made as to the level at which he should start his study. Since each pupil must take tests for each area in each subject, a considerable period of time (up to two weeks) at the start of the school year is spent in placement testing. However, since this procedure provides so much information about each pupil, it is looked upon as a wise investment of time.

The placement testing makes it possible to say of each pupil, "He should start at level D-Numeration, level D-Addition, level C-Subtraction, . . . [and so on]." That is, the process places the pupil at his proper level in the curriculum sequence in every subarea of reading, of arithmetic, and of science.

However, placing a pupil in the proper unit does not entirely solve the problem of assigning the exact lesson materials with which he should start working. Within each unit there are a number of objectives, and, although he is placed in a given unit, it may still be true that the student already has command of one or more of the unit objectives. To provide exact information concerning his command of objectives, each pupil is given a pretest over the materials of a unit before he starts work in it. The pretest contains items covering every objective in the unit and, hence, provides information concerning the pupil's command of *each* objective. This information permits the teacher to determine what a student needs to study and where he should begin work. On the basis of this information the teacher develops a "prescription" which lists a certain limited number of instructional exercises on which the pupil is to work. An example of a listing of needed instructional materials, such as would be found on an actual prescription form, is shown in Table 3.2.

TABLE 3.2

Example of the type of data entered on a pupil prescription blank

Name	John Smith		Class	2
Level	C		Unit	Addition

Date of prescription	Prescriber's initials	Page number	Skill number	(Description*)
4/5/66	JOB	C-184	1	(Illustration of how to add 3 single-digit numerals)
		C-185	1	(Extension of C-184)
		C-186	1	(Pupil supplies missing numerals, then adds this sum to a third numeral)
		C-188	1	(Pupil finds sum of 2 numerals, then adds this sum to a third numeral)
		C-189	1	(Curriculum-embedded test)
4/11/66	JW	C-190	1	(Illustration of how to add 3 single-digit numerals with parentheses instead of pictures)
		C-195	1	(Pupil adds 3 single-digit numerals in parentheses. No pictures)
		C-196	1	(Pupil supplies missing numerals when combining digits in adding 3-digit numerals)
		C-203	1	(Curriculum-embedded test)

* Descriptions of exercises are added here for clarification but would *not* be shown on prescription.

. . .

For individualized instruction, conditions must be provided which permit each pupil to progress through a learning sequence at a pace determined by his own work habits and by his ability to master the designated instructional objectives. Under Individually Prescribed Instruction, when a pupil has been given his prescription and has secured the materials with which he is to work, he takes his place at his own desk or some other type of study station (language laboratory booth, science laboratory area, chair in the library, or the like) and begins his independent study. With the types of materials that are used, most students can proceed quite readily with little or no assistance from a teacher. However, most of this individual study will be done in a large study area accommodating some 50 to 60 students and having 2 to 3 teachers (assisted by 3 or 4 teacher-aides) present to provide individual help to those pupils who need it. In this way a pupil who is having trouble with a particular question or problem can rather quickly have his difficulty straightened out and then proceed with his study.

A typical student prescription contains enough lesson material for a day's work or to teach one objective, if the latter requires less than a day's time. It provides, as a final objective, a "curriculum-embedded test." This test, which the pupil may look upon as only another work-sheet, is something of a "final examination" on that one objective and is used as the principal basis for determining whether or not the pupil has mastered the objective. As the pupil works through his material for a given objective, he stops periodically to have his lessons scored either by himself or by a clerk. This scoring is typically done by one of the teacher-aides who is working in the study area, although some use is being made of self-scoring by pupils. The results of the scoring and the actual exercise sheets themselves are then given careful scrutiny by one of the teachers as a basis for preparing the next prescription for the student. If the student has done satisfactory work, his next prescription will probably call for him to go on to study the next objective in the unit. If he displays some weakness, the teacher will probably prescribe additional work on the same objective.

. . .

When a pupil has covered all of the objectives within a given unit, he is given a unit posttest to determine the extent to which he has mastered and retained all of the content of the unit. If he does not show the prescribed mastery on this test, he will be given further work which will help him to make up his deficiencies. When he successfully completes the posttest, he is moved on to some new unit. This will probably be the next unit in the level at which he is working, but in some cases the teacher may have reason to give him work at some other point in the curriculum sequence. Again, when he enters a new unit, he is first given a pretest so that the teacher can see whether or not what he has learned previously has given him a basis for extrapolation so that he already actually has command of some of the abilities included in the new unit.

Through this procedure of carefully monitoring a pupil's progress through the use of a variety of evaluation devices and then developing prescriptions tailored to the individual, the IPI procedure attempts to keep each pupil working with materials that are a continual challenge to him but that are not too difficult to prevent him from making steady progress. . . .

If instruction is to be effective, it must make provisions for having the student actually carry out and practice the behavior which he is to learn. This principle, whether expressed in the rather classic phrase that "we learn by doing" or in the programer's term, "active responding," is of basic importance in identifying instructional activities for use in IPI. It alerts one to the fact that if pupils are to acquire a skill or an ability, they must not merely read about it or be told about it. Rather, they must be provided with an activity that gives them actual practice in what they are to learn. The emphasis is not on "How can I tell him about this?" or "How can I explain this to him?" but rather on "How can I get the pupil to do something that will give him actual experience, insight, and practice in this desired behavior?"

Of course, the major guide in developing materials and activities that will achieve this end is the actual behavioral objectives. That is, since these objectives are expressed in terms of what the pupil should be able to do after he has mastered the objective, the essential element in instruction is to provide conditions under which the pupil can practice this behavior. If the objective states that the pupil is to be able to solve problems of a particular type, the lesson materials must provide guided practice in the solving of such problems. If it states that he is to be able to derive certain principles from simple science experiments, he must be given work in performing experiments and deriving principles.

Identifying and developing curriculum materials in this way poses a real challenge to persons responsible for doing so. In cases in which the needed learning experience is particularly difficult to produce, the temptation is strong to merely "tell the student about this" or have him "read something about it" and hope that he acquires the needed ability in this way. For example, it is much simpler to have the student read about a scientific experiment and the conclusions to be drawn from it than it is to have him perform an experiment and attempt to draw his own conclusions. However, if the latter behavior represents the ability that the student is expected to acquire, the effective way by which he can learn it is to actually have experience in doing it. This is the principle that the IPI staff has attempted to follow in developing the exercises that teach each objective.

Learning is enhanced if students receive rather immediate feedback concerning the correctness of their efforts in attempting to approximate a desired behavior. A basic principle in most types of programed instruction has been that of "immediate confirmation," letting the student see the correct response to a frame almost immediately after he has made his own response to it or, in some way, informing him concerning his success. Too frequently under typical procedures in most classrooms a pupil works problems, answers questions, or takes a test and then must wait for a day or more to learn whether or not what he has done is correct. This can result in a lack of reinforcement for correct performances or, conversely, in some tendency for the student to learn incorrect responses because of the delay in informing him of his error. In any case, this delay in feedback to the student probably makes for inefficient learning.

In the IPI procedure, the attempt is made to keep the student rather continuously informed regarding his goals and his performance. His worksheets are scored, either by himself or by a teacher-aide, almost immediately after completion. In this sense each worksheet is comparable to a "frame" or a short series of frames in a program to which a student makes an "active response," which in turn is given "immediate confirmation" when the paper is scored. Further feedback is given to the student in the form of his scores on curriculum-embedded tests, his scores on unit tests, and the less formal remarks of the teacher. Every effort is made not only to monitor the progress of each student quite carefully but also to see that the student immediately receives information concerning his progress.

The final criterion for judging any instructional sequence must be its effectiveness in producing changes in pupils, and feedback concerning pupil performance should be used in the continuing modification and improvement of materials and procedures. Certainly another major contribution of the programed-instruction movement to the improvement of educational curricula has been its emphasis on the need for repeated trials of a program with students and the revision of the program on the basis of results from these trials. Most other procedures for curriculum development have called attention to the need for this type of trial, but programed instruction has outlined procedures for it as an essential step in the program-development process.

With rather conventional teaching procedures, weaknesses in materials and techniques may be overlooked if these affect the performance of only a minority of students in a class, or compensations for such weaknesses may be made through supplementary explanations by the teacher. However, procedures involving individualization and self-instruction make such weaknesses glaringly apparent. If an individual pupil is halted in his progress through the curriculum because he cannot work a given exercise or because he repeatedly fails a particular test, something must be done to remedy this situation. The curriculum developer is essentially forced to revise materials on the basis of this feedback from pupils.

The revision of materials and procedures on the basis of pupil performance has been an important feature of the IPI project. All instructional materials have been looked upon as being on trial until they have been tried out with, at least, a limited number of pupils. The person developing a lesson has asked himself the question, "Can pupils learn from this?" and then has used the lesson with a small sample of children to obtain an answer. After materials have been made an integral part of the program, they are still subjected to this type of scrutiny. In many cases the feedback on pupil performance has been rather informal in nature. Teachers have merely reported that "Pupils are having difficulty with this exercise." Frequently, such appraisals have been accompanied by suggestions as to what changes should be made, and it has been relatively simple to make rather immediate revisions. In other cases, the necessary revision has been much more extensive. At certain points it has involved a rather wholesale reordering and revision of the sequence of objectives as well as of the lesson materials. For example, at the end of the first year of trial of the IPI program at the Oakleaf School, the mathematics sequence was given a careful examination, certain objectives were changed, new ones were added, and the needed teaching materials were developed. This type of broad-scale re-examination of the curriculum, in the light of empirical data, is an essential feature of the IPI project and should probably be a part of any curriculum-development effort.

Steps have also been taken to develop a rather formal procedure for using test results to locate needed revisions.

INDIVIDUALLY PRESCRIBED INSTRUCTION AS AN APPLICATION OF THESE PRINCIPLES

Individually Prescribed Instruction may be considered as the application of the foregoing principles to develop and carry out a program for the individualization of instruction. It will be noted that these principles contain no mention of the subject-matter content that is to be taught or of the source of the objectives stressed. The IPI procedure is not limited to any particular type of content objectives, nor is it a curriculum project developed for the purpose of teaching some new and different subject matter. Rather, it is a procedure for planning and carrying out instruction that can be applied to any content for which objectives can be defined in specific behavioral terms and organized in some meaningful sequences.
. . .

SUMMARY

Implicit in our discussion has been the assumption that the basic principles of programed instruction should be applied more comprehensively and with greater continuity in schools. Such application will necessitate a restructuring of the total curriculum and of the instructional system.

We have noted that it has been difficult for educators to observe a broad application of programed instruction because school utilization has been limited almost entirely to a patchwork pattern of available programed materials stitched onto the regular curriculum. We reviewed briefly these patterns of use and the positive findings and problems encountered in this limited application of the potential of programed instruction. Although we recognized the gains from even this limited use, we expressed our belief that for the real advantages of programed instruction to be realized in the schools there must be a broad-scale application of the *principles* of instructional programing.

As an illustration of what is involved in a broad-scale application, we have drawn upon our experience in applying programing principles to curricular and instructional planning in the Oakleaf Elementary School of the Baldwin-Whitehall School District. We described "Individual Prescribed Instruction," a project which implements programing principles in several subject fields in this school. We showed how its theoretical rationale incorporates fundamental principles of programing, and we described the steps in the development of Individual Prescribed Instruction. We identified these steps in the development of the program: describing in detail the specific behavioral objectives; analyzing and sequencing the behaviors for effective learning; developing an extensive inventory of self-managed instructional materials and environments suitable for individual learning by learners who vary greatly in their competencies and attitudes and abilities; providing an accurate and efficient system by which teacher and learner determine specific abilities and needs of individual learners; establishing conditions that set for the learner an attainable goal and that induce, support, and confirm the requisite behaviors; and providing feedback and readjustments in the entire curriculum design, administrative procedures, and instructional practices.

In its attention to each learner's progress, in its individually prescribed learning tasks, and in its systematic materialization of the curriculum into predictable instructional practices, this project illustrates what we believe will be in the future the broader application of programed instruction in the schools. Surely individual teachers and many schools will continue to make their limited uses of programed instruction—from the adoption of an available program to the development of short programs or units. But we hopefully foresee more schools adopting the general principles of programed instruction.

QUESTIONS

1. Lindvall and Bolvin state that Individually Prescribed Instruction exemplifies the application of the principles of programmed instruction to curriculum development in an elementary school. Give an overview of the IPI program outlining (a) the theoretical bases and the procedures, and (b) the steps in the development of the curriculum.

2. The diagnostic and placement features of IPI are an important aspect of their individualized system. Describe the IPI procedures designed to adapt curriculum to individual differences.

3. Describe how each of the following principles from the experimental analysis of behavior is incorporated in IPI:
   a) immediate reinforcement
   b) behavior is learned when it is emitted and reinforced
   c) gradual progression
   d) the student is always right.

UNIT

4

Contingency Management

Content

Mechner, F. "Behavioral Contingencies." From "Science Education and Behavioral Technology." In R. Glaser, ed., *Teaching Machines and Programed Learning,* Vol. 2. Washington, D.C.: National Education Association, 1965, pp. 441–508. (a selection)

Stachnik, T. J. "The Use of Behavior Modification by Individual Classroom Teachers." In R. Ulrich, T. Stachnik, and J. Mabry, eds., *Control of human behavior,* Vol. 3. Glenview, Ill.: Scott, Foresman, 1974, pp. 96–106. (a selection)

 The program on contingencies is designed to clarify the technical use of this term. The article demonstrates an application of the principles of the experimental analysis of behavior to problems of classroom management.

Objectives

Students will define and give an example of a behavioral contingency, describe how behavioral principles are applied to change behavior, and note similarities between techniques of behavior modification and the principles of programed instruction.

Instructions

1. Read the objectives and the introduction.
2. The program on behavioral contingencies is optional. If you decide to include it, do it first.

3. Read the article, then write your answers to the questions that follow.

4. Check your answers.

5. Review your work with your instructor or your group before beginning Unit 5.

INTRODUCTION

Behavior modification and contingency management are terms currently used to describe the application of principles of operant psychology to problems in everyday life which require behavior change. A contingency is similar to a cause-effect relation between two events. In psychology, a contingency means: if behavior occurs, then a consequence will follow. Managing contingencies, then, means arranging or rearranging the consequences of behavior. The basic principle of operant psychology involved in contingency management is that behavior is modified by its consequences. In the following article you will notice that the children's behavior is most effectively modified by immediate, consistently applied consequences. If you are interested in further reading on the subject of contingency management in everyday life, we recommend *CONtingency MANagement,* a basic text in comic-book format, published by Behaviordelia Press (1971).

Accompanying the article is a short program by Francis Mechner on the particular meaning of behavior contingencies in psychology. If you are not familiar with the technical use of this term, work through the program before reading the article.

Behavioral Contingencies

Francis Mechner

Directions: Cover the right-hand side of the text. Write your answer in the left box. After answering *all* the questions in a box, check your answer by uncovering the right-hand side of the text.

Francis Mechner, "Science Education and Behavioral Technology, in *Teaching Machines and Programmed Learning,* vol. 2, ed. R. Glaser (Washington, D.C.: National Education Association, 1965), pp. 441–508. Reprinted by permission of the Association for Educational Communication & Technology.

1

Your being born *was not* a "response-event" for you. That is, it *was not* an action you initiated.

Your throwing your rattle out of your crib, however, *was* an action initiated by you. It *was* a "response-event" for you.

CHECK each sentence below that describes a response-event for the person or animal named in the sentence (note that there is no limit to the number of sentences you can check):

☐ a. Clara dyed her hair red.

☐ b. Herman died of old age.

☐ c. The dog has fleas.

☐ d. The cat meowed.

a

d

2

When you hit someone, it (☐ is ☐ is not) your action. It (☐ is ☐ is not) your response-event.

When the other person hits you back, it (☐ is ☐ is not) your response-event.

CHECK each sentence below that describes a response-event for the person or animal named in the sentence:

☐ a. Philip ran fast.

☐ b. Gregory was run over.

☐ c. Alice cheated on the exam.

☐ d. Mary was reprimanded for cheating.

☐ e. The canary lost all its feathers.

☐ f. The parrot said "Polly wants a cracker."

is

is

is not

a

c

f

3

The sentence, "The officer gave Mr. Smith a summons," *describes* the officer's giving the ticket, but merely *implies* Mr. Smith's speeding or going through the red light.

Does the sentence describe a response-event for Mr. Smith? ☐ yes ☐ no

no

CHECK the statements below that describe, not merely imply, response-events for *you:*

    ☐ a. You solved a hard math example.

a

    ☐ b. Your teacher gave you a good grade in math.

    ☐ c. You are a doctor.

    ☐ d. You are studying to be a doctor.

d

4

Psychology is often called the science of behavior. That is, it is the study of how living creatures behave, how they act, what response-events they initiate under what circumstances.

The sentence "The telephone rang" does *not* refer to a response-event, because only people or animals can initiate response-events.

CHECK the response-events below:

    ☐ a. The hurricane struck here yesterday. (for the hurricane)

    ☐ b. Tom struck Harry. (for Tom)

b

    ☐ c. Tom struck Harry. (for Harry)

    ☐ d. The clock struck ten. (for the clock)

5

COMPLETE the definition of the term "response-event" below. Your definition should include the word "action."

A response-event is ——————.

any action initiated by a person or animal (*or* by a living creature).

(or equivalent response)

6

When you get into the bathtub, your environment changes: you get wet.

When you are just sitting in the bathtub, your environment does *not* change: you are already wet.

When you are standing on the corner and the traffic light is red, your environment (☐ changes ☐ does not change).

does not change

When you are standing on the corner and the traffic light turns from red to green, your environment (☐ changes ☐ does not change).

changes

When you are standing on the corner and someone right behind you calls your name, your environment (☐ changes ☐ does not change).

changes

7

The sentence "Tommy finished his spinach" *describes* the response-event "finishing the spinach," but it merely *implies* the environmental changes "The spinach disappeared from the plate" and "Tommy's stomach got fuller."

CHECK the sentences below which describe, not merely imply, *changes* in your environment:

- ☐ a. You have a scar on your forehead.
- ☐ b. You are walking along and a ladder comes into view.
- ☐ c. Your alarm clock goes off in your ear.
- ☐ d. You set the alarm for 8:00.

b

c

8

We call a change in someone's environment a "stimulus-event" for that person.

Consider this sentence: Fred is stretched out on a sandy beach.

Does it describe a change in Fred's environment?
☐ yes ☐ no

no

Does it describe a stimulus-event for Fred? ☐ yes
☐ no

no

Consider this sentence: Fred is stretched out on the beach and a wave washes over him.

Does it describe a change in Fred's environment?
☐ yes ☐ no

yes

Does it describe a stimulus-event for Fred? ☐ yes
☐ no

yes

9

CHECK the stimulus-events below:

☐ a. The rat is sitting in a cage with a light bulb in front of him.

☐ b. The light goes on.

☐ c. He presses the bar in front of him.

☐ d. The pellet dispenser drops him a pellet of food.

☐ e. He eats the pellet.

b

d

10

The action of John hitting Al on the nose is a (☐ response-event ☐ stimulus-event) for John and a (☐ response-event ☐ stimulus-event) for Al.

response-event
stimulus-event

In front of each sentence below, WRITE:

"R" if it describes (not just implies) a response-event for *you*

"S" if it describes (not just implies) a stimulus-event for *you*

"O" if it describes neither a response-event nor a stimulus-event for *you*

_____ You pick up the telephone receiver.   R

_____ A dial tone sounds.   S

_____ Your mother-in-law, who is listening in on the extension phone, hears the dial tone, too.   O

_____ You dial your friend's number.   R

_____ You get a busy signal.   S

11

To summarize: For a given individual, a stimulus-event can be initiated by:

☐ that individual
☐ another individual
☐ the inanimate world

A response-event can be initiated by:

☐ that individual
☐ another individual
☐ the inanimate world

ALL THREE CHOICES:

that individual
another individual
the inanimate world

that individual

12

If you walk in the rain, then you'll get wet.
      R   S

In the sentence above, the response-event has been underlined and labeled _____.

The stimulus-event has been underlined and labeled _____.

R

S

13

In the sentences below, UNDERLINE each response-event and LABEL it with an "R." Also UNDERLINE each stimulus-event and LABEL it with an "S," as in the example.

Example: Unless you cash your check within
                 R
   thirty days, it will become void.
                S

a. Your hand will turn pale if you hold it above your head for a long time.

b. Arnold goes to the doctor once a year and never gets a serious disease.

a. Your hand will turn pale
            S
  if you hold it above your head for a long time.
        R

b. Arnold goes to the doctor once a year
          R
  and never gets a serious disease.
         S

14

Unless <u>you cash your check</u> within thirty days, <u>it</u>
R

<u>will become void.</u>
S

Unless R within thirty days, S.

In the model above, we have rewritten the sentence, substituting "R" for the whole response-event and "S" for the whole stimulus-event.

REWRITE the sentences below according to the model:

a. <u>Your hand will turn pale</u> if <u>you hold it above</u>
S$$R

<u>your head</u> for a long time.

$\overline{}$

b. <u>Arnold goes to the doctor</u> once a year and
R

<u>never gets a serious disease.</u>
S

$\overline{}$

a. S if R for a long time.

b. R once a year and never S.

15

Consider this sentence:

If you flick the light switch, then the light will go on.

It states that the light will go on:

☐ whether or not you flick the switch
☐ since you will flick the switch
☐ only on the condition that you flick the switch

only on the condition that you flick the switch

16

Sometimes a change in the environment *follows* behavior without being *conditional upon* (or *contingent upon*) the behavior.

For example, in both sentences below an S-event (environmental change) follows an R-event (behavior). CHECK the one that states a relation of conditionality or contingency between the R-event and the S-event that follows it:

☐ John pushed button "6" and then the elevator stopped at the sixth floor.

☐ If John pushes button "6" then the elevator will stop at the sixth floor.

If John pushes button "6" then the elevator will stop at the sixth floor.

17

First, UNDERLINE and LABEL all response-events and stimulus-events in the sentences below.

Second, REWRITE the sentences, substituting "R" for the whole response-event and "S" for the whole stimulus-event.

Third, CHECK the sentence if it *states* (not merely *implies*) that the S-event is contingent upon the R-event.

☐ a. A recorded announcement of the time played on the phone once when Alice dialed ME 7-1212.

　　 REWRITTEN: _____

☐ b. A recorded announcement of the time plays on the phone whenever Alice dials ME 7-1212.

　　 REWRITTEN: _____

☐ a. A recorded announcement of the time played on the phone once when
   <u>S</u>
   Alice dialed ME-7-1212.
   <u>R</u>
   S once when R.

☑ b. A recorded announcement of the time plays on the phone whenever
   <u>S</u>
   Alice dials ME 7-1212.
   <u>R</u>
   S whenever R.

18

Below are four types of statements. As psychologists, we are interested only in situations in which an environmental change is contingent upon behavior.

CHECK the one sentence that represents this type of situation:

☐ If R then R.　　　(*or:* R if R.)
☐ If R then S.　　　(*or:* S if R.)
☐ If S then R.　　　(*or:* R if S.)
☐ If S then S.　　　(*or:* S if S.)

If R then S. (*or:* S if R.)

19

As psychologists, we are interested in situations in which _____-events are contingent upon _____-events.

Why do we call such situations "behavioral contingencies"? (Include the words *behavior* and *contingent* in your answer.) _____

stimulus (*or* S)
response (*or* R)

because an environmental change (*or* stimulus-event) is *contingent* upon *behavior*.

(or equivalent response)

20

First, REWRITE each sentence below, substituting "R" for any response-event and "S" for any stimulus-event.

Then, CHECK a sentence only if it describes a behavioral contingency, that is, if it describes a situation in which an *S* is contingent upon an *R*.

☐ a. The radio will go on if you turn the knob to the right.

   REWRITTEN: _____

☐ b. The trees will get smashed if the hurricane comes this way.

   REWRITTEN: _____

☐ c. If you behave yourself all year long, then there'll be nice presents under the tree for you on Christmas morning.

   REWRITTEN: _____

☐ d. If it snows this weekend, then I'll go skiing.

   REWRITTEN: _____

☑ a. The radio will go on
       S
   if you turn the knob
   to the right.
       R
   S if R.

☐ b. The trees will get
   smashed if the hurri-
       S   S
   cane comes this way.
   S if S.

☑ c. If you behave your-
   self all year long,
       R
   then there'll be nice
   presents under the
   tree
       S
   for you on Christmas
   morning.
   If R, then S.

☐ d. If it snows this week-
           S
   end, then I'll go
   skiing.
       R
   If S, then R.

21

UNDERLINE and LABEL the R-event and the S-event in the following sentence:

   If the swelling in Mrs. Jones's leg gets worse, then she'll go to a doctor.

In this sentence, the _____-event is conditional upon the _____-event.

Therefore, the sentence (☐ describes ☐ does not describe) a behavioral contingency.

If the swelling in Mrs.
Jones's leg gets worse,
           S
then she'll go to a doctor.
                   R
R
S

does not describe

22

When deciding whether a sentence does or does not describe a behavioral contingency, it is important to look for the R and S in relation to the SAME person.

Consider, for example, the sentence, "If John hits Tom, then Tom will hit John."

REWRITE the sentence, substituting "R" for John's response-event and "S" for John's stimulus-event: _____

If R, then S.

REWRITE the same sentence, substituting "R" for Tom's response-event and "S" for Tom's stimulus-event: _____

If S, then R.

For whom does the sentence "If John hits Tom, then Tom will hit John" describe a behavioral contingency?

☐ for Tom
☐ for John

for John

23

Behavioral contingencies are often described in the form(s):

☐ a. A stimulus-event occurs when a response-event occurs.

a

☐ b. If a stimulus-event occurs, then a response-event occurs.

☐ c. If a response-event occurs, then a stimulus-event occurs.

c

☐ d. If one response-event occurs, then another response-event occurs.

☐ e. If one stimulus-event occurs, then another stimulus-event occurs.

☐ f. A response-event occurs when a stimulus-event occurs.

24

REWRITE the sentence below, substituting "R" for the response-event and "S" for the stimulus-event:

Unless you put that cat down, you'll get a spanking.

REWRITTEN: _____

Do the same for this sentence:

If you do not put that cat down, you'll get a spanking.

REWRITTEN: _____

Unless R, S.

If not R, S.

25

Unless you put that cat down, you'll get a spank-
       R   S
ing.

Unless R, S.

If you do not put that cat down, you'll get a spank-
           R   S
ing.

If not R, S.

The two sentences above are equivalent, because in both cases, the occurrence of the stimulus-event is contingent upon:

- ☐ the occurrence of the response-event, "put that cat down."
- ☐ the non-occurrence of the response-event, "put that cat down."

the non-occurrence of the response-event, "put that cat down"

26

REWRITE this sentence, substituting "R" for the response-event and "S" for the stimulus-event.

You'll get hurt if you do not cross streets carefully.

REWRITTEN: _____

In the sentence above, *whether or not* the _____ occurs depends upon *whether or not* the _____ occurs.

Thus, we say that the sentence (☐ describes ☐ does not describe) a behavioral contingency.

S if not R.

S

R

describes

27

CHECK the behavioral contingencies below:

☐ a. If you put off that visit to the dentist, your cavity will grow bigger.

☐ b. More people take their vacations in summer than in winter.

☐ c. You get the weather report when you dial WE 6-1212.

☐ d. If it rains tomorrow, I will go for a walk.

☐ e. If we go to the beach, then we'll take a picnic lunch.

☐ f. Your wish will come true if you wish on the first star you see at night.

☐ g. If someone is born in New York, then he is a native New Yorker.

☐ h. If I were you, I'd tell him a thing or two!

a

c

f

The Use of Behavior Modification by Individual Classroom Teachers

Thomas J. Stachnik

During the fall term of 1969, I taught a masters'-level course at Oakland University in Rochester, Michigan, titled, Mental Health of School Children. The class met

Thomas J. Stachnik, "The Use of Behavior Modification by Individual Classroom Teachers," from *Control of Human Behavior,* Vol. III, by Roger Ulrich, Thomas Stachnik, and John one evening a week since virtually all the participants had full-time teaching positions, mostly in elementary and junior high school settings. The course began with some discussion about what constituted "mental health," followed by considerable debate as to what role teachers should play in promoting the mental health of their students. Initially, a few of the teachers felt that they should do little more than make referrals to psychiatric professionals when a child exhibited some deviant behavior. But as the discussion progressed, it became more apparent that mental health could be defined behaviorally (the presence of certain behaviors and the absence of others), and that a child's teacher was perhaps in a better position than anyone else to help strengthen appropriate behaviors and weaken others.

At that point substantial interest arose about acquiring techniques which would enable the teacher to intervene effectively. Therefore, the balance of the course was designed to meet two objectives: (1) to introduce the teachers to the principles of behavior upon which behavior modification strategies are based, and (2) to give the teachers some experience in adapting those principles into effective classroom behavior management techniques.

The first objective was met in a traditional, didactic fashion which included readings, discussions, films, etc. The second objective was met largely through a classroom behavior modification project assigned to each teacher. The guidelines for the project were clear: Identify, objectively measure, and record the behavior of an individual student or the entire class, and then modify that behavior in an appropriate direction. At the end of the term, each teacher orally described his project and submitted a written report. The balance of this paper contains a sampling of those reports.

In reviewing the reports and reflecting upon the discussion which occurred during the course of the term, the following conclusions seem warranted:

1. The teachers enrolled in the course were very receptive to learning the rudiments of behavior modification. They also showed considerable skill in translating the principles they learned into useful classroom techniques.

2. Teachers can be made to readily recognize that their historical role of automatically referring troubled children to mental health professionals can be improved upon. They can be made to see that deviant social behavior in the classroom or unsuccessful academic performance is often the precursor to more serious problems, and that the classroom is often the chosen intervention setting.

3. Although all the teachers in the course had received bachelor degrees from accredited teacher-training institutions, they were woefully unprepared to deal effectively with problem behaviors in any specific way. The implication is obvious: Undergraduate teacher-training programs must begin to include the technology of contingency management in their curricula. That addition would insure the produc-

Mabry. Copyright © 1974 by Scott, Foresman and Company. Reprinted by permission of the publisher.

tion of more competent action-oriented teachers and simultaneously contribute toward the prevention of a variety of mental health problems among their students.

"A PROBLEM IN MATHEMATICS" BY CAROL BLUMENSTOCK

Problem

One of the problems a classroom teacher is faced with is what to do about the child who understands the concepts presented, knows how to do the work, but never seems to complete his daily work. It was this problem that led me to select Leigh, a student in my class, as the subject for my project.

Leigh is a "normal" seven-year-old child, who seems to be very well adjusted. She possesses an average intelligence and has no apparent learning disabilities. But, since Primary I, she has had difficulty completing each day's work.

Procedure

After careful observation of Leigh's daily work, I discovered that she very seldom completed her math assignment. She would leave the page unfinished or haphazardly fill in any answer. There were two behaviors that I wanted to establish:

1. complete each day's assignment;
2. discontinue the practice of filling in any number for an answer to a math problem.

I established a baseline by keeping a record of Leigh's daily math assignments and the progress she made. I kept a record of the following items:

1. whether or not the assignment was finished;
2. the number of problems per day;
3. the number of correct answers per day;
4. the number of errors per day;
5. the number of unfinished problems per day.

These are my findings:

	(X) Finished assignments	Number of problems	Number correct	Number of errors	Number unfinished
Monday		14	3	3	8
Tuesday	X	18	11	7	0
Wednesday		27	13	4	10
Thursday	X	14	6	8	0
Friday		32	11	9	12

Before intervening with a behavior modification technique, I wanted to discover whether Leigh had difficulty knowing what to do or how to do it. I found that she understood the concepts presented and knew how to do the problems. The technique I chose to use was the token system. I chose this technique for two reasons. From past experience, I learned that Leigh was a child who needed to be highly motivated and that what once served as motivation often did not work if used again. I explained the token system to Leigh in the form of a game, and she agreed that she would like to play. We decided that one token would be given for every correct answer. Leigh selected what were to be her rewards by naming activities she liked to participate in if given a free choice. The rewards that Leigh chose for herself were:

1. to have recess on gym day;
2. to have five extra minutes of recess;
3. to have show-and-tell for the class;
4. to cut-out and draw using colored paper;
5. to choose a game or a puzzle to play with for ten minutes at the end of the day;
6. to bring a snack for the class;
7. to have no boardwork for a day;
8. to help make things for the bulletin boards;
9. to play a math game at the end of the day with the class.

I assigned a token value to each of the above rewards and made a copy of these items for Leigh and taped the list to her desk.

Results

At the end of the first day I checked Leigh's math assignment. There were 23 problems and she had 5 correct, 11 errors, and 7 unfinished problems. Needless to say, I was not impressed with the results of the first day, and so at this time I added another dimension to the experiment. Leigh was told she would be awarded two extra tokens for each page of math that she completed. This contingency should have been included in the beginning, since it applied to one of the behaviors to be modified. I continued to record Leigh's progress for the next seven days. Here is the information that I obtained.

	(X) Finished assignments	Number of problems	Number correct	Number of errors	Number unfinished
Monday		23	5	11	7
Tuesday	X	36	36	0	0
Wednesday		29	16	6	7
Thursday	X	20	17	3	0
Friday	X	32	26	6	0
Monday	X	34	33	1	0
Tuesday	X	30	28	2	0
Wednesday	X	25	25	0	0

Of course, I am very pleased with the results, but of more importance is the great pride Leigh now takes in completing her math pages. I intend to continue using this technique with Leigh and gradually move from using the tokens to using social reinforcers.

. . .

"MODIFICATION OF SOBBING BEHAVIOR" BY BEVERLY BLESSINGER

Problem

A second-grade teacher, a friend who works in another school system, requested my aid as a reading clinician in a reading-discipline problem. One of the children in her class, Kirman, sobbed daily throughout the reading period. This behavior did not particularly disturb the other children since Kirman stayed in her seat with her head on her desk, sobbing softly. But her behavior was disturbing the teacher. Besides the annoyance of the actual sobbing, the teacher knew that Kirman was not doing her work at this time, and she was troubled that the child appeared so unhappy.

Kirman's teacher explained to me how she already had attempted to modify the child's behavior. At first, she had gone to the sobbing Kirman and attempted to find out why she was crying. The child said that the work was too hard for her. Although her teacher thought that the assignments were at Kirman's instructional level, she gave her easier work to do. But the sobbing continued. Then the teacher tried what she called punishment. When Kirman sobbed instead of doing her work, Kirman had to stay in the room during recess. But the sobbing continued.

Method

First, I asked the teacher to observe the amount of time Kirman sobbed each day and to report the result at the end of each day. I recorded these times for five days; this and subsequent records of sobbing appear in Fig. 4.1. The average sobbing time was thirty minutes. This behavior only occurred during the forty minutes Kirman was supposed to be doing independent-reading seat-work while the teacher was holding directed reading lessons with the other two reading groups. When Kirman's reading group was called, she came to the reading table quietly and did adequate work.

Thinking that the teacher's attention was the reinforcing agent for Kirman's behavior, I told Kirman's teacher to ignore her completely during the sobbing. I explained that Kirman, wanting the teacher's attention, was not being punished but rewarded when allowed to stay with the teacher during recess. (This was especially true since the teacher tended to chat with her during the "punishment.") Paying attention to Kirman while she sobbed was actually strengthening the sobbing behavior. I suggested that the teacher reward Kirman whenever she was working without sobbing by giving her some small, overt form of attention: smiling at her, glancing approvingly over her work, or by giving her a word or two of praise. This, hopefully, would reinforce the working, nonsobbing behavior.

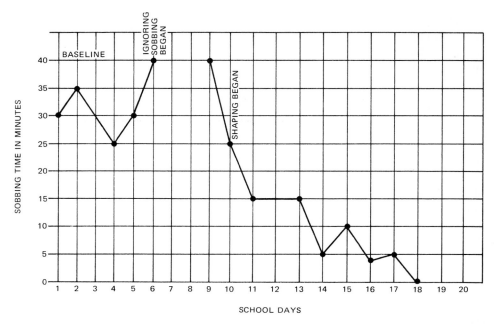

Fig. 4.1. Number of minutes a second-grade girl spent sobbing during baseline, ignoring of sobbing, and attention for not sobbing.

For fifteen days, Kirman's teacher ignored Kirman's sobbing. On the first day, when another child informed her of Kirman's crying, the teacher quietly told the class not to pay attention to it and not to tell her about it. At the end of each day, the teacher reported the amount of time Kirman sobbed.

For the first four of the fifteen days, Kirman sobbed for the entire forty minutes of independent reading. There seemed to be no opportunity to reward her with attention since she cried the entire time. Kirman's teacher began hinting that she was not going to "put up with this much longer" but was going to attend to Kirman when she was crying. Rather than attempting to explain to the teacher how rein-forcing this would be, I tried to think of some way to shape Kirman's behavior. Using successive approximations, I told the teacher to attend to Kirman at the very start of the forty minutes, right before Kirman began whimpering. With this en-couragement, Kirman started her work; the teacher praised her, and smiled at her about three minutes later. Kirman cried for only twenty-five minutes that day. From then on, there was always an opportunity to pay attention to Kirman. Each day, Kirman's teacher rewarded her with a smile or praise after she had worked without sobbing a little longer than she had the day before.

Results and Discussion

The effects of these procedures are shown on the graph (see Fig. 4.1). After fifteen days during which Kirman's sobbing was consistently ignored and her nonsobbing behavior reinforced, Kirman spent the entire forty minutes working without sobbing. For the first four days of the modification attempt, Kirman's sobbing behavior actually increased. Perhaps this increase was due to the teacher's previous unwitting intermittent reinforcement of Kirman's behavior; the teacher periodically had paid attention to Kirman's sobbing behavior. Perhaps Kirman felt that now she had to "cry harder" to be rewarded with attention. If I had suggested shaping Kirman's working behavior at the start of the experiment, the sobbing behavior might have been extinguished earlier.

Although the experiment was officially over on the twentieth day and the teacher no longer reported to me, I suggested to her that Kirman would not have to be reinforced every day. Instead, Kirman could be reinforced "every once in a while" or more intermittently. A few days later, Kirman's behavior was not only work-oriented, but, as an extra benefit, the other children were friendlier to her since she was no longer a "crybaby." Thinking that the new friends' attitudes would also reinforce Kirman's nonsobbing behavior, I heartily agreed with Kirman's teacher that everything was "just great."

"REDUCING DISRUPTIVE OUTBURSTS" BY CAROL CALLAHAN

Problem

My second-grade (Team 2) class of 13 boys and 6 girls were grouped according to the Gesell performance test. Their overall social and academic performance in September indicated they were working at a first-grade level. Two of the boys in the group had loud overpowering voices. They blurted out anything at anytime and rarely raised their hands or awaited a turn to speak. In September, I began ignoring them when they talked without raising their hands and immediately smiled and called on them when their hands were up. When I decided to record their talking-out-of-turn episodes in October, I discovered that they had begun to raise their hands. This allowed quieter-speaking children to talk out and, in fact, I even reinforced that behavior by acknowledging their questions. Thus, I decided to try to reduce the frequency of disruptive outbursts of the entire class.

Procedure

For five consecutive half-day sessions (both morning and afternoon) I kept a tally of the number of times the children talked without raising their hands in all but very small group work, talking while someone else was talking, or loudly calling out to me or another student. The children's arithmetic teacher also kept a tally of outbursts.

As I occasionally kept the tally on the board, the children began to guess why and would often stop to count the marks. (On the fifth day, I verified what they had guessed, and they agreed they sure talked out an awful lot!) The frequency of outbursts ranged from 35 to 45 per half-day session.

Since some children preferred recess more than others and most of the class valued having free time to play or socialize before the tardy bell rang, I decided to use both activities to help reduce the frequency of disruptive outbursts. I explained that, beginning the next morning, the class would have 40 points to work with each half-day. Each time they talked out, talked while someone else was talking, or were shouting or loudly talking while I was working with others, I would "X out" a number. If their outbursts exceeded 20, they would lose their free time before the bell the next session, and if they exceeded another 20 (total of 40 for a half-session), they would lose recess the next session. In other words, the activities they earned depended upon the appropriate behavior exhibited in the preceding session.

Under the circumstances, it was difficult to reinforce appropriate behavior immediately. Therefore, I displayed two charts, numbered from 1 to 20, with a sign attached to each which indicated the activity on one side and the loss of the activity on the other (Fig. 4.2). By looking at the charts and the signs, the children knew before they went home each session which activity they had earned for the next session. If the children were able to keep the outbursts below 20 each session, they would not lose either activity. After losing one free-time period, their outbursts dropped considerably. At point A (see Fig. 4.3), I lowered the criterion for each activity to 10 points per half-day session, and strengthened the desirability of these activities by allowing the children to bring their favorite games to play during free time and recess if they desired.

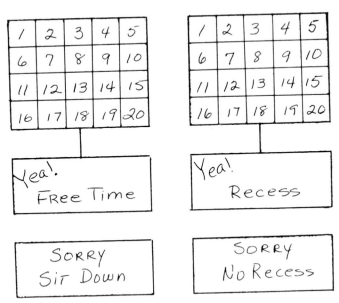

Fig. 4.2. Charts that illustrate a point system and consequences used to control disruptive behavior of a second-grade class. When disruptive behavior occurred, the teacher would "X" out a number. When all numbers were "X-ed" out, the reversible sign at the bottom would be turned from the positive to the negative consequence.

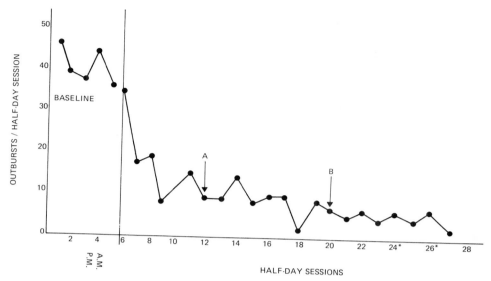

* Total of A.M. and P.M. sessions below 10.

Fig. 4.3. Frequency of outbursts of a second-grade class during baseline and loss of points for disruptive behavior.

At point B (see Fig. 4.3), I again lowered the criterion for each activity to 5 points per half-session. By this time, the children had sufficiently lowered their voices and raised their hands so frequently that I counted only loud or disturbing outbursts, and thus did not feel the criterion was too stiff. I also added Reinforcing activities at this time by asking the children to suggest things they would like to do if they could. These suggestions included: taking walks, having longer recesses, getting drinks without asking, having surprise treats hidden around room (this was done before), playing a game in the gym when it was free, listening to records using earphones, and playing their favorite games when their work was finished. These suggestions were written on small pieces of paper, combined with a few blank pieces, and placed in what we called "The Special Box." Using the idea of intermittent reinforcement, they could draw a slip from the box and would have a chance to do one of the desired activities. If the paper was blank, they could have another chance the next time outbursts totaled less than 10 per day.

Results and Discussion

The effects of this technique are dramatically indicated in Fig. 4.3. The children did not earn free time on several occasions, but they never lost recess. Most significant was the low frequency of disruptive outbursts.

There also were many other equally good effects. The children were pleased to earn special activities and liked the fact that they rarely lost free time or recess. I

rarely needed to single out any one person or raise my voice. When I witnessed disruptive behavior, I would calmly and quietly mark off a number. The child who
caused the disruption did not become angry or sullen—common in the case of being
reprimanded—but usually smiled or indicated a "whoops, I goofed" reaction. On
the whole, the children appeared to be more attentive in large-group discussions,
awaiting their turn to speak, or listening rather then talking to someone. There were
no incidents in which anger was directed at one child in particular who might have
caused more than his share of disruptions. The class was extremely honest about the
number of outbursts made. They kept their own record in arithmetic class and
during unit-study, which included all 90 children in the Team. Thus, hopefully they
learned to identify disruptive behavior.

The decline of disruptive behavior enabled the children to participate in many
more small-group experiences, to work individually, to use audio-visual aids, and
to work with a partner. The technique, I feel, was effective. Besides, I haven't even
had laryngitis yet this year.

QUESTIONS

1. Define and give an example of a behavioral contingency.
2. For Leigh's math-completion behavior, describe:
   a) the behavioral analysis of the desired change;
   b) the contingencies of reinforcement which brought about the desired change;
   c) how the teacher knew when to deliver reinforcement.
3. For Kirman's sobbing behavior, describe the behavioral analysis, the effective contingencies, and the method of observation.
4. The frequency of outbursts in Carol Callahan's classroom ranged from 35 to 45 per
   half-day session when the baseline for this operant was established. Under the first
   criterion, the children would receive some reinforcement if outbursts were kept below 40 per half-day session, and additional reinforcement if outbursts were below
   20 per half-day session.
   a) What was the effect of this double criterion on the likelihood that the children
      would perform some behavior which would be reinforced.
   b) Explain why establishing a criterion that can be met is important in changing
      behavior.
5. Briefly describe the similarities between the techniques used here to modify behavior
   and the principles of programmed instruction described in Unit 1.

UNIT

5

The Technology
of Teaching

Content

Skinner, B. F. "The Technology of Teaching." *Proceedings of the Royal Society,
B* 162 (1965): 427–443. (a selection)
Solomon, Carol. "Bringing Behavior under Stimulus Control."

    This unit emphasizes that teaching is the arrangement of contingencies of rein-
forcement. To clarify this concept, several examples are presented which illustrate
the application of behavioral principles to establish new forms of behavior, to
modify existing behavior, to bring behavior under control of stimuli, and to maintain behavior under infrequent reinforcement.

Objectives

Students will define a three-term contingency, identify examples of the various programs of contingencies, and describe in general terms how complex behavior is
established.

Instructions

1. Read the objectives.
2. Do the program on bringing behavior under stimulus control.
3. Read the article, then answer the questions following.

4. Check your answers.

5. Review your work with your instructor.

Bringing Behavior under Stimulus Control

C. Solomon

Directions: Write your answers to the questions in the space allotted. Then check your response with the answer given at the end of the article.

1. In the Mechner program in Unit 4 you learned that a behavioral contingency involves two terms, a(n) (1a) _____ -event and a(n) (1b) _____ -event.

2. A behavioral contingency can be defined as a situation in which a(n) (2a) _____ _____ change for some person or animal is contingent upon the (2b) _____ of that person or animal. (If necessary, see Unit 4, Behavioral Contingency program, frames 18 and 19.)

3. "Whenever John looks in the cookie jar, he sees the picture of an overweight man."
Under these conditions, we may observe that John looks in the cookie jar very seldom—less than once an hour.

"Whenever John looks in the cookie jar, he sees his favorite cookies."
Under these conditions we may observe that John looks in the cookie jar frequently—about five times an hour.

In the second case, the stimulus-event, seeing the cookies, (increases, decreases) the frequency of the response-event, looking in the cookie jar.

4. Any stimulus-event which increases the frequency of a response-event is called a reinforcer, or reinforcing stimulus. Judging from the rate of John's response, seeing his favorite cookies (4a—is, is not) a reinforcer for looking in the cookie jar. Seeing the picture of the overweight man (4b—is, is not) a reinforcer for looking in the cookie jar.

5. When we notice that in a given behavioral contingency, the rate of the response-event increases, the stimulus-event of that contingency is called a(n) _____
_____

6. What can we do to *increase* the rate of a selected response, such as looking in the cookie jar? _____
_____
_____

7. What can we do to *decrease* the rate of a selected response?
_____
_____

8. Suppose the cookie jar has contained only the picture of an overweight man for

several months. What has probably happened to the rate of John's response, looking in the cookie jar? _____

_____

9. Now suppose that one day after John has "learned" not to look in the cookie jar, he comes home and smells a delicious odor. When trying to locate the source of the odor, he happens to look in the cookie jar and sees freshly baked cookies. Next day, John comes home and sniffs as hard as he can, but he notices no delicious odor. He looks in the cookie jar anyway and sees a picture of an overweight man. If these contingencies continue to operate, John will soon look in the cookie jar only when _____

_____

10. John has learned to discriminate between situations when looking in the cookie jar will be reinforced and situations when that response will not be reinforced. "Whenever John smells a delicious odor, he often looks in the cookie jar and sees his favorite cookies." In this sentence, what describes John's response-event? (10a)

_____

10b. In that same sentence, what describes John's stimulus-event, or the reinforcement contingent upon his response? _____

_____

10c. What describes the occasion upon which a certain response is likely to be reinforced?

_____

11. "Whenever John does not smell the delicious odor, he does not often look in the cookie jar and see the picture of an overweight man." What part of the above statement describes John's response-event? (11a)

_____

11b. What part describes the stimulus-event contingent upon John's response?

_____

11c. What part describes an occasion in which a certain response is not likely to be reinforced? _____

_____

12. The contingencies described in frames 10 and 11 have three parts or *terms:*
   1) a discriminative stimulus, or the occasion on which a response will be reinforced;
   2) a response-event, or behavior;
   3) a stimulus-event, which may be a reinforcer.

   Underline and label the three parts of the following contingencies:
   a. "Whenever the light is red, the pigeon pecks the disk and the mechanism delivers a food pellet."
   b. "Whenever the child sees the small furry animal, she says CAT and her mother smiles at her."
   c. "When asked, 'What year did Columbus discover America?' Sara answers, '1492,' and the teacher says, 'Right!' "

13. In the article you will read, Skinner describes the three-term contingency as "bring-

ing behavior under the control of stimuli." How was John's behavior (looking in the cookie jar) brought under the control of a stimulus, the presence of the delicious odor? _____

_____

Answers

1a   and 1b: stimulus, response—in any order.

2a. environmental   2b. behavior or response

3.   increases

4a. is   4b. is not

5.   reinforcer or reinforcing stimulus

6.   arrange for a reinforcing stimulus-event to be contingent upon the response.

7.   arrange the environment so that no reinforcing stimulus-events are contingent upon the response.

8.   It will decrease radically, or disappear altogether.

9.   he smells the delicious odor.

10a. "he often looks in the cookie jar"

10b. "and sees his favorite cookies"

10c. "whenever John smells a delicious odor"

11a. "he does not often look in the cookie jar"

11b. "and see the picture of an overweight man"

11c. "whenever John does not smell a delicious odor"

12a. Whenever the light is red   the pigeon pecks the disk

    discriminative stimulus   response
    and the mechanism delivers a food pellet.

                  reinforcement

12b. Whenever the child sees the small furry animal   she says CAT

            discriminative stimulus   response
    and her mother smiles at her.

              reinforcement

12c. When asked, "What year did Columbus discover America?"

                  discriminative stimulus

    Sara answers, "1492"

            response

    and the teacher says, "Right"

              reinforcement

13.   Looking in the cookie jar was only reinforced by the appearance of cookies when

the odor was present. When the odor was not present, looking in the cookie jar resulted in seeing an unpleasant picture.

The Technology of Teaching

B. F. Skinner

(A Review Lecture delivered to the Royal Society, 19 November 1964.)

OPERANT CONDITIONING

. . .

An important process in human behavior is attributed, none too accurately, to "reward and punishment." Thorndike described it in his Law of Effect. It is now commonly referred to as "operant conditioning"—not to be confused with the conditioned reflexes of Pavlov. The essentials may be seen in a typical experimental arrangement. Figure 5.1 shows a hungry rat in an experimental space which contains a food dispenser. A horizontal bar at the end of a lever projects from one wall. Depression of the lever operates a switch. When the switch is connected with the food dispenser, any behavior on the part of the rat which depresses the lever, is as we say, "reinforced with food." The apparatus simply makes the appearance of food *contingent upon* the occurrence of an arbitrary bit of behavior. Under such circumstances the probability that a response to the lever will occur again is increased (Skinner 1938).

. . .

The relation between a response and its consequences may be simple, and the change in probability of the response is not surprising. It may therefore appear that research of this sort is simply proving the obvious. A critic has recently said that King Solomon must have known all about operant conditioning because he used rewards and punishment. In the same sense his archers must have known all about Hooke's Law because they used bows and arrows. What is technologically useful in operant conditioning is our increasing knowledge of the extraordinarily subtle and complex properties of behavior which may be traced to subtle and complex features of the contingencies of reinforcement which prevail in the environment.

We may arrange matters, for example, so that the rat will receive food only when it depresses the lever with a given force. Weaker responses then disappear, and exceptionally forceful responses begin to occur and can be selected through further differential reinforcement. Reinforcement may also be made contingent upon the presence of stimuli: depression of the lever operates the food dispenser, for example, only when a tone of a given pitch is sounding. As a result the rat is much more likely to respond when a tone of that pitch is sounding. Responses may also

---

B. F. Skinner, "The Technology of Teaching," *Proceedings of the Royal Society, B* 162 (1965): 427–443. Reprinted by permission.

Fig. 5.1. Rat pressing a horizontal bar attached to a lever projecting through the wall. The circular aperture below and to the right of the bar contains a food dispenser.

be reinforced only intermittently. Some common schedules of reinforcement are the subject of probability theory. Gambling devices often provide for the reinforcement of varying numbers of responses in an unpredictable sequence. Comparable schedules are programmed in the laboratory by interposing counters between the operandum and the reinforcing device. The extensive literature on schedules of reinforcement (see, for example, Ferster & Skinner, 1957) also covers intermittent reinforcement arranged by clocks and speedometers.

. . .

The application of operant conditioning to education is simple and direct. Teaching is the arrangement of contingencies of reinforcement under which students learn. They learn without teaching in their natural environments, but teachers arrange special contingencies which expedite learning, hastening the appearance of behavior which would otherwise be acquired slowly or making sure of the appearance of behavior which might otherwise never occur.

A teaching machine is simply any device which arranges contingencies of reinforcement. There are as many different kinds of machines as there are different kinds of contingencies. In this sense the apparatuses developed for the experimental analysis of behavior were the first teaching machines. They remain much more complex and subtle than the devices currently available in education—a state of affairs to be regretted by anyone who is concerned with making education as effective as possible. Both the basic analysis and its technological applications require instrumental aid. Early experimenters manipulated stimuli and reinforcers and recorded responses by hand, but current research without the help of extensive apparatus is unthinkable. The teacher needs similar instrumental support, for it is impossible to arrange many of the contingencies of reinforcement which expedite learning without it. Adequate apparatus has not eliminated the researcher, and teaching machines will not eliminate the teacher. But both teacher and researcher must have such equipment if they are to work effectively.

ESTABLISHING NEW FORMS OF BEHAVIOR

Programmed instruction also made its first appearance in the laboratory in the form of programmed contingencies of reinforcement. The almost miraculous power to change behavior which frequently emerges is perhaps the most conspicuous contribution to date of an experimental analysis of behavior. There are at least four different kinds of programming. One is concerned with generating new and complex patterns or "topographies" of behavior. It is in the nature of operant conditioning that a response cannot be reinforced until it has occurred. For experimental purposes a response is chosen which presents no problem (a rat is likely to press a sensitive lever within a short time), but we could easily specify responses which never occur in this way. Can they then never be reinforced?

The programming of a rare topography of response is sometimes demonstrated in the classroom in the following way. A hungry pigeon is placed in an enclosed space where it is visible to the class. A food dispenser can be operated with a handswitch held by the demonstrator. The pigeon has learned to eat from the food dispenser without being disturbed by its operation, but it has not been conditioned in any other way. The class is asked to specify a response which is not part of the current repertoire of the pigeon. Suppose, for example, it is decided that the pigeon is to pace a figure eight. The demonstrator cannot simply wait for this response to occur and then reinforce it. Instead he reinforces any current response which may contribute to the final pattern—possibly simply turning the head or taking a step in, say, a clockwise direction. The reinforced response will quickly be repeated (one can actually see learning take place under these circumstances), and reinforcement is then withheld until a more marked movement in the same direction is made. Eventually only a complete turn is reinforced. Similar responses in a counterclockwise direction are then strengthened, the clockwise movement suffering partial "extinction." When a complete counterclockwise movement has thus been "shaped," the clockwise turn is reinstated, and eventually the pigeon makes both turns in succession and is reinforced. The whole pattern is then quickly repeated. Q.E.D. The process of "shaping" a response of this complexity should take no more than five or ten minutes. The demonstrator's only contact with the pigeon is by way of the handswitch, which permits him to determine the exact moment of operation of the food dispenser. By selecting responses to be reinforced he improvises a program of contingencies, at each stage of which a response is reinforced which makes it possible to move on to a more demanding stage. The contingencies gradually approach those which generate the final specified response.

This method of shaping a topography of response has been used by Wolf, Mees & Risley (1964) to solve a difficult behavior problem. A boy was born blind with cataracts. Before he was of an age at which an operation was feasible, he had begun to display severe temper tantrums, and after the operation he remained unmanageable. It was impossible to get him to wear the glasses without which he would soon become permanently blind. His tantrums included serious self-destructive behavior, and he was admitted to a hospital with a diagnosis of "child schizophrenia." Two principles of operant conditioning were applied. The temper tantrums were extinguished by making sure that they were never followed by reinforcing consequences. A program of contingencies of reinforcement was then designed to shape the desired behavior of wearing glasses. It was necessary to allow the child to go hungry so that food could be used as an effective reinforcer. Empty glasses frames were placed about the room and any response which made contact with them was reinforced with food. Reinforcement was then made contingent on picking up the frames, carrying them about, and so on, in a programmed sequence. Some difficulty was encountered in shaping the response of putting the frames on the face in the proper position. When this was eventually achieved, the prescription lenses were put in the frames. Wolf *et al.* publish a cumulative curve showing the number of hours per day the glasses were worn. The final slope represents essentially all the child's waking hours. [The cumulative curve, not reproduced here, shows that the number of hours the glasses were worn increased from an average of two hours per day to twelve per day over a thirty-day program of contingencies.]

MODIFYING EXISTING BEHAVIOR *

A second kind of programming is used to alter temporal or intensive properties of behavior. By differentially reinforcing only the more vigorous instances in which a pigeon pecks a disk and by advancing the minimum requirement very slowly, a pigeon can be induced to peck so energetically that the base of its beak becomes inflamed. If one were to begin with this terminal contingency, the behavior would never develop. There is nothing new about the necessary programming. An athletic coach may train a high jumper simply by moving the bar higher by small increments, each setting permitting some successful jumps to occur. But many intensive and temporal contingencies—such as those seen in the arts, crafts, and music—are very subtle and must be carefully analyzed if they are to be properly programmed.

BRINGING BEHAVIOR UNDER STIMULUS CONTROL

Another kind of programming is concerned with bringing behavior under the control of stimuli. We could determine a rat's sensitivity to tones of different pitches by reinforcing responses made when one tone is sounding and extinguishing all responses made when other tones are sounding. We may wish to avoid extinction, however; the organism is to acquire the discrimination without making any "errors."

---

* Editors' note: Modifying existing behavior is very similar to establishing a new form of behavior, so we will treat them similarly in the questions for this unit.

An effective procedure has been analyzed by Terrace (1963). Suppose we are to condition a pigeon to peck a red disk but not a green. If we simply reinforce it for pecking the red disk, it will almost certainly peck the green as well and these "errors" must be extinguished. Terrace begins with disks which are as different as possible.* One is illuminated by a red light, but the other is dark. Although reinforced for pecking the red disk, the pigeon is not likely to peck the dark disk, at least during a period of a few seconds. When the disk again becomes red, a response is immediately made. It is possible to extend the length of time the disk remains dark. Eventually the pigeon pecks the red disk instantly, but does not peck the dark disk no matter how long it remains dark. The important point is that it has never pecked the dark disk at any time.

A faint green light is then added to the dark disk. Over a period of time the green light becomes brighter and eventually is as bright as the red. The pigeon now responds instantly to the red disk but not to the green *and has never responded to the green*.

A second and more difficult discrimination can then be taught without errors by transferring control from the red and green disks. Let us say that the pigeon is to respond to a white vertical bar projected on a black disk but not to a horizontal. These patterns are first superimposed upon red and green backgrounds, and the pigeon is reinforced when it responds to red-vertical but not to green-horizontal. The intensity of the color is then slowly reduced. Eventually the pigeon responds to the black and white vertical bar, does not respond to the black and white horizontal bar, *and has never done so*. The result could perhaps be achieved more rapidly by permitting errors to occur and extinguishing them, but other issues may need to be taken into account. When extinction is used, the pigeon shows powerful emotional responses to the wrong stimulus; when the Terrace technique is used it remains quite indifferent. It is, so to speak, "not afraid of making a mistake." The difference is relevant to education, where the anxiety generated by current methods constitutes a serious problem. There are those who would defend a certain amount of anxiety as a good thing, but we may still envy the occasionally happy man who readily responds when the occasion is appropriate but is otherwise both emotionally and intellectually disengaged. The important point is that the terminal contingencies controlling the behavior of both anxious and nonanxious students are the same; the difference is to be traced to the program by way of which the terminal behavior has been reached.

The discriminative capacities of lower organisms have been investigated with methods which require very skilful programming. Blough (1956), for example, has developed a technique in which a pigeon maintains a spot of light at an intensity at which it can just be seen. By using a range of monochromatic lights he has shown that the spectral sensitivity of the pigeon is very close to that of man. Several other

---

* Terrace used one disk that was illuminated sometimes by a red light and sometimes by a green light.

techniques are available which make it possible to use lower organisms as sensitive psychophysical observers. They are available, however, only to those who understand the principles of programming.

Some current work by Murray Sidman provides a dramatic example of programming a subtle discrimination in a microcephalic idiot. At the start of the experiment Sidman's subject was 40 years old. He was said to have a mental age of about 18 months. He was partially toilet trained and dressed himself with help. To judge from the brain of his sister, now available for post-mortem study, his brain is probably about one-third the normal size. Sidman investigated his ability to discriminate circular forms projected on translucent vertical panels. Small pieces of chocolate were used as reinforcers. At first any pressure against a single large vertical panel (Fig. 5.2A) operated the device which dropped a bit of chocolate into a cup within reach. Though showing relatively poor motor co-ordination, the subject eventually executed the required, rather delicate response. The panel was then subdivided into a three by three set of smaller panels (represented schematically in Fig. 5.2B), the central panel not being used in what follows. The subject was first reinforced when he pressed any of the eight remaining panels. A single panel was then lit at random, a circle being projected on it (Fig. 5.2C). The subject learned to press the lighted panel. Flat ellipses were then projected on the other panels at a low illumination (Fig. 5.2D). In subsequent settings the ellipses, now brightly

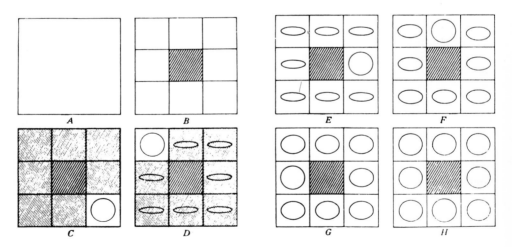

Fig. 5.2. A program designed to teach subtle form discrimination. Reinforcement was contingent on: (A) a response moving a large panel; (B) a response moving any one of nine smaller panels (with the exception of the center panel); (C) a response moving only the one panel on which a circle is projected; (D) as before except that flat ellipses appear faintly on the other panels; (E,F,G) a response to the panel bearing a circle, appearing in random position among ellipses the shorter axis of which is progressively lengthening; (H) a response to the panel bearing a circle among ellipses closely approximating circles.

illuminated, progressively approached circles (Fig. 5.2E to G). Each stage was maintained until the subject had formed the necessary discrimination, all correct responses being reinforced with chocolate. Eventually the subject could successfully select a circle from an array approximately like that shown in Fig. 5.2H. Using similar shaping techniques Sidman and his associates have conditioned the subject to pick up and use a pencil appropriately, tracing letters faintly projected on a sheet of paper.

The intellectual accomplishments of this microcephalic idiot in the forty-first year of his life have exceeded all those of his first 40 years. They were possible only because he has lived a few hours of each week of that year in a well programmed environment. No very bright future beckons (he has already lived longer than most people of his kind), and it is impossible to say what he might have achieved if he had been subject to a similar program from birth, but he has contributed to our knowledge by demonstrating the power of a method of instruction which could scarcely be tested on a less promising case. (The bright futures belong to the normal and exceptional children who will be fortunate enough to live in environments which have been designed to maximize *their* development, and of whose potential achievements we have now scarcely any conception.)

MAINTAINING BEHAVIOR UNDER INFREQUENT REINFORCEMENT

A fourth kind of programming has to do with maintaining behavior under infrequent reinforcement. A pigeon will continue to respond even though only one response in every hundred, say, is reinforced, but it will not do so unless the contingencies have been programmed. A fresh pigeon is no more likely to peck a disk a hundred times than to pace a figure eight. The behavior is built up by reinforcing every response, then every other response, then every fifth response, and so on, waiting at each stage until the behavior is reasonably stable. Under careful programming pigeons have continued to respond when only every ten-thousandth response has been reinforced, and this is certainly not the limit. An observer might say that the pigeon is "greatly interested in his work," "industrious," "remarkably tolerant to frustration," "free from discouragement," "dedicated to his task," and so on. These expressions are commonly applied to students who have had the benefit of similar programming, accidental or arranged.

The effective scheduling of reinforcement is an important element in educational design. Suppose we wish to teach a student to read "good books"—books which, almost by definition, do not reinforce the reader sentence by sentence or even paragraph by paragraph but only when possibly hundreds of pages have prepared him for a convincing or moving dénouement. The student must be exposed to a program of materials which build up a tendency to read in the absence of reinforcement. Such programs are seldom constructed deliberately and seldom arise by accident, and it is therefore not surprising that few students even in good universities learn to read books of this sort and continue to do so for the rest of their lives.

In their pride, schools are likely to arrange just the wrong conditions; they are likely to maintain so-called "standards" under which books are forced upon students before they have had adequate preparation.

Other objectives in education need similar programming. The dedicated scientist who works for years in spite of repeated failures is often looked upon as a happy accident, but he may well be the product of a happy if accidental history of reinforcement. A program in which exciting results were first common but became less and less frequent could generate the capacity to continue in the absence of reinforcement for long periods of time. Such programs should arise naturally as scientists turn to more and more difficult areas. Perhaps not many effective programs are to be expected for this reason, and they are only rarely designed by teachers of science. This may explain why there are so few dedicated scientists. Maintaining a high level of activity is one of the more important achievements of programming. Repeatedly, in its long history, education has resorted to aversive control to keep its students at work. A proper understanding of the scheduling of reinforcement may lead at long last to a better solution of this problem.

PROGRAMMING EDUCATIONAL TASKS

Let us look at these principles of programming at work in one or two traditional educational assignments. Instruction in handwriting will serve as one example. To say that a child is to learn "how to write" tells us very little. The so-called signs of "knowing how to write" provide a more useful set of behavioral specifications. The child is to form letters and words which are legible and graceful according to taste. He is to do this first in copying a model, then in writing to dictation (or self-dictation as he spells out words he would otherwise speak), and eventually in writing as a separate nonvocal form of verbal behavior. A common method is to ask the child to copy letters or words and to approve or otherwise reinforce his approximations to good copy. More and more exact copies are demanded as the hand improves—in a crude sort of programming. The method is ineffective largely because the reinforcements are too long deferred. The parent or teacher comments upon or corrects the child's work long after it has been performed.

A possible solution is to teach the child to discriminate between good and bad form before he starts to write. Acceptable behavior should then generate immediate, automatic self-reinforcement. This is seldom done. Another possibility is to make reinforcement immediately contingent upon successful responses. One method now being tested is to treat paper chemically so that the pen the child uses writes in dark blue when a response is correct and yellow when it is incorrect. The dark blue line is made automatically reinforcing through generous commendation. Under such contingencies the proper execution of a letter can be programmed; at first the child makes a very small contribution in completing a letter, but through progressive stages he approaches the point at which he composes the letter as a whole, the chemical response of the paper differentially reinforcing good form throughout. The model to be copied is then made progressively less important by separating it in both time and space from the child's work. Eventually words are written to dictation, letter by letter, in spelling dictated words, and in describing pictures. The same kind of differential reinforcement can be used to teach good form, proper spacing, and so on. The child is eventually forming letters skillfully under continuous automatic reinforcement. The method is directed as much toward motivation as toward good form. Even quite young children remain busily at work for long periods of time without coercion or threat, showing few signs of fatigue, nervousness, or other forms of escape.

As a second example we may consider the acquisition of a simple form of verbal behavior. A behavioral specification is here likely to be especially strongly resisted. It is much more in line with traditional educational policy to say that the student is to "know facts, understand principles, be able to put ideas into words, express meanings, or communicate information." In *Verbal Behavior* (Skinner, 1957) I tried to show the behavior exhibited in such activities could be formulated without reference to ideas, meanings, or information, and many of the principles currently used in programming verbal knowledge have been drawn from that analysis. The field is too large to be adequately covered here, but two examples may suggest the direction of the approach.

What happens when a student memorizes a poem? Let us say that he begins by reading the poem from a text. His behavior is at that time under the control of the text, and it is to be accounted for by examining the process through which he has learned to read. When he eventually speaks the poem in the absence of a text, the same form of verbal behavior has come under the control of other stimuli. He may begin to recite when asked to do so—he is then under control of an external verbal stimulus—but, as he continues to recite, his behavior comes under the control of stimuli he himself is generating (not necessarily in a crude word-by-word chaining of responses). In the process of "memorizing" the poem, control passes from one kind of stimulus to another.

A classroom demonstration of the transfer of control from text to self-generated stimuli illustrates the process. A short poem is projected on a screen or written on a chalkboard. A few unnecessary letters are omitted. The class reads the poem in chorus. A second slide is then projected in which other letters are missing (or letters erased from the chalkboard). The class could not have read the poem correctly if this form had been presented first, but because of its recent history it is able to do so. (Some members undoubtedly receive help from others in the process of choral reading.) In a third setting still other letters are omitted, and after a series of five or six settings the text has completely disappeared. The class is nevertheless able to "read" the poem. Control has passed mainly to self-generated stimuli.

As another example, consider what a student learns when he consults an illustrated dictionary. After looking at a labelled picture, as in Fig. 5.3, we say that he knows something he did not know before. This is another of those vague expressions which have done so much harm to education. The "signs or symptoms of such knowledge" are of two sorts. Shown the picture in Fig. 5.3 without the text the student can say "caduceus" (we say that he now knows what the object pictured in

caduceus

Figure 5.3

the figure is called) or, shown the word *caduceus,* he can now describe or reconstruct the picture (we say that he now knows what the word *caduceus* means). But what has actually happened?

The basic process is similar to that of transferring discriminative control in the Terrace experiment. To begin with, the student can respond to the picture in various ways: he can describe it without naming it, he can find a similar picture in an array, he can draw a fair copy, and so on. He can also speak the name by reading the printed word. When he first looks at the picture and reads the word, his verbal response is primarily under the control of the text, but it must eventually be controlled by the picture. As in transferring the control exerted by red and green to vertical and horizontal lines, we can change the control efficiently by making the text gradually less important, covering part of it, removing some of the letters, or fogging it with a translucent mask. As the picture acquires control the student can speak the name with less and less help from the text. Eventually, when the picture exerts enough control, he "knows the name of the pictured object." The normal student can learn the name of one object so quickly that the "vanishing" technique may not be needed, but it is a highly effective procedure in learning the names of a large number of objects. The good student learns how to make progressive reductions in the effectiveness of a text by himself: he may glance at the text out of the corner of his eye, uncover it bit by bit, and so on. In this way he improvises his own program in making the text less and less important as the picture acquires control of the verbal response.

In teaching the student "the meaning of the word *caduceus*" we could slowly obscure the picture, asking the student to respond to the name by completing a drawing or description or by finding a matching picture in an array. Eventually in answer to the question *What is a caduceus?* he describes the object, makes a crude sketch, or points to the picture of a caduceus. The skillful student uses techniques of this sort in studying unprogrammed material.

"Knowing what a caduceus is" or "knowing the meaning of the word caduceus" is probably more than responding in these ways to picture or text. In other words, there are other "signs of knowledge." That is one reason why the concept of knowledge is so inadequate. But other relevant behavior must be taught, if at all, in substantially the same way.

These examples do scant justice to the many hundreds of effective programs now available or to the techniques which many of them use so effectively, but they must suffice as a basis for discussing a few general issues. An effective technology of teaching, derived not from philosophical principles but from a realistic analysis of human behavior, has much to contribute, but as its nature has come to be clearly seen, strong opposition has arisen.

OBJECTIONS TO PROGRAMMING IN EDUCATION

A common objection is that most of the early work responsible for the basic formulation of behavior was done on so-called lower animals. It has been argued that the procedures are therefore appropriate only to animals and that to use them in education is to treat the student like an animal. So far as I know, no one argues that because something is true of a pigeon, it is therefore true of a man. There are enormous differences in the topographies of the behaviors of man and pigeon and in the kinds of environmental events which are relevant to that behavior—differences which, if anatomy and physiology were adequate to the task, we could probably compare with differences in the mediating substrata—but the basic processes in behavior, as in neural tissue, show helpful similarities. Relatively simple organisms have many advantages in early stages of research, but they impose no limit on that research. Complex processes are met and dealt with as the analysis proceeds. Experiments on pigeons may not throw much light on the "nature" of man, but they are extraordinarily helpful in enabling us to analyze man's environment more effectively. What is common to pigeon and man is a world in which certain contingencies of reinforcement prevail. The schedule of reinforcement which makes a pigeon a pathological gambler is to be found at race track and roulette table, where it has a comparable effect.

Another objection is to the use of contrived contingencies of reinforcement. In daily life one does not wear glasses in order to get food or point to circles in order to receive chocolate. Such reinforcers are not naturally contingent on the behavior and there may seem to be something synthetic, spurious, or even fraudulent about them. The attack on contrived contingencies of reinforcement may be traced to Rousseau and his amazing book, *Émile*. Rousseau wanted to avoid the punitive systems of his day. Convinced as he was that civilization corrupts, he was also afraid of all social reinforcers. His plan was to make the student dependent upon *things* rather than people. John Dewey restated the principle by emphasizing real life experiences in the schoolroom. In American education it is commonly argued that a child must be taught nothing until he can reap natural benefits from knowing it. He is not to learn to write until he can take satisfaction in writing his name in his books, or notes to his friends. Producing a purple rather than a yellow line is irrelevant to handwriting. Unfortunately, the teacher who confines himself to natural reinforcers is often ineffective, particularly because only certain subjects can be taught through their use, and he eventually falls back upon some form of punishment. But aversive control is the most shameful of irrelevancies: it is only in school that one parses a Latin sentence to avoid the cane.

The objection to contrived reinforcers arises from a misunderstanding of the nature of teaching. The teacher expedites learning by arranging special contingencies of reinforcement, which may not resemble the contingencies under which the behavior is eventually useful. Parents teach a baby to talk by reinforcing its first efforts with approval and affection, but these are not natural consequences of speech. The baby learns to say *mama, dada, spoon,* or *cup* months before he ever calls to his father or mother or identifies them to a passing stranger or asks for a spoon or cup or reports their presence to someone who cannot see them. The contrived reinforcement shapes the topography of verbal behavior long before that behavior can produce its normal consequences in a verbal community. In the same way a child reinforced for the proper formation of letters by a chemical reaction is prepared to write long before the natural consequences of effective writing take over. It was necessary to use a "spurious" reinforcer to get the boy to wear glasses, but once the behavior had been shaped and maintained for a period of time, the natural reinforcers which follow from improved vision could take over. The real issue is whether the teacher prepares the student for the natural reinforcers which are to replace the contrived reinforcers used in teaching. The behavior which is expedited in the teaching process would be useless if it were not to be effective in the world at large in the absence of instructional contingencies.

Another objection to effective programmed instruction is that it does not teach certain important activities. When required to learn unprogrammed material for an impending examination the student learns how to study, how to clear up puzzling matters, how to work under puzzlement, and so on. These may be as important as the subject-matter itself. The same argument could have been raised with respect to a modern experimental analysis of learning when contrasted with early studies of that process. Almost all early investigators of learning constructed what we now call terminal contingencies of reinforcement to which an organism was immediately subjected. Thus, a rat was put into a maze, a cat was put into a puzzle box, and so on. The organism possessed little if any behavior appropriate to such a "problem," but some responses were reinforced, and over a period of time an acceptable terminal performance might be reached. The procedure was called "trial and error." A program of contingencies of reinforcement would have brought the organism to the same terminal performance much more rapidly and efficiently and without trial and error, but in doing so it could have been said to deprive the organism of the opportunity to learn how to try, how to explore—indeed, how to solve problems.

The educator who assigns material to be studied for an impending test presents the student with an opportunity to learn to examine the material in a special way which facilitates recall, to work industriously at something which is not currently reinforcing, and so on. It is true that a program designed simply to impart knowledge of a subject-matter does not do any of this. It does not because it is not designed to do so. Programming undertakes to reach one goal at a time. Efficient ways of studying and thinking are separate goals. A crude parallel is offered by the current argument in favor of the cane or related practices on the ground that they build character; they teach a boy to take punishment and to accept responsibility for his conduct. These are worthwhile goals, but they should not necessarily be taught at the same time as, say, Latin grammar or mathematics. Rousseau suggested a relevant form of programming through which a child could be taught to submit to aversive stimuli without alarm or panic. He pointed out that a baby dropped into a cold bath will probably be frightened and cry, but that if one begins with water at body temperature and cools it one degree per day, the baby will eventually not be disturbed by cold water. The program must be carefully followed. (In his enthusiasm for the new science, Rousseau exclaimed "Use a thermometer!") Similar programs can teach a tolerance for painful stimuli, but caning a boy for idleness, forgetfulness, or bad spelling is an unlikely example. It only occasionally builds what the eighteenth century called "bottom," as it only occasionally eliminates idleness, forgetfulness, or bad spelling.

It is important to teach careful observation, exploration, and inquiry, but they are not well taught by submitting a student to material which he must observe and explore effectively or suffer the consequences. Better methods are available. There are two ways to teach a man to look before leaping: he may be severely punished when he leaps without looking or he may be positively reinforced (possibly "spuriously") for looking before leaping. He may learn to look in both cases, but when simply punished for leaping without looking he must discover for himself the art of careful observation, and he is not likely to profit from the experience of others. When he is reinforced for looking, a suitable program will transmit earlier discoveries in the art of observation. (Incidentally, the audiovisual devices mentioned earlier which undertake to attract attention do not teach careful observation. On the contrary, they are much more likely to deprive the student of the opportunity to learn such skills than effective programming of subject-matters.)

Learning how to study is another example. When a teacher simply tests students on assigned material, few ever learn to study well, and many never learn at all. One may read for the momentary effect and forget what one has read almost immediately; one obviously reads in a very different way for retention. As we have seen, many of the practices of the good student resemble those of the programmer. The student can in a sense program material as he goes, rehearsing what he has learned, glancing at a text only as needed, and so on. These practices can be separately programmed as an important part of the student's education and can be much more effectively taught than by punishing the student for reading without remembering.

PROGRAMMING CREATIVE BEHAVIOR

It would be pleasant to be able to say that punishing the student for not thinking is also not the only way to teach thinking. Some relevant behaviors have been analyzed and can therefore be explicitly programmed. Algorithmic methods of problem-solving are examples. Simply leading the student through a solution in the traditional way is one kind of programming. Requiring him to solve a series of problems of graded difficulty is another. More effective programs can certainly be prepared. Unfortunately, they would only emphasize the rather mechanical nature of algorithmic problem-solving. Real thinking seems to be something else. It is sometimes said to be a matter of "heuristics." But relevant practices can be formulated as techniques of solving the problem of solving problems. Once a heuristic device or practice is formulated and programmed, it cannot be distinguished in any important way from algorithmic problem-solving. The will-of-the-wisp of creative thinking still leads us on.

Human behavior often assumes novel forms, some of which are valuable. The teaching of truly creative behavior is, nevertheless, a contradiction in terms. Original discovery is seldom if ever guaranteed in the classroom. In Polya's little book, *How to Solve It* (Polya, 1945), a few boys in a class eventually arrive at the formula for the diagonal of a parallelopiped. It is possible that the teacher did not tell them the formula, but it is unlikely that the course they followed under his guidance resembled that of the original discoverer. Efforts to teach creativity have sacrificed the teaching of subject-matter. The teacher steers a delicate course between two great fears—on the one hand that he may not teach and on the other that he may tell the student something. Until we know more about creative thinking, we may need to confine ourselves to making sure that the student is in full possession of the contributions of earlier thinkers, that he has been abundantly reinforced for careful observation and inquiry, that he has the interest and industry generated by a fortunate history of successes.

It has been said that an education is what survives when a man has forgotten all he has been taught. Certainly few students could pass their final examinations even a year or two after leaving school or the university. What has been learned of permanent value must therefore not be the facts and principles covered by examinations but certain other kinds of behavior often ascribed to special abilities. Far from neglecting these kinds of behavior, careful programming reveals the need to teach them as explicit educational objectives. For example, two programs prepared with the help of the Committee on Programmed Instruction at Harvard—a program in crystallography constructed by Bruce Chalmers and James G. Holland and a program in neuroanatomy by Murray and Richard Sidman—both reveal the importance of special skills in three-dimensional thinking. As measured by available tests, these skills vary enormously even among scientists who presumably make special use of them. They can be taught with separate programs or as part of crystallography or neuroanatomy when specifically recognized as relevant skills. It is possible that education will eventually concentrate on those forms of behavior which "survive when all one has learned has been forgotten."

FUTURE USES OF THE TECHNOLOGY OF TEACHING

The argument that effective teaching is inimical to thinking, whether creative or not, raises a final point. We fear effective teaching, as we fear all effective means of changing human behavior. Power not only corrupts, it frightens; and absolute power frightens absolutely. We take another—and very long—look at educational policy when we conceive of teaching which really works. It has been said that teaching machines and programmed instruction will mean regimentation (it is sometimes added that regimentation is the goal of those who propose such methods), but in principle nothing could be more regimented than education as it now stands. School and state authorities draw up syllabuses specifying what students are to learn year by year. Universities insist upon "requirements" which are presumably to be met by all students applying for admission. Examinations are "standard." Certificates, diplomas, and honors testify to the completion of specified work. We do not worry about all this because we know that students never learn what they are required to learn, but some other safeguard must be found when education is effective.

It could well be that an effective technology of teaching will be unwisely used. It could destroy initiative and creativity, it could make men all alike (and not necessarily in being equally excellent), it could suppress the beneficial effect of accidents upon the development of the individual and upon the evolution of a culture. On the other hand, it could maximize the genetic endowment of each student, it could make him as skillful, competent, and informed as possible, it could build the greatest diversity of interests, it could lead him to make the greatest possible contribution to the survival and development of his culture. Which of these futures lies before us will not be determined by the mere availability of effective instruction. The use to which a technology of teaching is to be put will depend upon other matters. We cannot avoid the decisions which now face us by putting a stop to the scientific study of human behavior or by refusing to make use of the technology which inevitably flows from such a science.

The experimental analysis of behavior is a vigorous young science which will inevitably find practical applications. Important extensions have already been made in such fields as psychopharmacology and psychotherapy. Its bearing on economics, government, law, and even religion are beginning to attract attention. It is thus concerned with government in the broadest possible sense. In the government of the future the techniques we associate with education are most likely to prevail. That is why it is so important that this young science has begun by taking its most effective technological step in the development of a technology of teaching.

Preparation of this lecture has been supported by Grant K6-MH-21,775-01 of the National Institute of Mental Health of the U.S. Public Health Service, and by the Human Ecology Fund.

REFERENCES

Ayllon, T., and N. H. Azrin (1965). "An Objective Method for the Measurement and Reinforcement of Adaptive Behavior of Psychotics. *J. Exp. Anal. Beh.* (in press.)

Barzun, J. (1963). "Review of Bruner, J. S., *Essays for the Left Hand.*" *Science* 25:323.

Blough, D. (1956). "Dark Adaptation in the Pigeon." *J. Comp. Physiol. Psychol.* 49: 425–430.

Ferster, C. B. and B. F. Skinner (1957). *Schedules of Reinforcement.* New York: Appleton-Century-Crofts.

James, W. (1889). *Talks to Teachers on Psychology.* New York: Henry Holt.

Lindsley, Ogden R. (1960). "Characterization of the Behavior of Chronic Psychotics as Revealed by Free Operant Conditioning Methods." *Diseases of the Nervous System,* Monograph Supplement 21:66–78.

Polya, G. (1945). *How to Solve It.* Princeton, New Jersey: Princeton University Press.

Pressey, S. J. (1926). "A Simple Apparatus which Gives Tests and Scores—and Teaches." *Sch. Soc.* 23:373–376.

Rousseau, J. J. (1762). *Émile ou de l'Éducation.* Le Haye: Néaulme.

Skinner, B. F. (1938). *The Behaviour of Organisms.* New York: Appleton-Century-Crofts.

Skinner, B. F. (1957). *Verbal Behavior.* New York: Appleton-Century-Crofts.

Sidman, M. (1964). "Personal communication."

Terrace, H. S. (1963). "Errorless Transfer of a Discrimination across Two Continua." *J. Exp. Anal. Behav.* 6:223–232.

Wolf, M., H. Mees, and T. Risley (1964). "Application of Operant Conditioning Procedures to the Behaviour Problems in the Autistic Child." *Behav. Res. Therapy* 1:305–312.

QUESTIONS

1. What is a three-term contingency of reinforcement?

2-7 Each of the following questions is a description of a program of contingencies designed to teach a particular behavior. Read over each and decide if it represents a program that:
   a) modifies existing behavior to establish a new form of behavior (see editors' note on page 80 of the Skinner article);
   b) brings behavior under stimulus control;
   c) develops behavior which will be maintained under infrequent reinforcement.

2. The task is to draw freehand from a still-life model. Early in training, a simple vase is used as the model. At first, drawing lines that only approximate the lines of the model is reinforced. Then, a more and more exact likeness is required for reinforcement.

3. The task is to tell the difference between the letters *b* and *d*. The two letters are first made as different as possible: the *b* has a red arrow superimposed on it pointing to the right; the *d* has a green arrow pointing to the left. When the *b* appears in the window of the teaching machine, a button on the right should be pressed; and when the *d* appears, the left button should be pressed. Gradually the colors of the arrows fade to grey, and then the arrows themselves gradually fade out, while the child continues to make the appropriate left or right response.

4. The task is to name letters of the alphabet as each letter is presented. Saying "A" in

the presence of the symbol A is reinforced. All other letter names spoken in the presence of the symbol A are not reinforced.

5. The task is to read great works of literature. The skills required for "appreciating" such literature are enumerated—such skills include recognizing plot parallels, foreshadowing, use of irony and understatements, etc. Then a series of reading materials exemplifying each device is developed. Early in each series, students need read only one brief paragraph to find the ironic parallels (or whatever) and be reinforced. Later, one or two pages, then a whole short story, and finally longer and longer stories must be read before the ironic parallel can be found.

6. The task is to clap hands in time with the rhythm of certain songs. At first all claps occurring within three seconds of the correct rhythmic time are reinforced. Claps occurring outside this tolerance are not reinforced. Gradually the tolerance is reduced, until only claps occurring at the exactly correct rhythmic time are reinforced.

7. The task is to pronounce a Chinese word. At first, any approximation to the correct sound is reinforced. Later, closer and closer approximations are required for reinforcement. Finally, the student must pronounce the word correctly to be reinforced.

8. Briefly state how you get an organism (human or otherwise) to emit some complex behavior.

Summary of Units 1–5

These units have introduced the basic principles of the experimental analysis of behavior and also have described certain general characteristics of educational materials developed in accord with this science. You'll remember that the most important basic principle is: The student should be active in learning. To put this principle in operation, we are suggesting that you summarize these units yourself. The following are some questions to answer in writing your summary:

1. Describe the characteristics of instructional methods based on the experimental analysis of behavior.
2. Control of the learning environment is critical in the learning process: What must be controlled? Who controls what and how? Why is this control needed?
3. What are the primary advantages of teaching students individually?

PART

II

Behavior Theory in Practice

The first five units described several particular educational applications of behavior theory. However, in order to develop the ability to design materials appropriate for a range of educational goals, an understanding of the basic behavioral principles is required. Students of the technology of cooking do not confine themselves to reading recipes. They must learn the basic processes involved in cooking in order to develop the ability to devise new recipes appropriate to the type of cuisine to be prepared. Similarly, students of educational technology should not learn only about particular instructional design models. Developing the ability to design effective instructional materials suitable for a wide variety of to-be-learned behaviors requires use of the fundamentals of a science of behavior rather than a mere cookbook approach. Units 6–10 present readings in basic behavioral principles as well as educational applications of these principles. When you complete this part of the course, you should be able to describe in some detail the experimental analysis of behavior, including schedules of reinforcement and stimulus control.

For your study of behavior theory, you will use selections from *one* of the following four books:

1. J. G. Holland and B. F. Skinner. *The Analysis of Behavior.* New York: McGraw-Hill, 1961.

2. C. B. Ferster, S. Culbertson, and M. C. Perrott Boren. *Behavior Principles*. Englewood Cliffs, N.J.: Prentice-Hall, 1975; or the 1968 edition from Appleton-Century-Crofts.

3. D. L. Whaley and R. W. Malott. *Elementary Principles of Behavior*. Englewood Cliffs, N.J.: Prentice-Hall, 1971.

4. G. S. Reynolds. *A Primer of Operant Conditioning*. Glenview, Ill.: Scott, Foresman, 1975 or 1968.

(If you have not already selected a supplementary text, you will find a brief description of each in the introduction of this book, page 5).

Each unit in this section consists of a reading from your selected supplementary text, an additional reading describing or illustrating the basic principles applied to education, and some unit questions which usually concern these educational applications. You should not assume that correct answers to the unit questions indicate sufficient knowledge of the basic science. A thorough grounding in the science depends on a correct use of your selected supplementary text. If you are using the Holland-Skinner text, be sure to write the response to each frame before checking it. Ferster *et al.,* and Whaley and Malott provide questions at the end of each chapter which should be answered before beginning a new chapter. And, if you are using Reynolds, be sure to write a summary of each chapter before going on.

Each unit cover sheet indicates the chapters or sets from each supplementary text to be read at that time. A unit question marked with an asterisk (*) indicates that students using Reynolds or Whaley and Malott will have difficulty with the answer. Nevertheless, all students should attempt an answer to each unit question before checking the suggested answers at the back of the text.

UNIT

6

Operant Conditioning

Content

Follow the appropriate directions for your selected supplementary text (one of these four):

1. Holland and Skinner—Work sets 7–13.

2. Ferster *et al.*—Read each of the following parts and answer the probe questions:

1968 ed.	*1975 ed.*
Ch. 1, parts 1, 3, and 4	Ch. 2, parts 1, 3, and 4
Ch. 2, parts 1 and 2	Ch. 3, parts 1 and 2
Ch. 3, part 1	Ch. 4, parts 1 and 5
Ch. 5, parts 1 and 2.	Ch. 6, parts 1 and 2.

3. Whaley and Malott—Read each of the following chapters (including the "Notes" section) and answer the chapter questions: Chapters 1, 2, 3, 15, and 20.

4. Reynolds—Read Chapters 1 and 2 and write a summary of each.

The reading is adapted from an article by Helen Craig and Audrey Holland, "Reinforcement of Visual Attending in Classrooms for Deaf Children," which appeared in the *Journal of Applied Behavior Analysis* 3 (1970): 97–109.

In this unit, students begin an extensive, detailed exploration of the science that underlies the principles of behavior control they have already learned. Topics covered are operant behavior, operant conditioning, shaping, and extinction. The Craig and Holland adaptation illustrates an application of the principle of reinforcement to the control of attending behavior.

Objectives

Students identify basic learning principles, especially reinforcement, in both a laboratory learning situation and a classroom application.

Instructions

1. Read the designated sections of your selected supplementary text and respond as suggested above.
2. Read the adaptation of the Craig and Holland article.
3. Answer the unit questions, check your answers, and confer with your instructor.

Reinforcement of Visual Attending in Classrooms
for Deaf Children

(adapted from an article by H. Craig and A. Holland)

This study applied methods of behavior modification to visual attending responses of deaf children in the classroom.

Because deaf children are cut off from auditory stimuli, visual attending is especially important in their classroom education. Yet deaf children in school frequently do not look at the teacher or the appropriate information-bearing stimulus. Instead, competing stimuli from fellow students and the surroundings distract the child.

The authors of this study proposed that part of the problem lay in the fact that reinforcement for appropriate attending responses was often delayed because of the absence of immediate aural feedback. They proposed to increase the frequency of appropriate observing responses in a class of deaf children by providing immediate, tangible reinforcement for these responses.

The procedure paralleled, as much as possible, everyday classroom activities. The class consisted of seven children in a large residential school for the deaf. The children were nine to ten years old.

Observations were made of classroom behaviors before the experiment began, and attending and nonattending behaviors were listed. Attending behavior consisted of a child being seated with eyes oriented toward the relevant information-bearing stimulus for the full observation period of ten seconds. Some nonattending behaviors were: looking someplace other than at the teaching stimulus; fiddling with hands, feet, shoes, class materials, etc.; looking at the right thing at the wrong time, and so on.

Two observers were introduced into the classroom. They wore dark glasses to minimize the children's ability to see where the observers were looking. Baseline measurements of attending and nonattending responses were made. The children were observed in serial sequence. This approach introduced the possibility of a time discrimination on the part of the children due to a fixed-interval schedule, but, in practice, the observing and reinforcing sequence was variable rather than fixed, since if a child being observed stopped attending during the ten-second period, the observer immediately began observing the next child.

After the baseline responses had been recorded, the reinforcement procedure began. The reinforcing apparatus consisted of a small box containing a light. The light could be flashed by the observer, contingent upon the child's attending for 10 seconds. The light flash was the immediate reinforcer. The number of light flashes subsequently earned for the child a corresponding number of M & M's or tokens.

A box was placed on each child's desk three days before the reinforcement procedure began to allow the children to adapt to the presence of the apparatus. The children were then told the purpose of the boxes and reinforcement began. The reinforcement procedure continued for sixty-six class sessions.

The number of attending responses was tallied for each child and the teacher then counted out M & M reinforcers. After the twenty-fourth session, a token reinforcement system was begun. A mark was recorded for each light flash and fifteen marks earned the child a red card. The children could spend their red cards on a variety of primary reinforcers, such as candy, toys, and special privileges, each labelled as to cost.

RESULTS

The baseline for appropriate attending was merely 25 percent. That is, when the children were observed prior to initiating reinforcement procedures, approximately 75 percent of their classroom behaviors were *not* directed toward the appropriate teaching stimulus. However, when reinforcement of appropriate attending behaviors was introduced, behaviors indicating attention to the teaching stimulus increased immediately to 85 percent of the total.

The authors note that, "Differences across sessions were generally minimal, suggesting that attending behaviors remained constant from one time of day or one type of educational activity to another, once the reinforcement procedure had been instated" (Craig and Holland, 1970, p. 101).

In two subsequent experiments with different classes, reinforcement was withdrawn after conditioning of attending behavior had been achieved. Attending behavior returned to the original baseline level. But in the third experiment social reinforcement provided a middle ground between conditions of no reinforcement and of tangible reinforcement. The authors feel that "with more systematically scheduled social reinforcement [and . . . with provisions for making the instructional stimuli as reinforcing as the stimuli competing for attention], the increased attending behavior may very well be maintained without constant tangible reinforcement" (Craig and Holland, 1970, p. 107).

QUESTIONS

1. The first rule for teaching (humans or other animals) is to structure the environment so the desired behavior is likely to occur, for behavior must be emitted before it can be learned. As an example from an educational setting, what changes in the environment did Keller (Unit 2) make to increase the probability of desired behaviors?

*2. Name at least three factors affecting the speed of conditioning. Relate them to the way Helen Craig increased visual attention in deaf children.

3. Distinguish between positive and negative reinforcement. How do they affect the rate of response? Which did Helen Craig use?

4. Place a check (for yes), or an X (for no) in each cell to indicate whether the given characteristic of operant conditioning applies to the given learning situation.

	Organism being conditioned in standard experimental space	A teaching machine	Helen Craig's procedure
Arranges for specific identifiable response			
Provides immediate reinforcement			
Reinforcement contingent upon response; i.e., reinforcement occurs only when specific response criterion is met.			

5. a) How does one identify an effective reinforcer?
   b) How do we know the objects Helen Craig used where reinforcing?
   c) Identify some of the reinforcers used in an educational situation you are familiar with, and indicate how you can be certain they are reinforcers.

UNIT

7

Shaping Complex Behavior

Content

Follow the appropriate directions for your selected supplementary text (one of these four):

1. Holland and Skinner—Work sets 14–16 and 18–20.
2. Ferster *et al.*—Read each of the following parts and answer the probe questions:

   1968 ed.
   Ch. 8, parts 1, 2, and 3
   Ch. 9, part 1
   Ch. 10, parts 3 and 4
   Ch. 11, part 3.

   1975 ed.
   Ch. 9, parts 1, 2, and 3
   Ch. 10, part 1
   Ch. 11, parts 1 and 2
   Ch. 12, part 3.

3. Whaley and Malott—Read each of the following chapters (including the "Notes" section) and answer the chapter questions: Chapters 4–7.
4. Reynolds—Read Chapters 3 and 6 and write a summary of each.

Skinner, B. F., and S. Krakower. *Handwriting with Write and See.* Chicago: Lyons and Carnahan, 1968. (one sample page.)

This unit continues the detailed exposure to principles of operant conditioning. Topics covered are shaping a complex behavior and schedules of reinforcement. Students examine a sample of curriculum material that applies shaping.

Objectives

Students discuss successive approximation and differential reinforcement in laboratory learning and classroom situations. They also analyze an accidental or superstitious contingency.

Instructions

1. Read the designated sections of your supplementary text and respond as suggested above.
2. Look over the sample page from the *Handwriting with Write and See* program.
3. Answer the unit questions, check your answers, and confer with the instructor.

Figure 7.1

Handwriting with Write and See

B. F. Skinner and S. Krakower

Figure 7.1 is a sample from *Handwriting with Write and See* by Skinner and Krakower. From this sample, you can observe the gradual withdrawal of stimulus support.

Unfortunately, this reproduction cannot show the effect of the specially treated paper and special felt-tipped pens provided with the books which provide immediate reinforcement for correct responses. If the mark the student makes stays within the bounds of a well-formed letter, the letter appears in brown ink. If the line strays outside the bounds, it appears in yellow ink.

QUESTIONS

1. In the Skinner and Krakower handwriting program, how is *differential* reinforcement provided? How is correct letter form successively approximated?

2. What is an accidental reinforcing contingency? Give an example.

3. A teacher in a classroom may be sensitive to "attentive" and "knowledgeable" facial expressions of some children in dispensing signs of approval. Since there is no necessary relationship between looking "attentive" or looking "knowledgeable" and being attentive or being knowledgeable, what may result?

4. Review the section of Skinner's *Technology of Teaching* which describes the process of getting the blind "schizophrenic" child to wear his glasses. (See Unit 5, pp. 79–80.)

   a) What was the effect of withholding reinforcement?

   b) How was a strong reinforcer established?

   c) Describe the shaping procedure.

B. F. Skinner and Sue Ann Krakower, *Handwriting with Write and See* (Chicago: Lyons and Carnahan, Inc., 1968), p. 44. Reprinted by permission of the publisher.

UNIT

8

Generalization and Discrimination

Content

Follow the appropriate directions for your selected supplementary text (one of these four):

1. Holland and Skinner—Work sets 21 and 22.
2. Ferster *et al.*—Read each of the following parts and answer the probe questions:
   1968 and 1975 editions
   Ch. 14, parts 1, 2, and 3
   Ch. 15, parts 1 and 2.
3. Whaley and Malott—Read each of the following chapters (including the "Notes" section) and answer the chapter questions: Chapters 8–11.
4. Reynolds—Read Chapter 4 and write a summary.

The reading is adapted from an article by Sidney Bijou, "Systematic Instruction in the Attainment of Right-Left Form Concepts in Young and Retarded Children," which appeared in J. G. Holland and B. F. Skinner, eds., *An Analysis of the Behavioral Processes Involved in Self-Instruction with Teaching Machines* (final report to the U.S. Office of Education, Grant number 71-31-0370-051.3, 1965.)

Topics covered in this unit include stimulus discrimination and generalization. The reading describes a program that teaches a difficult form discrimination.

Objectives

Students discuss stimulus control and analyze pertinent examples, such as the Bijou program.

Instructions

1. Read the designated sections of your supplementary text and respond as suggested above.
2. Read the adaptation of the Bijou article.
3. Answer the unit questions, check your answers, and confer with the instructor.

Systematic Instruction in the Attainment of Right-Left Form Concepts in Young and Retarded Children

(adapted from an article by Sidney Bijou)

This investigation was concerned with teaching nonverbal concepts involving discrimination of geometric forms with left-right orientational differences. Programed-instruction techniques were used in the teaching. This series of learning tasks demonstrates especially the principle of gradual progression.

The apparatus, shown in Fig. 8.1, consisted of a box with a panel of touch-sensitive windows to display the stimuli and register selections. A geometric shape projected from behind onto the large upper window was designated as the sample. Geometric shapes projected onto the five smaller windows were the choices. The sample was presented first. The choices only appeared after the learner pressed on the sample window.

The child pressed on one of the small windows to select the match for the sample. If the choice was correct, a red light glowed, a chime sounded, the sample and five choices disappeared, and the next sample appeared. Again the child had to press the sample window to make the five choices appear. Then he made his next choice of a match, and so on. In the case of an incorrect choice, the light and chime did not operate but the choices disappeared. The child had to press on the sample window once more to make the choices reappear. Then he had a second opportunity to choose a match. This sequence would be repeated until the correct choice was made. Thus, the last response made to a problem was always the correct response. For those slides on which errors were made, after the last and necessarily correct response, the slide tray backed up to the previous item. If this item was answered correctly on the first attempt, the slide tray advanced, and the child was given another opportunity to respond to the item on which he had made an error. Thus, advancement through the program was contingent upon a correct response on the first attempt.

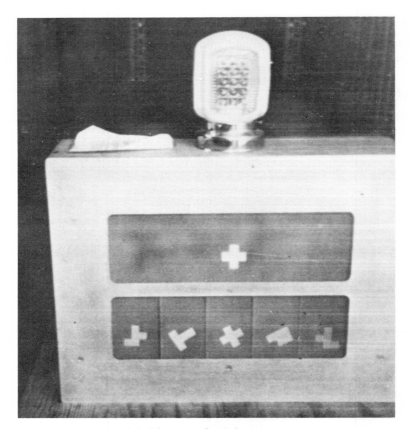

Fig. 8.1. Photograph of the apparatus.

The stimuli consisted of ten shapes colored either red, yellow, green, or blue (see Fig. 8.2). Note that three of the shapes have mirror-image possibilities: **⌐** , **⌐** , **⌐** , **⌐** , **⌐** , **⌐** . Two versions of the program were constructed, one with sample and matches all one color and the other with four colors mixed within a slide. The program was divided into Elementary, Intermediate, and Advanced Sets.

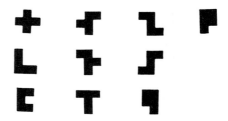

Fig. 8.2. Forms used in mirror-image training.

ELEMENTARY SET

The Elementary Set started with simple problems involving only three familiar shapes: a colored circle, square, and triangle. These easy problems allowed the children to become acquainted with the operation of the apparatus and instructed the children in appropriate attending behavior for making the matching response.

In the first few trials only three choices were presented (see Fig. 8.3, slide 1-1.) Then two of the experimental forms were added, so that from sixth trial on, five choices were presented. Gradually the other experimental forms replaced the circle, square, and triangle (Fig. 8.3, slide 1-10.)

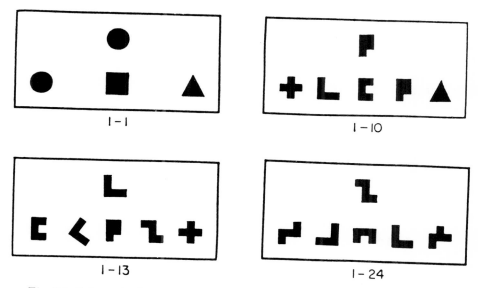

Fig. 8.3. Schematic drawings of representative slides from the Elementary Set.

Clockwise and counterclockwise rotation of the forms was irrelevant to the final objective of discriminating mirror images, so rotation was introduced to insure that this factor did not become an inadvertent cue for responding.

From slide 13 (see Fig. 8.3, 1-13) to the end of the Elementary Set, the correct match was gradually rotated, while the sample was always presented in the upright position. The degree of rotation (to the left or right) began at 30 degrees and was gradually increased to 90 degrees.

INTERMEDIATE SET

The Intermediate Set was designed to train discrimination when both the sample and the match are rotated. The range of possible rotation was increased to 180 degrees. Two slides in the Intermediate Set are shown in Fig. 8.4. Slide 1-20 (the

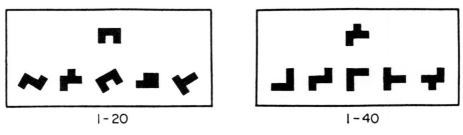

Fig. 8.4. Schematic drawings of representative slides from the Intermediate Set.

middle slide in the set) presents the sample at plus 90 degrees and the correct match at plus 60 degrees, with a difference in rotation between them of 30 degrees. Slide 1-40 (the last slide in the set) shows the sample at plus 90 degrees and the correct match at minus 90 degrees, with a difference in rotation between them of 180 degrees.

ADVANCED SET

The Advanced Set was designed to train discrimination between mirror images and non–mirror images of forms, first presented in upright positions and then with rotations. In this set only the **Ⴔ**, **Ⴑ**, and **⊥** , were samples. Half the time they were presented oriented in the opposite direction, i.e., as **◖**, **Ⴑ**, and **⊥**. Because of its length, the Advanced Set was divided into five units.

Unit 1

Gradual progression was used to introduce the mirror image of the sample as an *incorrect choice*. In successive slides the mirror image of **◖** was developed by gradually raising the lower horizontal arm of **Ⴑ**. (See Fig. 8.5, slides 1-1, 1-29, 1-35.)

The mirror image of **Ⴑ** was gradually developed in successive slides by lowering the left-hand arm of **ᚲ**. (See Fig. 8.5, slides 1-8, 1-14.)

And the mirror image of **⊥** was gradually formed by lowering the left arm of **⊦** . (See Fig. 8.5, slide 1-22.)

In other words, changes were made in three *incorrect* non–mirror-image forms to make them into *incorrect* mirror images of the forms **◖**, **Ⴑ**, and **⊥**. The purpose of this procedure is to reduce error by reducing the likelihood that the learner will ever select the inappropriate mirror image as a match.

Unit 2

This unit provided further training in discriminating a mirror image from a non–mirror image when the sample and its match were rotated. On the assumption that discriminations are facilitated when similar forms are close to each other, the mirror

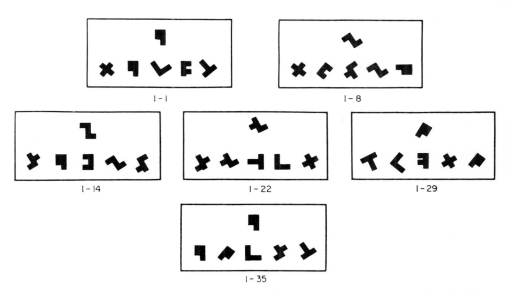

Fig. 8.5. Schematic drawings of representative slides from Unit 1 of the Advanced Set.

image of the sample was first placed in the window adjacent to the correct match, and then, on later items, was separated by one, two, and three windows.

Unit 3

Unit 3 increased the complexity of the discrimination by introducing a greater degree of rotation, and by presenting a greater discrepancy in rotation between the correct match and the mirror image of the sample. Again the match and the mirror image initially were presented in adjacent windows and on later items were presented farther and farther apart.

Units 4 and 5

In Unit 4, *two* mirror images of the sample appeared among the incorrect choices. And in Unit 5, three and four mirror images appeared. In Fig. 8.6, slide 5-3 shows a problem with three mirror images among the incorrect choices and rotations to 90 degrees, and slide 5-38 shows four mirror images and rotations to 120 degrees.

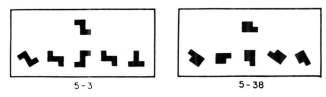

Fig. 8.6. Schematic drawings of representative slides from Unit 5 of the Advanced Set.

Note in slides 5-3 and 5-38 that the correct match is rotated while one of the mirror images is shown in the same rotational position as the sample. These items represent the terminal behavior in which the child selects a match even though it is rotated and does not select mirror images even though they may be presented in the same rotational position as the sample.

RECORDS OF LEARNING

Figure 8.7 shows the cumulative record of the responses of a boy, nearly six years old, during this training program. He was started on the Intermediate Set. Time is plotted in 20-second units on the horizontal axis and the order number of slides on the vertical axis. A step up represents a correct response. The length of each horizontal line represents duration of response time. A vertical stroke represents an error. A step down represents a return to the previous slide, following a slide on which an error was made.

As shown in the upper left graph, this boy's rate was slow and fairly constant in the Intermediate Set. In the same session he was given Units 1 and 2 of the Advanced Set. The cumulative records show that his rate steadily decreased and that he made four errors on Unit 1 and one error on Unit 2.

In session 2, he was given only Unit 3 of the Advanced Set. His rate slowed down even more but he made only one error.

In session 3, Units 4 and 5 were given. The slow rate of responding continued, but again the error rate was quite low, only one error on Unit 5, none on Unit 4.

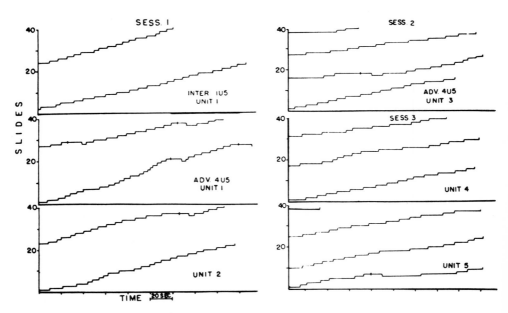

Fig. 8.7. Performance of a boy, 5 years 11 months, on the Intermediate and Advanced Sets administered in four sessions.

QUESTIONS

1. How can we determine when a pigeon or other nonverbal organism is able to discriminate between two stimuli?

2. What are the parts of a three-term contingency? Give an example of conditioning an operant using a three-term contingency.
   (*Note:* see Unit 5 for a definition of a three-term contingency if that term isn't used in your selected text.)

3. Read the following anecdote, then answer the question on it.

   "Later, in music class, the children were asked to touch their toes when the teacher played a C. The teacher then played a little march, to which the children walked around. Every time she came to a C, she held it. Naturally the children touched their toes each time. Just as naturally, they touched them if any note other than C was held, and when C was played without being held, they ignored it. And this woman thought she was teaching them C!"

   John Holt, *How Children Fail,* p. 145.

   What is the unintended three-term contingency in this example?

   (*Note:* the reinforcer is not specified above but you can make your own statement of one or two likely reinforcers in this typical classroom situation.)

4. Describe the gradual progression procedures used in the Bijou program. Include at least five points.

5. What does the response data presented in Fig. 8.7 of the Bijou adaptation tell you about the error rate of this program?

6. How did the Bijou program achieve an abstraction?

7. A child learns to read using a single given primer. Afterward, how well can we expect him to do in reading: (a) different print sizes, (b) different fonts or type styles, (c) cursive, or handwriting? What basic behavioral phenomenon is involved?

UNIT

9

Sequences or Chains

Content

Follow the appropriate directions for your selected supplementary text (one of these four):

1. Holland and Skinner—Work sets 23–25.

2. Ferster *et al.*—Read each of the following parts and answer the probe questions:

1968 ed.	*1975 ed.*
Ch. 7, parts 1, 2, and 3	Ch. 8, parts 1, 2, and 3
Ch. 15, part 3	Ch. 15, part 3
Ch. 17, parts 1, 2, and 3.	Ch. 17, parts 1, 2, 3, and 4.

3. Whaley and Malott—Read each of the following chapters (including the "Notes" section) and answer the chapter questions: Chapters 12, 13, 16, 17 and 22.

4. Reynolds—Read Chapters 5 and 10 and write a summary of each.

Holland, A., and J. Matthews. "Application of Teaching Machine Concepts to Speech Pathology and Audiology." *Asha* 5 (1963): 474–482. (a selection)

This is the last unit of a series presenting the basic behavior principles. Topics covered include chaining of behaviors and the role of discrimination training in establishing continuous behavior repertoires. The selection describes a program designed to teach auditory discrimination. It is followed by a note from the editors on the role of discrimination training in production.

Objectives

Students describe how principles of behavior control are applied in an [s] sound discrimination program, and discuss how discrimination of a sound can lead to improved production of that sound.

Instructions

1. Read the designated sections of your supplementary text and respond as described above.

2. Read the selection from the Holland and Matthews article and the note following it.

3. Answer the unit questions, check your answers, and confer with your instructor.

Application of Teaching Machine Concepts to
Speech Pathology and Audiology

Audrey L. Holland and Jack Matthews

The purposes of this study were to develop a series of experimental teaching machine programs for teaching discrimination of the [s] phoneme to children with defective [s] articulation, to develop an experimental teaching machine suitable for presenting the programs, and to evaluate the relative effectiveness of each of the programs.

. . .

The teaching machine developed for this study presented the auditory problem (single words, pairs of words or isolated sounds) by tape recorder. The subject's response to each problem (item) was to press one of three buttons. An incorrect response resulted in the tape recorder's immediately rewinding and replaying that problem. On correct responses the tape recorder simply continued to play uninterrupted. The clatter of the rewinding recorder was sufficient to delineate incorrect items without the assistance of auxiliary stimuli. Hence, the instrument meets qualifications for a teaching machine in presenting short problems, requiring the student to respond, and giving immediate information as to whether the response was correct or incorrect.

. . .

The subject depressed one of the three large wooden buttons which operated electrical switches. The buttons, which were colored blue, red and green and had large white numerals (1, 2 and 3 respectively) painted upon them, were placed in

A. L. Holland and J. Matthews, "Application of Teaching Machine Concepts to Speech Pathology and Audiology," *Asha* 5 (1963): 474–482. Reprinted by permission.

a row on a metal panel. Each of the three types of response labeling (position, color and number) was of use in some particular phase. . . .

. . .

[The program] . . . had four distinct phases. Phase 1 involved discrimination of [s] in isolation from other isolated speech sounds. This was the grossest type of auditory discrimination within the program. For the 62 items in this phase, the subject pressed the blue button every time he heard [s] and pressed the red button when he heard any other sound. Isolated sounds were recorded so that there was a period of 5 seconds between the presentation of one sound and the sound following it. Good teaching machine programs are constructed so that in as many instances as possible the student is right. They attempt to shape complex forms of behavior by proceeding in small steps from quite simple material to more and more difficult material. The material in Phase 1 was thus constructed so that early presentations of [s] were longer and louder than non-[s] sounds. This was gradually faded until all the sounds were of roughly equal length and loudness. The earliest discriminations involved [s] and other speech sounds phonetically quite different from [s]. As this phase of the program continued, sounds which required finer discriminations were incorporated into the program.

In Phase 2, the subject was required to discriminate the sound in words. Again, an attempt was made to evolve from simplest to more complex discriminations. Since it is easier to discriminate sounds at the beginning of words, the first 83 items in this part of the program required the child to determine which one of a pair of words began with the [s] sound. If word number 1 began with the [s] sound, pressing button number one was correct. If word number 2 began with the [s] sound, pressing button number two was correct. Early items in the program stressed the word which began with the [s] sound. This emphasis was gradually eliminated (faded) as the program progressed. This part of the program began with items in which non-[s] words were much different from the [s] words, gradually progressed through items in which the non-[s] words rhymed with the [s] words but began with much different sounds, went on through items where the initial sound of the non-[s] words was similar to [s] but which differed in the remaining phonetic context, and finally included items where the non-[s] words rhymed with the [s] words and in addition had initial consonants which were hard to discriminate from [s].

Following this, the child listened for words which ended in [s]. Pairs of words were again used, and a progression similar to the above was used, differing only in that final, rather than initial, [s] sounds were under consideration. After 81 items for discriminating final [s], the child was next exposed to problems of discriminating medial [s] sounds from other medial sounds. Pairs of words were again used. The same general principles of emphasis and fading out were followed here, and again the other word of each item gradually progressed toward greater and greater similarity to the paired [s] word.

. . . the next discrimination task should be that of identifying the position of the [s] sound within words. However, some transition items were included to insure that the child listen to the whole word again, rather than concentrating on a part of a word, and to begin to establish his ability to recognize the position of sounds in words. The child was instructed that he would hear some words one at a time. Some of the words had one [s] sound in them, some had two. He was to decide how many, and push the appropriately numbered button. There are only 30 items in this part of the program. However, gradual progression was an important factor. Early items had one or two quite obvious [s] sounds. Close to the end, the items required that the child discriminate between sounds which are similar to [s] in order to count the correct number of [s] sounds.

In Phase 3, the child was asked to identify the position of [s] within a word. The 95 items in this phase of the program forced the child to listen carefully enough to respond to the position of the [s] sound in each word. He had, by now, been trained in discriminating the [s] sound in every position in words; but now he had to respond differentially to the position taken by [s] in a given word. He pressed the first button for an initial [s], the middle for a medial [s], and the end button for a final [s]. The earliest items had exaggerated [s] sounds, were easily recognizable as to [s] position, and furnished systematic practice with all three positions before the words were randomized as to position of [s] within them. Gradually, the changing of [s] position in a similar word was presented, and lastly final discriminations were forced with words which have within them, in addition to [s] sounds, sounds similar to that phoneme.

Phase 4 involved discrimination of correctly articulated from misarticulated [s] sounds within words. Omission of the [s] sound, nine substitutions of other phonemes, and four [s] distortions formed the basis for the program. All were discriminable on the tape recorder. These were arranged from most audibly different from [s] to least audibly different from [s]. Three initial [s] words, three medial [s] words, three final [s] words, and three [s]-blend words were assigned to each "error." There were 168 items in all.

For each item, the child heard the same "word" twice, once correctly and once misarticulated. Pressing button number one was the correct response if the first word was correctly articulated, while pressing button number two was correct if the second word was correctly articulated.

Two types of gradual progression were built into this phase. The first type was the gradual progression from most obvious to most subtle type of misarticulation. In addition, within each misarticulated segment the most discriminable items occurred first, and effort was made to exaggerate the misarticulation in early items. This was gradually faded out.

In accordance with good teaching machine technique, the program progressed through a finely graded series of more and more difficult auditory discriminations. Care was also taken throughout the program to insure that the items sampled [s] sounds adjacent to all possible vowels and all [s] blends. This follows programming technique, which suggests that we include as wide a variety of examples as possible in order to adequately establish a discrimination (Lumsdaine & Glaser, 1960). All of the words used in the program were checked with the Thorndike-Lorge (1944) lists. Words which did not appear in the first 3,000 were not used unless it was clear that children would be familiar with them. Partial randomization within the items of the program determined which of a pair of words was correct. Initial, medial, and final words were also randomized for Phase 3. Restrictions were applied so that not more than six successive items were keyed to a particular button. For all items following Phase 1, the time from beginning of one item to the beginning of the next was eight seconds.

After Phase 1 of the program, every problem had at least one good [s] sound in it. This program format was chosen because such items forced the child to listen to at least one good [s] per item and furnished much more [s] stimulation than otherwise would have been available.

. . .

The programmed instruction was administered individually, in most cases during school time. At the beginning of the first session, the child was taught to operate the teaching machine. Throughout the entire program, each child was responsible for all of the operations involved in playing the recorder. Each child worked as long as he wanted to at each session. He was also allowed to hear items over again if he wished. The average time per session was 40 minutes; average time for completing the programs was 2 hours, 15 minutes. [Editors' note: The authors determined the effectiveness of the programmed instruction by testing the children before and after instruction in their ability to discriminate sounds generally, to discriminate [s] sounds, and to articulate [s] sounds. The subjects showed a statistically significant improvement in [s] discrimination after training. The children also showed a statistically significant improvement in ability to articulate the [s] sound. The authors found this latter result surprising and recommended a cautious interpretation of it.]

. . .

. . . an "improved" score on this test does not indicate that the child who could not previously articulate [s] now could do so. It means, merely, that in the 24 phonetic contexts in which [s] was tested, the child was able to articulate [s] correctly more often. In order to satisfactorily modify his [s] sound for testing purposes, a child would have had to score 24 on the post-test. No child modified his [s] to this degree; all still had [s] problems, even in the testing situation, at the end of the study.

It is well known that few persons who misarticulate sounds do so in all possible phonetic contexts (Spriestersbach and Curtis, 1951). Twenty of the children in this study initially showed such inconsistency. The significant increase in correct [s] production . . . reflects simply an ability to articulate [s] within a few more phonetic contexts, not correct and stable [s] production. This gain is a beginning sign in articulation improvement and must be regarded as nothing more.

REFERENCES

Lumsdaine, A. A., and R. Glaser. *Teaching Machines and Programmed Learning*. Washington, D.C.: National Education Association, 1960.

Spriestersbach, D. C., and F. F. Curtis. "Misarticulation and Discrimination of Speech Sounds." *Quarterly Journal of Speech* 37 (1951):483–491.

Thorndike, E. L., and I. Lorge. *The Teacher's Workbook of 30,000 Words.* New York: Columbia University Press, 1944.

A Note on the Relationship of Discrimination Training to Production

A very large portion of the problem in teaching deaf children to talk involves the lack of an immediate reinforcement mechanism for the self-produced sound. Deaf children cannot hear their own speech production, and so are deprived of automatic differential reinforcement when their production of a sound matches a stimulus sound.

The children in the [s]-sound discrimination program were not deaf. In fact, their hearing was normal. Yet, before taking the program, they could not distinguish between a correctly articulated [s] sound and a misarticulated [s] sound. The program trained [s]-sound *discrimination,* and yet, without intervening training, [s]-sound *production* improved. How can this improved production be explained?

The process of speech production may be analyzed as a three-term contingency:

S^D—sample sound ("say *tu*")

R—a particular muscular configuration of tongue, teeth, and vocal cords

S^R—learner-produced sound (*"tu"*) which matches the sample sound.

(The symbol S^R stands for reinforcing stimulus.) The auditory matching of a learner-produced sound to a sample sound reinforces the particular muscular arrangement that produced the sound (i.e., placement of teeth, tongue, muscular tension, etc.) If the learner cannot hear the difference between a correctly articulated [s] sound and a misarticulated [s] sound, the particular muscular arrangement that produces a correct [s] sound will not be differentially reinforced.

Since a correct muscular arrangement is only very slightly different from an incorrect muscular arrangement, it is difficult for a speech teacher to arrange another form of differential reinforcement. Of course, this is exactly what must be done in teaching deaf children to speak, since auditory matching of a self-produced sound to a sample sound is precluded. Deaf children may watch the teacher pronounce a sound, then, using a mirror, watch themselves pronounce the sound, attempting to match their lip movements to the teacher's. This is less effective than an auditory match as a reinforcer for correct speech production because apparently similar lip movements can produce different sounds.

Deaf children cannot "learn" to discriminate subtle differences in sounds. However, many normal children with an articulation problem also have a problem with the discrimination of that sound which can be overcome by programmed discrimination training. In the [s]-sound program, once discrimination of a correct [s] sound was established, production of a correct [s] sound "automatically" improved. As children learned to hear the difference between a "good" [s] sound and a "poor" [s] sound on the tape, they were also learning to hear the difference between their self-produced [s] sound and the correct or sample [s] sound. Establishing this discrimination allows immediate differential reinforcement of vocal muscle positions and movements which produce the sound. Such immediate differential reinforcement functions to allow improved production of the sound.

SPEECH PRODUCTION AND A CONTINUOUS REPERTOIRE

We have discussed discrimination of [s] sounds as if a correct [s] sound was one discrete stimulus and an incorrect [s] sound a different discrete stimulus. In fact, however, there is a continuum of [s]-like sounds, some points of which are "correct" [s] sounds and other points of which are "incorrect." There is a similar continuum in the muscular positions which result in [s] sound production. Very slight differences in these responses produce corresponding slight differences in the resulting [s] sound. A sizable portion of this continuum falls within the limits of acceptable or "correct" [s]-sound production. A talented vocal mimic has developed a continuous repertoire of vocal motor responses which produce sounds matching a similarly continuous stimulus dimension, the typical speech sounds of the mimicked person. A skilled mimic is able to:

1. discriminate subtle differences in the speech of others;
2. discriminate the degree of the match between his or her own response-produced speech sounds and the speech of others.

When these conditions are met, the stimuli resulting from the response (the sound and the particular muscular configuration which produced the sound) differentially reinforce closer and closer approximations to precise imitations.

OTHER EXAMPLES OF CONTINUOUS REPERTOIRES

Many commonplace behaviors involve the control of a continuous response dimension by a continuous stimulus dimension. In ordinary conversation, subtle changes of facial expression and slight body movements of the listener are a continuous stimulus dimension to which the speaker adjusts. The life-of-the-party type who is really boring everyone may have never developed a sufficient discrimination of this particular stimulus continuum. In driving a car, the driver's controlling stimulus for manipulation of the steering wheel is the position of the car on the road. Similarly, the artist's model is the controlling stimulus for the artist's brush strokes. In learning to compose "good" paragraphs, the student who is first trained to discriminate among a variety of good and not-so-good paragraphs then has available automatic differential reinforcement for a self-produced paragraph. In the development of a continuous repertoire of responses, specific training in the discrimination of the controlling continuous stimulus dimension is often necessary. Additional training along the response continuum itself is frequently also necessary, but this training is greatly facilitated when the necessary discrimination of the controlling stimulus dimension has already been established.

QUESTIONS

1. What reinforces the behaviors in the chain prior to the final behavior?
2. Describe, as fully as you can, how each of the following principles was represented in the [s]-sound discrimination program:
   a) immediate reinforcement,
   b) gradual progression,
   c) variety of examples to establish abstraction.
3. How are irrelevant cues for responding avoided in the [s]-sound discrimination program?
4. After successfully completing the [s]-sound discrimination program, many children showed some improvement in their production of the [s] sound, even though production was not specifically trained in the program. Explain how this learning came about. Be sure to include in your answer what the reinforcing mechanisms might have been. (But do not simply describe the procedures of the program.)
5. Learning to write is essentially a copying behavior. Before the learner can correctly copy the symbols, what three conditions must be present?
6. Why might a music teacher begin to teach singing from a score by teaching the student to discriminate various notes as sung by another person?

UNIT

10

Section Summary on Units 6-9

Content

A set of questions.

Objectives

The student will discuss a chain of behaviors, apply shaping techniques to a motor-learning situation, discuss how reinforcement history could account for behavior, analyze the behavior control existing in a situation, describe an example of three-term contingency, and analyze a program example for unintended contingencies.

Instructions

1. Answer the questions. (You may, if you wish, refer to the readings or to your answers for the preceding units.)
2. When you have reviewed your answers, see your instructor for a brief interview.

QUESTIONS

1. "Looking" or "attending" is often a component of a chain of behaviors. Explain why and discuss a chain of behaviors that includes this component.
2. Describe as completely as possible how you would use the technique of shaping to establish walking in a nonambulatory, nonverbal, retarded child who has no physical

disability. Make your answer sufficiently detailed so that a person not familiar with behavioral principles and technical terms could carry out the procedure. Include comment on the following points: (a) reinforcers, (b) analysis of the task, (c) environment, (d) gradual progression.

3. Person A can mimic any auditory pattern, can sing any note. Person B finds it impossible to sing a matching pitch or melody after hearing it, despite trying very hard to do so. Describe the possible histories of reinforcement experienced by Person A and Person B that might have resulted in their different competency in these skills.

4. Describe how children develop the practice of talking to their parents in a much louder tone of voice than is necessary for ordinary hearing. Analyze the effect of the child's loud voice on the parents' behavior as well as the effect of the parents' behavior on the child.

5. The following item is from a computer-assisted-instruction program teaching reading. The student sits before a touch-sensitive screen. On the screen there appears a box or cell with two letters above it (the last two letters of the word that belongs in the cell), one letter to the left of it (the first letter of the word that belongs in the cell), and four words below it. The student hears a recorded computer message, "Touch and say the word that belongs in the empty cell." If the correct one of the four words below the cell is touched (in this case, *ran*) the recorded message is, "Good, you have put 'ran' in the cell. Touch and say 'ran'."

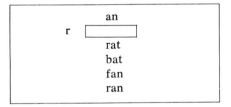

As part of a reading course the student is supposed to learn something about symbol-sound correspondence, or, if an incorrect alternative is chosen, to receive appropriate remedial material. This is one of many items identical in format. Describe any possible unintended contingency which could hamper the intended learning.

PART

III

Preparation for Teaching: Analysis of the To-Be-Learned Behavior

If instructional material is to be effective, it must suit the particular to-be-learned behavior. However, deciding *what* is to be taught is a very difficult task. Certain elements of the *what* decision which are dependent upon knowledge of the particular subject matter or discipline are beyond the scope of this book. However, Units 11–13 demonstrate generally useful methods of analyzing a discipline in preparation for teaching it effectively.

Once decisions about what is to be taught have been made, appropriate instructional strategies must be outlined. Units 14–16 provide exercises in selecting and devising instructional strategies suitable for different behavioral objectives.

Your work in Unit 17 will summarize this part of the course: you will select a topic, formulate behavioral objectives, design an achievement test, and describe an appropriate instructional strategy. Later (Unit 24) you will write instructional materials intended to achieve the objectives outlined.

UNIT

11

Preparing Behavioral Objectives

Content

Solomon, C. "Preparing Behavioral Objectives." (included with this unit); *or*

Vargas, J. S. *Writing Worthwhile Behavioral Objectives.* New York: Harper & Row, 1972.

Note: The Vargas book contains a much more detailed treatment of behavioral objectives and many more exercises. If further work in this area is desired, the Vargas programmed text is highly recommended.

This unit presents a rationale for behavioral objectives and some exercises to teach the writing of objectives that describe observable student behavior and specify a criterion or acceptable level of performance.

Objectives

The student will:

1. List advantages of behavioral objectives, differentiate between inferred mental activities and observable actions, and defend the use of behavioral objectives.
2. Given a list of objectives, decide which conditions for a good behavioral objective each does *not* meet.
3. Given a list of objectives which do not meet all the conditions for good behavioral objectives, rewrite them so that they do meet those conditions.

Instructions

1. Look over the objectives, then read the first section of the article and answer the questions. Check your answers.
2. Read the next section and do the exercises. Check your work.
3. Discuss your work with the instructor.

Preparing Behavioral Objectives*

Carol Solomon

RATIONALE

Most people would agree that objectives are vital in education. With objectives in hand, we know where we're going and can map out an appropriate route. And further, if we know the objectives, we'll know when (and if) we've arrived.

To be of maximum use, objectives must be stated behaviorally. As an illustration, consider a nonbehavorial objective for a fictional American history course: "The student will be familiar with the role of the United States in World War II."

This objective gives the curriculum designer or the teacher a general idea of the content of the course in question. In terms of "mapping out a route," however, this sort of objective is more useful in ruling out certain obvious material (books on Chinese history, for example) than in choosing between similar possibilities (newsreels of the attack on Pearl Harbor or the book *Day of Infamy*). For deciding whether the student has arrived, the objective is useless. How does the designer or teacher know when the student has become sufficiently "familiar" with the material to pass the course? The student must do something which is acceptable as a demonstration of "familiarity." The teacher or designer of this fictional American history course probably had some acceptable student behavior in mind when that objective was written—but exactly what that behavior is will become apparent only when the final examination is given.

Students, teachers and designers need to know their objectives much earlier than that. A student must know the teacher's objectives to study efficiently. So, if the teacher doesn't make the objectives clear at the start, many students will expend great time and energy ferreting them out. They will look up old tests, talk to students who have taken the course, and (to the teacher's dismay) continually ask what will be on the test. If the teacher *does* know what he or she wants the students to do, but won't tell them, the students will spend time "psyching the teacher out" rather than studying. If the teacher is *not* clear on course objectives, the student's search will be futile. Either way, the teacher has wasted the students' time and misdirected their energies.

---

* This short introduction to behavioral objectives parallels the fuller development by Julie Vargas in *Writing Worthwhile Behavioral Objectives*. The author is indebted to Ms. Vargas but is herself responsible for this description.

A clear statement of behavioral objectives is equally vital for the teacher and designer. When they know what they want the students to be able to *do,* they can better select appropriate learning experiences, can let the students know what is expected of them, and can give themselves and the students standards for evaluating progress. Compare two objectives with regard to these functions:

A. The student will grasp the significance of Shakespeare's *Hamlet.*

B. Without reference to text or notes, the student will describe, in an essay of his or her own, the formal plot structure of *Hamlet,* especially delineating (1) the comic parallels to tragic action, and (2) alternations of formal and informal scenes. The essay will be written during the two-hour final-exam period.

Which of the following activities would be irrelevant to objective A?

1. producing a scene from *Hamlet*;

2. hearing a lecture on Christ-figures in *Hamlet*;

3. reading about great actors' interpretations of Hamlet;

4. reading *Rosencrantz and Guildenstern Are Dead* by Tom Stoppard (a contemporary play focusing on minor characters in *Hamlet*).

Each of these activities could be defended as contributing something to someone's idea of the significance of *Hamlet.* Objective A is useless in providing criteria for a selection. The teacher/designer must decide what is "significant" in *Hamlet* and how they feel the student should demonstrate a "grasp" of it in order to make an informed choice of activities that will achieve the objective.

Objective B does reveal what one teacher or designer thinks is significant about *Hamlet* and how students should demonstrate their understanding of the play. A reading of objective B reveals that none of the above activities would be relevant to its achievement, and a closer reading suggests some activities that *would* be appropriate. For example, a teacher or designer might have students find *Hamlet*'s comic and tragic scenes, and its formal and informal scenes; they might be asked to write a plot summary of one act; or, given a formal plot-structure description for that act, they might discuss how it differs from their plot summary and then describe the formal plot structure of another act, etc.

Which of these two objectives tells students what is expected of them? If students know objective B, they can see the relevance of the planned activities and can plan pertinent study activities of their own. Given objective A, students cannot determine which study activities would be valuable and may easily study inappropriate material or spend valuable study time trying to discover what will be on the test.

When objectives are clear, they provide a measure of achievement. A good behavioral objective states clear standards for student performance which must be met before the student is reinforced. How would a teacher and student know when the student had met the contingencies described in objective B? When the student has written an essay in the allotted time period, covering the specified points, the contingency has been met. By contrast, how would a teacher know when to re-inforce for meeting the contingency described in objective A? The following essay fulfills that objective:

> "*Hamlet* is a very significant play. It has been written about and produced for over 300 years. Many people still discuss it. It is a very important work."

Yet most teachers would be reluctant to reinforce that meager performance. A description of the standards of performance which will meet the contingency should be included in the objective.

A behavioral statement of the terminal objective helps both teachers and curriculum developers design relevant learning tasks. What students should be equipped to do when they have completed the curriculum should determine the overall design of the curriculum. It should be obvious that a terminal objective such as "solving quadratic equations" requires that the designer develop a series of learning tasks in which students solve quadratic equations. Yet many texts, despite objectives indicating students will be able to perform activities upon completion of the curriculum, ask only that students *talk about* the activities. Suppose the terminal objective for a chemistry curriculum is "the students use the scientific method to solve various problems, such as the analysis of an unknown chemical in solution." Which of the following general designs would be appropriate to achieve that objective?

A. A curriculum in which the student reads about how scientists work and memo-rizes the four steps of the scientific method.

B. A curriculum in which the student performs a graded series of experiments analyzing for unknowns in chemical solutions.

B is obviously a more appropriate design since the learning tasks most nearly approximate the desired terminal performance.

A designer's terminal objective can be easily rewritten to become the final criterion task of the curriculum, just as a teacher's terminal objectives may become a test question. However, terminal objectives are not the only kinds of behavioral objectives. Generally, the terminal performance is achieved through mastery of a series of relevant learning tasks, each of which may be described by a behavioral objective. For example, one terminal objective of the course you are now taking requires that you criticize existing programs with regard to certain principles of programming. To achieve this terminal objective you must first be able to perform various other tasks. So, in the first unit of the course, you were required to simply state the programming principles. Later, you identified these principles as they were applied in various educational situations (Keller, IPI math). And later you will examine material to find good and poor applications of these principles. Each of these sub-tasks can be formulated as a behavioral objective. The readings and other learning activities which help students achieve mastery of that sub-task can then be chosen.

Once the curriculum writer has stated the terminal objective and the behavioral objectives which contribute to mastery of the terminal task, the basic framework of the curriculum is complete. Behavioral objectives need not be simple just because they must be specific. On the contrary, it is possible to hide trivial educational activities behind high-sounding, but vague, general objectives. A teacher can claim to be teaching the "significance" of *Hamlet* while asking only that students repeat back a plot summary given them in class. If the objective of the course were stated behaviorally in terms of what the students actually do, its insignificance would become immediately apparent. Still, that insignificance would hardly be the result of stating the objective behaviorally.

However, it is not always easy to spot simple memory objectives, even when they apparently specify a particular student behavior. What if this teacher had stated the objective as follows:

> The student will write an essay in the class period which demonstrates an understanding of the significance of *Hamlet*. The essay must include a plot summary and a discussion of how *Hamlet* fits into the Elizabethan revenge-tragedy genre. The student may use notes.

Now suppose that on the day before the exam the teacher had given a complete lecture on this very subject. Would the fact that students could reproduce this lecture (with the aid of notes) demonstrate an understanding of the significance of Hamlet? Certainly that point could be argued. This statement of the objective presents two problems. First, it does not describe what the students actually do, i.e., reconstruct a lecture from notes. Second, it identifies a particular activity as a "demonstration of an understanding of significance. . . ." What general understanding the activity demonstrates should be clear from the description of the activity. Phrases like "demonstrate an appreciation . . ." are merely excess verbiage in behavioral objectives. Despite its apparent "correctness," the objective above is a poor description of the learning taking place. If the student is to memorize certain information on *Hamlet,* and present that information in essay form, that activity should be clearly specified. Since that activity does not necessarily demonstrate the student's understanding of *Hamlet's* significance, that section of the objective should be eliminated.

It is easier to write behavioral objectives which require only that the student give back exactly what he or she has been given. Some rote-memory work is a necessary part of every discipline, but most teachers and designers want to provide other kinds of learning tasks as well. When objectives are stated behaviorally, the amount of time devoted to rote memory should be apparent. Thus the teacher and designer have some guidance if they want to change the ratio of rote-memory activities to other student activities.

Other learning tasks that can be described by behavioral objectives involve having students paraphrase information, analyze situations or solve problems that differ from those in the text, create a unique product using certain techniques, or evaluate given products using their own criteria. With some effort and imagination many rote-memory objectives can be revised. For example, the following rote-memory objective, "Without the use of the text, the student will list four of the six reasons given for the Civil War," could be revised to: "State in your own words four of the six reasons given by the text for the Civil War and make up your own fictional 'historical' example to clarify each reason." The first objective requires only that the student repeat certain portions of the text; given the second, the student must remember the text, restate it, and demonstrate some understanding of each reason given. Although these kinds of objectives may take more effort to write and to teach, they are certainly worth the energy spent. (Please answer the following questions before going on.)

QUESTIONS

1. What are three advantages to the teacher and designer of behavioral objectives? Explain each, using examples if necessary.

2. Being able to write good behavioral objectives depends on understanding the difference between observable behavior and unobservable, inferred, mental activities or states of knowledge. For example, we can infer that students *know* algebra because we observe them *solving* linear equations, *graphing* curves, and *translating* verbal problems into algebraic formulae. List at least five verbs that indicate inferred mental activities or states, and five other verbs that indicate observable activities.

3. The unbeliever says, "If you can state all your objectives in terms of observable student behavior, you're not teaching anything really important. The goal of a good teacher is to give students an understanding of and appreciation for the subject, rather than to require rote recitation of facts." How would you answer this?

4. Rewrite the following objective from the article so that it describes what the students *actually* did: "Students will write an essay in the class period which demonstrates their understanding of the significance of *Hamlet*. The essay must include a plot summary and a discussion of how *Hamlet* fits into the Elizabethan revenge tragedy genre. Students may use notes."

WRITING BEHAVIORAL OBJECTIVES

From the above discussion, you should have some idea of the criteria for writing good behavioral objectives. You know that a good objective describes observable student behavior and specifies a criterion or an acceptable level of performance.

When describing the student's behavior, remember that it will take place at a particular time, in a particular place, and will have a particular form. When these variables are relevant, they should be stated in the objective. For example, *how* the student is expected to perform—whether orally, on an essay test, with or without notes or text, on a multiple-choice or true-or-false test—is a critical dimension that should be explicitly stated in the objective.

Specifying a criterion or acceptable level of performance often involves stating how many mistakes and what kinds of mistakes are permissible. Often an acceptable time period for completion is also a necessary criterion—e.g., "The bandage must be applied according to specifications in p. 15 of the text, and the bleeding stopped within two minutes." As the form of the task changes, so do the specifications or criteria for acceptable performance.

Finally, since behavioral objectives are designed to clarify the teaching process, care should be taken to state them clearly and succinctly. Eliminate vague or unnecessary wording. If necessary, rewrite the objective completely (see example A) so that it:

a) Refers to observable student behavior.

b) Specifies a criterion or acceptable level of performance.

QUESTIONS (continued)

A. Here are some objectives which do not refer to observable student behavior. Rewrite each so that it refers to observable student behavior. (Do not be concerned with a criterion at this point.)

Example: The student will be exposed to a film on Italian Renaissance art.

Answer: In the half hour after the film, the student will write a short essay recapitulating the theme of the film and mentioning at least two of the artists dealt with in the film.

5. The teacher will explain the technique of cross-hatching used in Durer's etchings.
6. The student will have confidence in his or her ability to solve linear algebraic equations.
7. The student will understand the major causes of the Great Depression in the United States.
8. The student will be shown how to mix a burnt-orange color from red, yellow, and brown oil paints.
9. The student will comprehend written Spanish at the second-year level as used in the high-school Spanish reader.

B. The following objectives do not specify a criterion or acceptable level of performance. Rewrite them to include both these features. If you are not familiar with the subject, invent criteria.

Example: Without looking at the keyboard, the student will retype the letter on page 12 of the typing book.

Answer: Without looking at the keyboard, the student will retype the letter on page 12 in ten minutes, with no more than five errors.

10. The student will stitch the sleeve in the armhole neatly.
11. Students will write an essay describing their summer vacation. They may use the dictionary and the grammar handbook. The essay should demonstrate their command of correct English.
12. The student will name orally the parts of a typical flower as the instructor points to them on the diagram.

C. Decide if each of the objectives below meets *both* requirements. State which requirements any objective fails to meet. Rewrite the defective objectives so that they meet both requirements for a behavioral objective.

Example: The student will know how to use the tape recorder.

Answer: No criterion, no observable student behavior. "Without guidance, the student will place the tape cassette in the tape recorder, rewind the cassette if necessary so that it is at the beginning of the tape sequence, and play the tape forward at normal speed for 1 minute."

13. In class the student will recite the Gettysburg address without using text or notes.

14. The student will demonstrate a grasp of the significance of Picasso's cubist period for modern art.

15. With a yardstick, the student will measure five objects in the room to within one-half inch accuracy.

16. The student will design and construct a hinged wooden jewelry box, using the appropriate shop tools.

17. In class time and without notes the student will write a clear and succinct paragraph explaining why behavioral objectives are valuable.

18. Students will observe a demonstration of the titration process so that they will understand how carefully it must be carried out.

19. The student will be assisted in locating quickly a specified book in the library.

20. In an essay of at least 500 words written during class time, the student will analyze a given poem from Ciardi's *How Does a Poem Mean?* in terms of its mood and the technical devices used to evoke that mood. Correspondences between the mood and the device must be explicated as Ciardi does for Robert Frost. At least three different poetic devices must be discovered. No notes may be used.

21. This course will instill in the student an appreciation of the complexity of the economic issues involved in the formation of the European Common Market. The student will understand why the Common Market developed so slowly and why Britain was anxious to join and yet was excluded. At the conclusion of the course the student should be able to read intelligently about the Common Market and make some predictions about its future.

22. The student will recognize the need to have standard measuring units.

UNIT

12

Writing Terminal
Objectives for Curricula

Content

Mechner, F. "Science Education and Behavioral Technology." In R. Glaser, ed., *Teaching Machines and Programed Learning, II*. Washington, D.C.: National Education Association, 1965, pp. 441–508.

The first section of the above article, which illustrates a method of analyzing a subject matter into terminal objectives, is presented.

Objectives

Students will prepare a similar analysis for either cooking or auto mechanics, and will also write other appropriate behavioral objectives for science education.

Instructions

1. Read the objectives, then read the selection from the Mechner article.
2. Answer the questions and compare your answers with those provided.
3. Discuss your work with the instructor.

Science Education and Behavioral Technology
(first part)
Francis Mechner

I. INTRODUCTION

When the behavioral technologist approaches the problem of science teaching, he must begin by asking the question, "What does one teach when one teaches 'science' and to whom does one teach it?" In his technical jargon, he would ask, "What are the terminal behavior specifications and the target population?" The answer to this question is becoming increasingly dependent on whom one asks. Should one ask scientists? School principals? State boards of education? Research directors in industry? Foremen in factories? Science teachers on the grass-roots level? Perhaps the students themselves? Publishers of scientific literature? Clearly, each of these authorities will provide a different answer. This dilemma is not a trivial one. The problem of science education cannot be considered independently of the frame of reference.

Each frame of reference imposes a different set of terminal behavioral specifications and is concerned with a different target population. Our educational system attempts to accommodate these varying requirements with trade schools, specialized vocational schools, technical institutes, curricula based on "major subjects" in high schools, colleges, and professional schools. These specialized curricula always end with some form of practical training, called "on-the-job" training, "doctoral thesis," or "internship," depending on the field.

This article is addressed to two groups: the educators, educational administrators, and educational planners who will significantly control what is produced; and the behavioral technologists and subject matter experts who will actually produce the science education systems of the future.

The main emphasis of the article will be the objectives of science education, and the application of behavioral technology to the implementation of these objectives. It is hoped that the present article, by presenting in perspective what has been accomplished to date and the tasks that lie ahead, will help science educators and educational planners to chart the course of science education in the future.

II. THE APPLICATION OF BEHAVIORAL TECHNOLOGY TO EDUCATION

Readers for whom this is familiar terrain may skip this section and proceed directly to Section III, TERMINAL BEHAVIOR FOR SCIENCE EDUCATION. For readers who are not familiar with the principles of behavioral technology, the description below will provide a summary of the basic methodology and mode of thought.

Behavioral technology involves the detailed application of learning theory to

Francis Mechner, "Science Education and Behavioral Technology," in *Teaching Machines and Programmed Learning,* vol. 2, ed. R. Glaser (Washington, D.C.: National Education Association, 1965), pp. 441–508. Reprinted by permission of the Association for Educational Communication & Technology.

practical problems of training and education. Much as an aeronautical engineer feels that he can design an airplane by applying a few basic physical principles plus a little art and intuition, so, too, a behavioral technologist feels that he can design a complex repertoire of knowledge or behavior by applying a few basic principles of learning theory plus a little art and intuition. The behavioral technologist approaches his task with a basically deterministic and operational attitude. This attitude may be characterized as follows:

1. We wish to cause an individual to "understand x," "know x," "be able to do x."
2. First, we must find an acceptable way of determining whether an individual "understands x," "knows x," "can do x."
3. We must operationally specify the conditions which we will accept as evidence that the individual "understands x," "knows x," "can do x."
4. The specification of these conditions always involves the specification of BE-HAVIOR. The specifications are met when the individual does or says certain things under certain conditions.
5. We bring about the conditions which we have specified by operating on the individual's BEHAVIOR in accordance with known principles of behavior theory (or learning theory).
6. When the individual exhibits the specified behavior under the specified conditions, we then say that he "understands x," "knows x," "can do x."

The reader should note that the behavioral technologist equates "knowledge" and "understanding" with behavior. The behavioral technologist argues that we need not worry whether knowledge is basically behavior or not. The significant consideration is that the only tangible evidence of "knowledge" we ever have is behavioral evidence. The only way to determine whether an individual "knows" something is to see what he does or says under certain conditions. "Well, then," the reader may argue, "suppose I teach one of my students mechanically to wire up some dry cells and resistors to an ammeter, and then to vary the resistance so as to show a change in current. I then teach him in equally robot-like fashion to substitute the correct values in the equation $E = IR$ and to solve for I. He has then exhibited a lot of behavior, and yet I would not be willing to say that he 'understands' Ohm's law." True enough. But the fault here lies not in the fact that the student merely exhibited behavior. The fault lies, rather, in the way in which the behavior that was supposed to constitute evidence of "knowledge of Ohm's law" was specified. If the behavior specifications had included solving a set of well-chosen problems in which Ohm's law had to be applied, and the manipulations of the dry cell-resistor circuit with accompanying verbal explanations of the principle being demonstrated, then the behavioral evidence of an "understanding of Ohm's law" would have been much more convincing.

To sum up, then, the behavioral technologist approaches a problem by going through the following basic steps:

1. He specifies the behavior which the student is to acquire. (Behavior may be considered as evidence of knowledge.)
2. He specifies the relevant characteristics of the student, including the student's present level of knowledge.
3. He performs a behavioral analysis of the material to be taught. This involves "atomizing" the knowledge to be imparted according to learning theory principles. The knowledge is broken down into concepts, discriminations, generalizations, and chains.
4. He constructs a teaching system or program by which the behavior may be built into the student's repertoire.
5. He tests the teaching system on sample students, and revises it according to the results, until the desired result is obtained reliably in student after student.

The operational specification of the educational objectives, which is the first step in the application of behavioral technology to an educational problem, offers the following benefits which are particularly significant in science education:

1. It provides a way of determining and measuring the extent to which the objectives of the course have in fact been met, after a student has completed the course.
2. It provides a set of guidelines for anyone wishing to teach the course, whether by means of a behaviorally designed instructional system or by conventional means.
3. It provides a concise, and yet exhaustive, summary of the content of the course for anyone who wishes to know what the course teaches. This feature is of particular significance in connection with evaluation.
4. It provides a discussion framework and a set of working documents on which science educators and designers of the course can reach agreement prior to making a major investment of time and effort in developing the course itself.
5. It can serve as a final examination, in the event that such an examination should be desired.

A behaviorally designed course may be thought of as an instructional system for attaining the course objectives as efficiently as the resources of modern behavioral technology allow, without commitment to any particular set of media, techniques, or modes of administration.

III. TERMINAL BEHAVIOR FOR SCIENCE EDUCATION

A. Gross Categorization of Terminal Behavior

Educators are accustomed to thinking about terminal behavior from two complementary points of view: the functional point of view, which considers the ultimate occupation or profession of the student; and the substantive point of view, which considers the subject matter which the student is to master. This dual approach will be taken here, in preparation for the more detailed treatment used in the following sections.

Table 12.1 is a matrix which combines the functional with the substantive categorization. It distinguishes five occupational categories corresponding to different types of involvement in science, and crosses these with five terminal behavior classes.

1. Occupational or Functional Categories

It must be understood that the occupational categories are not mutually exclusive; they merely designate the type of involvement with science for which the student is being prepared. The categories may be described as follows:

a. The Consumer of Science. The consumer of science is the car owner, the television set owner, the individual who is called upon to vote on such matters as fluoridation of drinking water and atomic testing, the individual who must decide when he should go to see a doctor and whether or not his house needs a lightning rod.

b. The Skilled Worker. He may be an automobile mechanic, a carpenter, a plumber, a draftsman, a television or radio repairman, an electrician, or a printer.

c. The Technician. The technician is essentially the assistant to the scientist and the technologist. He carries out routine functions in laboratories, such as setting up equipment and carrying out procedures. He may install and program computers, make measurements in a physics laboratory, carry out chemical syntheses, administer new drugs to experimental animals, perform blood tests, or carry out statistical calculations.

d. The Technologist. The technologist is the engineer who applies scientific knowledge to the solution of practical problems. Electrical engineers, mechanical engineers, nuclear engineers, chemical engineers, doctors, dentists, are all technologists. They all turn the findings of science to the service of society.

e. The Scientist. He is the producer of science. While there is considerable division of labor among scientists, the scientist's functions include the identification of problems that deserve attention, the formulation of these problems in a manner that makes them susceptible to the scientific approach, and the solution of these problems.

The above are the five broadest occupational categories from the science education standpoint. The teacher and administrator of science are not classified separately because they cut across all of those categories. In a sense, each of the five groups has its own teachers and administrators. It is impossible to consider the training of a teacher or an administrator without specifying whom he is to teach or administer.

TABLE 12.1

Categories of terminal behavior for science education by occupation and area of training

	Formal descriptive and analytic systems	Current body of scientific knowledge	Empirical and theoretical bases of scientific knowledge	Scientific method and research skills						Scientific personality traits		
				Deductive	Inferential	Generating hypotheses	Selecting hypotheses	Testing hypotheses	Formulating problems for attack by science	Patience	Perseverance	Scientific curiosity
Consumer of science	elementary	elementary		elementary	elementary							
Skilled worker	elementary	elementary		elementary	elementary					✓	✓	
Technician	intermediate	intermediate	elementary	intermediate	intermediate	elementary				✓	✓	
Technologist	advanced	advanced	intermediate	advanced	advanced	intermediate		✓	✓	✓	✓	✓
Scientist	advanced	advanced	advanced	advanced	advanced	advanced	✓	✓	✓	✓	✓	✓

2. Substantive or Behavioral Categories

Below are the five major classes of terminal behavior in which each of the five occupational groups must be trained to various degrees. The five categories are called "categories of terminal behavior" in Table 12.1. It should be noted that they are certainly not "terminal behavior specifications"; they are merely gross classes. The various forms the terminal behavior specifications for these classes might take are described in Section III B, "Terminal Behavior Specifications in the Five Substantive Categories."

a. Formal Descriptive and Analytic Systems. The most significant descriptive and analytic system used by scientists is mathematics, which includes logic and statistics as well as arithmetic and various specialized techniques like information theory and differential equations.

b. Current Body of Knowledge. This includes all the generalizations and principles that have become accepted, and that are said to constitute our "body of scientific knowledge."

c. Experimental and Theoretical Bases of Scientific Knowledge. The distinction between category (b) above and this category is the distinction between the statement "$F = ma$" and the reasons we believe that $F = ma$. In science, the reasons why we accept a principle or hold a theory are always given in terms of the experimental procedures by which the principle or theory is demonstrated, or in terms of the theoretical framework within which the principle or theory may be deduced.

d. Scientific Method and Research Skills. This is a broad category, which includes the ability to formulate problems so that they may be attacked scientifically, skill in experimental design, techniques of measurement, techniques for generating hypotheses, skill in selecting fruitful hypotheses, criteria for deciding which experiments to perform, skill in designing "crucial test cases," and all the various data evaluation techniques, including the proper application of logic and statistics.

e. Generalized Traits Useful in Scientific Activity. It takes more than just skill and knowledge to make a scientist. Certain personality traits and thought habits are necessary also. Science teachers often cite such traits as "scientific curiosity," "perseverance," "patience," and "a logical mind" (the disposition to think logically) as desirable traits for scientists to possess. While these terms may sound rather vague, it is nevertheless possible to identify and specify a set of behavior patterns to which these terms somewhat loosely refer.

Table 12.1 is intended to illustrate how the educational requirements of various gross occupational categories may be stated in terms of these five terminal behavior classes. It must be emphasized that the table is intended merely as an illustration; the positions of the check marks are not to be interpreted as proposals or recommendations regarding the occupational requirements of different occupations. They are intended only to illustrate a method of analysis and categorization in an area in which methods of analysis and categorization are still largely lacking. They are also intended to illustrate the types of decisions that must be made before behavioral technology can have its full impact.

B. Terminal Behavior Specifications in the Five Substantive Categories

1. *Formal Descriptive and Analytic Systems*

Mathematics is the language of science in two senses: It is the means for summarizing and codifying knowledge, and it is the means for deducing the implications of the summaries and codifications. In the broadest sense, mathematics may be understood to include logic, arithmetic, statistics, and applied specialties such as information theory and differential equations.

Different branches of mathematics are used by members of different occupational categories: The consumer of science certainly needs to be skilled in arithmetic, and could probably benefit from an understanding of statistics, probability theory, and algebra. A working research scientist, on the other hand, usually puts to use as much mathematics as he knows; the more he knows, the more he uses.

The terminal behavior specifications for programs on formal descriptive and analytic systems can take many different forms, depending upon the functional and substantive categories involved. They could form the subject of an entire article, and will therefore not be treated in great detail here. Some of the broadest skill categories are suggested by the following problems:

a. *Exercises in Applying Mathematics*

1) Convert 1.5 miles into inches.
2) Three pencils cost 15 cents. How much does 1 pencil cost?
3) Problems in probability theory.
4) Problems in operations research.
5) Problems in calculus and differential equations.
6) Exercises in applying algebra to practical problems.

b. *Pure Mathematics*

1) Devising proofs of theorems.
2) Stating previously learned proofs of theorems.
3) Developing derivations.
4) Discovering relationships.

c. *Descriptive Mathematics*

1) Which function would you use to describe the data below?
2) Fit a parabola to the points of this graph, using the method of least squares.
3) Use the appropriate transformation of axes in the graph below to simplify the functional relationship.

4) What transformation would you want to apply to these data so as to summarize them best?

5) Derive the equations that follow from assumptions A, B and C, so that you may test the theory against the data given below.

6) What simplifying assumptions would you want to make in theory X before testing this theory against the data obtained in the experiment described below?

d. Exercises in Deciding Which Branch of Mathematics
to Use in Particular Applications

1) In solving the following problem, would you use algebra or calculus?

2) Is the following a statistics or a probability theory problem?

3) What branch of mathematics would help you solve the problem below?

2. Current Body of Scientific Knowledge

Almost all of the "science" programs developed thus far fall into this category. The distinction is here being made between "scientific knowledge proper" and "the empirical basis for scientific knowledge." The distinction is more traditional than real. Working scientists often do not make the distinction, although the distinction has traditionally been made in science education.

Examples of terminal behavior specifications for teaching scientific knowledge are:

a. In which case is a covalent bond more likely: when the two atoms in the molecule are similar in electronegativity, or when they are different in electronegativity? Explain.

b. A gun shoots a bullet up into the air at an angle of 30 degrees to the ground. The bullet leaves the muzzle at 100 miles per hour. How far away will the bullet land?

c. Draw the circuit diagram for a circuit which you could use to make a temperature measurement using a thermistor and a Wheatstone bridge, and describe in words the procedure which you would use to make the measurement.

d. Define electrical power in terms of energy, and use this definition in conjunction with Ohm's Law to derive the power equation.

e. Name three important genera in each animal phylum, and show their approximate placement in the evolutionary tree.

f. Name four important substances in female endocrinology, and describe their role in the control of the ovulatory cycle.

g. Sketch the curves that show the graphic relationship between visual sensitivity and frequency of light, for high and low illuminations. Label the axes and show the approximate scales on the axes.

h. Write the chemical reactions you would use to synthesize trinitrotoluene from chemicals that are easily available, using ordinary laboratory equipment.

3. Experimental and Theoretical Bases of Scientific Knowledge

The reforms which science education is currently undergoing are of two separate kinds: (a) modernization of curricula, and (b) introduction of scientific knowledge to the student by stressing the empirical and theoretical bases for the acceptance of the "knowledge." The present section is concerned with the latter kind of reform.

The major contributions have come during the past few years from curriculum study groups. Such groups as the Physical Sciences Study Committee under Zacharias, and the Biological Sciences Curriculum Study of the American Institute for Biological Science, have devised tests and measuring instruments that represent perhaps the most significant forward steps in defining the goals of science teaching. One important reason for the quality of these contributions is the fact that terminal behavior objectives are being developed by scientists who are conscious of the interplay between knowledge and experimental findings, and who appreciate, more than professional educators can, the fact that all scientific knowledge is tentative. From the behavioral technologist's standpoint, the advent of actual scientists upon the science education scene is an essential development. If we are to accept the premise, as it appears we must, that science is what scientists do and know, then we are forced immediately to the corollary conclusion that scientists are the best-qualified experts on science. It is from them that the terminal behavior specifications must be obtained.

That this point of view is gaining rapidly is evidenced by the increasing number of curriculum study groups in which scientists are active members, and the increasing experimentation with curriculum alterations and laboratory approaches to science teaching, in primary schools, secondary schools and colleges. National and international organizations that have responsibility for science education and manpower development, including NSF, Ford, Carnegie, UNESCO, and the Organization for Economic Cooperation and Development, are appropriating increasing funds for experimentation with science instruction that stresses the skills which approximate those of the scientist.

Examples of terminal behavior specifications for this type of science teaching are:

a. What are the main pieces of supporting data for the theory of the evolution of species?

b. Describe the experiment you would perform to persuade somebody that water is made up of hydrogen and oxygen in the ratio of 2 to 1. Give the accompanying reasoning.

c. Describe one experiment that would lead us to accept the wave theory of light and one experiment that would lead us to accept the particle theory of light. Give an explanation of each feature of your experimental design, and, for each experiment, explain why the result would lead you to one theory or the other.

This last question is taken from the terminal behavior specifications being developed for a behaviorally designed physics course in São Paulo, Brazil. The project is being supported by UNESCO as a demonstration of the modern approach to physics teaching and the applications of behavioral technology. It should be noted that question (c.) above does not require the student to conceive the experiments, or even to design them. He will have been taught and shown these experiments during the programmed course. But in order to answer the question satisfactorily, he must be able to reason his way through all the phases of the experiments, and also through the logic that leads to one theory of light propagation or the other. The student must understand the experimental bases for the theoretical formulations. The theories are not handed to him in a dogmatic, authoritarian fashion. Rather he is taught *why* we hold these theories, why we have two alternative theories, and that his confidence in either of them should be only as strong as his experimental evidence.

4. Scientific Method and Research Skills

This is an area in which relatively little progress has yet been made, but in which some work is now beginning to appear. Many science educators have pointed out that science is what scientists do; it is an approach to the solution of problems; it is a method by which problems may be attacked; it is a philosophic attitude. The subject matter of science, they point out, is the knowledge that has already been obtained as a result of the application of the scientific method. It is the method, however, not the knowledge so far obtained, which is the important and distinguishing aspect of science. This point of view, widely accepted among scientists, suggests that scientific method is an area that demands more emphasis than it is usually given.

The area of scientific method and research skills must be subdivided into more manageable pieces before it can be treated successfully. The following are some possible subdivisions:

a. Deductive Reasoning Skills. The skills implied by this category include both informal deduction and the sophisticated application of mathematics or logic. Terminal behavior specifications for these skills might take the following forms:

1) The dog was given one injection of drug X per day. After two months, the dog died. What can you conclude? Explain.
2) Given data X, Y, and Z, what can you conclude about W? Why can you not conclude A?

b. Inferential Reasoning Skills. The scientist's formal tool for making inferences is, of course, statistics. It would therefore seem that this aspect of science education belongs more properly under Formal Descriptive and Analytic Systems as discussed on page 140. However, a scientist's skill in the use of statistics must extend beyond the ability to apply statistics to his data. Scientists must also possess "statistical intuition," which is the ability to make good guesses about the likely outcomes of rigorous statistical analyses and thereby save enormous time and effort. Examples of terminal behavior specifications for statistical intuition are: (Each of these questions is to be answered within ten seconds, without formal statistical calculation.)

1) Out of fifty tubes you tested, three were defective. What would you guess is the probability that 10% of all tubes in the batch are defective?

2) The distribution shown below is slightly bimodal. The number of cases is 56. What do you think is the probability that the bimodality would persist if the number of cases were increased to 1,000,000?

3) Each of the curves shown in the graph below represents the number of errors for successive learning trials in teaching six rats to learn a maze. You will note that rat number 5 learned the maze faster than any of the other rats. At which probability level do you think that the difference between this rat and the other rats is statistically significant?

4) You have made four determinations under each of two conditions, A and B. How many more determinations do you think you will need so that the difference between the two means will be statistically significant at the .01 level of confidence?

condition A	condition B
3	4
6	9
2	11
4	6

5) You have obtained a time-course function for blood pressure following injection for six animals that had received drug, and for six animals that had received saline. The time-course functions are shown below. What do you think is the probability that the drug affects blood pressure? How many more animals do you think you would need in each group to bring your confidence up to the .01 level? To the .001 level?

A scientist makes many judgments of this type every day, without applying formal statistics. Clearly, his skill at making these judgments accurately determines the effectiveness and efficiency of his research activities.

c. Skill in Generating Hypotheses. Good scientists are often distinguished from poor ones in their ability to generate useful or interesting hypotheses. Some scientists claim that they spend a great deal of their time thinking up "crazy" ideas and then refuting them. Refuting a hypothesis involves scanning the available data of previous experimental findings, and seeing whether the hypothesis is in accord with these data. One time in a thousand, one of these "crazy" ideas turns out not to be so crazy after all.

It should be noted that this hypothesis-generating activity in which scientists claim to engage is often largely covert. When they test their hypotheses, they do most of it mentally. Only when they are unable to refute the hypothesis in a reasonable time do they begin to talk to people about it or to suggest physical experiments.

It appears likely that claims of the "It came to me in a flash" variety are often true. What these scientists usually neglect to mention are the other 999 ideas that had come to them in similar flashes, but were promptly dismissed by them as absurd.

This type of activity may be described as a type of scanning, like free association, except that it always involves statements about the world. Each statement is checked against experience until it is refuted. If it is not refuted, it becomes a scientific contribution. This process is, in a sense, mechanical. The skill involved can certainly be specified in operational terms, and measured. This skill is one of the elements of what is frequently termed "imagination" or "creativity." The terminal behavior test for this skill would require the student to generate and test, at a certain minimal rate, hypotheses about a universe with which he has had some previous experience. The programmer, in developing the terminal behavior specifications, would have to (1) make the behavior overt rather than covert, (2) circumscribe the universe for the hypotheses, and (3) circumscribe the range of data against which the successive hypotheses are tested by the student. Here, the use of a computer suggests itself. It should be possible to develop a program for the computer that would make the computer behave like a small, artificial, circumscribed universe. This universe would be described by a set of specific input-output relationships, some of them determined and others probabilistic. The student of "creativity" would start out by learning his "subject matter," i.e., how this computer behaves under various specific conditions. At the end of this subject matter training, there would still be a great deal about the computer-universe that would be unknown to him. Here he must begin to generate hypotheses and test them. It is easy to see how a program could be designed to develop this skill. The program would teach the student in the standard step-by-step fashion how to generate hypotheses on the basis of some available data, and then to test the hypotheses in brute force manner against other available data until the hypothesis is refuted or until the data are exhausted. At the end of the program, the student would be generating and testing hypotheses at the desired rate.

d. Skill in Selecting "Fruitful" Hypotheses. A higher-order skill in this category is how to discriminate between alternative hypotheses before starting to test any of them. Great scientists seem to have a peculiar ability to pick out "fruitful" hypotheses. The behavioral technologist, in developing a specification of "ability to choose fruitful hypotheses," would have to interview scientists and try to get them to verbalize what criteria they employ. It is likely that there exist criteria that cut across different disciplines. Structured interview techniques, in which the scientists are given sets of hypotheses among which to choose, might be used to supplement the interview data.

In the final terminal behavior specification, the student's task would be to answer questions of the form, "Which of the following hypotheses is the most promising on the basis of present knowledge?" The development of this type of skill is certainly a much more formidable problem than that of generating hypotheses indiscriminately.

e. Skill in Testing Hypotheses and in Deciding Which Experiments to Perform. Skinner and other scientists who have attempted to describe their own thought processes have pointed out that the research process does not generally follow the lines advocated by the logicians or the philosophers of science. Very often, scientists engage in a type of experimental activity which may be characterized as "I wonder what will happen if I change this variable," or "Let's see what happens if . . ." This type of exploratory activity appears to be a very important component of scientific research, and can be performed with varying degrees of skill. It may be thought of as a physical extension of the type of activity described in (d.) above. Skinner, in his paper, "A Case History in Scientific Method," impresses the reader with his remarkable "luck," as it would seem. Good scientists know, however, that only good scientists are lucky, just as only good poker players seem always to be lucky. What must be examined is how scientists decide which variables to play with, in what direction and over what range to vary them. Again, a structured interview technique or even a behavioral analysis by naturalistic observation may help in the identification of the criteria that good scientists use, consciously or unconsciously.

Once some of these criteria have been identified, the next step is to program them into our computer-mediated artificial universe, and to pose the students such problems as "Given what you know now, which variable would you manipulate at this point, and in which way?" This is perhaps the most important skill for an experimentalist to develop.

Another important skill which the experimentalist must have is the ability to find "crucial test cases" for tentative hypotheses. An experimentalist looks at a set of data and says, "I seem to notice the same phenomenon here, here, and also here. I wonder if this is a universal phenomenon." Now he must formulate some stringent test cases. Frequently, this involves taking extreme values of some variables in the experimental situation, and seeing whether the phenomenon still holds up. Sometimes it involves introducing a new variable. At other times it may involve eliminating a variable. In any case, there are rules which may be applied in the design of crucial tests that challenge the generality of a finding. The process is similar to the process used by a mathematician in determining whether a new theorem he has just thought up is true. He may start out by letting x equal zero, and then letting it equal infinity. If the theorem then still holds up, he may put other strains on it, such as choosing a value of x such that the function is maximized or minimized, etc. A mathematician usually goes through all this empirical testing before he undertakes any formal proofs.

The terminal behavior test for this type of skill would include such items as: "On the basis of the data you have been given so far, it would seem that x is always true. What experiment would you do to determine whether this finding is general?"

f. Skill in Formulating Problems so that They Can Be Solved by the Scientific Method. When a problem is stated in the form of a general empirical question (e.g.,

What is the effect of salary on productivity?), the statement always requires further elaboration. To make the problem susceptible to experimental attack, the independent variable, the dependent variable, and the overall experimental setting must be operationally defined. This type of refinement of an experimental question is a necessary skill for a scientist. (An experienced scientist can usually offer several alternative refinements of any general statement of an experimental question within his own field.)

Some examples of terminal behavior specifications for this skill are:

1) What effect does alcohol have on thought processes?

   The student's answer will have to include a specification of the behavior to be used as the dependent variable, the manner in which the independent variable will be controlled and administered, and the species of organism used.

2) Which is harder, wood or chalk?

   Here, the student must specify how he will define and measure hardness, and how he will decide what type of wood and what type of chalk to use.

The skill of reformulating problems is, of course, related to experimental design but stops short of the details of equipment and design and meticulous control of variables, which would fall more properly under the category of experimental technique.

5. Generalized Traits Useful in Scientific Activity

Scientific knowledge and technical skill are only part of the scientist's behavioral armamentarium. There is almost universal agreement among scientists and science teachers alike that certain personality traits and temperamental characteristics are just as important to the scientist, if not more so. The terminology used to describe these traits is, of course, still very loose. Rigor becomes necessary only when there is a desire to measure, predict, and control. Some of the terms that are most commonly associated with the scientific personality are "logical mind," "scientific curiosity," "perseverance," and "patience." Everyone feels that he knows more or less what these things are, but few individuals could offer operational definitions that would receive widespread acceptance. In spite of this, teachers of science claim that it is these traits that they try to teach, rather than mere facts and subject matter knowledge.

Advocating the teaching of these desirable traits is somewhat like advocating righteousness. Because most educators know so little about the measurement or establishment of these traits, such advocacy is relatively safe: Teachers of "logical thought," "scientific curiosity," etc., are always doing a good thing. Because these traits are so difficult to specify or measure, the teacher runs little risk of being held accountable for not succeeding.

All this is no reason to deny the importance of teaching these traits, or even to reduce the amount of emphasis placed upon them. The behavioral technologist's task is, clearly, to develop adequate terminal behavior specifications for these traits. The question he must pose is, "How can we determine, by testing, whether and to what degree an individual has 'a logical mind,' 'perseverance,' or 'patience'?" The behavioral technologist feels that once he is able to specify and measure these traits in an operational manner, he can then apply the methods of behavioral science to generate them. If the methods of behavioral science have been successful in teaching scientific subject matter or mathematics, it is because we have been able to specify our objectives. If the methods of behavioral technology do not at present seem applicable to the teaching of scientific personality traits, this is not a failing of behavioral technology, but rather a failing in our ability to specify in operational and measurable terms what these traits are.

Few educators are aware of the large amount of excellent work and thought that already has been devoted to the problem of specifying in operational terms what we mean by "perseverance," "patience," and "scientific curiosity." Most of it has, once again, been done by B. F. Skinner and his students, especially in connection with the traits of perseverance and patience.

a. Patience. Scientists are subject to the contingencies imposed by the physical universe. A real-life contingency in which "patience" or "waiting ability" is required, and to which many of us have been exposed at one time or another, is fishing. A fisherman is considered patient if he keeps fishing in spite of long intervals between catches. It is not difficult to think of a variety of situations that test patience, and any combination of these may be used as the terminal behavior specifications for the teaching of patience as a personality trait. We shall return later to the question of how patience may be taught.

b. Perseverance. A related trait is "perseverance." In his *Behavior of Organisms* (1938) Skinner introduced the concept of "schedules of reinforcement for free operants." He showed that behavior can be maintained at high strength even if reinforcement is the exception rather than the rule. Some responses are reinforced, but most responses are allowed to go unreinforced. In 1957, Ferster and Skinner published a major research report on the subjects of schedules of reinforcement. They showed, among other things, that extreme tolerance of non-reinforcement may be built up in an organism by gradually increasing the number of responses that are allowed to go unreinforced. By means of a carefully designed program of schedules, an animal may be brought to a state where it will continue to respond for weeks and months without a single reinforcement, just as scientists do. A pigeon trained in this manner may peck at a key thousands and tens of thousands of times before finally quitting. This may well be called extreme perseverance. Skinner implies in his *Science and Human Behavior* (1953) that human beings develop perseverance and tolerance for non-reinforcement in much the same way: They are exposed to longer and longer stretches of non-reinforcement. Later in training, very little of the behavior is reinforced, yet the strength of the behavior remains high. There are many different names for the resulting behavioral state, including "frustration tolerance," "resistance to extinction," and "high ratios." The layman usually settles for "perseverance." Again, perseverance tests are easy to construct. All sorts of games and puzzles provide straightforward tests of perseverance. The problem of teaching perseverance as a generalized trait will be considered in the next section.

c. Scientific Curiosity. The trait of "curiosity" has received attention from many psychologists besides Skinner. Some of the work in this area has been done by Harry Harlow and his co-workers. Psychologists generally define curiosity as the capacity to be reinforced by novel stimuli. Monkeys will work long and hard for an opportunity to peek out of a window and watch a toy train, or to play with a lock. The "novelty" of stimuli appears to be closely related to their predictability for the observer. Exploration behavior is based upon the reinforcing effect of bringing novel stimuli under predictive control. When an animal explores a novel environment, stimuli which are initially unpredictable become predictable. Developmental psychologists point out that when children are very young, they too have a natural capacity to be reinforced by the ability to predict and control. Children are forever exploring and playing. When they explore, they learn to predict. Apparently, they like to be able to predict. Children also spend a lot of time playing. When they play, they are learning to control aspects of their environment. The improved ability to control probably reinforces play. Further evidence that children are strongly reinforced by the ability to control their environment is that many young boys take great delight in "making things happen," such as producing sounds, causing people to pay attention to them, building startling contraptions (building involves modifying and thus controlling the environment), and transporting themselves about at high speeds. It would certainly seem, then, that children are strongly reinforced by the ability to predict and control.

Prediction and control are, of course, the main objectives of scientific activity. Scientists are particularly susceptible to the reinforcement inherent in the ability to predict and control. We say that such people have "scientific curiosity." It would seem that we could develop what we call scientific curiosity by developing the capacity to be reinforced by the ability to predict and control. Here, classical learning theory is of relatively little help, for there has been virtually no research in this area. The developmental psychologist claims that children have a natural capacity to be reinforced by this ability. They point out further that the socialization process is often the enemy of these capacities. Children are intermittently punished for playing, especially when the kind of control they are imposing on the world begins to conflict with the kind of control their elders wish to impose on the world. "Stop that noise" or "Don't touch that" are familiar admonitions.

O. K. Moore (1960), in his experiments with teaching young children how to read and write, utilizes the child's natural exploratory activity. The child's main reinforcement is his increasing ability to control the environment in which Moore allows him to "play." In short, it appears that the problem of creating "scientific curiosity" is less a problem of building a trait, than a problem of not destroying a trait that all children start out with. It may be that permissiveness and encouragement of exploratory activity and play, on the part of parents and school teachers, would achieve a great deal more than any conceivable form of imposed training. [References follow the second part of this article, Unit 22.]

QUESTIONS

1. Mechner illustrates a method of analyzing a subject matter in preparation for teaching it. The analysis begins with a categorization of the occupations of those using the subject matter and a categorization of the subject matter itself. (See section IIIA of the reading.) Many subject areas can be fruitfully analyzed in this fashion, although, of course, the particular categories Mechner developed for science will not be the same for all subjects. Prepare an analysis similar in outline to Mechner's (including a matrix) for *one* of the following:

   a) cooking, meal planning, nutrition, etc.

   b) automobile engine design, mechanics, etc.

2. Mechner outlines a variety of general goals for science education and describes a number of specific terminal behaviors (or tests for achievement of behavioral objectives). For each substantive behavior category, Mechner provides one or more examples of an exercise (or test item.) For each of these, write a new one not given by Mechner:

   A. *Formal Descriptive and Analytic Systems:*

   a) exercises in applying mathematics

   b) pure mathematics

   c) descriptive mathematics

   d) exercises in deciding which branch of mathematics to use in particular applications

   B. *Current Body of Scientific Knowledge*

   C. *Experimental and Theoretical Bases of Scientific Knowledge*

   D. *Scientific Method and Research Skills*

   a) deductive reasoning skills

   b) inferential reasoning skills

   c) skill in generating hypotheses

   d) skill in selecting "fruitful" hypotheses

   e) skill in testing hypotheses and deciding which experiments to perform

   f) skill in formulating problems so that they can be solved by the scientific method

   E. *Generalized Traits Useful in Scientific Activity*

   a) patience

   b) perseverance

   c) scientific curiosity

UNIT

13

Writing Terminal
Objectives for Curricula

Content

This unit continues work on writing terminal objectives.

Objectives

The student chooses a discipline, analyzes it into functional and substantive categories, and writes a terminal task for each category.

Instructions

1. Follow the directions given in the question.
2. When you have finished answering the question, compare your work to the three examples of student answers given at the back of the text.
3. See your instructor.

QUESTIONS

1. Prepare for a discipline other than science a treatment like Mechner's. Begin, as he does, with gross categorization into functional categories and substantive categories, and continue with terminal-behavior specifications, giving at least one example of a task for each substantive category.

    Mechner's outline may be a good guide and your answer may begin with a reworking of it. For example, in the discipline of art, Mechner's "consumer of science" may become "a museum visitor." If needed, though, add new categories and omit inappropriate ones. Be sure not only to outline the categories, but also describe at least one sample task for each category.

Very soon you will begin work on your curriculum project, so in this unit you may want to analyze a discipline that relates to your selected project. However, you should not feel bound to relate this unit to your project. Some possible disciplines for analysis in this unit include:

history	sociology
literature	political science
mathematics	music
art	education

UNIT

14

Designing an Appropriate Instructional Procedure

Content

The reading for this unit, written by the editors, is a summary and adaptation from many sources, but it is most indebted to an article by Philip Tiemann and Susan Markle (1973). The reading differentiates among various learning tasks and describes different instructional procedures for achieving these tasks.

Objectives

Students will analyze behavioral objectives in terms of a three-term contingency, describe instructional procedures appropriate for various tasks, differentiate between verbal fluency on a topic and the ability to make valid judgments about the topic, and describe the relationship between teaching the discrimination of good form and teaching the student to perform with good form. Finally, students will analyze a complex task into smaller tasks, then describe effective instructional procedures for these tasks.

Instructions

1. Read the article.

2. Read over all of the questions following the article before attempting to answer any of them.

3. Answer the questions. Take your time with these answers, refer back to the reading as necessary, and be as detailed as possible in your replies.

4. Check your responses with the suggested answers at the back of the book.

Designing an Appropriate Instructional Procedure

INTRODUCTION

A behavioral description of the desired terminal objective, such as you produced in Unit 13, is the first step in the creation of a teaching program. The second step is the development of an instructional procedure appropriate to the desired behavior. In developing guidelines for the selection or invention of appropriate instructional procedures, educational psychologists have constructed various "task taxonomies" in which tasks described by behavioral objectives are analyzed and categorized according to the conditions necessary for learning the particular task. An analysis of the task itself involves an analysis of the entry behavior of the learner.

Many task taxonomies have been written to describe instructional procedures that have proved effective in establishing particular kinds of behaviors. Among the most well known are Benjamin Bloom *et al., A Taxonomy of Educational Objectives* (1956) and Robert Gagné, *The Conditions of Learning* (1965). This unit is based on a taxonomy developed by Philip Tiemann and Susan Markle (1973) which benefits from the work of Bloom, Gagné, and other educational psychologists as well. If, after having completed this reading, you are still unsure of the function of task taxonomies (or would like to know more about them), we recommend further reading in Bloom, Gagné, and Tiemann and Markle.

OVERVIEW OF THE TAXONOMY

The major value of a taxonomy of learning tasks is its usefulness in suggesting instructional techniques. Tasks that benefit from particular teaching methods should be grouped accordingly in a taxonomy. However, tasks often do not fit neatly into the categories of any taxonomy; and similarly, instructional procedures must often be newly devised to fit a particular problem. Nevertheless, some guidance in selecting appropriate instructional procedures is better than none at all. Even if you initially feel rather mechanical in your use of this taxonomy, as your experience broadens the taxonomy should become simply a tool to clarify your thinking about the desired learning task. The complete taxonomy is briefly outlined first; then, each category is discussed in terms of type of task and its appropriate gradual progression.

The following is an outline of the nine learning types suggested by Tiemann and Markle. The Roman numerals indicate the three major categories of learning types:

psychomotor, memory, and cognitive. The letter A under each category represents the smallest, simplest units of behavior for that category. The letter B represents groups of related units of behavior, and the letter C represents examples of flexible and original regroupings of the units. A description or an example is given in parentheses beside each category and subcategory.

Outline of the Taxonomy

I. PSYCHOMOTOR LEARNING (training the form of a particular behavior)

    A. Responses (winking)

    B. Response chains (in golf, sinking a level, 4-foot putt)

    C. Kinesthetic repertoire (in golf, the ability to sink a putt from anywhere on the green)

II. MEMORY LEARNING (emitting established responses in the presence of discriminated stimuli)

    A. Associations

        1. paired associates (associating a name with a particular dog, Fido)
        2. multiple discriminations (picking Fido out of a group of similar dogs)

    B. Sequences (responding in a prescribed order)

        1. serial memory (reciting a poem from memory)
        2. algorithms (solving a long division problem)

    C. Verbal repertoire (restating an article in one's own words)

III. COMPLEX COGNITIVE LEARNING (responding appropriately to properties of stimuli, including examples never seen before)

    A. Concepts (classifying examples of dogs, triangles, instances of reinforcement)

    B. Principles (relating two or more concepts, given a definition, such as identifying acids by using blue litmus paper)

    C. Strategies (discovering principles by examining individual instances, such as discovering that blue litmus turns red in acids)

I. INSTRUCTIONAL PROCEDURES FOR PSYCHOMOTOR LEARNING

This category involves training the form or topography of a response. The smallest unit of learning within this category is a single motor response. Single responses are linked together to form response chains, the second stage in the psychomotor category. The highest stage in this category is the development of a kinesthetic repertoire, which involves the ability to perform a range of response chains, some of which have never been practiced before.

A. Response Learning

The most basic kind of learning task in the psychomotor category is response learning, in which the form or topography of the response is not currently in the learner's repertoire. Examples of response learning include learning to wink, to wiggle one's ears, or to pronounce the French *u* sound or the German guttural *ch* sound. Such tasks as a child learning to write, an American adult learning to write the characters of shorthand or of Chinese, or a baby's learning to say "Da-Da" are also illustrations of response learning.

One teaching technique appropriate for establishing a new response form is shaping, a method whereby the reinforcement contingency is gradually altered. For example, in teaching the German guttural *ch* sound, the instructor would first accept any *ch* approximation. Later, however, closer and closer approximations would be required for reinforcement, and finally only production of the precisely correct sound would be reinforced.

If reinforcement is delivered by an expert who determines the "correctness" of each response, as when a parent decides which approximations to "Daddy" he will reinforce and which he will ignore, there may be little need to give the learner prior training in discrimination of the correct response. However, when close monitoring is impractical, a first step in response learning may well involve discrimination training. If the learner is first trained to discriminate a correct German guttural *ch* sound from incorrect guttural sounds, the behavior that produces the sound can be immediately reinforced by the discriminated sound. Immediacy of reinforcement is vital in response learning, as in all kinds of learning. You may recall that teaching children to discriminate the *s* sound in Unit 9 resulted in improved pronunciation even without formal training in *s*-sound production. Prior training in discrimination frequently leads to more efficient response learning.

B. and C. Chains and Kinesthetic Repertoires

The second and third types of learning tasks in the psychomotor category are chains and kinesthetic repertoires. A chain is a series of responses in which the reinforcer for completing one response is also the discriminative stimulus for beginning another response. Athletic skills involve response chains, as do such skills as dancing, carpentry, threading a needle, tying a shoelace, and setting up complex electronic equipment. Kinesthetic repertoires are developed from specific response chains. Chains and kinesthetic repertoires are related in a particular way, best described by Tiemann and Markle (1973, p. 152):

> Any lower level chain—for example, sinking free throws in basketball—may be practiced until a learner attains virtually 100 percent proficiency. But a kinesthetic repertoire, in addition to proficiency, reflects an ability to perform a range of related chains, some of which may not have been specifically practiced before. Having practiced shooting baskets at 10 feet and 20 feet, the individual with such a repertoire can interpolate to 12 feet or 18 feet at an equivalent level of proficiency. A

kinesthetic repertoire is reflected in some level of proficiency, not necessarily maximum, across a continuum of related tasks rather than at one or more unique tasks within such a range.

When first establishing a chain, the learner practices in nearly identical situations. For example, in shooting a basket, the learner should practice from one particular spot. As that one chain is perfected, however, practice at shooting baskets from other areas of the floor should begin. As the learner becomes proficient at several related chains, a kinesthetic repertoire will develop. Since a kinesthetic repertoire is the ability to execute similar chains which have not been specifically practiced, we will concentrate here on the teaching of response chains.

Teaching a response chain involves shaping each individual response. In addition, it is necessary to establish the correct discriminative stimuli for each response in the chain, whether the stimuli are external or internal. It is usually easier to ensure that the learner is attending to the correct S^D if the stimulus is external and available to both the instructor and the learner. Consider this chain: observe a red light; remove foot from gas pedal; press foot down on brake pedal. In this example the first S^D, the traffic light, is available to both the instructor and the learner. The instructor can directly prompt bringing one part of the response chain under stimulus control by saying, "Look at the traffic light."

But another part of the chain, lifting the foot from the gas pedal and pressing on the brake pedal, must come under control of internal S^D's which are available only to the learner, i.e., muscle tension and pressure of the brake pedal on the foot. The instructor can provide verbal prompts which may help the learner in the task of discriminating the correct S^D's, e.g., "Rest your heel on the floor and slowly lower the ball of your foot until you feel some pressure from the brake pedal." In fact, good instructors are usually distinguished by their ability to describe the proper internal "feel" of the particular response topography in a way that is helpful to the learner. Instructors acquire this "talking through" skill by attempting to describe their own internal kinesthetic stimuli during the performance of the response.

An instructor who is able to prompt the learner's discrimination of internal S^D's will spare the student much trial-and-error learning. Such prompting is expected when the S^D is external—few students would patronize a driving instructor who let them discover by trial-and-error that a red light was an S^D for stopping. However, when the S^D's are internal, some trial-and-error learning is still expected since there is a stronger possibility of a discrepancy between the instructor's verbal description and the learner's internal experience. And so, the learner frequently must experience the car lurching to a stop to punish certain braking responses, and a smooth stop to reinforce other braking responses. With the combination of verbal prompting for both internal and external S^D's and some trial-and-error experiences, the learner will eventually make the correct discriminations for each response in the chain, whether the discrimination involves internal or external stimuli.

To establish the proper S^D's in animal training, response chains are taught backwards; that is, the last step in performance of the chain is taught first, the next-to-last step is taught second, and so on. For the hungry pigeon, pecking the lighted key is followed by the appearance of food. Once the lighted key is established as an S^D, the lighted key can be used to reinforce another behavior, as when stepping on a small box is followed by the illumination of the key (the S^D for pecking the key). It would be impossible to "reinforce" stepping on the small box by the appearance of the lighted key before the lighted key has been first established as an S^D. Animal chains of behavior must be built backwards because the primary reinforcer follows the final step, and all other stimuli in the chain derive their reinforcing value from the primary reinforcer.

Backward chaining may be used in much human response-chain learning also. However, it is not an absolute necessity for humans as it is for animals because an instructor working with humans can use an already established reinforcer, like praise, to shape each individual response in the chain in any order. If responses are taught out of order, additional care must be taken to bring each response under proper stimulus control.

A choreographer may begin shaping a particular response in dancers with verbal praise. Dancers can also make use of a practice-room mirror to shape their responses if they know what a movement should look like but are not sure of what it should feel like. Eventually, however, the response must come under control of each dancer's self-produced stimuli. The choreographer's praise and the practice-room mirror must be faded out, that is, must eventually be completely eliminated. Each dancer can control the fading of the mirror by glancing away more and more frequently and for longer and longer periods during practice sessions. Once the dancer has learned to execute a particular response and to discriminate the kinesthetic stimuli produced by that response, being in a proper position to execute the learned response can function as a reinforcer for an earlier response in the dance movement. This would imply that long or complex response chains should be learned gradually, beginning one response as another response is perfected, rather than practicing the whole chain at once. Of course, the size of an appropriate unit of behavior varies according to the current repertoire of the learner.

In summary, the two important factors in teaching response chains are shaping the individual responses and arranging the environment to promote proper stimulus control, through use of any suitable aids, such as mirrors, tape recorders, and verbal instructions about the kinesthetic stimuli produced by good form.

II. INSTRUCTIONAL PROCEDURES FOR MEMORY LEARNING

The second category, memory learning, is based on the task of associating particular stimuli with particular responses. The smallest unit of this category is association learning in which one particular stimulus is associated with one particular response, as when a certain dog is named Fido. The next level of this category involves a sequence of associations usually in a particular order, for example, learning to recite a poem from memory without glancing at the text. The highest level, the establishment of a verbal repertoire, describes the flexible ordering and reordering of language that marks a good storyteller, radio personality, or sports announcer.

A. Association Learning

In association learning, the most basic in the memory category, a stimulus comes to be associated with a response in such a way that in the presence of the stimulus, the response occurs with a high probability. The form of the response is already in the learner's repertoire; the instructional problem is having the response occur reliably in the presence of a particular stimulus. And unlike concept formation, the stimulus for a particular response in association learning is the same for each presentation, including all test presentations.

Children have acquired associations when they have learned the names of particular objects or creatures. Other examples include learning new words in a foreign language and learning various facts and historical dates. In typing, particular finger movements are associated with certain letters or characters.

Associations often require much practice. In the case of typing, and other tasks that involve large numbers of associations, the principal learning problem is interference among the separate associations. The appropriate gradual progression for such rote-learning problems is to master only a few associations at first and practice these extensively. Practice periods should be short with many rest periods between sessions. New associations should be introduced gradually, together with a review of old associations, until all of the associations have been learned. For an excellent example of programming principles applied to rote-learning, see *The Living Method Typing Course,* by Lewis Robins and Reed Harris (1958).

At the beginning of association learning the typical learner generally behaves differently in the presence of the different stimuli. The typical beginning typist can distinguish the various letters in the copy he's typing from; for example, he can name them, can group all the A's, and all the B's. The instructional problem is to pair these stimuli with new responses, i.e., the appropriate finger movements at the typewriter. Thus, Tiemann and Markle call typing an example of paired-associate learning.

Frequently, however, the typical learner at first makes no differential response when presented with the stimuli of a task. In these situations, for example, in teaching four-year-olds to name the alphabet letters, or adults to identify new car models, evergreen trees, or wild mushrooms, the first task is to teach the typical learner to discriminate among the various stimuli. One might begin training, for example, by teaching the learner to say "same" or "different" when given two stimuli, or to match a sample stimulus given several alternative choices, or to sort similar stimuli into one pile and dissimilar stimuli into another.

If a beginning botany student cannot sort various species of mushrooms, the to-be-learned task first involves discriminating among many similar stimuli. The usual instructional procedure for these multiple discrimination tasks involves exaggerating the critical differences among the stimuli, and then gradually fading out the exaggeration. One might, for example, present this beginning botany student with plastic models of mushrooms that have the critical distinguishing features painted in a variety of bright colors. The learner could sort these mushrooms according to their very obvious critical features. Gradually, the highlighting of critical features is decreased, until the learner is finally classifying actual mushrooms as they appear in nature. Learning the names of the classified species may occur during or after this discrimination training. Of course, short practice periods and frequent rest periods as suggested for rote-learning are important if there are many multiple discriminations.

If a beginning botany student can already respond differentially to the various species of mushrooms, the instructional problem is getting the student to respond by giving the name of a particular species, a rote-learning task. You'll remember that the appropriate instructional procedure for rote-learning (the learning of many similar paired-associates) involves beginning with a few species of mushrooms which are obviously different and having the learner practice their names extensively. Gradually other, more similar, species are introduced, until all the associations are mastered.

B. Sequences

Serial memory tasks are comprised of a string of discrete verbal responses in a particular order, for example, recitation of a poem or of the alphabet. Algorithms are logical step-by-step tasks, frequently involving a choice between alternative next steps, like solving long-division problems, following a recipe, filling out an income-tax form, or using a classification key to identify a botanical specimen. The psychomotor components of serial memory tasks and algorithms are known to the learner; the order of the steps is to be learned.

A form of gradual progression appropriate for many serial learning tasks and algorithms is fading. In fading, the response given at the beginning of learning is formally identical to the response given at the end; but the stimulus situation changes considerably. The response is at first highly supported, but the supports are gradually removed. For example, in Unit 5, Skinner describes a fading program used to teach the memorization of a short poem. First, the whole poem is written on the blackboard, and the class recites it. Then a few words are erased, and the class again recites the poem. More and more words are erased, until finally the class recites the whole poem from memory. This fading progression is designed to teach recitation of the words of the poem in a particular order; of course, it is not designed to teach "understanding" of the poem as demonstrated by the students' ability to restate it in their own words. A similar fading program for a math algorithm like long division will teach the order of the steps, but not the reason why these steps work.

Such performance without comprehension is a frequent educational problem for serial memory tasks. In some cases it is possible to remedy this problem by developing a fading program in which the correct answer can only be achieved when the student has understood the reasoning behind the algorithm or word order. When the development of such a fading program is impossible or impractical, it is important to remember that successful recitation of a poem or completion of a long-division problem does not indicate comprehension of the reasoning behind the order of associations.

Teaching students to restate a poem in their own words or to discuss the reasons for the various steps in a long-division problem involves the establishment of a verbal repertoire. And building a student's verbal repertoire requires a very different kind of instructional procedure than the fading process appropriate for learning serial memory tasks.

C. Verbal Repertoire

Before discussing the instructional conditions for establishing a verbal repertoire, it is useful to elaborate on the distinction between verbal repertoires and concepts. Learning the definition of "fjord" is a typical association memory task. The task is successfully accomplished if the learner, given the word "fjord," responds with the definition, "a narrow inlet of the sea between cliffs or steep slopes." If the learner then uses the word correctly in a composition describing Norway, and can talk about such things as the effect of living in a land of wild fjords on the emotions of certain characters in Ibsen, the word has become part of the student's verbal repertoire. If this same student then stumbles across a real fjord in Sommes Sound, Maine, would he now identify the Maine fjord? Perhaps he would, but not from his training as we have described it.

Suppose a different student goes to Norway and notices, in traveling, that places with certain characteristics are marked with one prominent kind of Norwegian sign, which he cannot read. After much experience with these places and with places not marked by the sign, he might learn which characteristics are always present when the sign is present, and which are only occasionally present. He may even learn to predict the occurrence of the sign, given the presence of those characteristics in a new place. Let us assume that, unknown to the student, the sign identifies fjords. The student has no verbal repertoire in Norwegian or in English with regard to fjords. He still cannot read the sign and cannot name the places. But when he decides that a particular new place has the characteristics of other "sign" places, and correctly predicts the appearance of the sign, he demonstrates possession of the concept called "fjord" in the English language.

A verbal repertoire involves talking knowledgeably and fluently about things; a concept involves identification of instances and noninstances. When doctors look at specific patients with specific sets of symptoms and make diagnoses, they are exhibiting mastery of the concepts of various diseases. When they discuss a diagnosis with the patient, they are using a verbal repertoire. A verbal repertoire does not guarantee mastery of the concept. Nor is mastery of the concept acceptable evidence of a corresponding verbal repertoire. Nevertheless, people who have mastery of a concept can usually also talk about it, although they may not be fluent if the specific conditions for developing such fluency were not also present in their training. And some people trained only in verbal definitions of "fjord" might correctly classify actual fjords *if* they had prior mastery of important concepts in the definition like "inlet," "sea," and "cliffs."

An adequate test for possession of a verbal repertoire involves answering questions about some verbal material when either the questions or the answers are phrased substantially differently from the instructions. This means that if students are taught a particular definition of "fjord," a test which merely required them to repeat or select that identically worded definition would be simply a test of association learning. To test whether or not the word is in the learner's verbal repertoire would require the learner to use other words in defining it, or to select a paraphrased definition of "fjord." If the language of instruction is, "A fjord is a narrow inlet of the sea between high cliffs," a test for a verbal repertoire would involve the presentation of a paraphrased definition, like "a slender finger of the ocean with steep slopes on either side," to which the learner can also respond with the newly learned word, "fjord." For a description of a theoretical basis for the distinction between these two kinds of tests, and an extensive treatment of acceptable methods of paraphrasing for such testing, see Richard C. Anderson, "How to Construct Achievement Tests to Assess Comprehension" (1972).

Appropriate methods of establishing a verbal repertoire involve such traditional school activities as reading a passage and answering paraphrased questions about it, summarizing verbal material in one's own words, and writing comparisons and contrasts of two positions. The program on behavioral contingencies by Francis Mechner (see Unit 4) is an excellent example of teaching material designed to establish a verbal repertoire. Here is the first frame of that program:

> Your being born *was not* a "response-event" for you. That is, it *was not* an action you initiated.
>
> Your throwing your rattle out of your crib, however, *was* an action initiated by you. It *was* a "response-event" for you.
>
> Check each sentence below that describes a response-event for the person or animal named in the sentence:
>
> _____Clara dyed her hair red.
> _____Herman died of old age.
> _____The dog has fleas.
> _____The cat meowed.

Notice that this frame cannot be answered correctly by finding a definition of response-event in the text and matching it to an answer below. Instead, a correct answer is contingent upon comparing each of the possible answers with the sample response-event and the sample non–response-event.

Gradual progression in programs of this sort involves carefully building on established behavior. In this first frame of Mechner's program, a sample response-event and a sample non–response-event are present as new response-events are selected. Then the samples are withdrawn and the learner continues to select response-events. By frame five, the learner gives a definition of "response-event" based on the discriminations made so far. Only when the learner is able to discriminate descriptions of response-events and stimulus-events does Mechner introduce the relationship between these two events, described as a behavioral contingency (frame 18). This is a good program to review carefully as an example of gradual progression in building a verbal repertoire.

III. INSTRUCTIONAL PROCEDURES FOR COMPLEX COGNITIVE LEARNING

The third category, complex cognitive learning, is derived from the task of discriminating the stimulus. The basic unit of the complex cognitive category is concept learning, in which many different stimuli come to be identified as having one particular attribute.

Concept learning and association learning are essentially on opposite ends of a continuum of stimulus "sameness." In pure association learning, a particular, single stimulus is associated with a particular response, as when one person is named Mary. The test for association learning involves presenting this particular stimulus and waiting for the correct response. In pure concept learning, one aspect of many stimuli is associated with a particular response, as when a child responds with the word "red" to red carts, red balls, red dresses, and red roses. The test for concept attainment involves presenting a new stimulus not used during training to see if, indeed, this abstract quality of the stimulus has come to control the response.

Principle applying is the second level of the complex cognitive category and requires learning the relationships among two or more concepts. For example, the boiling point of a liquid is defined as a relationship between the vapor pressure of the liquid and atmospheric pressure. The highest level, strategies, involves the ability to make inductive discoveries of principles and concepts from an examination of a series of specific instances. For example, given blue litmus paper and a variety of known liquids, the student concludes that blue litmus turns red in acids.

A. Concepts

Concept formation is the basic form of learning in the complex cognitive category. A child who correctly identifies *new* examples of dogs and correctly excludes *new* examples of cats, squirrels, rabbits, etc. has formed the concept "dog." The concept "dog" is not completely embodied in any one particular dog, so seeing one dog is not sufficient to establish it. (In association learning, however, you remember that one particular dog comes to be associated with the response, "Fido.") Concepts are abstractions of particular objects, which have additional attributes not important to the concept in question; for example, all dogs have four legs, but all four-legged animals are not dogs. Therefore, in establishing a concept it is important to present a variety of instances and noninstances of the concept to prevent accidental features of the examples from controlling the response. To ensure that responding is not based upon accidental features of the examples used in teaching the concept, a test of concept attainment requires the presentation of examples not used in teaching. Some of the new examples are instances that do not have the particular accidental feature; some are noninstances that do have the particular accidental feature.

The basic instructional procedure for concept formation is the same for "concrete" and "defined" concepts. (In concrete-concept learning the learner is presented only with instances and noninstances of the concept. In defined-concept learning the student is given a verbal definition of the concept which may then be used to classify examples and nonexamples of the concept.) The appropriate instructional procedure involves presentation of a wide variety of instances and noninstances of the concept in a gradual progression from most obvious to most subtle, while requiring the learner to respond to the relevant property of each example. Lack of sufficient variety in examples and nonexamples is one frequent instructional failure, resulting in an inability to correctly discriminate new instances and non-instances of the concept. Curriculum developers particularly interested in this problem are referred to a study by Robert Tennyson, F. Ross Woolley, and M. David Merrill (1972). Unit 22 discusses another frequent weakness in concept teaching —when a correct response is possible without attention to the relevant property of each example.

B. Principles (Rule Applying)

A principle is a relation between two or more concepts. Principles include most rules of science, grammar, mathematics, etc. Examples include "gases expand when heated," "unlike electrical charges attract," "the pronoun *each* takes a singular verb," "force equals mass times acceleration," "If *R*, then *S*."

In teaching principles, prior learning of the individual concepts is necessary. Then the relationship among the concepts is explicitly taught and the learner practices applying the principle. This practice may include such activities as:

given Boyle's law, solve these gas expansion problems;

select from this description the specific information needed to solve a gas expansion problem;

from the following problems, select those that can be solved by applying Boyle's law;

given this information, set up the problem so that it can be solved by use of Boyle's law.

It is important that practice in using the principle be as varied as possible, and include situations in which the learner decides whether or not the principle should apply.

C. Strategies

Tiemann and Markle note that strategies operate when the learner solves problems for which the principles are not provided but must be discovered. Examples of use of strategies might include such things as logically thinking through a new puzzle, development of a model for the atomic structure of a new molecule, creation of a work of art, production of a play, as well as more mundane tasks like mapping out a new route through traffic, or a child learning to speak the native language.

Strategies can best be taught by first giving the learner a problem that can be solved by a slightly changed use of a known principle, and then gradually presenting problems with solutions that require greater and greater transformations of known principles.

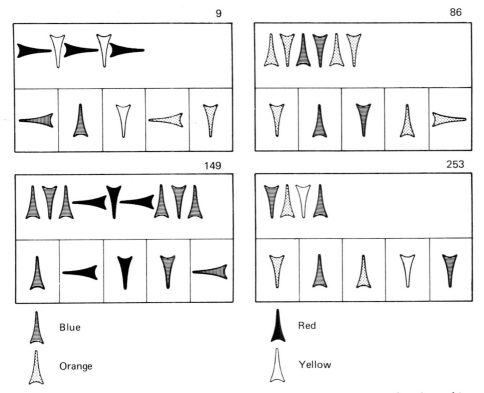

Fig. 14.1. Frames from an inductive reasoning program—an example of teaching a strategy.

For example, Fig. 14.1 presents four items from an inductive reasoning program for children aged six to nine (Holland, 1962). In the apparatus used in the program, a logical series of elements varying in color and orientation appears in the upper rectangle. From the five choices below, the child selects the element appropriate in color and orientation to continue the series.

Item number 9 appears early in the program. Color and orientation of each element vary together, i.e., red always points to the right, yellow always points down. Also, four of the five possible answers can be eliminated on the basis of color alone, since their colors do not appear in the sample sequence.

Item 149 appears later in the program. The pattern is more complex, with six elements before the series begins to repeat. Also, none of the possible answers can be eliminated on the basis of color alone.

Item 253 appears near the end of the program. Here color alternates in a three-element sequence (blue-orange-yellow) and orientation alternates in a two-element sequence (down-up). In addition, the sample series repeats itself every six elements, but the child is given only the first four elements, and not the complete series. A correct answer to this item involves a projection of the series rather than a matching-to-sample response.

For those interested in further reading on the teaching of strategies, we recommend an article by Anderson (1965) in which first graders are taught the problem-solving strategy of varying only one attribute at a time while holding all other elements constant.

SUMMARY

When using this taxonomy, it is necessary to pay particular attention to the three-term contingency operating in each learning task. The three terms of the contingency are:

1. discrimination of the stimulus—S^D,
2. production of the response,
3. reinforcement.

Three different instructional problems may be present:

1. learning to discriminate the stimulus,
2. learning to execute the response,
3. forming the association between stimulus and response.

The first step in analyzing any behavioral objective is to place it in the context of a three-term contingency. The second step is to decide which (if any) of the three potential instructional problems is *not* a problem for your typical learner. You now have a very specific idea of what must be taught. The next step is to devise an instructional program appropriate to this particular task.

For example, dancers must discriminate the rhythm of music, execute the particular steps of the dance, and associate certain steps with a particular musical pattern. In the actual skilled execution of the dance, these activities appear to occur simultaneously, but they probably should not be taught simultaneously. Practically, however, often only one of these three aspects must be taught. Most skilled dancers have developed good discrimination of musical rhythm and have learned to execute various standard dance movements. For them, the most frequent instructional problem is forming the association between a particular new musical pattern and a dance movement. In this case, instructional methods appropriate for association learning may be modified to apply to this particular task. Beginning with a short musical section, the desired part of the dance is practiced. Gradually more and more parts are added, while continuing to review the learned association, until the whole has been learned.

However, in teaching aspiring but unskilled dancers, specific instruction in all three aspects may be needed. Appropriate instructional procedures for teaching discrimination of rhythmic patterns are very different from appropriate instructional procedures for shaping particular dance movements. Shaping, the appropriate strategy for establishing new dance responses, has already been described in some detail in the section on learning response chains. Compare that strategy to the following possible strategy for teaching rhythmic discriminations.

Children are to learn to clap hands to the rhythm of any tune. The first tunes have very obvious, simple rhythmic beats, accentuated by an accompanying drum beat. All claps within three seconds of the drum beat are reinforced; all other claps are unreinforced. Gradually this tolerance is decreased, until only claps that coincide with the drum beat are reinforced. Then the drum beat is faded, and the children clap in rhythm to some simple tunes without this aid. The tunes then become more complex rhythmically. If necessary, drumbeats are reintroduced, and the time tolerance for the clap is increased as more complex tunes are introduced; these aids, however, must finally be faded out. Note that the drum beat functions as a cue for correct responding, like prolonging the s in the s-sound discrimination program, and like the bright colors for various mushroom parts described earlier in this unit.

Given the behavioral objective, "With a running start, the student will clear a four-foot-high hurdle," and given the fact that the average beginning student can only clear a three-foot-high hurdle, this task can be analyzed as requiring the establishment of a new response form for the typical learner. An appropriate instructional procedure for establishing a new form of response is shaping. To shape this response, first the hurdle is lowered and three-foot jumps are reinforced, but gradually the reinforcement contingency is altered (the hurdle is raised) to favor higher and higher jumps. A similar procedure is described by Skinner in Unit 5 to teach the young boy to wear his glasses and to teach a pigeon to pace a figure eight. You might review these examples for details about the relationship between the original behavior of the boy and the pigeon and their terminal behavior.

If, however, the behavioral objective requires that the student correctly answer a question about when Columbus discovered America, the form of the response (writing or saying "1492") is usually assumed to be in the typical learner's repertoire. We may also assume that the typical learner can discriminate the stimulus, i.e., read the question. In this case, the instructional problem is to associate a certain stimulus, like "Columbus discovered America in the year ____," with a particular response, "1492." With only one association there are few instructional problems. However, with many similar associations, as in a history class, a simpler but related behavior would be making the responses in the presence of the appropriate stimuli *and* a prompt. The familiar flashcard technique provides an example of this procedure.

Yet another kind of behavior may be involved in teaching the objective, "The student will identify the species of examples of common deciduous trees of the Northeastern United States." Here again we usually assume that the form of the response (saying or writing the tree names) is already in the typical learner's repertoire. However, we *cannot* usually assume that the typical learner can discriminate the stimulus, which in this case means recognizing the differences among different species of trees. Many beginning botany students must first be taught to distinguish oaks, maples, and elms before they can learn to associate a particular name with each variety. If the typical learner cannot discriminate the stimuli, instructional situations requiring simpler discriminations should be designed. For example, the critical differences between the stimuli might be highlighted to simplify the discrimination. Gradually the highlighted cues must be faded out. The Skinner article in Unit 5 describes how this strategy was used to establish an error-free red-green discrimination in pigeons.

An instructional procedure appropriate for establishing many associations is not appropriate for establishing a new response form. If the gym teacher attempted to teach hurdle jumping by requiring a four-foot jump in the presence of the hurdle (the S^D), no response in the typical novice's repertoire would be reinforced. Under these conditions, the novice would probably soon give up learning to jump hurdles. And, conversely, it would be inappropriate to attempt to establish history-date associations by reinforcing closer and closer approximations to the correct date in the presence of the historical description. Similarly, a coach trying to teach a new response form, jumping a four-foot hurdle, would hardly begin by teaching students to discriminate between a three-foot hurdle and a four-foot hurdle.

The decision whether the to-be-learned task involves shaping a response, establishing differential responses at elementary levels, or forming associations depends upon the behavior of the learner at the start of teaching. Once you have decided upon the to-be-learned task based on your assumptions about the entering behavior of the student, you can begin to devise an appropriate instructional procedure.

REFERENCES

Anderson, R. C. "Can First Graders Learn an Advanced Problem-Solving Skill?" *Journal of Educational Psychology* 56(1965):283–294.

Anderson, R. C. "How to Construct Achievement Tests to Assess Comprehension." *Review of Educational Research* 42 (1972):145–170.

Bloom, B. S., M. D. Englehart, E. J. Furst, W. H. Hill, and D. R. Krathwohl. *A Taxonomy of Educational Objectives: Handbook I, Cognitive Domain.* New York: David McKay, 1956.

Gagné, R. M. *The Conditions of Learning.* New York: Holt, Rinehart and Winston, 1965.

Holland, J. G. "New Directions in Teaching-Machine Research." In J. E. Coulson, ed., *Programmed Learning and Computer-Based Instruction.* New York: Wiley, 1962, pp. 46–57.

Robins, L., and R. Harris. *The Living Method Typing Course.* New York: Crown, 1958.

Tennyson, R. D., F. R. Woolley, and M. D. Merrill. "Exemplar and Nonexemplar Variables Which Produce Correct Classification Behavior and Specified Classification Errors." *Journal of Educational Psychology* 63(1972):144–152.

Tiemann, P. W., and S. M. Markle. "Remodeling a Model: An Elaborated Hierarchy of Types of Learning." *Educational Psychologist* 10(1973):147–158.

QUESTIONS

1. Analyze the following tasks in terms of a three-term contingency. For each task, identify a discriminative stimulus, a response, and a reinforcer for the learner.

   Task A. The student will hear two pronunciations of each word on the tape, i.e., "pencil, penthil." If the first pronunciation is correct, button one should be pressed. If the second pronunciation is correct, button two is pressed. For each correct choice an M&M will be dispensed.

   Task B. The learner will pronounce words like "then, with, arithmetic" after the teacher has pronounced them. The learner is praised for each correct pronunciation.

   Task C. When the teacher points to a long, slender object used for writing, the student correctly calls it a pencil, and the teacher says, "right."

2. Each of the three tasks described in question 1 represents a terminal behavior. Suppose you are to achieve Task A with an otherwise normal child who doesn't hear any difference between the pronunciation of *s* and *th*. Classify this learning task, using the taxonomy. Then describe an appropriate gradual progression specific to this particular task.

3. Suppose you have a child who has no organic speech impediment or hearing problem, but who does not pronounce the *th* sound correctly. You want to achieve the terminal Task B of question 1. Classify this learning task and describe an appropriate, specific gradual progression.

4. You are teaching English to foreign students who already have concepts like "pencil" in their own language. You want to teach a new vocabulary word, like *pencil*. You are not currently concerned with correct pronunciation. Your terminal task is Task C of question 1. Classify this task and describe an appropriate instructional strategy.

5. You want a class of children to write any letter of the alphabet as you pronounce it. Describe the skills the children must have learned in order to perform this task.

6. Select a particular topic. Describe the basic difference between a verbal repertoire on the topic and mastery of concepts in the topic. Include a description of the kind of test suitable for evaluating possession of a verbal repertoire and the kind of test suitable for evaluation of mastery of concepts.

7. Look over the Mechner program on behavioral contingencies from Unit 4. After successfully completing this program, do you think a college student could identify a behavioral contingency in his or her environment? Why?

8. You want students to define various poetic metrical feet, so that given the name of the foot, they can state its metrical characteristics. (For example, given the word *iamb,* they state that it is a metrical foot of one unstressed syllable followed by one stressed syllable; the student will similarly give definitions for trochee, anapest, dactyl, and spondee.) Classify this learning task and describe an appropriate instructional strategy.

9. You want students to write essays in their own words describing the characteristic poetic meter of various authors. (For example, Shakespeare and Elizabethan dramatists usually favored iambic pentameter, while the dactyl and the spondee were most frequently used by Roman authors.) Classify this learning task and devise an appropriate instructional strategy.

10. You want to give students unidentified lines of poetry and have them identify the meters. Classify this learning task and describe an appropriate instructional strategy.

11. Why are chains of responses in animals built backwards? Are human response chains always built backwards? Why?

12. In teaching students to write good paragraphs, why is it often better to begin by teaching them to discriminate well-written from poorly written paragraphs?

13. What prior learning must dancers have before being able to use a practice-room mirror to shape their own dance movements?

14. You have decided to teach your students to discriminate well-written and poorly written paragraphs. Write a terminal behavioral objective for this task, and then describe, in general terms, an appropriate instructional strategy.

15. When dancers no longer use practice-room mirrors, how do they know if they are performing correctly? In other words, what stimuli now control their responses? Describe one way that this transfer of control (from seeing the movement in the mirror to the new stimuli) might be accomplished.

16. In association learning a child learns to call one particular horse "Trigger." In concept learning a child learns to identify a certain class of animals as horses. What would be an appropriate test for formation of the association "Trigger"? What would be an appropriate test for formation of the concept "horse"?

17. Describe the difference between a paired-associate task and a multiple discrimination task in terms of the entry behavior of the learner.

18. What is a frequent flaw in instructional procedures for teaching concepts?

19. You must design materials to teach native English-speaking high-school graduates to take phonetic transcription. The target population can read and write but have had no experience with phonetics. The terminal task is: Given a tape recording of twelve English sentences, the student will make an accurate phonetic transcription in less than one hour, using no notes or reference aids.

    Analyze this task, identify the learning types involved, and describe specific instructional procedures.

UNIT

15

Learning Hierarchies

Content

Resnick, L. B., M. C. Wang, and J. Kaplan. "Task Analysis in Curriculum Design: A Hierarchically Sequenced Introductory Mathematics Curriculum." *Journal of Applied Behavior Analysis* 6 (1973): 679–709. (a selection)

After terminal behavioral objectives are identified, they must be broken down into component skills and prerequisite skills, and these skills then must be sequenced in a way that facilitates learning. This unit presents one approach to this sequencing task.

Objectives

The student describes the steps in constructing a learning hierarchy and also constructs learning hierarchies for a task.

Instructions

1. Read the introduction and the selection from the Resnick, Wang, and Kaplan article.
2. Answer the questions.
3. Confer with your instructor.

INTRODUCTION TO LEARNING HIERARCHIES

Construction of a learning hierarchy, another tool developed by educational psychologists to analyze behavioral objectives, has proved very useful in developing an optimal sequence of tasks leading to performance of the terminal objective. Given a description of the terminal task, an informal hierarchy may be constructed by asking questions like, "What behaviors must be in the learner's repertoire before he or she can successfully perform this task?"

For example, a terminal objective might be: Given five blocks of different sizes, the child can place them in order according to size. Some prerequisite behaviors for this task include being able to say which of any two blocks is the larger (or smaller), and being able to place blocks or other objects in a row. These may not be the only prerequisites, but it should be clear that a child who can't tell which of two blocks is larger also won't be able to order five blocks according to size. Furthermore, if you teach this child to tell which of two blocks is larger, he will then be able to use this behavior in the performance of the terminal objective. In addition, although the child may understand size relationships, he may not be able to place objects in a row. If he's taught to place objects in rows (as opposed to placing them in circles or in disorderly arrangements), he will again use this behavior in the performance of the terminal task.

It makes sense, then, to teach prerequisite behaviors *before* teaching terminal behaviors. Creating a learning hierarchy is a tool for achieving a sensible instructional sequence. (It is still necessary, however, to use a task taxonomy to classify the prerequisite behaviors in order to develop appropriate instructional strategies for them. Placing objects in rows, for example, is another instance of response learning.)

In the task just described (arranging blocks in order according to size) the hypothesized hierarchy is extremely informal, simple (some might say simplistic), and obvious. It is, nevertheless, very useful for developing an instructional sequence to teach this terminal task. In general, it is extremely helpful for the curriculum developer to ask what behaviors are prerequisites for successful performance of the terminal objective, and then to begin testing instructional sequences based on the answer. Many find this relatively informal outline of behaviors a sufficient basis for preparing instruction, while others use more formal procedures for developing a learning hierarchy.

The Resnick, Wang, and Kaplan reading in this unit is an excerpt from a complex and formal learning hierarchy, constructed when the authors were developing a grade-school math curriculum. The behavioral objectives for the curriculum were derived by specifying certain behaviors that math teachers would generally accept as evidence of attainment of the abstract concept of number. These objectives were then analyzed in a particular way. The authors hypothesized a skilled performance routine that would accomplish the objective and then analyzed this routine into discrete components. Each component of the skilled routine was then examined to discover its particular prerequisite behaviors. As an example, consider this terminal objective: Given two sets of blocks, each set containing from one to five blocks, the child can state which set has more blocks.

Resnick, Wang, and Kaplan (1970) construct a learning hierarchy by describing a particular routine to accomplish the objective. This routine has three components:

1. each block from one set is paired with a block from the other set;
2. the sets are examined to find any extra objects;
3. if there are extra objects in one set, that set is identified as having *more* objects.

A child using this routine will successfully perform the task. The authors propose to teach the task by teaching this particular solution routine. Each component in the routine is analyzed for prerequisite tasks that would facilitate learning. Hypothesized prerequisite tasks for the pairing component of the terminal task are:

a. If the child is given a set of blocks and a row of marked-off spaces, he can place the blocks in the marked-off spaces.
b. If the child is given a set of blocks, he can place them in a row without the additional aid of having the spaces marked-off.
c. If the child is given two sets of blocks, he can keep the sets separate while he is arranging each set in a row.

Prior learning of these tasks should facilitate learning to pair each block from one set with a block from the other set.

A hierarchy begins as a curriculum developer's hypothesis about the sequence of various tasks. There are several methods of validating this hypothesis. One method involves teaching the tasks in the hypothesized optimal sequence and in various nonoptimal sequences, and comparing rates of learning. Providing that teaching methods are the best possible and constant for all groups, users of the optimal sequence should learn faster. If they don't, a revision of the hierarchy is in order. In another method of validation, individuals who can successfully perform the terminal task are tested on the hypothesized prerequisite tasks. If these tasks are really prerequisites, success on the terminal task should accurately predict success on the prerequisite tasks.

The Resnick, Wang, and Kaplan detailed method of task analysis is useful when teaching a particular solution method. In the example given here, the child must pair blocks from two sets in order to say which set has more blocks. However, when teaching a particular solution method is not desirable, the use of an instructional strategy derived from an analysis of the to-be-learned behavior allows the learner to develop his or her own solution method. For example, a user of the Tiemann and Markle taxonomy described in Unit 14 would categorize this particular behavioral objective as an example of concept learning, the concept being "more." An appropriate instructional strategy for concept learning is to begin with very obvious examples of the concept and progress to more subtle examples. Instruction might begin by comparing five blocks to one block, seven blocks to two blocks, six blocks to three blocks, etc., with the child learning to respond to the obviously larger set of blocks as "more." It may be necessary to artificially cue this correct response by some additional difference between the sets (color or size of blocks). All such cues must be faded out gradually but completely, as the difference in number of blocks for the two sets is gradually reduced. By the end of training, the child has developed his or her own method of attending to number, the only difference between the two sets relevant to the concept of "more."

REFERENCES

Resnick, L. B., M. C. Wang, and J. Kaplan. "Behavior Analysis in Curriculum Design: A Hierarchically Sequenced Introductory Mathematics Curriculum." Pittsburgh: University of Pittsburgh, Learning Research and Development Center, 1970, Monograph 2.

Resnick, L. B., M. C. Wang, and J. Kaplan. "Task Analysis in Curriculum Design: A Hierarchically Sequenced Introductory Mathematics Curriculum." *Journal of Applied Behavior Analysis* 6 (1973):679–709.

Task Analysis in Curriculum Design: A Hierarchically Sequenced Introductory Mathematics Curriculum[1]

Lauren B. Resnick, Margaret C. Wang, and Jerome Kaplan

The curriculum presented in this paper is an intermediate result of a research program exploring application of detailed task-analysis procedures to the problem of designing sequences of learning objectives. The aim of this research program is to develop a systematic method of specifying and validating learning hierarchies so that instructional programs can be designed that provide an optimal match for a child's natural sequence of acquisition. It is assumed that curricula that closely parallel this sequence will facilitate learning under a wide variety of specific teaching methods.

The basic rationale for the methods employed here has been presented in papers by Resnick (1967) and by Resnick and Wang (1969). Briefly, the strategy is to develop hierarchies of learning objectives such that mastery of objectives lower in the hierarchy (simpler tasks) facilitates learning of higher objectives (more complex tasks), and ability to perform higher-level tasks reliably predicts ability to perform lower-level tasks. This involves a process of task analysis in which specific behavioral components are identified and prerequisites for each of these determined (*cf.* Gagné, 1962, 1968). Detailed procedures of analysis are explicated in the course of this paper.

An introductory mathematics curriculum must present the fundamental concepts of mathematics, or operations leading to them, in forms simple enough to be

L. Resnick, M. C. Wang, and J. Kaplan, "Task Analysis in Curriculum Design," *Journal of Applied Behavior Analysis* 6, no. 4 (1973): 679–709. Copyright © 1973 by the Society for the Experimental Analysis of Behavior, Inc. Reprinted by permission.

[1] Preparation of this paper was supported by a grant from the Ford Foundation. Reprints may be obtained from Lauren B. Resnick, Learning Research and Development Center, University of Pittsburgh, Pittsburgh, Pennsylvania 15260.

learned by very young children. Methodologically, this requires that target concepts be identified, and that hierarchies of specific objectives then be constructed to guide the child from naivete to competence in understanding and using these concepts. Finally, empirical studies, both laboratory and classroom, must be undertaken to validate the sequences of objectives and study the functioning of the curriculum in an applied setting. The first two sections of this paper deal with the problems of defining and analyzing early mathematical content. The final section describes a program of classroom research in which the characteristics of the behaviorally derived curriculum are examined.*

CONTENT OF AN INTRODUCTORY MATHEMATICS CURRICULUM

The Concept of Number

. . .

The basic goal of the present mathematics curriculum is the development in children of a stable concept of number. Many developmental psychologists are skeptical of the possibility of directly teaching these concepts, stressing instead the role of "general experience" in inducing the state of "concrete operations," which includes mathematical operations along with classificatory logic and related concepts (Kohlberg, 1968). Our work, however, operates from a broad assumption that operational number concepts can be taught, believing that "general experience" is in fact composed of a multiplicity of specific experiences, certain ones of which are critical in the acquisition of an operational number concept. The problem, both for psychological research and educational design, is to discover which experiences are the crucial ones; that is, which early behaviors form the building blocks of the higher-level competence one seeks to establish.

Behavioral Definition of the Number Concept

The first step in developing a hierarchy of curriculum objectives leading to an operational concept of number was to specify in behavioral terms a number of specific components of the number concept. The behaviors thus specified comprise an operational definition of the number concept in the form of concrete performances, which, taken together, permit the inference that the child has an abstract concept of number. . . . These behaviors comprise the actual objectives of the curriculum.

There are eight units in the introductory curriculum, each made up of a series of specific objectives. Units 1 and 2 cover counting skills to 10, and simple comparison of sets by one-to-one correspondence. Units 3 and 4 cover the use of numerals. Units 5 and 6 include more complex processes of comparing and ordering sets. Unit 7 introduces the processes of addition and subtraction, while Unit 8 uses equations to establish more sophisticated understanding of partition and combina-

---

* Editors' note: In this selection, the first two sections have been shortened and the final section eliminated.

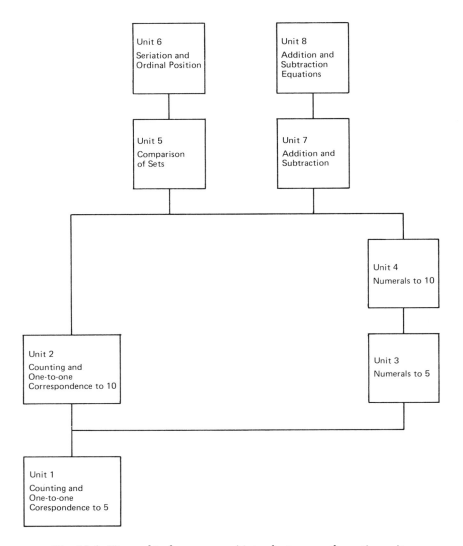

Fig. 15.1. Hierarchical sequence of introductory mathematics units.

tion of sets. The numbering of the units is for reference purposes, and does not imply a linear order of instruction. Figure 15.1 shows the pattern of hierarchical relationships among the units and the order in which they can be presented without skipping prerequisites.

. . .

In determining possible teaching sequences, the charts are read from the bottom up. The earliest units appear at the bottom and are considered prerequisite to those appearing above and connected by a line. Unit 1, for example, is prerequisite to 2

and 3; and 3 is prerequisite to 4. Units 2 and 3, however, have no prerequisite relation to each other, and can be taught in either order. Unit 5 has two prerequisites,
2 and 4, and according to this analysis would not normally be taught until both of
these units were mastered.

. . .

Table 15.1 lists the objectives that comprise the current curriculum.* Each
objective listed defines a terminal objective of the curriculum—an objective deemed

TABLE 15.1

Objectives of the curriculum

Units 1 and 2: Counting and One-to-One Correspondence

A. The child can recite the numerals in order.
B. Given a set of moveable objects, the child can count the objects, moving them out of
the set as he counts.
C. Given a fixed ordered set of objects, the child can count the objects.
D. Given a fixed unordered set of objects, the child can count the objects.
E. Given a numeral stated and a set of objects, the child can count out a subset of stated
size.
F. Given a numeral stated and several sets of fixed objects, the child can select a set of
size indicated by numeral.
G. Given two sets of objects, the child can pair objects and state whether the sets are
equivalent.
H. Given two unequal sets of objects, the child can pair objects and state which set has
more.
I. Given two unequal sets of objects, the child can pair objects and state which set has
less.

Units 3 and 4: Numerals

A. Given two sets of numerals, the child can match the numerals.
B. Given a numeral stated and a set of printed numerals, the child can select the stated
numeral.
C. Given a numeral (written), the child can read the numeral.
D. Given several sets of objects and several numerals, the child can match numerals with
appropriate sets.
E. Given two numerals (written), the child can state which shows more (less).
F. Given a set of numerals, the child can place them in order.
G. Given numerals stated, the child can write the numeral.

---

important enough to be subjected to direct measurement in assessment of the child's
progress through the curriculum. Figure 15.2 shows the hierarchical relationship
between the specific objectives in each unit. . . .

---

* Editors' note: Units 5 through 8 and their corresponding objectives have not been included
in this selection.

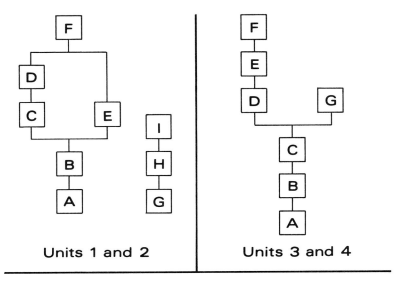

Fig. 15.2. Hierarchical sequence of individual objectives, by unit.

ANALYSIS AND SEQUENCING OF THE OBJECTIVES

The ordering of objectives within each unit is based on detailed analyses of each task. These analyses are designed to reveal component and prerequisite behaviors for each terminal objective, both as a basis for sequencing the objectives and to provide suggestions for teaching a given objective to children who are experiencing difficulty. The detailed analyses identify many behaviors that are not part of the formal curriculum, but which underlie the stated objectives and may need to be taught explicitly to some children. Often, two superficially similar tasks differ with respect to their demands on some basic function such as memory or perceptual organization. These differences between tasks provide the basis for ordering tasks according to complexity, and thus for predicting optimal instructional sequences. The detailed rationale for such sequencing will be described in the following sections, which discuss each of the units in some detail. Figures showing the detailed analyses of some of the objectives are included in order to exemplify the method of analysis. The full set of analyses are available from the authors.[2]

To interpret the figures that follow, it is necessary to understand the procedures followed in performing the analyses and the conventions used in displaying them. In [Figs. 15.3 and 15.4*], the top box contains a statement of the objective being

[2] Write to Lauren B. Resnick requesting a copy of "Behavior Analysis and Curriculum Design: A Hierarchically Sequenced Introductory Mathematics Curriculum," Learning Research and Development Center, University of Pittsburgh, Pittsburgh, Pa. A charge of $1.00 covers the cost of printing and handling.

* Editors' note: Only two of the twelve original figures are included in this selection.

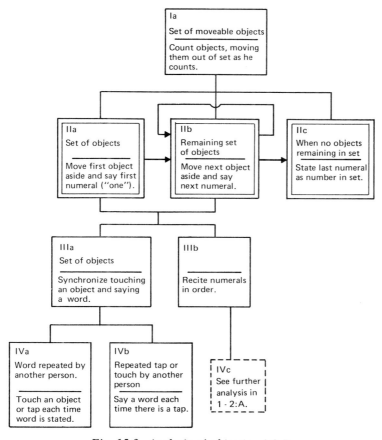

Fig. 15.3. Analysis of objective 1-2:B.

analyzed. In this box, and throughout the analysis charts, the entry above the line describes the stimulus situation with which the child will be presented, and the entry below the line describes the child's response. Thus, in Fig. 15.3, box Ia should be read as, "*Given* a set of movable objects, *the child can* count objects, moving them out of set as he counts." Box IIIa would be read, "*Given* a set of objects, *the child can* synchronize touching an object and saying a word." Adherence to this convention assures that each box in the analysis will contain a behaviorally defined task, one that can be tested by direct observation.

The first step in performing an analysis is to describe in as much detail as possible the actual steps involved in skilled performance of the task. The analyses generated share certain features of "process models" used in studies of computer simulation of thinking (see Newell and Simon, 1972; Klahr and Wallace, 1970), but are less formalized. The results of this "component analysis" are shown in level

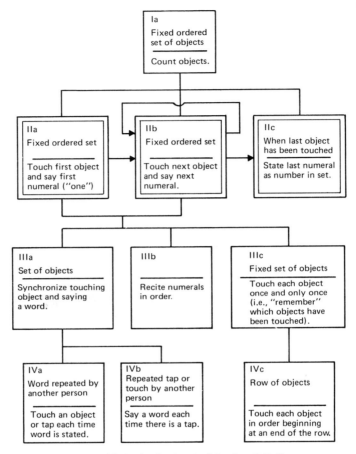

Fig. 15.4. Analysis of objective 1-2:C.

II of each chart. The double lines around the boxes indicate that these behaviors are *components* of the terminal behavior; it is hypothesized that the skilled person *actually performs* these steps (although sometimes very quickly and covertly) as he performs the terminal task. The arrows between the boxes indicate that the component behaviors are performed in a temporal sequence. Sometimes (*e.g.,* Fig. 15.3) there are "loops" in the chain, indicating that it is necessary to recycle through some of the steps several times to complete the task. . . .

Once the components are identified, a second stage of analysis begins. Each component that has been specified is now considered separately, and the following question asked: "In order to perform this behavior, which simpler behavior(s) must a person be able to perform?" Here, the aim is to specify *prerequisites* for each of the behaviors. Prerequisite behaviors, in contrast to component behaviors, are not actually performed in the course of the terminal performance. However, they are thought to *facilitate* learning of the higher-level skill. More precisely, if A is prerequisite to B, then learning A first should result in positive transfer when B is learned, and anyone able to perform B should be able to perform A as well. The first set of prerequisites appear in level III of each of the charts.

Continuing the analysis, identified prerequisites are themselves further analyzed to determine still simpler prerequisite behaviors.

. . .

Analysis stops when a level of behavior is reached that can be assumed in most of the student population in question. . . .

Sometimes a single behavior is prerequisite to more than one higher-level behavior. Conversely, a given component or prerequisite can have more than a single prerequisite. In reading the charts, it is necessary to remember simply that a given behavior is prerequisite to all behaviors above it and connected to it with a line.

Counting: Units 1 and 2

Units 1 and 2 specify several different kinds of counting behavior (Objectives A to F). Analyses of these behaviors [Figs. 15.3 and 15.4] suggest that each type of counting task has certain unique components and prerequisites. Because the tasks are behaviorally different, they have been included as separate objectives in the curriculum.

Figure 15.3 shows the analysis for Objective 1-2:B, counting a set of moveable objects. The key component is moving an object out of the set while saying a numeral (boxes IIa and IIb). This behavior has two prerequisites: synchronizing touches with counts (box IIIa) and reciting the numerals in order (box IIIb). Because he can move objects out of the set as he counts them, the child has no problem of remembering which objects have been counted.

In counting a fixed set (Objective C; Fig. 15.4), on the other hand, the child must touch the objects in a fixed pattern in order not to miss any objects nor touch any of them twice (*cf.* Potter and Levy, 1968). This additional prerequisite is shown in Fig. 15.4 in box IIIc. Since Objective C has all the prerequisites of B plus an additional one, C was placed above B in the unit hierarchy (see Fig. 15.2). This indicates a hypothesis that learning B first will facilitate the learning of C.

. . .

At the same time as he is learning to count, the child can be working on another basic aspect of the number concept, one-to-one correspondence. In Objectives G, H, and I, he learns to pair objects from two sets to determine whether the sets are equivalent or which set has more (or less) objects. The analyses of Objectives G ("equivalent") and H ("more") showed nearly identical components. The child must: (a) pair the objects, one from each set; (b) decide whether there are extra (*i.e.,* unpaired) objects in either set; and (c) if there are no extra objects, state that the sets are equivalent; *or* if there are extra objects, state that the sets are not equivalent. The only difference among the three objectives appears in the third component. To determine which set has more objects, the child must correctly select the set with extra objects, while, to decide whether the sets are equivalent, he need only determine whether there are extra objects in *either* set. On the basis of this slight additional complexity, Objective H was placed above G in the unit hierarchies.

To determine which of two sets has fewer objects (Objective I), it is necessary to determine which set has extra objects, and then choose the other set. This is behaviorally analogous to using negative information, which is known to be difficult for young children. Thus, the task analysis suggested that the concept "less" should be more difficult to learn than the concept "more." For this reason, Objective I was placed above H in the unit hierarchy, yielding a predicted learning sequence for one-to-one correspondence tasks in which "equivalent" (G) is prerequisite to "more" (H), which is in turn prerequisite to "less" (I).

The sequence G-H-I is supported empirically in a study by Uprichard (*unpublished*) in which "equivalent to," "greater than," and "less than" was shown to be the optimal order for teaching these three concepts. On the other hand, data from a scaling study by Wang (1973) suggest that preschool children normally learn the concept "more" before they learn "equivalent."

Thus, there is some doubt as to the appropriate sequence for Objectives G and H; it may, in fact, be likely that both objectives will be learned most easily when taught simultaneously, as "contrast" cases for one another. The Uprichard and the Wang findings are in agreement concerning the dependency of the concept of "less than" on "more" and "equivalent." In addition, Donaldson and Balfour (1968) found that children at about age four typically respond to the term "less" as if it were synonymous with "more." Thus, for this concept, existing empirical data support the predictions derived from task analysis. . . .

SUMMARY

A method of systematic task analysis is applied to the problem of designing a sequence of learning objectives that will provide an optimal match for the child's natural sequence of acquisition of mathematical skills and concepts. The authors begin by proposing an operational definition of the number concept in the form of a set of behaviors which, taken together, permit the inference that the child has an abstract concept of "number." These are the "objectives" of the curriculum. Each behavior in the defining set is then subjected to an analysis that identifies hypothesized components of skilled performance and prerequisites for learning these components. On the basis of these analyses, specific sequences of learning objectives are proposed. The proposed sequences are hypothesized to be those that will best facilitate learning, by maximizing transfer from earlier to later objectives.

REFERENCES

Donaldson, M., and G. Balfour. "Less Is More: A Study of Language Comprehension in Children." *British Journal of Psychology* 59(1968):461–471.

Gagné, R. M. "The Acquisition of Knowledge." *Psychology Review* 69 (1962):355–365.

Gagné, R. M. "Learning Hierarchies." *Educational Psychologist* 6(1968):1–9.

Klahr, D., and J. G. Wallace. "An Information Processing Analysis of Some Piagetian Experimental Tasks." *Cognitive Psychology* 1(1970):358–387.

Kohlberg, L. "Early Education: A Cognitive-Developmental View." *Child Development* 39 (1968):1013–1062.

Newell, A., and H. A. Simon. *Human Problem Solving.* Englewood Cliffs, N.J.: Prentice-Hall, 1972.

Potter, M. C., and E. Levy. "Spatial Enumeration without Counting." *Child Development* 39(1968):265–272.

Resnick, L. B. *Design of an Early Learning Curriculum.* Working Paper 16. Pittsburgh: Learning Research and Development Center, University of Pittsburgh, 1967.

Resnick, L. B., and M. C. Wang. "Approaches to the Validation of Learning Hierarchies." *Proceedings of the Eighteenth Annual Western Regional Conference on Testing Problems.* Educational Testing Service, 1969.

Uprichard, A. E. "The Effect of Sequence in the Acquisition of Three Set Relations: An Experiment with Preschoolers." Unpublished paper presented at a meeting of the American Educational Research Association, March, 1970.

Wang, M. C. "Psychometric Studies in the Validation of an Early Learning Curriculum." *Child Development* 44(1973):54–60.

QUESTIONS

1. What general question should curriculum developers ask themselves when trying to plan an instructional sequence to achieve a particular objective?

2. Describe some probable prerequisite behaviors for this task: The child names the letter of the alphabet as the teacher points to the printed letter.

3. What are the steps recommended by Resnick *et al.* in analyzing a curriculum objective to develop an instructional sequence? (Include identification of component and prerequisite behaviors.)

4. How could a learning hierarchy be validated?

5. Figure 15.5 is a possible hierarchy chart with color names in place of task descriptions. Answer these questions based on your reading of that chart:
   a) What is the terminal task?
   b) If an individual can do task Black, theoretically what other tasks are in his repertoire?
   c) Task Yellow is a prerequisite for what other tasks on the chart?
   d) Is task Orange a prerequisite for task Brown?

6. Fig. 15.6 is a partially filled-in hierarchy diagram for the elementary numeration skills described in Table 15.1 of the article (Units 3 and 4, Objectives A through G). On

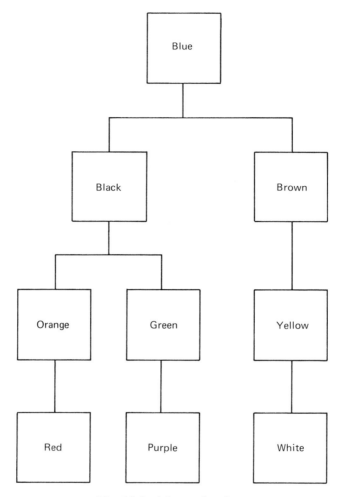

Fig. 15.5. A hierarchy chart.

the right are numbered objectives that belong in the blank spaces. Look at these objectives, decide upon a logical teaching order, then put the appropriate numbers in the hierarchy blanks. Check your work with the chart given for Units 3 and 4 in Fig. 15.2 of the article.

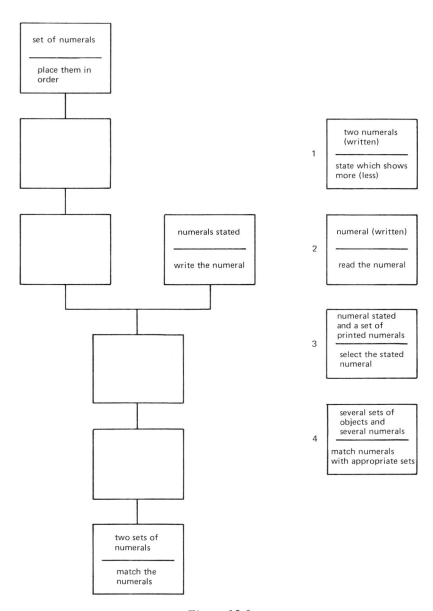

Figure 15.6

UNIT

16

Instrumentation

Content

Holland, J. G., and J. Doran. "Instrumentation of Research in Teaching." In R. Travers, ed., *Second Handbook of Research on Teaching*. Chicago: Rand McNally, 1973, pp. 286–317. (a selection)

The selected reading for this unit describes several examples of instrumentation of the learning cycle.

Objectives

Students describe the three aspects of a learning cycle and then specify how each of these aspects is instrumented in three different teaching programs. They discuss the instrumentation of two learning tasks in terms of the two kinds of gradual progression appropriate for the type of task being taught. They also examine the general value of instrumentation of the learning process.

Instructions

1. Read the objectives and use them to guide your reading of the article.
2. Answer the questions, then compare your answers to the suggested answers.
3. See your instructor for a brief interview.

Instrumentation of Research in Teaching[1]

James G. Holland and Judith Doran

Via the television we have recently watched men as they walked on the moon. Many aspects of their physiological and psychological states were monitored with occasional information passed on to the millions who watched as it was happening. This is in stark contrast to educational settings in which we seldom know much more than whether or not the student is present. The space flight was the culmination of a long history of development of methods and instrumentation in the physical, biological and behavioral sciences. Man was preceded into orbit by a chimpanzee named Ham who performed a set of complex learning tasks during flight. The tasks required automated control not simply because Ham was alone but because of the subtle contingencies of reinforcement which cannot easily be done without proper instrumentation (cf. Rohles, 1966).

Progress in science has often depended on the development of new instruments. Consider the importance of the lens to astronomy, the cyclotron to modern physics or the electrical amplifier to physiology. It is unlikely that Pavlov would have demonstrated adequately the conditioned reflex without developing his harness and the controlled environment, but having done so he opened the way to investigation of an important phenomenon since others could repeat or elaborate his experiments with the same care for precise measurement and careful control. The greater objectivity and reliability of measurement made subsequent studies of the reflex cumulative. Similarly the study of learning and motivation saw a sizable advance with Skinner's (1938) operant analysis and the manifestation of that analysis in instruments and procedures. Skinner identified his measure of behavior (the operant) as the probability of an arbitrary response and searched for those events in the environment which control the probability (or frequency) of the response. These events which control behavior are principally contingent relationships describable in contingency statements like "if x, then y," or "if the child picks from a set of forms a form which is identical to a sample form, he has completed the task and is reinforced," or "if in his speech the child produces the subtle and complex pattern of inflective rhythm and sound frequency distribution, his social environment acts appropriately and his behavior is reinforced." The contingent relationships between discriminative stimuli, responses and reinforcing stimuli are rich in variety and subtlety even though the principles of reinforcement describing them are simple.

James G. Holland and Judith Doran, "Instrumentation of Research in Teaching," in *Second Handbook of Research on Teaching*, ed. R. M. W. Travers (Chicago: Rand McNally, 1973). Copyright © 1973 by American Educational Research Association. Reprinted by permission.

[1] Much of the time for the preparation of this chapter was made possible by the Learning Research and Development Center supported in part as a research and development center by funds from the United States Office of Education, Department of Health, Education and Welfare. The opinions expressed in this publication do not necessarily reflect the position or policy of the Office of Education and no official endorsement should be inferred.

The power of Skinner's analysis and the pervasiveness of its influence are in large part attributable to the nature of the instrumentation he developed and the precise way that the instrumentation embodied the concepts. Skinner's standard experimental chamber and the use of electro-mechanical equipment for the automatic control of all contingencies made possible an analysis of behavior of such precision that the science of behavior could often deal with the behavior of individuals rather than average trends and could move from prediction to control of its subject matter. The precision of control and measurement provided by instrumentation led to discoveries not otherwise possible. A few milliseconds delay of reinforcement can result in changes in the form of the response, and seemingly minor changes in a reinforcement schedule will change the pattern of response frequency. Therefore, variable error would be large if these factors were not controlled with the precision good instrumentation makes possible.

In systems in which all stimulus presentation and reinforcement contingencies are automated, much of the strength of instrumentation comes in the communication among scientists. In the style of McLuhan, "the equipment is the message." When the conditions of an operant conditioning experiment are described, the critical aspects of the environment are detailed by describing the nature of the apparatus including the electro-mechanical control circuits. A schedule of reinforcement is in no way a description of behavior; it is a description of the wiring of the equipment and thus a description of the environmental conditions. A second investigator can exactly replicate the reinforcement contingencies or can add his own elaboration. Again, in the case of the science of learning, instrumentation has made possible identification and measurement of phenomena that would have been difficult or impossible without it. Instrumentation has also made the science more precisely communicable and hence cumulative, and the findings and approaches have gradually been extended both to research in educational problems and to the use of instrumentation in education.

As educational research moves forward in the use of better instrumentation, precise, subtle relationships are discovered and new discoveries can more easily be converted into practice. "Equipment as message" is particularly important in the transmission of new educational techniques into practice. Teachers have taken learning courses as part of their training for years with at best modest success in identifying the behavioral characteristics of each individual learning task, identifying when each student has met each contingency and reinforcing it. Such a feat is impossible because of the subtlety and number of such behavioral events in the classroom on the one hand and the size of the teacher-training problem on the other. But with the introduction of teaching machines, direct transmission of good teaching became possible.

The progress of technical development in education is all too slow, however. Consider the irony of a nation gradually turning over the conduct of a war to electronic devices placed in a field to detect movement of people; these devices telemeter information back to computers which in turn can direct fire at the electronically designated targets (Kirchener, 1971). By contrast, educational research is in a most primitive state, a contrast which is a sad commentary on the priorities of our society and which raises concern in an educational researcher who might contribute to the store of technical knowledge that in turn might be used under the same system of priorities which has given us electronic battlefields. On the positive side, the classroom researcher can now draw upon the sizable technology developed by the scientist working on problems of human learning in the laboratory as well as the rich store of technical devices developed for uses in other contexts. The aim of this chapter is to explore the possibilities not only of instrumentation already being used in classroom research but also of instrumentation being used in the experimental analysis of behavior in other contexts than education which might in turn be profitably used in classroom research.

THE PROBLEM—THE PROCESS OF LEARNING

The core problem in a science of instruction is the process by which the individual student learns. Instrumentation has potential for each step of this process. The learner is exposed to some material or stimuli; he must interact with that material in some active fashion as writing, talking, thinking or reasoning; and the adequacy of the interaction must in some way be evaluated and reinforced. It is this basic learning cycle that the operant conditioning laboratories have demonstrated for us. This learning cycle stands at the basis of programmed instruction, contingency management, behavior modification and behavior therapy. Each of the separate components in this learning cycle can be instrumented. Controlled presentation of material is very commonly instrumented in audiovisual language laboratories and in audiovisual equipment in the classroom. Tape recorders, one-way mirrors and video cameras aid in the measurement of student responses in the classroom and language lab. The principal focus of the present chapter, however, will be on the instrumentation of the total, contingent relationship including the control of the stimulus, the assessment of the response, the determination as to whether the response has met the criteria for reinforcement, and the delivery of reinforcement. Extensively discussed elsewhere are the areas of audiovisual instruction (cf. Allen, 1960, or Brown, Lewis, & Harcleroad, 1964) and educational television (cf. Chu & Schramm, 1967). Only instances in which elements are relatively new and not yet used in common practice, e.g., new stimulus presentation devices or new modes of recording responses, will be discussed. Primary emphasis will be given to systems in which instrumentation is used for the control of contingencies of reinforcement under controlled stimulus conditions. But the most important reason for concentrating on the contingent relations between the student's response and the material is that the basis for learning, when learning occurs, is in the contingent relationship among stimuli, responses, and the resulting reinforcement.

Conventional classrooms have presented material either via textbooks, lecture or audiovisual equipment. Traditionally, learning has been left to the unspecified activity of the student when exposed to the materials. But since Skinner's article,

"The Science of Learning and the Art of Teaching" (1954), educators have become increasingly aware of the importance of students' responses. This process of constructing repertoires of verbal and nonverbal behavior in the student has benefited by the laboratory experimentation in the analysis of behavior, and it is the use of instrumentation in this process which is the most profitable line of research and development for those interested in furthering the ends of education.

Each of the various components of the learning cycles can be illustrated with a program to teach preschool children to classify an array of objects a variety of different ways (Holland & Doran, 1972). A teaching program was developed to further the ability to classify on the basis of relationships that exist between or within classes. Photographs of a variety of stimulus materials included abstract shapes and pictures of objects which in a given slide could differ in color, size, function, etc. These were presented by a 35mm carousel projector onto a touch-sensitive display which is a computer interface device that transmits the location of a touch by the child to the computer. This device is constructed by using two sets of fine wires, some running in the vertical direction, others in the horizontal direction. The wires are covered by a flexible plastic material which serves as a projection screen and at the same time transmits the pressure of the child's touch to the wires underneath. The press of the child will bring the vertical and horizontal wires appropriate to a given location into contact with each other, completing a circuit which is specific to the location of the press (cf. Fitzhugh & Katsuki, 1971). Early items in the program familiarized the child with the categories to be included in later multiple-category items. Auditory messages were presented by a random-access auditory device. In late items in the program, the child was presented with a picture of an array of objects having a variety of different properties and permitting different classifications on the basis of color, shape, size, function, etc. The child was asked by the taped message presented through a speaker to "Touch all the things that are alike." He could then proceed to touch all of the objects of the given color, for example. If the child failed to touch an object within 15 seconds, the original message was repeated. When the child completed a set, for example, touched all the things that were blue, he saw a light flash. He was then instructed to "Find some more things that are alike." If he again selected objects that were blue, he would hear, "You already did that. Try again." Then he might touch all of the things that were green, for example. If he began touching several given objects but did not complete the set, after ten seconds he heard, "You didn't find all of them. Try again." When he completed the green set, the light flashed. He was again instructed to "Find some more things that are alike." He might then go on classifying on the basis of color, or he might shift to classifying on the basis of another dimension such as touching all of the circles, all of the large objects, all of the objects used for transportation, or all of the objects that were hot. In each instance, when the child completed a given set, the light flashed. When he finished all of the required attributes, a bell sounded and a marble which was exchangeable with other marbles for a toy at the end of the session was presented. If the child failed to classify on the basis of some attributes, the computer presented each uncompleted set independently with the message, "Find all the Xs." After completing all of the missed sets in this fashion, the original instruction was again presented, "Find all the things that are alike," and the child started again to classify the objects in a variety of different ways. The number of possible sets in a multiple-category item ranged from two to six. Items of the complexity described were eventually reached in a low error rate program of 160 items. The children, therefore, were able to complete even the difficult multiple-category items with a low error rate. To determine, in each instance, what subsequent message was to be presented and whether the contingency for reinforcement had been met required apparatus as sophisticated as a computer. With each touch by the child, the computer had to determine whether a permissible category was being followed, and, as the touches proceeded, whether it was a category already completed or not, and which categories remained or if all the possible categories had been completed.

The computer, then, successfully managed reinforcement contingencies for a task which would be difficult or impossible to arrange with more simple devices or without instrumentation. Keeping track of such contingencies would be extremely difficult for a teacher operating without instrumentation, particularly in view of the need for immediate feedback. The use of automatic equipment provided the careful control of contingencies which made possible the establishment of this rather sophisticated skill several years earlier than it normally appears in children. The control of these difficult contingencies would not have been possible without instrumentation; moreover, the program sequence could be put through several revisions because the precise instrumentation removed the ambiguity of early difficulties with the program. Hence, again, the instrumentation made possible the direct transmission of the procedure into practice in the admittedly improbable event that some kindergarten class has a computer at its disposal. This example illustrates the three components of all problems of instrumentation of reinforcement contingencies: first, the production of environmental events as in the presentation of the stimulus material via slides or tape and the presentation of the reinforcement through operation of the marble dispenser; second, "sensing" and "transducing" the response as in using the touch-sensitive display to provide a separate electrical signal for each area the child touches; and third, the "logic" or control circuit to determine when a designated set of events has occurred and to provide control signals for the consequent events in the environment, as in using the computer to determine when admissible sets of objects were touched by the child. The old-style educational researcher turned gadgeteer finds the nature of his difficulties dependent upon the state of the art in these separate problem areas. And as the technical developments in each area became more sophisticated they also became more easily used by the relatively inexperienced.

INSTRUMENTED INSTRUCTION

To survey a variety of learning tasks it will be convenient to classify them in terms of the predominant aspect to be established. Learning tasks differ as to whether different response forms or topographies are being shaped, whether new stimulus control is being established, whether hierarchical textual relationships or a rote series of unrelated associations is being taught. Each of these presents somewhat different problems for the programmer or the researcher and different problems for instrumentation.

Shaping Response Topography

When an especially difficult response topography must be shaped, extremely crude approximations are at first accepted for reinforcement and on subsequent occasions the criterion for differential reinforcement is gradually increased until the skilled response is shaped. To instrument for such procedures, provision for measuring the response and automatically making decisions as to its acceptability for differential reinforcement must be made. A demonstration of shaping response topography is provided by a procedure to develop rhythmic skill in young children (Skinner, 1961). The child strikes a key in synchrony with a series of auditory stimuli; a bell sounds or a light flashes when the key is struck close enough in time to the sound. At first the response is reinforced even if the beat is poorly matched, but gradually closer and closer approximation between response and stimuli is required until a nearly perfect match is obtained. Control for this procedure was obtained by modifying an ordinary phonographic turntable by adding a metal plate on which a paper disk could be overlaid. The paper disk had slits cut in it. These slits were swept by two metal contacts, one controlling the presentation of the stimulus, the other the allowable reinforcement contingency. The stimulus sequence was arranged by cutting a series of holes in the paper in a rhythmic pattern. When the metal contact passed over one of these holes, it made contact with the underlying metal disk, completing a circuit which presented the auditory stimulus; a second longer slit corresponded with each stimulus, preceding it somewhat in time and following it somewhat in time. If the child struck the key during the time that the appropriate contact passed over this slit, the bell and light would operate. A series of pairs of patterned slits in the paper could provide different rhythms and different tolerances for reenforcement.

A similar problem saw a different solution when Ihrke (1971) developed an instrument to train a student to perform rhythmic patterns. The rhythmic stimuli were presented by an ordinary tape player and the student responded on the keyboard of an electric organ. The test for the adequacy of the response was provided by an especially designed electronic rhythm monitor which compared signals from the prerecorded tape with those from the student's electric organ. The electronic rhythm monitor informed the student if his response was early or late. The margin of allowed error could be varied from 0.25 second to 0.1 second. Thus there are many potential solutions to provide essentially the same result. Skinner used a primarily mechanical system for control of the stimulus and reinforcement contingencies supplemented by a simple relay control circuitry, whereas Ihrke provided this control through an electronic device he designed.

. . .

Discrimination Training

With the advent of new developments in educational technology with the emphasis on carefully defined behavioral objectives, discrimination training has become an increasingly important part of educational systems from the preschool, where the emphasis is on the learning of many perceptual concepts, to the advanced sciences and medical training, where it is becoming increasingly apparent that learning "about" things through textbooks is not a substitute for acquiring the various perceptual repertoires that are necessary. Therefore, discrimination training has become an important area for educational research, both as a testing ground for the extension of basic learning principles to the classroom and in discovering new basic information beginning from an applied educational problem.

Visual Discrimination Training

In discrimination training a simple arbitrary response such as a touch that operates an electrical switch is sufficient and control circuitry is simple standard equipment. Any challenge found is in arranging for the necessary variations in stimulus material, and even here the well-developed technology of photography and projectors makes this simple.*

There are a top window and five small choice windows. The windows serve both as stimulus displays and response keys. The windows are transilluminated by a 35mm slide projector. When the top window is pressed, a small microswitch mounted behind it and along an edge is operated; the shutter then opens, exposing the projected images on the five small choice windows. Each of these choice windows has a small microswitch mounted along its lower edge inside the instrument. Photocells, mounted inside the projector near the slide frame, are operated by light passing through a hole-punch coding system (or the photocells may be mounted near the keys and operated by exposed areas on the film). The photocell coding system determines which of the five bottom windows will be scored correct. When a correct bottom window is pressed, the shutters close, the slide changes to present the next frame, a red light mounted at the top of the instrument flashes, and a gong sounds for reinforcement. If, however, an incorrect window is pressed, only the bottom shutter closes. The subject must then press the top window again to open the bottom shutter. He responds again to the same problem. If in this case he is correct, the slide changes, the light flashes and the gong sounds; but instead of receiving the next frame in the sequence, the projector presents the previous frame. If he is correct on this frame, the material advances to the frame he has previously missed. If he is then correct on his first choice, the material advances to the next frame in the sequence. Detailed construction information and photographic pro-

---

* Editors' note: A typical instrument of this type is described in the Bijou program in Unit 8.

cedures are provided by Hively (1964) for a response and display unit for this type of machine.

A particularly useful form of recording has been used with this instrument (described in Sidman & Stoddard, 1967). A standard cumulative recorder common in operant conditioning work was modified by attaching the pen directly to the slide tray with a cord. With each initial correct response, the slide tray advances, moving the pen upwards on the paper. With time the paper moves horizontally under the pen. A series of correct responses gives a series of steps. The slope described by the steps gives the rate of correct responding, the distance between successive steps is a measure of the time taken by the subject for a given frame. On a correct response following an error the slide tray backs up one frame, producing a downward step of the pen. It is common in materials in which the subject hits a point at which he has great difficulty for the slide tray to move backward and forward past a given frame, recycling as he finally gets a slide correct, backs up to the previous slide, repeats the difficult slide, again missing it, backs up to the previous slide, etc. Such areas of difficulty are readily apparent and the data can be interpreted at a glance.

. . .

Teaching discrimination skills involving visual materials often requires special effects. In some cases the task analysis demands the use of motion pictures which may be used much like any other stimulus material (Gropper, 1966; Schrag & J. G. Holland, 1965). Schrag and Holland instrumented a Physical Sciences Study Committee (PSSC) film teaching the concept of relativity. A movie projector was modified so that it is automatically stopped on a signal coded in the margin of the film and turns off the projector. The student reads a printed question which he can answer if he has properly observed the film or, in some instances, he makes predictions as to the outcome of an experiment and the film is used to confirm his prediction. The teaching of concepts of the relativity of motion required temporal variation of spatial events and hence film was indicated.

Another special problem arises when three-dimensional views are necessary. Such a case arises in medical education when training visual discriminations necessary for operative procedures. The authors have observed interesting use of projections of filmed stereo views of eye operations prepared by Kenneth Richardson of the Pittsburgh Eye and Ear Hospital for a sophisticated teaching machine using a computer for control. A recent technological development called *holography* offers another solution to the presentation of three-dimensional views (Barson & Mendelson, 1969). In this procedure, a picture in depth with full three-dimensionality is made using a special photographic plate and laser light. When the resulting slide is projected by a laser beam, it represents an image possessing full three-dimensionality. This opens new possibilities for use of three-dimensional stimuli. It will be easy to store libraries of holography slides which would serve the purpose of the often needed but rarely practical three-dimensional models. Moreover, these can be used in instrumented instructional settings more easily than models because of the greater ease of automatic presentation and control of the stimulus. Teaching machine programs in biology, geometry or similar areas may use laser projectors to provide three-dimensional stimuli.

Video tape is now a convenient alternative to film and has been used in some interesting research on training teacher-trainees in discriminating the properties of good and poor teacher interaction. In one study (Johnson, 1968), trainees viewed their video tape with an accompanying programmed booklet that, through the questions asked, provided cues as to which aspects of the scenes to focus upon, gave the trainees an opportunity to report their observations, and gave corrective feedback as to the accuracy of the reports. Another group of trainees, who viewed the video tape without questions, performed on a posttest like the nontreatment control group. Johnson concluded that video-taping teacher-pupil interactions is a useful training device if the trainees are taught what to observe in the video tape. Resnick and Kiss (1970) and Reynolds and Millmore (1971) similarly demonstrated the usefulness of video-taped teacher-student interactions. The material chosen for the video tape showed appropriate contrast between adequate and inadequate performance and was programmed to establish such a discriminative repertoire in the trainees. They demonstrated that discrimination training was reflected in the teacher's behavior and that discrimination training provided the possibility of self-editing of behavior.

Auditory Discrimination Training

The problems faced in discrimination training of visual stimuli are paralleled by the problems faced in discrimination training of auditory stimuli.

Instrumented speech correction

An interesting example of the usefulness of instrumentation in research on auditory discrimination training is found in the "ear training" of children who have articulation difficulties. It is a common practice for school speech therapists to work with children in the third or fourth grades who misarticulate certain speech sounds. For example, a child might substitute the /th/ for the /s/ in his typical speech behavior. It is commonly found that such children not only misarticulate these sounds, but also fail to discriminate the sound from their substitute sound. Children with demonstrated articulation and discrimination difficulties normally spend many hours with the therapist learning to discriminate these sounds in words. But now a machine form of discrimination training has been developed (A. L. Holland & Matthews, 1963). After completing a program which usually required about two hours, the discrimination problem was completely corrected and the articulation significantly improved without intervening articulation therapy.

The instrumentation used for this discrimination-training procedure is best seen in a film prepared on the technique (A.L. Holland, 1965). Figure 16.1 is a photograph of the subject's response panel which consisted of a box with three keys coded differently for the various response requirements in different phases of the discrimination procedure. The auditory material was presented via a stereo tape player

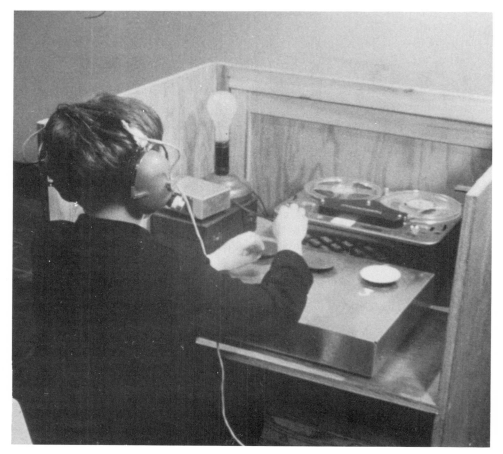

Fig. 16.1. Child working at a teaching machine with an auditory discriminaton program. The child presses one of three buttons in response to each discrimination problem. If the choice is correct, a counter advances, a light flashes, and the tape recorder presents the next item. If the choice is incorrect, the tape recorder rewinds to replay the item.

which was modified so that one track served to present the stimulus and the second track presented a coded signal to the equipment in the form of a pulse train to signal the control circuit as to which of the response keys was correct. After either an error or the lack of a response in a five-second period, the tape recorder rewound a sufficient distance and replayed the missed item. All events—the rewinding of the player, the recording of responses, and the presenting of reinforcement—were automatically controlled by relays and other electro-mechanical equipment. The child used the appropriate one of 11 programs for the sound he misarticulated. Each program followed a careful, gradual progression of tasks. The final task in a program had the child discriminate which of a pair of productions of the same word contained the correct sound compared with misarticulated sounds. Within this section of the program among the misarticulated alternatives were representations of all the possible misarticulations of the sound. Each of the 11 programs underwent repeated tests and revisions using the automated equipment. This enabled gradual refinement of the programs in a way that would have been difficult without well-instrumented procedures to pinpoint ambiguity and sources of difficulty. After completion of the development of the programs, an alternative form of instrumentation was devised to make the programs more widely available (A. L. Holland, 1969). The New Century Audio-Frame-System with "Write and See" was employed (see Fig. 16.2). In this system a small cassette recorder of a type readily available is used for the presentation of stimuli and a simple added circuit detects a tone recorded at the end of each frame and stops the cassette. A response button lights when the cassette stops and a press on this button presents the next frame. The student uses a response booklet with portions printed in an invisible ink and a special pen which reacts chemically with the ink on the booklet. An incorrect response produces a pale yellow, but a correct response produces a distinctly different dark brown.

Fig. 16.2. Child using the New Century Audio Frame System. At the end of each frame the cassette stops and a white button at the lower right of the machine lights. When the child is ready to hear the next frame he presses this button to advance the tape.

In addition to providing a handy solution to the difficult problem of articulation therapy, the sound-discrimination program illustrates a process with wide potential educational application. The reason discrimination training influences production is that the subject acquires the ability to discriminate correct and incorrect productions of his own speech, enabling rapid correction and automatic reinforcement of correct productions. Many important educational tasks have this property. Examples include singing, drawing from copy (or arts and crafts generally), articulation in second languages, handwriting and English composition. Teaching production often requires one-to-one tutorial help to identify the adequacy of the response. The programmed speech therapy, however, suggests that any of these tasks might benefit from instrumented discrimination training which would provide the means for the automatic reinforcement of discriminably correct productions.

. . .

Rote Associations

When all of the stimuli in a given domain have been well discriminated and all of the needed responses well differentiated, there may remain a problem in the association between stimuli and responses. A single individual association of this sort is easily learned and in most educational problems rote association has little if any role to play. When such problems do arise, there is a rich literature from the verbal learning laboratories. The principal problem in learning rote associations is interference among new associations. Hence, the length of the list of items to be learned is a major consideration, and similarity between stimuli and responses is a major variable leading to interferences among the elements. Spaced practice decreases such interference and hence becomes important when many rote associations must be learned. In most educational settings new associative elements should be few and, where necessary, new associations can usually be spaced so that the literature on rote associations is seldom relevant. There are occasional exceptions to this such as learning the typewriter keyboard in beginning typing, some aspects of initial reading, and learning the alphabet.

A very worthwhile and well-designed example of the use of paired associate learning is illustrated in a program which teaches typing to beginners (Robins & Reed, 1958). They use a phonograph and a typewriter in which all of the keys are covered so that the subject never associates the letter name with a visual position. The subject begins with his fingers on the home keys and is taught just four keys at first, practices these for a while, then adds two more keys to his repertoire. Designed into the program are many required rest pauses and a gradual pyramiding of the number of letter-name-finger movement (striking a key) associates. Robins and Reed keep the number of new associations low while the student practices the old associations. The subject quickly learns keying to proficiency.

Another task which takes a rote form is a drill and practice type of computer-assisted instruction. Suppes (1966) described such a procedure in drilling students in arithmetic problems. A problem is presented to the subject on a cathode ray screen such as, $(6 \times 8) + 10 = $. The student responds using a teletype keyboard and types in the numerical answer. If the student's answer is wrong, it is indicated to him and the question is repeated. If a second error is made, the statement of error is followed by the printing of the correct answer. The problem is then repeated for a third time. The student may copy the correct answer. The computer then provides the next question. An elaboration on this procedure in spelling drills (Block, 1971) has the computer select differentially from the set of words, depending upon the subject's performance on the words. Hence, the words which he consistently spells correctly do not reappear while he is more frequently drilled on the words with which he has difficulty. Although the limited role found in education for rote learning limits the usefulness of drill and practice, the studies are valuable as explorations into computer control of research in learning.

MIXED CASES: DISCRIMINATION, RESPONSE DIFFERENTIATION AND ASSOCIATIVE LEARNING

In many of the more challenging teaching problems, the tasks are not neatly divided into discrimination, response differentiation, and rote association. The problem rather represents a mix of functional categories. Language or reading are examples of such a mix. In learning a language the student must learn auditory discriminations for the sounds of the language, visual discriminations for the pattern of printed characters, higher level discriminations like discrimination of syntactic characteristics, and also various associations like grapheme-phoneme correspondences in reading. He must learn vocabulary words for objects and relationships. He must undergo response shaping for production of sounds and for writing.

Language Teaching

In research spanning all aspects of language teaching the equipment needs to be highly flexible. Garvey, Johansen, and Noblitt (1967) made good use of an extremely flexible machine, the Portable Laboratory System distributed by Appleton-Century-Crofts publishing company.

The subject faces a console with a viewing area slightly smaller than an IBM card. This area is divided into four window-keys behind which material printed on cards appears automatically. The windows can also serve as response areas. Beneath three of the windows are three button-operated electric switches which may also be illuminated. To the right is an opening to a reel of paper tape for write-in responses. A microphone with a signal light around it serves to record the voice and operate a voice-operated relay. A tape player is capable of presenting four different messages with each frame. For all of the presentations, the features and response possibilities are controlled by the logic unit, which consists of circuits based on small quiet relays and an interchangeable plugboard for changing the nature of operation of the equipment. Each stimulus card contains a punched-hole code which operates photocells that indicate to the logic circuit which alternative is correct and what mode of operation is called for on the particular card.

With this flexible machine, response requirements can differ from frame to frame. A few examples from the French program will illustrate the flexibility of the equipment. In teaching auditory discrimination the tape player presents a word or phrase, the alternative windows light up indicating that they would react to a press, under the windows is a card with the numbers 1 and 2, the subject presses one of these windows and hears either the same word or phrase or a mispronunciation of the word or phrase. After listening to both as many times as he wishes, he indicates his choice by pressing one of the two buttons beneath the windows. If he is correct, he hears confirmation in the form of an appropriate French sentence. If he is incorrect he hears a buzzer and the original stimulus is represented and he must choose again. After finally answering correctly, he hears the usual confirmation and the machine presents the previous item. In a "production" frame a printed French sentence or phrase appears in the left window with an oral instruction such as "Transform to negative," the light on the microphone then comes on and after the student has formulated his response he speaks into the microphone. The voice-operated relay in the microphone signals the logic unit when speech is occurring and when it has ended. When the subject's response is completed, it is confirmed by audio presentation of the correct form and the program advances to the next frame. The next frame might be a visual discrimination frame. In that case, the card in the left window shows perhaps a question written in French, the alternative windows indicate written French answers. For example, the choice between a masculine or feminine answer could hinge on the ending of a word in the question. Lights appear on the alternative windows and the student presses a window to indicate his chosen answer. If the choice is incorrect, a buzzer indicates an error and feedback is presented by the tape, for instance, "The spelling tells you that it must be a man." The student then chooses again. If the answer is correct, he hears confirmation in the form of a complete sentence answering the question and, after the microphone lights, the student repeats the confirmation sentence. Thus the Portable Laboratory System allows many contingent relationships between the types of stimuli and the types of response requirements. With such adequate and flexible instrumentation, Garvey, Johansen and Noblitt (1967) were not only able to produce a French program and a procedure readily transferable to other settings but also to contribute to the process of language teaching. The program was intended to serve as a prototype for future language programs.

The Portable Laboratory System resulted from considerable collective experience of many who had worked with instrumentation in educational research, but Mace (1967) was responsible for much of the development of the equipment and has described the scenario of his "cut-and-try" experiences in the evolution of the Portable Laboratory System. His attempts to program English as a second language determined the features of the equipment. He described his experiences beginning with a simple carousel projector and coordinated tape recorder and, over a period of years, extending the equipment to obtain greater control over the necessary response contingencies. After various tryouts with Chinese students learning English in his program, he gradually modified his equipment, adding stimulus lights to windows, adding the voice-operated relay and so forth until the details of the Portable Laboratory System were gradually shaped by interaction among the equipment, the experimental subjects and Mace, the modifier of the equipment. His scenario is characteristic of the evolution of instrumentation in any new and difficult area.

REFERENCES

Allen, W. H. "Audio-Visual Communication. In C. W. Harris, ed., *Encyclopedia of Educational Research*. 3rd ed. New York: Macmillan, 1960, pp. 115–137.

Barson, J., and G. B. Mendelson. "Holography—A New Dimension for Media." *Audio-Visual Instruction* 14(1969):40–42.

Block, K. K. "Computer-Assisted Instruction." In A. Kent and H. Lancour, eds., *Encyclopedia of Library and Information Science*. Vol. 5. New York: Marcel Dekker, 1971, pp. 515–538.

Brown, J. W., R. B. Lewis, and F. F. Harcleroad. *A-V Instruction: Materials and Methods*. 2nd ed. New York: McGraw-Hill, 1964.

Chu, G. C., and W. Schramm. *Learning from Television: What the Research Says*. Stanford, Calif.: Stanford University, Institute for Communication Research, 1967.

Fitzhugh, R. J., and D. Katsuki. "The Touch-Sensitive Screen as a Flexible Response Device in CAI and Behavioral Research." *Behavior Research Methods and Instrumentation* 3(1971):159–164.

Garvey, C. J., P. A. Johansen, and J. S. Noblitt. "A Report of the Developmental Testing of a Self-Instructional French Program." Washington, D.C.: Center for Applied Linguistics, 1967.

Gropper, G. L. "Learning from Visuals: Some Behavioral Considerations." *AV Communication Review* 14(1966):37–69.

Holland, A. L. *Programmed Auditory Discrimination Training for Children Who Misarticulate*. Washington, D.C.: Office of Education, Bureau of the Handicapped, 1965. Sixteen millimeter sound motion picture.

Holland, A. L. *Speech Sound Discrimination*. New York: New Century, 1969.

Holland, A. L., and J. Matthews. "Application of Teaching Machine Concepts to Speech Pathology and Audiology." *Asha* 5(1963):474–482.

Holland, J. G. "New Directions in Teaching Machine Research." In J. E. Coulson, ed., *Programmed Learning and Computer-Based Instruction*. New York: Wiley, 1962, pp. 46–57.

Holland, J. G., and J. Doran. "Teaching Classification by Computer." *Educational Technology* 12(1972):58–60.

Ihrke, W. R. "A Modular Station for Automated Music Training." *Educational Technology* 11, no. 8 (1971):27–29.

Johnson, R. B. "The Effects of Prompting, Practice and Feedback in Programmed Video-tape." *American Educational Research Journal* 5(1968):73–79.

Kirchener, D. P. "Antiguerrilla Armament." *Ordnance* 56(1971):127–130.

Mace, L. "The Role of Flexible Laboratory Equipment in Verbal Learning Research." Paper presented at a colloquium at the Center for Research in Language and Language Behavior of the University of Michigan. Ann Arbor, Michigan, July 1967.

Resnick, L. B., and L. E. Kiss. "Discrimination Training and Feedback in Shaping Teacher Behavior." Paper presented at the meeting of the American Educational Research Assocation. Minneapolis, March 1970.

Reynolds, J., and M. Millmore. "Analysis of the Teacher's Role in Individualized Evaluation." Paper presented at the meeting of the American Educational Research Association, New York, February 1971.

Robins, L., and H. Reed. *The Living Method Typing Course*. Long Island City, N.Y.: Crown, 1958.

Rohles, F. H., Jr. "Operant Methods in Space Technology." In W. K. Honig, ed., *Operant Behavior: Areas of Research and Application*. New York: Appleton-Century-Crofts, 1966, pp. 677–717.

Schrag, P. G., and J. G. Holland. "Programming Motion Pictures: The Conversion of a PSSC Film into a Program." *AV Communication Review* 13(1965):418–422.

Sidman, M., and L. T. Stoddard. "Programming Perception and Learning for Retarded Children." In N. R. Ellis, ed., *International Review of Research in Mental Retardation*. Vol. 2. New York: Academic Press, 1966, pp. 151–208.

Sidman, M., and L. T. Stoddard. "The Effectiveness of Fading in Programming a Simultaneous Form Discrimination for Retarded Children. *Journal of the Experimental Analysis of Behavior* 10(1967):3–15.

Skinner, B. F. *The Behavior of Organisms*. New York: Appleton-Century, 1938.

Skinner, B. F. "The Science of Learning and the Art of Teaching." *Harvard Educational Review* 24(1954):86–97.

Suppes, P. "The Uses of Computers in Education." *Scientific American* 215, no. 3 (1966):206–220.

QUESTIONS

1. What is the basic learning cycle as demonstrated by operant-conditioning laboratories?

2. For the classification-computer program (Holland and Doran, 1972), describe in detail how each aspect of this learning cycle was instrumented.

3. For the program to develop rhythmic skill in young children (Skinner, 1961), describe in detail how:

    a) the discriminative stimuli were presented to the learner (describe the instrumentation);

    b) the learner responded to these stimuli;

    c) the learner's response was evaluated and reinforced (describe the instrumentation).

4. How does this device for teaching rhythmic skill allow for a gradual progression in the shaping of the response?

5. Do you think the response contingencies for establishing such rhythmic responding in children could be easily managed without instrumentation? Explain your answer.

6. For the typical instrument used in visual discrimination training describe how:

   a) stimulus presentation is instrumented;

   b) learner interacts with stimulus;

   c) learner interaction is evaluated and reinforced.

7. The instrument that you have described in question 6 does *not* allow shaping of the motor response. That is, the amount of force that the learner must use to press a window remains constant throughout the program. Also, pressing a window that is merely close to the correct match window is never reinforced. (Compare this to the reinforcement contingencies described in your answers to questions 3 and 4.) Why does this instrument not allow such response shaping? What form of gradual progression does it allow?

8. In your answers to the above questions, you have described some ways in which instrumentation is an invaluable aid in controllng complex stimulus presentation and in monitoring complex response contingencies. Another value of instrumentation was described by Holland and Doran as follows: "But with the introduction of teaching machines, direct transmission of good teaching became possible." Explain what is meant by that statement.

UNIT

17

Project, Part I

At various points in this book, you will be instructed to work on successive parts of your curriculum design project. Now is the time to begin.

In the section just completed (Part III), you have written formally correct behavioral objectives, analyzed a discipline into a series of terminal tasks, classified tasks according to appropriate instructional strategies, devised learning hierarchies, and discussed appropriate instrumentation for various kinds of tasks. However, each particular skill was developed in a separate unit, by completing a separate set of exercises. At this point these skills will be put together in an exercise that allows their interrelatedness to come into focus.

For your work in this unit, select a topic for your curriculum project, taking into account: (1) your interest in this topic, (2) your competence to design a lesson on this topic, and (3) your ability to complete the lesson within the time limits of this course. You may wish to select for your project work *one* of the terminal behaviors you outlined in Unit 13.

After selecting the topic, formulate the behavioral objectives you wish to achieve. Design a test to measure mastery of these objectives, and remember to include an indication of the criteria used to evaluate performance on this test. Describe the intended users of your material, including prerequisite behaviors and expected entering behaviors. Finally, describe the instructional strategy and form of gradual progression appropriate to each behavioral objective.

You will find it helpful to discuss your work in all project units with your peers. If such discussion is not possible, plan to set your completed project work aside for a week or so, and then review it objectively.

PART

IV

Teaching: Selecting and Writing Instructional Materials

Units in this section (Units 18–26) focus on the actual teaching process in formal instructional materials. A few units are primarily didactic (Units 18 and 25), but most ask that you make judgments about various types of instructional materials. In Unit 24 you will also write instructional materials for the curriculum project you began in Unit 17.

UNIT

18

Techniques for Identifying Response Contingencies

Content

Margulies, S. *Some General Rules of Frame Construction*. New York: Basic Systems, 1963.

Holland, J. G. "A Quantitative Measure for Programmed Instruction." *American Educational Research Journal* 4 (1967): 87–101. (a selection)

This unit develops the implications of response contingency (or the critical-response principle) in programming. The blackout ratio is introduced as a means of demonstrating the amount of textual material which must be read to produce a correct response.

Objectives

Students will define the concept of contingency in programming, identify various contingencies, define the blackout ratio, and use the blackout technique. They will explain the implications of the concepts of response contingency and errorlessness for curriculum materials, and will produce a frame of instructional material which has a low blackout ratio.

Instructions

1. Read the objectives.
2. Read the articles.
3. Answer the questions and confer with your instructor.

Some General Rules of Frame Construction

Stuart Margulies

INTRODUCTION

The present paper is directed to the identification and analysis of some general rules of frame construction. These rules allow us to recognize and correct the deficiencies in such frames and frame sequences as the ones below.

1. a) Because of its inefficient cutting arm, the Layman reaper can perform only 120 operations. 360 operations would require _____ reapers.

   b) The Layman reaper is restricted to 120 operations because of inadequacies in the _____ _____.

   c) Because of the cutting arm, only 120 operations can be obtained from the _____ reaper.

2. The immediate use of goods in return for the promise to pay later is characteristic of a purchase made on credit.

   "Fly now, pay later" is an example of a purchase made on _____.

3. Cortical convolutions increase as we ascend the phylogenetic scale. Thus as we ascend the phylogenetic scale, we observe an _____ (increase/decrease) in the number of cortical convolutions.

ANALYSIS OF SIMPLE FRAMES

Before examining the faults in the frames above, let us consider frames 4 and 5 below. These two frames illustrate in an exaggerated fashion two contrasting philosophies of frame construction. The purpose of both frames is to teach the information that the symbol * is the equivalent of plus.

4. * is the equivalent of plus   5. * is the equivalent of plus
   $4 * 3 =$ _____ $4 + 3 =$ _____

Both of these frames adhere to generally accepted tenets of programming technique. They present small units of information, require active responses, and give immediate reinforcement. Yet most people would intuitively select frame 4 as preferable to 5; they would agree that frame 5 can teach, but would feel that frame 4 can teach better.

Stuart Margulies, *Some General Rules of Frame Construction* (New York: Basic Systems, 1963). Copyright © by Xerox Corporation. Reprinted by special permission of Xerox Corporation.

This intuitive preference is amply supported by the theoretical arguments of the learning theorist. The shaping process requires that the experimenter build only on established behavior. Frame 4 is satisfactory because a correct response requires mastery of the material presented; the writer is therefore able in later frames to build upon the concept that has been taught. Frame 5 must be rejected because a correct response need not indicate understanding of the new information.

CRITICAL PROCEDURE VS. EVERYTHING PROCEDURE

Implicit in the preceding discussion is the following principle, which is held here to be the fundamental rule of efficient frame construction:

> In each frame, a student can be held responsible only for that portion of the presented material to which he has responded correctly. Subsequent frames may build only upon such material.

This principle will be referred to as the "critical-response" or "critical" principle and may be contrasted with a second position, which will be called the "everything-is-learned" or "everything" principle. The "everything" principle—of which frame 5 is an illustration—may be stated as follows:

> In each frame, a student may be held responsible for all material presented whether or not he utilizes this information in making an immediate response. Subsequent frames may build upon all material presented.

An analysis of the following simple frame sequence may be useful in illustrating the differences between the two contrasting principles.

6a. * is equivalent to plus.
   * was used by the Greek, Thesalius.
   3 * 4 = _____

6b. Name the Greek who used the symbol *. _____

This frame sequence is consistent with the everything principle but violates the critical principle because material called for in frame 6b has not been responded to in the preceding frame. Violations of this fundamental rule occur quite frequently in the work of inexperienced program writers, but are rarely so blatant as in frames 6a and 6b. A more typical example is given on page 208 and is reproduced below:

1a) Because of its inefficient cutting arm, the Layman reaper can perform only 120 operations. 360 operations would require _____ reapers.

b) The Layman reaper is restricted to 120 operations because of inadequacies in the _____ _____.

c) Because of the cutting arm, only 120 operations can be obtained from the _____ reaper.

Again, material called for in frames 1c and 1b has not been correctly responded to in preceding frames.

PROGRAMS VS. TEXTBOOKS

Learning from textbooks is based on much the same principles as learning from programs constructed on the everything-is-learned rule, because in both cases the student is expected to read and retain all presented material. The active response required by the everything program is not very important; the student is responsible for material to which he has not made an active response. Theoretically, then, a student might learn as well by reading such programs with the response blanks filled in as by going through the programs and making all the correct responses.

This fact may partially explain those surprising research results which indicate that students who read through a "program" with the response blanks filled in do as well in post-test performance as students who go through the program making all the required responses. These studies invariably conclude that student responses are not critical to learning; such results may actually be attributable to the fact that the programs thus studied have utilized everything-is-learned, rather than critical-response, procedures.

In an everything program, there may be no significant difference in the post-test performances of those students who are required to respond and of those students who are given no opportunity to respond. In a critical program, the student required to respond may be expected to achieve better results than the student who merely reads.

In other words, in a critical program, the active responses are integral to the learning, while in an everything program, they are not.

COMPARISON OF "EVERYTHING" VS. "CRITICAL" PROGRAMS

The everything-is-learned program can result in satisfactory post-test performances, just as inefficient textbooks may result in learning. However, it is the contention of this paper that everything-is-learned procedures result in less motivationally sound and less pedagogically efficient learning than do critical-response procedures. Critical-response program sequences employ the laboratory principle of shaping in that they build upon reinforced behavior. Everything-is-learned programs, on the other hand, require an inefficient expenditure of student time and demand study skills which few readers possess. The student must painfully read and reread each frame, attempting to master any element which might be significant. He may discover that he will later be asked about some, but not all, of the material which is included in a frame. In this event, he may begin to learn selectively. And he must decide which information, apart from that which is required in the response, is important and most likely to be called for in subsequent frames, even though, as Mechner has pointed out, the student is often new to the subject-matter area, and far less competent than the writer to judge what is important.

USE OF SUPPORTING MATERIAL

It may seem that the writer of everything frames has greater opportunity to introduce illustrative supporting material; after all, he counts on the student to read, study and retain every element in every frame. Paradoxically, the contrary is true. The everything writer must often limit himself to a sparse presentation because he may otherwise cause the student to devote himself to learning material intended only for illustrative purposes. Consider the following frames which teach that delivery of material requires 10 days.

7. It requires 7 days to pack and assemble material after the request is made.
   It will require 3 days to label the material for delivery.
   How long is the total time between request and delivery? _____

This frame offers no problem for the critical-response writer, who holds the student responsible only for learning that delivery takes 10 days. However, the everything-is-learned writer who introduces such material faces the problem that the student will study all the supporting information in preparation for subsequent frames which may ask how much time is required for labeling, or which operation requires 7 days. This information may be useful for illustrative purposes but unworthy of retention.

RULE OF CUEING

According to the critical-response rule, a student may be held responsible for material to which he has responded correctly. It is clear, however, that a correct response may indicate only a limited mastery of the presented material. This leads to an important corollary to the critical-response rule. It is formally stated below.

A student is held responsible only at the minimum level of understanding required for a correct response to a frame.

The practical implication of this rule is that the programmer may not assume conceptual understanding when the student is responding to extraneous cues. The following frame illustrates this danger.

8. All Gaul was broken into THREE Divisions.
   Thus Gaul consisted of T_ _ _ _ _ parts.

Here the student can respond correctly without really reading or understanding any of the material presented in the frame. This frame is functionally identical to a frame which reads:

9. Copy the word THREE. _____

For this reason, several writers have termed such frames as 8 "copy-response frames." The disadvantage of such frames is that they are inefficient—in the example above, the student receives practice only in copying the word "three" rather than in learning that Gaul is divided into three parts. More efficient ways of writing the above frame are:

10.

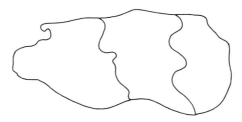

    This map shows the division of Gaul.
    Into how many parts was Gaul divided? _____

11. Gaul was divided into parts occupied by the Celts, the Belgae and the Aquitani.
    Into how many parts was Gaul divided? _____

(Note that by the critical-response rules given above, the reader need not learn the names of the Gallic tribes.)

DANGERS OF INADVERTENT COPY FRAMES

Learning theorists point out that concept formation is dependent upon maximum generalization within a class. Copy frames adhere to the antithesis of this principle because the student reading a copy frame repeats the information presented; he does not sample from the wide range of instances which define the class.

    The failure to properly develop conceptual understanding is not limited to frames employing such blatant cues as T _____. Markle and Mechner* have pointed out that there are many subtle ways in which a frame writer can inadvertently give away the correct response and thereby transform what might otherwise be a well-cued frame into a copy frame. (This topic has also received extensive treatment in the field of test construction.) The following frame contains an example of a subtle giveaway cue:

12. The immediate use of goods in return for the promise to pay later is characteristic of a purchase made on credit.
    "Fly now, pay later" is an example of a purchase made on _____.

    Here, the phrase "purchase made on" preceding the word "credit" in both sentences clearly gives away the desired response, and serves to reduce the frame to a copy frame.

---

* Editors' note: This reference is to Susan Meyer Markle, author of the book, *Good Frames and Bad,* and to Francis Mechner, author of the article, "Science Education and Behavioral Technology."

TECHNIQUE FOR APPROPRIATE CUEING

The relationship between a copy frame and a properly cued frame is continuous rather than dichotomous; a frame may be more or less cued, and the desired response may be more or less given away. A useful technique which maximizes generalization and serves to ensure meaningful utilization of new material is to require that each restatement of a concept utilize news terms and, when possible, new perspectives. Consider the examples below, each of which attempts to teach the concept that cortical convolutions increase as we ascend the phylogenetic scale. (It is assumed in these examples that all the pertinent terms are familiar to the target population.)

13. Cortical convolutions increase as we ascend the phylogenetic scale. As we ascend the phylogenetic scale, cortical convolutions _____ (increase/ decrease).

14. Cortical convolutions increase as we ascend the phylogenetic scale. As we ascend the phylogenetic scale, cortical convolutions become _____ (greater/smaller).

15. Cortical convolutions increase as we ascend the phylogenetic scale. As we go from lower organism to higher organisms, the number of cortical convolutions becomes _____ (smaller/greater).

16. Cortical convolutions increase as we ascend the phylogenetic scale. A platypus is a mammal. Which has a greater density of brain furrows, a platypus or a duck? _____

17. Cortical convolutions increase as we ascend the phylogenetic scale. The diagram below represents cortical sections from a lizard, a duck and a rat. Write the name of the appropriate organism below each diagram.

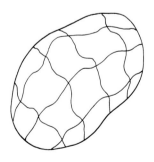 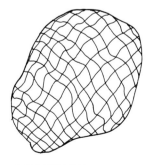 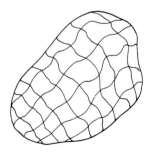

_____   _____   _____

Frame 13 is clearly a copy-response frame. Frame 14 represents a slight improvement because it used the words "becomes smaller" instead of the word "decreases." Similarly, frame 15 is a considerable improvement because many of the terms in its second sentence have been changed, while frames 16 and 17 contain sufficient variation to be considered acceptable.

SUMMARY AND CONCLUSIONS

Critical-response procedures employ laboratory-derived principles of shaping. The student is held responsible only for material to which he has responded correctly and, as a corollary, only at the minimum level of understanding required for such responses. Conceptual understanding is aided by the presentation of each restatement of a concept in new terms and, when possible, new perspectives.

In a critical program, responses are, then, an integral part of learning. In an everything-is-learned program, they are not, and the student reads and rereads frames, attempting to master even unessential illustrative material. Critical-response principles can be used to correct a wide range of deficiencies in frames and frame sequences. Programs that employ these principles build upon reinforced behavior. They are motivationally sound and pedagogically efficient.

A Quantitative Measure for Programmed Instruction[1]

James G. Holland

Programmed instruction, at its best, is an applied science in that it rests on fundamental principles of the learning laboratory. However, the principles as they have been related to matters of program design have been all too vague and general. They have lost much of the precision of operational statements so necessary to experimental research. The loss is unfortunate because exact meanings and empirically identifiable processes distinguish technology from craft. Further development of a technology of programmed instruction awaits the return to exact specifications for the important variables. It is the task of applied research to sharpen the description of fundamental variables needed in application and to forge useful measuring instruments for these variables.

Although most programmers would agree that not all sets of short completion items are programs, there are as yet no unequivocal criteria for identifying the

---

James G. Holland, "A Quantitative Measure for Programmed Instruction," *American Educational Research Journal* 4 (1967): 87–101. Reprinted by permission.

[1] The research reported in this paper was sponsored by the Air Force Systems Command, Electronic Systems Division, Decision Science Laboratory, under contract No. AF 19 (628)—2404 with Harvard University. The paper is identified as ESD—TR—65—543. Further reproduction is authorized to satisfy the needs of the United States Government. Much of the research was conducted in the facilities provided by the Harvard Committee on Programmed Instruction which is supported by the Carnegie Corporation. The work was completed in the Learning Research and Development Center of the University of Pittsburgh.

point when material can be termed "programmed." If the programmer had at his disposal clear cut measures of the degree to which material is programmed, he would have powerful help in designing material. Also, program editors could easily identify well-done programs, and could easily communicate their evaluations to authors. Experimenters with questions as to comparisons of programs and conventional techniques, or those with questions as to best presentation modes for programs or best response modes for programs would be able to identify first whether or not they were using real programs. Strangely, many experimenters have rushed to make such comparisons without first being able to demonstrate that they were in fact dealing with a program.

THE MEASURE

The present paper describes a series of experiments which attempts to provide a measure of the degree to which material is programmed. Programming has been defined by Skinner (1963) as "the construction of carefully arranged sequences of contingencies leading to the terminal performances which are the object of education." A key concept in this definition is *contingency*. Programs establish behavior through differential reinforcement; a correct answer can be reached only after some precursory behavior. Only that precursory behavior which had to occur is assured; only that unavoidable behavior constitutes the contingency for a correct answer. Material is, then, programmed only to the extent that the correct answer is contingent upon (i.e., depends upon) appropriate preceding behavior. A problem must be solved, a sentence or two carefully read, etc. This implies that when the precursory behavior has occurred, the student answers correctly and a low error rate results, but a low error rate, although a necessary condition for a program, is not a sufficient condition. Only those things which the student must do to reach the correct answer are a part of the program.

In the case of verbal knowledge programs (or programs designed to teach content), the response-contingent, or programmed, portions are those which must be read if the question is to be answered. Response contingency is the basis for what follows. The measure consists of determining what portions of a given set of material answers depend upon and what portions play no necessary role in evoking correct answers. The first step is simply to obliterate everything that can be obliterated without changing the program's error rate. All phrases which do not support the answer are covered by black crayon. Use of a heavy coating of black crayon makes these words invisible and readily suggests the term "blackout" technique for the procedure. In choosing the material to be covered by black crayon, all those portions of each item judged to be unnecessary for any student to attain a correct answer are physically obliterated. Usually only whole phrases are blacked out and articles, prepositions, and auxiliary words are blacked out only when the whole phrase is blacked out.

The blackout is next validated by testing the blacked-out and normal (unblacked-out) programs to demonstrate that error rate has not been influenced to a statistically significant extent. Should error rate be affected the blackout must be revised and retested until no effect is found. In practice the first attempt usually proves adequate. The unit used in calculating the blackout percentage of predominantly textual material is simply words. The percentage of the total number of words blacked out is the index of the amount of material which bears no contingent relation to the answer. Thus, the lower the percentage that can be blacked out, the more highly programmed the material.

The blackout technique not only can indicate whether verbal material is programmed but can indicate which portions of graphs, photographs, and models or instruments are programmed in material in which these play an important role. Unfortunately, as yet no quantitative measure is possible for non-textual material because there is no generally meaningful unit for such material. The concept of a contingent relationship between material and subject's response applies fully for programs in any medium, but the quantitative blackout ratio is at present applicable only to verbal and mathematical material.

It should be emphasized that the blackout measure is not a direct measure of whether the material teaches well or poorly, nor is the blacked-out version considered to be an improvement over the original version. The blackout ratio is only intended as a measure of the extent to which the original material is programmed.

DEMONSTRATION OF THE BLACKOUT TECHNIQUE

This technique was first developed (Holland and Kemp, 1965) using a program in which responses were largely determined by abundant formal prompts. The program was used in training bank personnel and dealt with monetary instruments. Two items from this program are shown in Fig. 18.1. The top item is Number 22

Normal	*Blacked out*
22. A B--- of Exchange (Draft) is convenient for the payment of debts.	22. A B--- of Exchange (Draft) ▬▬▬▬▬▬▬ ▬▬▬▬▬▬▬
23. The seller of merchandise by sending a Bill of E------- drawn on the buyer and attaching the shipping documents to a bank for collection can be assured that the merchandise will not be delivered to the buyer until the buyer pays for it.	23. ▬▬▬▬▬▬▬ ▬▬▬▬ a Bill of E------- ▬▬▬▬ ▬▬▬▬▬▬▬ ▬▬▬▬▬▬▬ ▬▬▬▬▬▬▬ ▬▬▬▬▬▬▬ ▬▬▬▬▬▬▬ ▬▬

Fig. 18.1. Samples of normal and blacked-out items from the monetary program.

and not the first time the concept "bill of exchange" has been introduced. Item 23 is filled with information which the programmer surely must have intended to teach. It can be seen, however, that much material can be obliterated without influencing the subject's ability to answer. In all, a 140-item sequence in this program was subjected to the blackout procedure. Sixty-nine percent of the words in this material were blacked out. Then one group of 15 subjects went through this blacked-out material in a teaching machine (under controlled conditions) writing their answers by utilizing the information from the remaining 31 percent. A second group of 15 subjects used the regular version. The median error rate for the subjects using the blacked-out version was 12.9 percent as compared with a median error rate of 11.4 percent for subjects using the normal, unblacked-out, program. This difference was not statistically significant (t test or Kolmogorov-Smirnov two-sample test). . . .

Blacking out a full 69 percent of the words in this program, then, had little or no apparent effect on the subject's ability to answer. The remaining 31 percent was demonstrated to influence answers by an additional group using a "reverse-blackout" program in which this 31 percent was covered with black crayon and the 69 percent judged unrelated to the answer remained available to the subjects. . . . The median error rate in the reverse blackout was 72.5 percent, an increase of 61.1 percentage points over the error rate in the normal version. The application of the blackout procedure indicates that no more than 31 percent of the words were programmed while 69 percent were not programmed.

. . .

THE RANGE OF BLACKOUT RATIOS

The percentage blacked out theoretically can vary from zero percent to 100 percent. In the idealized case of completely programmed material obliterating a single word would increase the error rate, while in completely unprogrammed material all words in every item could be covered without affecting error rate. Neither of these extremes are generally found in practice (although the latter is sometimes approximated in sequences of items when items all have identical answers). An indication of the range of values which might normally be found is shown in a study (Kemp and Holland, 1966) which compared blackout ratios for segments of twelve sets of material which had been used in a number of experiments. The length for the segments of programs blacked out ranged from 17 items, in the one case for which no more material was available, to 375 items. In most cases the first 50 items were used. All were subjected to the blackout procedure and the blackout was validated using test subjects. The initial blackouts for four of the programs slightly altered error rates and the blackout for these were revised. The revision was then tested and shown not to differ significantly in error rate from the normal programs.

An item selected from each of four sets of material is shown in Fig. 18.2 both before and after being blacked out. The first item, from a statistics "program," is an extreme case of nearly completely unprogrammed material. The item can be an-

Normal	Blacked out

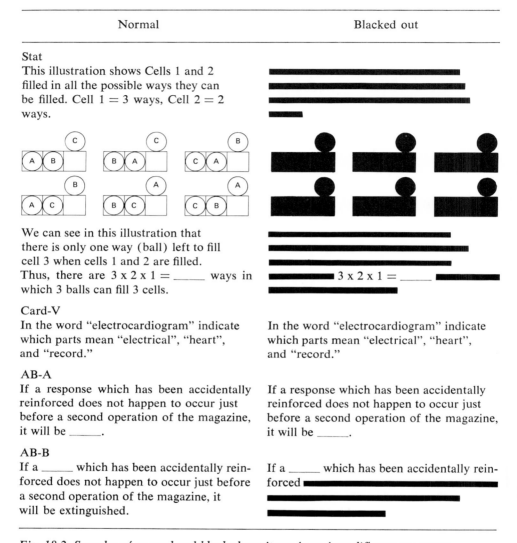

Stat
This illustration shows Cells 1 and 2 filled in all the possible ways they can be filled. Cell 1 = 3 ways, Cell 2 = 2 ways.

We can see in this illustration that there is only one way (ball) left to fill cell 3 when cells 1 and 2 are filled. Thus, there are 3 x 2 x 1 = _____ ways in which 3 balls can fill 3 cells.

3 x 2 x 1 = _____

Card-V
In the word "electrocardiogram" indicate which parts mean "electrical", "heart", and "record."

In the word "electrocardiogram" indicate which parts mean "electrical", "heart", and "record."

AB-A
If a response which has been accidentally reinforced does not happen to occur just before a second operation of the magazine, it will be _____.

If a response which has been accidentally reinforced does not happen to occur just before a second operation of the magazine, it will be _____.

AB-B
If a _____ which has been accidentally reinforced does not happen to occur just before a second operation of the magazine, it will be extinguished.

If a _____ which has been accidentally reinforced

Fig. 18.2. Samples of normal and blacked-out items from four different programs.

Fig. 18.3. Percent of the total number of words which could be blacked out of each of the 12 sets of material. The programs are arranged in rank order from lowest to highest blackout ratios.

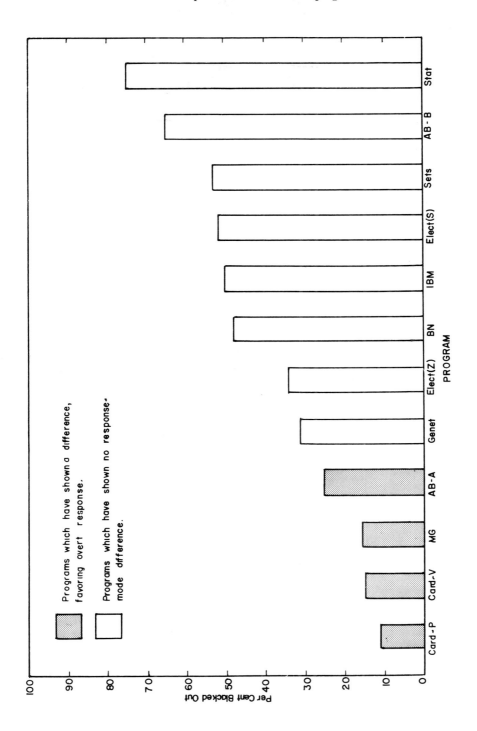

swered on the basis of the expression, "3 × 2 × 1 = ———," without regard to the major point of the item concerning the number of permutations of three events. Two of the items (labeled AB-A and AB-B) differ only in the word left blank; but this small difference in the design of the item makes the difference between programmed material which doesn't blackout and relatively unprogrammed material which blacks out substantially.

Figure 18.3 indicates the percent blacked out for each of the twelve sets of material. The wide range of percentages (11.1 percent to 74.6 percent) demonstrates that the measure is sensitive to differences in programs and can be expected to yield quite different values.

These twelve programs were chosen because they had been used in studies investigating the value of overt vs. covert responses. This problem has special relevance to the question of contingent relationships between the answer and the rest of the item. The rationale for programmed instruction demands that there be a response to every item. Responding is so central to the principles of programming that generally it is felt that responses should be overt (written, spoken, etc.) in order to assure that a response is given. An especially popular research question has focused on the question of the necessity of such an overt response. (For a review of the relevant literature see Holland, 1965). Posttest performances after writing an answer to every program item have been compared with posttest performances when either merely "thinking" the answer or when reading complete declarative sentences requiring no answer. The results of these studies have been inconsistent. Many have failed to find a statistically significant advantage to overt responding while a few have confirmed the claimed advantage for an overt response. It has been suggested (Holland, 1965; Eigen and Margulies, 1963) that many of the "programs" used in studies which failed to find an advantage for overt responding contained items in which much of the material failed to serve as contingencies for responses. At the time these studies were done, and this criticism first offered, no measure for this contingent relationship between answers and textual material was available.

The blackout measure was applied to twelve sets of material used in studies which evaluated the role of overt responses. Figure 18.3 summarizes the results of these blackouts. It can be seen that the four sets with the lowest blackout ratios were those which, in previous research, yielded results favoring an overt response. These had blackout ratios ranging from 11.1 percent to 25.4 percent. On the other hand, the eight sets of material which yielded no significant advantage for overt responding all had higher blackout ratios ranging from 31.0 percent to 74.6 percent. The conclusion to be drawn seems simple, indeed perhaps self-evident. When the answer given by the subject has little or no relationship to the critical content of the item it does not matter whether the subject writes an answer, thinks an answer, or answers not at all. It is only when the critical content serves as a contingency for correct answers that the overt response is important. A measure for the amount of contingent material insures that this variable can no longer be so easily overlooked in studies exploring the properties of programs.

POSTTEST PERFORMANCE AS A FUNCTION OF
VARIED BLACKOUT RATIOS

A program's blackout ratio indicates only the degree to which material is programmed. It is not a measure of educational value of the material, nor is it in itself a measure of how effectively the material teaches. Whether highly programmed material produces superior learning is a quite different question. Such a question, however, can be answered only to the extent that one can identify the degree to which material is programmed. A considerable advantage is, of course, expected to result through the technology of programmed instruction. It would, therefore, be reasonable to expect greater learning in programs yielding a low blackout ratio than with programs yielding a high blackout ratio.

. . .

A direct comparison of posttest performance for programs differing in blackout ratios requires that there be two or more programs differing in blackout ratio but having a single posttest equally applicable to the programs used. This is not a requirement ordinarily met by independently prepared programs. However, some earlier experiments (Holland, 1960; 1964) arranged an experimental modification of a program to create two forms which meet the condition. These experiments utilized the same posttest as well as material differing in the degree to which the subject's response depended on careful reading of textual material. A 377 item segment of a psychology program was altered by filling in the program's usual response blank and then selecting another word or words to be replaced by a blank for the subject to complete. In this modified version the blank was so chosen that the answer was highly cued and easy to answer but the cues which evoked the response had as little as possible to do with the important textual content of the item. In essence the modified version was designed to have a higher blackout ratio than the original version. Although the blackout measure had not been developed when this experiment was performed the modified program was subsequently shown to blackout 65.0 percent while the original version blacks out 25.4 percent.

Another modified version of this material was arranged to vary a different, but related, property of programs. This version (version C) also held the content of the material constant. However, the word or words chosen to be left blank were undetermined or "uncued." This version was designed so that the probability of responding correctly was low. However, the response term was highly dependent upon the critical content of the item.* This version had a relatively low blackout ratio (38.0 percent) and a high error rate (73.7 percent). As the reader may be aware, a traditional, and still applicable, measure of an essential feature of a program is a low error rate. The subject learns the thing he did in reaching an answer which he considers to be correct. Textual material is programmed when it serves as a contingency which *can be met* by the subject. Material is programmed (i) to the extent

---

* In other words, version C looked more like a test for mastery of the relevant concepts than like a program designed to teach these concepts.

that the critical performance must occur (i.e., low blackout ratio), and (ii) to the extent that the subject can successfully perform (i.e., low error rate).[4] The two modified versions of the psychology program are designed to evaluate these two propositions. Table 18.1 shows a sample of one statement as it appeared in each of the three versions.

TABLE 18.1

Sample item (set 11, item 5) as it appeared in experimental version

Condition A:

Reinforcement which consists of presenting stimuli (e.g., food) is called positive reinforcement. In contrast, reinforcement which consists of terminating stimuli (e.g., painful stimuli) is called _____ reinforcement.

Answer: negative

Condition B:

Reinforcement which consists of presenting stimuli (e.g., food) is called positive reinforcement. In contrast, reinforcement which consists of terminating _____ (e.g., painful stimuli) is called negative reinforcement.

Answer: stimuli

Condition C:

Reinforcement which consists of presenting stimuli (e.g., food) is called 1) _____ reinforcement. In contrast, reinforcement which consists of terminating stimuli (e.g., painful stimuli) is called 2) _____ reinforcement.

Answers: 1) positive 2) negative

Groups of six to eight subjects were compared on posttest performance after completing either the original material (condition A), the high blackout material (condition B), the high error-rate material (condition C), or material which had no blanks and required no response (condition D, a control). [Students using the original program, condition A, had an average error rate on the posttest of 18%. Students in each of the other three conditions had an average posttest error rate of 40%.] The original program, relatively low in both blackout ratio and error rate, produced substantially better posttest performance than any of the other conditions. Condition B, C, and D could not properly be considered programs, D because it consisted only of exposure to textual material without a response, B because of the high blackout ratio, and C because of the high error rate. There were no significant posttest differences among the three "non-programmed" conditions and each was

---

[4] This description of the role of low error rate is not intended to deprecate the legitimate use of diagnostic test items which, of necessity, have high error rates. Further, the author does not belittle the more popularly understood role correct answers play in providing positive reinforcement in contrast to the aversive control common to traditional education practice.

worse than the original programmed material. There is indeed an advantage for material which meets the requirements of a program.[5]

CONCLUSION

Now it is possible, even easy, for the programmer, the editor, the researcher, and the consumer of programmed materials to measure directly the extent to which material is programmed by determining the error rate and the blackout ratio. Both measure important defining properties of programs but neither alone is sufficient. Moreover, highly programmed material, as indicated by the combination of low blackout ratio and low error rate, teaches more effectively than relatively unprogrammed material.

Many statements regarding programming techniques presuppose contingent relationships between the material and the response. It should now be somewhat easier, therefore, to conduct research in developing procedures for sequencing material, or so to construct rules as to the characteristics of examples needed to form an abstraction efficiently, or to develop other useful guide lines for programming.

In the past, experiments on procedural matters such as programmed texts vs. teaching machine presentation, overt vs. covert responding, confirmation vs. no confirmation for answers, and tests of other hypotheses arising from the rationale of programmed instruction have frequently generated conflicting results. The confusions have often arisen because experiments test an hypothesis regarding some aspect of programs when, in fact, the material used is not a program. The measures of blackout ratio and error rate should correct this situation as they already have, in part, the overt vs. covert response issue.

The still young technology of programmed instruction has produced some highly effective materials for generating a high level of achievement in the user who finds the material challenging and interesting. Unfortunately, some of the negative judgments which have been passed upon programming are based upon a few, all too conspicuously, bad examples of "programs." Although these usually have low error rates they also usually have high blackout ratios. A program may seem boring or prove ineffective because trivial cues serve as the basis for answers; the subject simply is not asked to do anything of consequence. Inappropriate generalizations based on single bad examples should now become less common, not only because the deficiencies can now be recognized, but because deficient material should be produced less frequently.

---

[5] For additional evidence see M. A. Sherman (1965). This study used material specially designed so that each posttest item was based on material which served as a contingency in the program for half the subjects but not for the other half of the subjects. Posttest performance clearly favored material on which responses depended. See also L. D. Eigen and S. Margulies (1963).

REFERENCES

Eigen, Louis D., and Stuart Margulies. "Response Characteristics as a Function of In-formation Level." *Journal of Programed Instruction* 2:45–54; Spring, 1963.

Holland, James G. *Design and Use of a Teaching-Machine Program.* Paper read at American Psychological Association Convention. Chicago, September, 1960.

Holland, James G. "New Directions in Teaching-Machine Research." In *Programmed Learning and Computer-Based Instruction,* edited by J. E. Coulson. New York: John Wiley, 1962.

Holland, James G. "Response Contingencies in Teaching-Machine Programs." *Journal of Programed Instruction* 3: 1–8; Spring, 1964.

Holland, James G. "Research on Programming Variables." In *Teaching Machines and Programmed Learning: II Data and Directions,* edited by R. Glaser. Washington, D.C.: National Education Association, 1965, pp. 66–117.

Holland, James G., and Frederick D. Kemp. "A Measure of Programing in Teaching-Machine Material." *Journal of Educational Psychology* 56:264–269; December, 1965.

Kemp, Frederick D., and James G. Holland. "The Blackout Ratio and Overt Responses in Programmed Instruction: Resolution of Disparate Results." *Journal of Educational Psychology* 57 (April, 1966).

Sherman, Mark A. "The Relation of Posttest Performance to Response-Contingencies in Programmed Instruction." Report No. ESD-TR-65-543. New Bedford, Mass.: Air Force Systems Command, 1965.

Skinner, B. F. "Reflections on a Decade of Teaching Machines." *Teachers College Record* 65:168–177; November, 1963.

QUESTIONS

Answer questions 1 through 8 by referring to these two sample frames from the Mar-gulies article:

FRAME A

> * is the equivalent of plus
>
> 4 * 3 = _____

FRAME B

> * is the equivalent of plus
>
> 4 + 3 = _____

1. Could the majority of a group of high-school students correctly answer frame A without reading "* is the equivalent of plus"?

2. Could the majority of a group of high-school students correctly answer frame B without reading "* is the equivalent of plus"?

3. In the Mechner program in Unit 4 a behavioral contingency is defined as a situation in which a stimulus event (i.e., "The radio will go on") is contingent upon a response event (i.e., "if you turn the knob to the right.") This same concept of contingency is applicable to verbal learning programs and could be restated as, "You will get the right answer if you read this sentence, do this problem, copy this word, etc." In the article, "A Quantitative Measure for Programmed Instruction," this kind of verbal learning contingency is described as the precursory behavior which results in the right answer.

   a) Describe the precursory behavior which results in the right answer for frame A.

   b) Describe the contingency for the right answer for frame B.

4. Apply the blackout technique to frame B. Assume that two groups of high-school students will receive this frame. One group will receive your blacked-out version and one group will receive the normal version. Circle all the material that you expect could be blacked out in frame B without increasing the number of wrong answers the blacked-out group is likely to give as compared to the normal group.

5. Apply the blackout technique to frame A. Again, assume two groups of high-school students will receive this frame—one group the normal version and one group your blacked-out version. Circle all material that could be blacked out without affecting the error rate of the blacked-out group as compared to the normal group.

6. Look at frame B only. One behavioral objective of the lesson which uses this frame is: Given a problem in the form, A * B, the student will solve it by adding A and B. (Disregard the fact that this is a silly objective no one would ordinarily want to teach.) If that is the objective, what is wrong with frame B?

7. If you know the behavioral objective (given in question 6) and you have done a blackout on the teaching material (as in question 4), how does this information help you revise the frame?

8. The principle of gradual progression in shaping complex behavior requires that we build only on behavior that has been established (i.e., emitted and reinforced). Therefore, it is important to know what behavior has been emitted and reinforced in one item before designing a second item. If students have correctly answered frame B, we could *not* assume that they would be now able to answer this subsequent frame:

   @ means "perform the operation opposite
        to *"

   4 @ 3 = _____

Why not?

9. What is the contingency for a correct response to this frame from the Margulies article:

   All Gaul was broken into <u>three</u> divisions.
   Thus Gaul consisted of t ___ ___ ___ ___ parts.

10. Suppose that the "Gaul" frame from question 9 was a typical frame from a program used in an experiment to determine whether or not active responding is necessary for

learning. In this experiment, half the students worked through the program filling in the blanks, and half simply read through a version of the program which had the blanks filled in for them. On the posttest both groups performed comparably. According to Margulies and Holland, does this result prove that active responding is not necessary for learning? Explain your answer.

11. Explain why "everything-is-learned" type programs (as well as standard textbooks) are inefficient methods of teaching.

12. What is the purpose of the blackout ratio?

13. How do you determine whether the amount of material blacked out is correct?

14. If you find that a program has a high blackout ratio, what would you do to improve the program? What do you do with the material that blacked out?

15. Here is an early frame from a program to teach children some characteristics of plants: "*Plants* do not eat food. P __ __ __ __ __ make their own food." Given a correct answer to this frame, circle the only word you can be sure has been read.

16. There are a total of ten words in the frame from question 15. All but two of the words black out. (The response blank is counted as a word, and does not black out.) Calculate the blackout ratio for this frame.

17. The objective of the frame in question 15 is to teach that plants make their own food and do not eat food. A child should not be able to respond correctly to the frame without attending to this critical information. The following frame is rewritten so that a correct answer indicates use of this critical information: "Plants do not _____ food, plants _____ their own food." If this version replaced the frame in question 15 as a *teaching* frame, would you predict that it would be generally answered correctly? Why or why not?

18. Here is a third revision of the frame from question 15:

"Plants do not eat food, plants make their own food. A rose bush and a maple tree are kinds of plants. Does a rose bush eat food? _____. How does a maple tree get food? _____."

a) Apply the blackout technique to this version. What is the result?

b) Do you think this version of the frame is more likely to be answered correctly than the version in question 17? Explain why or why not.

19. a) Why is a low error rate a necessary condition for a good program?

b) Why is a low error rate not the only necessary condition for a good program?

20. Write a frame or frames to teach a second characteristic of plants: they need soil, water, and sunlight. Make sure that this critical information must be used in order to answer your frame correctly.

UNIT

19

The Blackout Program: Evaluating Whether Programs Are Well Written

Content

Program samples.

Objectives

Students evaluate each frame from the sample programs and mark the parts they consider unnecessary for correctly answering that frame or subsequent frames. They then check their decisions with the blacked-out versions of the samples.

Instructions

1. Read the introduction and the instructions carefully.
2. Work through the program samples as directed. Check your responses after each page rather than after completing the entire program.
3. Discuss your work with the instructor.

BLACKOUT PROGRAM—GENERAL INTRODUCTION

Programmed verbal material teaches by having the student complete sentences by filling in a missing word or words.

For example:

The sense organs used for hearing are the _____.

Answer: ears

Normally, students do not see the correct answer until after they have filled in the blank.

An item or frame contains sentences or phrases that the student must use to obtain a correct answer for that or other items; the item also might contain sentences or phrases giving information not directly necessary for a correct response. In this program, we would like you to identify the material that is necessary to ascertain the correct answer (the cues for the answer) and the unnecessary material which, if removed, will not affect the likelihood of responding accurately. You will be applying the blackout technique.

In the excerpts from programs that follow, you will be looking for the words and phrases that cue the correct answer. Remember that you are making a judgment, and your judgment may not always agree with ours. Keep in mind the criterion: Could a group of subjects using the blacked-out page have about the same average error rate as a matched group using the normal program? As an exercise in applying this criterion, answer the following frames. All material judged unnecessary for achieving the correct response has been blacked out. (Answers are below.)

1. ██
████████ when the wheel turns the axle also t__ __ __ __ .

2. When you turn the _____knob to open a door, ████████████████
████████████

3. ████████████████ exert a force ████████████████████████████
████████████████ exerts a _____ ████████████████████
██
████████████████████

Presumably you were able to answer these frames correctly, even though most of the important material the designer intended to teach has been obliterated. In well-designed material the learner should not be able to achieve a correct response without emitting behavior described by the designer's behavioral objectives for the lesson.

If your judgment as to the appropriate blackout material differs greatly from our judgment, you may want to put your judgment to an empirical test. Obliterate the material with a felt-tip marker and give the frames to a friend. If you have blacked out vital cues, or too much of an item, your friend will not be able to answer that item correctly.

(*Answers:* 1. turns; 2. door; 3. force.)

BLACKOUT PROGRAM INSTRUCTIONS

1. If you think a word, phrase, or sentence is unnecessary for the correct response, cross it out. (You need not actually black it out with heavy crayon.)

2. Don't be afraid of crossing out too much or too little of an item. Sometimes the whole item is necessary for the correct response; sometimes only a word or two is needed.

3. Single words such as articles, qualifiers, and auxiliary verbs are not crossed out unless the words they modify are crossed out.

4. Don't be afraid to cross out words, phrases, or sentences which contain information relevant to the subject matter of the program as long as this material is not needed to answer the item (or succeeding items) correctly.

5. The blackout procedure is not an editing procedure. It is not necessary to have grammatically correct sentences when you are done.

6. Assume that the following selections are the first frames in their respective programs. In making your blackout judgment do not assume prior teaching material, unless you are directed to do so.

7. If something in an early item is not necessary for that item but is necessary for a later item of that set, it *cannot* be blacked out—error rate would be affected. (Note: This is also a programming error, but it is not detectable by the blackout technique.)

8. As a final reminder, remember that the biggest mistake most people make is crossing out too little rather than too much of an item.

Work carefully on the following programs, then check yourself by looking at the approved blacked-out versions which follow.

Sample Program 1
Intended users—sixth graders

THE WHEEL AND AXLE

1. A *wheel and axle* is a simple machine. A w＿ ＿ ＿ ＿ and a＿ ＿ ＿ can be used to do work.

(wheel, axle)

2. You use a wheel and ＿＿＿＿＿＿ many times each day.

(axle)

3. A doorknob is an example of a ＿＿＿＿＿＿ and axle.

(wheel)

4.

This is a diagram of a wheel and axle. "A" is the wheel. "B" is the ＿＿＿＿.

(axle)

5. Look at this diagram of a doorknob.

The circumference of the wheel is (smaller/larger) than the circumference of the axle. A point on the circumference of the wheel travels a greater distance than does a point on the circumference of the axle.

(larger)

6. A force exerted on the wheel will cause the wheel to turn, and when the wheel turns the axle also t__ __ __ __ .

(turns)

7. When you turn the _____ knob to open a door, you are using a wheel and axle.

(door)

8. When you exert a force on the knob, the knob turns the shaft. The shaft exerts a _____ on the latch. The force exerted by the shaft is greater than the force exerted on the knob.

(force)

9. When you turn the knob one revolution, the shaft turns one revolution. How many times does the shaft turn when you turn the knob three times? _____

(three)

Sample Program 2
Intended users—tenth graders

THE SPANISH-AMERICAN WAR

1. Spanish misrule in Cuba led to repeated attempts by C_____ patriots to gain independence from Spain.

(Cuban)

2. In 1852, Great Britain and France joined in guaranteeing Spanish authority in Cuba. Millard Fillmore refused to join them in guaranteeing _____ authority in Cuba.

(Spanish)

3. Two European countries which supported Spanish authority in Cuba were _____ and _____ .

(Great Britain and France)

4. The United States, under Millard Fillmore, (did, did not) guarantee Spanish authority in Cuba.

(did not)

Sample Program 3
Intended users—tenth graders. For this program apply the blackout technique to non–response-contingent sections of the reading as well as to the questions.

MARS

Mars has two satellites. They are small, estimated to be about five and ten miles in diameter if their surfaces have properties similar to that of our moon. They were discovered in 1877 by Asaph Hall. The outer satellite is named Deimos and it revolves around Mars in about 31 hours. The inner satellite, Phobos, whips around Mars in a little more than seven hours, making three trips around the planet in each Martian day. (*The World Almanac & Book of Facts*)

Answer the following questions based on the passage you've just read. You may refer back to the passage.

1. Mars has ———— satellites, Phobos and Deimos.

(two)

2. Deimos, the outer satellite, takes (more/fewer) hours to revolve around Mars than does Phobos, the inner satellite.

(more)

3. Phobos makes three seven-hour revolutions each Martian day. Therefore, a Martian day is 7×3 or ———— hours long.

(21)

4. The satellites were discovered by ———————— in the year
————————.

(Asaph Hall, 1877)

Sample Program 4
Intended users—college students

ONOMATOPOEIA!

1. An onomatopoetic word sounds like what it means. Onomatopöeia is the naming of a thing by a vocal imitation of the sound associated with it. "Hiss" is an example of a/an ———————— word.

(onomatopoetic)

2. Say the word "hiss" aloud. The sound of the word imitates the sound of a snake or the sound of escaping gas. When the sound of a word ———————— the sound of the thing it names, that word is onomatopoetic.

(imitates)

3. An onomatopoetic word sounds like what it means. "Hiss" is an example of an onomatopoetic word. "Crash," "bang," and "ding-dong" are other examples. Underline other words from this list that are onomatopoetic:

MOTHER	BUS	BUZZ
ZING	WHAP	HURT
SING	THUD	SCREECH

(zing, whap, thud, buzz, screech)

4. Now you think of some words that are onomatopoetic. Write them down here:
_____.

(check your list with the instructor)

Sample Program 5
Intended users—beginning readers (These children have already learned that they are to underline the word or words that describe the picture.)

CAN   CAT

This is a trip.
This is a tree.

Mary sees a dog.
Joey sees a log.

Sample Program 6
Intended users—college students

HALLMARKS ON ENGLISH SILVER

1. Since 1300, England has had a law requiring the marking of silver objects to guarantee their purity. The hallmark is a m__ __ __ stamped on silver objects. It signifies that the object has passed the assay test.

(mark)

2. The hallmark, or town mark as it came to be known, denotes the t___ ___ ___ where the assay was made.

(town)

3. The London assay office is the oldest in England. At first, all silver objects made anywhere in England had to bear the London h___ ___ ___mark of the leopard's head.

(hall)

4. Later, seven assay offices were opened. Each _____ office has its own hallmark.

(assay)

5. The hallmark does not stand alone. Another mark is added to denote the year when the a___ ___ ___ ___ was made.

(assay)

6. A l___ ___ ___ ___ ___ of the alphabet is used to denote the year the assay was made.

(letter)

7. In the reign of Henry VIII, the purity of the silver coinage became less than the sterling standard. Silversmiths added a third mark to their wares to emphasize that they met the _____ standard.

(sterling)

8. The third mark is called the standard mark. The s_____ mark denotes that the silver meets the sterling standard.

(standard)

9. All assay offices in England must use the same standard mark. The standard mark used by all _____ offices in England is the lion *passant*.

(assay)

10. A fourth _____ denotes the maker of the silver object. This mark usually consists of the initials of the maker.

(mark)

11. This illustration shows two of the marks on a piece of silver:

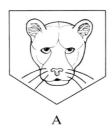

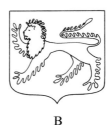

A   B

"A" is the London hallmark.
"B" is the standard mark.
Which mark shows where this piece of silver was tested? _____
Which mark shows that the silver meets the sterling standard? _____

(A, B)

Sample Program 7
Intended users—college students

BEHAVIORAL CONTINGENCIES

Francis Mechner

1. Your being born *was not* a "response-event" for you. That is, it was not an action you initiated. Your throwing your rattle out of your crib, however, *was* an action initiated by you. It *was* a "response-event" for you.

   Underline each sentence below that describes a response-event for the person or animal named in the sentence:
   a) Clara dyed her hair red.
   b) Herman died of old age.
   c) The dog has fleas.
   d) The cat meowed.

(a, d)

2. When you hit someone, it (is/is not) your action. It (is/is not) your response-event. When the other person hits you back, it (is/is not) your response-event.

   Underline each sentence below that describes a response-event for the person or animal named in the sentence:
   a) Philip ran fast.

b) Gregory was run over.
c) Alice cheated on the exam.
d) Mary was reprimanded for cheating.
e) The canary lost all its feathers.
f) The parrot said "Polly wants a cracker."

(is, is, is not, a, c, f)

3. The sentence, "The officer gave Mr. Smith a summons," *describes* the officer's giving the ticket, but merely *implies* Mr. Smith's speeding or going through the red light. Does the sentence describe a response-event for Mr. Smith? (yes/no)

Underline the sentences below that describe, not merely imply, response-events for *you:*
a) You solved a hard math example.
b) Your teacher gave you a good grade in math.
c) You are a doctor.
d) You are studying to be a doctor.

(no, a, d)

4. Psychology is often called the science of behavior. That is, it is the study of how living creatures behave, how they act, what response-events they initiate under what circumstances.

The sentence "The telephone rang" does *not* refer to a response-event, because only people or animals can initiate response-events. Underline the response-events below:
a) The hurricane struck here yesterday. (for the hurricane)
b) Tom struck Harry. (for Tom)
c) Tom struck Harry. (for Harry)
d) The clock struck ten. (for the clock)

(b)

5. Complete the definition of the term "response-event" below. Your definition should include the word "action." A response-event is _____
_____.

(any action initiated by a living creature—
or equivalent response)

This is the end of the blackout program.

UNIT

20

Evaluating a Chemistry Program

Content

Chemistry 1, Atomic Structure and Bonding. New York: Basic Systems, 1962, selected pages from the Teacher's Manual and frames 1–33 from the program.

This unit presents an example of programmed material for evaluation and analysis.

Objectives

Students observe some auxiliary information that should accompany published programs and apply the blackout procedure to part of a program. They examine individual frames and explain the learning principles illustrated. They describe what is wrong with two alternative forms of part of the program, decide whether certain frames achieve their objectives, and rewrite the poorer frames.

Instructions

1. Read the objectives carefully and use them to guide your reading of the text.
2. Quickly read over the preface, lesson plans, tests, drills, and tables from the Teacher's Manual.
3. Carefully *work* through the selection from the *Chemistry 1* program, writing your answers and checking them. Note that you should write your answer to frame 1, then, following the arrow, turn the page to check your answer and find the next frame.
4. Answer the questions that follow this material.
5. Check your answers, then discuss this unit with your instructor.

Chemistry 1

(from the Teacher's Manual)

GUIDE TO THE PERFORMANCE OF THE PROGRAM

As a program is developed, a number of students are utilized as test subjects at various stages. Each stage of revision requires a fresh group of subjects to obtain data on the program at that stage of progress, and to indicate what further revisions are necessary. These students are selected to sample the types of students likely to use the program when it is completed. In all, twenty-six such subjects were employed during the developmental stages of this program.

When the program nears its final form a validation test is given to gather data on the performance characteristics of the program as a whole. The validation test is carried out on a population selected so as to sample in a representative way the population for whom the program is intended.

The Test Group

The validation group for this program consisted of twelve students ranging in school grade from 10th through 12th (last grade completed), in age from 14–17 years, and in IQ (as measured by the appropriate form of the Wechsler) from 102–138. Table 20.1 summarizes the information for each subject.

Students were not recruited randomly, but were chosen so as to span representative points at roughly even intervals across the IQ range. It can be seen from the reported grades in mathematics and science that these students were doing average or better work in their schools.

Test Procedure

Each student participated in the entire validation test over a time period of about a week's length which contained three or four sessions of several hours' duration each on consecutive or near consecutive days. The steps were as follows:

1. Initial recruiting, screening, administration of IQ test.
2. Pre-test. Each student was asked to complete as many items of the final examination as he could before beginning the program.
3. Study by programmed instruction. The procedure for working on a program was explained and illustrated. Each student then began working on the program at his own pace under supervision of Basic Systems Testing Department personnel. Responses were made in separate notebooks which were retained for analysis. Frames completed were recorded at half-hour intervals. Sessions never exceeded two hours; there was one and sometimes two such sessions each day and reasonable breaks were given.

Chemistry 1, Atomic Structure and Bonding (New York: Basic Systems, 1962). Copyright © Xerox Corporation. Reprinted by special permission of Xerox Corporation.

TABLE 20.1

Student	1	2	3	4	5	6	7	8	9	10	11	12
Age	14	14	14	15	15	16	16	15	16	16	17	17
Last grade completed	10	10	10	10	10	10	10	11	11	11	11	12
IQ (Wechsler) WISC	109	120	135	127	138			127				
WAIS						102	105		125	117	113	115
Reported science background: Gen. Sci.		95	94	90	88	85	85	90	85	90	75	90
Elem. Alg.	65	92	95	98	85	75	90	80	70	75	78	75
Geometry	70	94	98	85	88		90	80	75		78	75
Int. Alg.						75		92		70		75
Trig.												75
Biology	85	85	98	90	85	80	85	95	90	90	75	90
Pre-test	**2%**	**11%**	**15%**	**2%**	**4%**	**4%**	**8%**	**6%**	**2%**	**0%**	**9%**	**8%**
Total time (in hours)	12.7	7.8	7.3	8.5	7.8	15.3	12.2	6.5	8.4	9.0	12.7	7.9
Frame rate (per hour)	65	106	114	98	106	54	68	127	99	92	65	103
Total errors	38	38	4	34	49	5	30	1	71	38	15	24
Error rate (per cent)	4.6	4.6	0.48	4.1	5.9	0.73	3.6	0.12	8.6	4.6	1.8	2.9
Final exam.	**87%**	**100%**	**100%**	**100%**	**100%**	**100%**	**100%**	**100%**	**100%**	**96%**	**98%**	**99%**

4. Interim quizzes. The three interim quizzes were administered at appropriate points in the program, and formed part of the regular sessions.

5. Final exam. When the student had completed the program, the final examination was administered in a separate session of its own, also under the supervision of the testing personnel.*

Achievement

This manual contains the three interim quizzes and the final examination which were employed in the validation of the program. The teacher may make use of these as he sees fit.

---

* The final examination is included in this selection from the Teacher's Manual.

Figure 20.1 shows the achievement (in percentage scores) on the three quizzes and the final examination of the twelve students who participated in the validation study. (The weighting employed in scoring the final exam is indicated with the exam.) The scores labeled F_1 are the scores on the final examination taken before students had worked through the program. Only two of them are above 10% in value, indicating little preparation in the field of atomic structure and the periodic table. In the upper part of the figure, the scores labeled *1, 2,* and *3* represent scores on the three quizzes respectively; the scores labeled *F* are the grades on the final examination taken after completion of the program. It can be seen that the achievement produced by the program is uniformly high. Of the 48 marks generated by the validation test (excluding, of course, the pre-test), only two are below 90%, and both of these are above 85%.

Most significant is the fact that this uniform high achievement is maintained in spite of the variations in IQ, which appear to have been "absorbed" by the time differences described above.

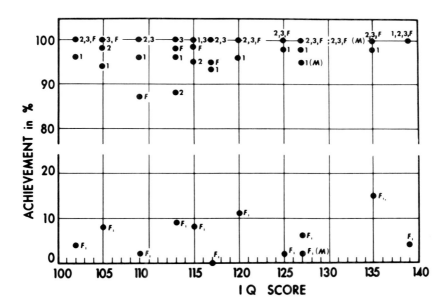

Figure 20.1

LESSON PLANS

Lesson 1

I. Assignment

Frames 1–117. Go through frames 1–4 or 5 in class so that students understand how program is to be used. You may wish to continue further or to take the next

complete class period to do a section of the program in class and use any time remaining for clarification of student questions.

II. Aims

Conceptual

1. Atoms are composed of smaller particles.
   a) Protons and neutrons in the nucleus
   b) Electrons in energy levels outside the nucleus
2. Atomic number is the number of protons in the atom.
3. Electrons, whose energies determine their most probable distance from the
   nucleus, are arranged in energy levels.
4. Energy levels are numbered in succession, the one nearest the nucleus, representing the least energy, being numbered 1.
5. Charged particles exert electrostatic forces on each other, particles of like
   charges repelling each other while those of unlike charge attract each other.

Fundamental Skills

1. Subatomic particles may be represented by symbols: e^- (electron), p^+ (proton), n^0 (neutron).
2. Diagrams (models) of atoms
   a) Show nucleus with the number of protons (atomic number) and the num-
      ber of neutrons.
   b) The successive energy levels may be represented by concentric arcs (or con-
      centric circles) and the electron population of each energy level represented
      by a number preceding the electron symbol.
3. Diagrams for representing forces acting between subatomic particles

TESTS, DRILLS, AND TABLES

Final Examination

(Student is to have periodic table available.)

I. 1. Name the three fundamental particles of which atoms are composed (2*).
      What is the charge of each of these particles (2)?

   Ans.   proton, +1
   electron, −1
   neutron, no charge (neutral)

   2. Draw a diagram of an atom with an atomic number of twelve, showing the
      correct number of electrons in each energy level (3). Label the energy levels
      of the atom you have drawn (1).

---

* The numbers following each question indicate weighting used in scoring. See page 239.

Ans.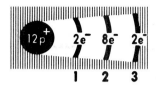

3. Phosphorus has an atomic number of 15. How many electrons does a phosphorus atom have in energy level 2 (4)?

   Ans.   *eight*

4. What is an element (4)?

   Ans.   *An element is a substance composed of atoms all of the same atomic number.*

5. What is meant by the term "stable structure" (4)?

   Ans.   *A stable structure is one that cannot be changed easily, that is, one in which an atom has 8 electrons in its outermost energy level.*

II. 1. What are two properties of the element argon (at. no. 18)? Use your periodic table (4).

   Ans.   *colorless, gaseous, or inert*

2. A certain element has the electron structure represented below. In what period does the element belong (3)?

Energy level	1	2	3	4
Number of electrons	2	8	18	5

   Ans.   *4*

3. Complete this chart (4). (See your periodic table.)

Name	Symbol	Atomic No.	Period	Group
		20		
Phosphorus			3	
	He			Inert Gas

   Ans.

Name	Symbol	At. No.	Period	Group
Calcium	Ca	20	4	IIA
Phosphorus	P	15	3	VA
Helium	He	2	1	Inert Gas

4. Draw diagrams to represent the electron structure of each of the following atoms: Zn (at. no. 30), Rb (at. no. 37), and Sc (at. no. 21) (9).

Ans.

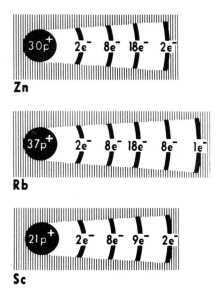

[This is the preface to the *Chemistry 1* program as it appears in the student's workbook. The selection from the program follows this preface.]

No matter where one begins the study of chemistry, he must come sooner or later to a study of the periodic table. Enunciated in 1869 by the Russian chemist Mendeleev, the *Periodic Table of the Elements* is surely one of the great summaries in all science. It consists of an arrangement of elements in the order of increasing atomic numbers, into rows and columns relating elements which have similar physical and chemical properties. This program is designed to give the student an understanding of the periodic table through a study of atomic structure and some aspects of bonding.

Chemistry is an experimental science, subject to continual additions and revisions. These changes are generally in the direction of greater exactness, better integration, and wider range. Keeping this fact in mind has led to the design of a program which should serve the student well in the face of further study and new discoveries.

Basic Systems, Inc.

New York

CHEMISTRY I Atomic structure and bonding

**BEGIN
HERE**

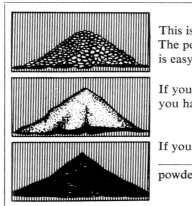

This is a pile of pebbles. The pebbles are large, so it is easy to see them.

If you make them smaller you have sand.

If you make them still _____ you have powder.

 1

11

Is it possible to see an electron? Why?

12

---

one

22

Complete the following statement. An atom has a center called the _____. The _____ travel about the _____ at various distances called _____ ergy levels.

23

smaller

➡

1

Why is it difficult to see powder particles?

➡

2

No, it is too small.
Since we cannot see an
atom we certainly could
not see an electron,
which is part of an
atom.

12

Electrons move about the _____ in complicated ways and paths we do not completely know
and understand.

13

---

nucleus
electrons
nucleus
energy

23

The electrons travel about the nucleus at various distances called _____ levels.

24

They are too small to
be seen easily.

2

Each powder particle is made up of millions of even
smaller particles, called atoms. Why can't you see an
atom?

3

nucleus

13

Do electrons travel around the nucleus in neat circles?

14

energy

24

The atom shown below has three _____.

25

It is too small.

3

A chair, a book, and a piece of fruit are all made of atoms. As you might guess, everything is made of _____.

4

no

14

In the diagram, the path of an electron about the nucleus is shown by a _____. Does this mean that we think the path is exactly this shape?

15

energy levels

25

Energy levels are numbered. Energy level 1 is closest to the nucleus. Number the next two energy levels in the diagram below. (There isn't room to show the complete circles for the energy levels.)

1 2

2e⁻ 8e⁻ 8e⁻ 1e⁻

26

atoms

4

Below are rough diagrams of atoms. The center of the atom is called the nucleus. Draw an x on the nucleus of each atom.

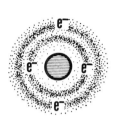

5

---

circle

no

15

This atom has _____ electrons.

(how many)

16

26

In the diagram below, the first energy level has 2 electrons in it, as shown by the symbol of $2e^-$. Using the electron symbol and a number, show that there are eight electrons in the second energy level.

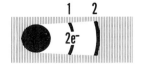

27

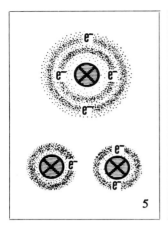

5

The nucleus is the center of the _____.

6

three

16

The particles that travel about the nucleus are called

_____.

17

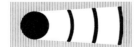

27

Show that there are 2 electrons in the first energy level, 8 in the second, and 4 in the third. Number the energy levels.

28

atom

6

Draw in the nucleus of this atom and label it.

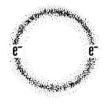

7

electrons

17

Label the parts of this atom.

18

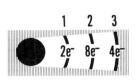

28

The farther away an electron is from the nucleus, the more energy it has. Which electron would have more energy, one in energy level 1, or one in energy level 2?

29

nucleus

e⁻   e⁻

7

The _____ is the center of the atom.

8

---

electrons

e⁻

e⁻   e⁻

nucleus

18

Where do electrons travel?

19

---

one in energy level 2

29

The greater the distance at which an electron travels about the nucleus, the _____ is its energy.
(greater/lesser)

30

nucleus

8

The plural of nucleus is *nuclei*. If one atom has one nucleus, then two atoms have two _____.

9

about the nucleus

19

Electrons travel about the nucleus at different distances. Which of the two electrons, *a* or *b,* is traveling at the shorter distance from the nucleus?

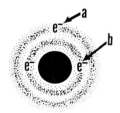

20

greater

30

Which of the three energy levels, 1, 2, or 3, has the electrons with the least energy?

31

nuclei

9

Write the word that means more than one nucleus.

10

b

20

The different distances at which electrons travel about the nucleus are called *energy levels*. How many energy levels are shown in the diagram below?

21

1

31

The name for the distances at which electrons travel about the nucleus is _____.

32

nuclei

10

Electrons are particles that move about the nucleus. The symbol for an electron is e^-. Draw two electrons around this nucleus.

To page 243 ➤

11

---

two

21

How many energy levels are shown below?

e^-

22

---

energy level

32

Draw two electrons moving about the nucleus of an atom. Use the symbol you have learned for the electron and put both electrons in the same energy level.

33

QUESTIONS

1. How can a consumer determine what this program teaches and how well it teaches it?

2. Analyze part of the program for blackout ratio. (You might try frames 24–33, or make your own selection of ten frames or so.) Is the material well programmed?

3. Look at frame 14 once again. Then try blacking out frame 13. Now examine frame 14 and explain why someone might have trouble responding to it.

4. Some people think of programmed texts exclusively in terms of writing a word in a blank. Programs are not so limited. What different forms of responses are called for in this program?

5. Examine frames 6 and 8. They are identical except for the position of the blank. Explain the purpose of this.

6. Frames 29, 30, and 31 teach this rule: Electrons traveling in the farthest energy levels have the most energy. What scientific concepts should a student know before being taught this rule? Are these concepts taught in this program before the rule is taught?

7. Frames 20–25 teach the concept of energy level. Could a college student unfamiliar with chemistry answer frame 25 *without* reading frames 20–24? Could such a student answer frame 25 after working frames 20–24? What does this suggest about the construction of this chemistry program?

8. Describe the progression in complexity of response to the concept "energy level" required in frames 20–25. (What does the student do in each frame and what cues that response?)

9. Teaching a concept or abstraction is not simply a matter of getting the student to parrot a definition. Frames 11–19 teach the concept of electrons. Describe the various kinds of responses a student makes in those frames.

10. Following are two revisions of frames 1–5 of this chemistry program. In its own way, each revision is inferior to the original program. Look at each carefully and compare it to the original five frames. Then explain why both chemistry 1A and chemistry 1B are worse than the original program.

CHEMISTRY 1A

frame A1.

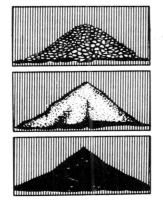

This is a pile of pebbles. The _____ are large, so it is easy to see them.

If you made them *smaller,* you have sand. If you make them still _____, you have powder.

(pebbles, smaller)

frame A2. It is difficult to see an individual powder particle because it is so

_____

(small, or tiny, little, etc.)

frame A3. Each powder particle is made up of millions of even s_____ particles called atoms. Atoms are very small.

(smaller)

frame A4. A chair, a book, and a piece of fruit are all made of *atoms*. As you might guess, everything is made of _____.

(atoms)

frame A5. Below are rough diagrams of atoms. The center of the _____ is called the nucleus.

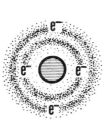

(atom)

CHEMISTRY 1B

frame B1.

This is a pile of pebbles. The pebbles are _____, so it is easy to see them.

If you make them _____, you have sand.

If you make them still _____ you have powder.

(large, smaller, smaller)

frame B2.   Why is it difficult to see powder particles?

(They are too small to be seen easily.)

frame B3.   Each powder particle is made up of millions of even smaller particles, which you cannot see with the naked eye. These small particles are called _____.

(atoms)

frame B4.   A chair, a book, and a piece of fruit are all made of atoms. As you might guess, _____ is made of atoms.

(everything)

frame B5.   Below are rough diagrams of atoms. The _____ of each atom is called the nucleus. Draw an x on the nucleus of each atom.

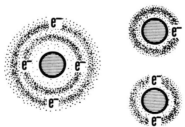

11. Frames 34–38 of the original chemistry program introduce the concept of protons. Following are the objectives for the introduction of this concept:

   a) Given a verbal description of a proton and a diagram with the symbols of protons marked on it, the student will identify the protons in the diagram.

   b) As a result of this diagram identification, the student will be able to verbalize that the nucleus is where protons are found.

   c) The student can then place the symbols for protons in the appropriate place in the nucleus of an unlabeled diagram.

   d) Given a diagram with proton symbols, but no verbal description of protons, the student can label the protons. To assure that proton is spelled correctly the word should appear in the text, however.

e) Finally, the student produces the word proton given only a verbal definition.

Assume you have received the following five frames as a first draft of the section teaching this concept. All the information you need to teach about protons is presented in these frames. Look the frames over in the light of the above objectives. Rewrite frames when necessary in order to achieve those objectives.

FIRST DRAFT: PROTONS

frame 34. The nucleus of this atom contains two particles called *protons*. There are two _____ in the nucleus of this atom.

frame 35. P ___ ___ ___ ___ ___ ___ are found in the nucleus of an atom.

frame 36. We use the symbol p+ to represent one proton, just as the symbol e— represents one electron. How many protons are in this atom?

frame 37. Complete the labeling of this diagram as to nucleus, protons, energy levels and electrons:

frame 38. P_____ are particles found in the nucleus of an atom.

12. The Teacher's Manual states that each stage of revision requires a fresh group of subjects. Why wouldn't it be desirable to test the revised version using the subjects whose past performance was the basis for the revision?

UNIT

21

The Wild Child of Aveyron

Content

Solomon, C. "An Adaptation and Partial Translation of Itard's Report on the Wild Child of Aveyron."

   This unit presents a factual account written in the early 1800s by Itard describing his attempts to educate a feral child found in the woods in Aveyron, France. The account affords the student the opportunity to apply principles of programing to Itard's behavioral analysis of teaching in a context far removed from the standard conception of programed instruction.

Objectives

Students identify behavior principles manifested in Itard's procedures. The principles include use of reinforcement or punishment, gradual progression, Itard's identification of the need for discrimination training and of the contingencies controlling the child's responses, and his task analyses.

Instructions

1. Read the question—in this unit, it *precedes* the reading.
2. Approach the selection as light pleasure reading. As you read, note on a separate sheet of paper the location of incidents illustrating the various principles, together with any comments you may have on these incidents.
3. Compare your list with ours, then discuss your work in this unit with the instructor.

QUESTIONS

1. In the course of your reading, look for incidents illustrating the following:

   a) Itard determining what things or activities could be used as reinforcers or punishers;
   b) identifying a need for discrimination training;
   c) identifying a need for gradual progression or shaping, and examples of Itard's use of gradual progression in his teaching procedures;
   d) Itard's task analysis, including examples of both good and poor analyses;
   e) establishing an abstraction;
   f) Itard identifying contingencies for responding, both appropriate and inappropriate.

   Note on a separate sheet the line number of your chosen incidents, and include any comments or criticisms you may have of the incident.

An Adaptation and Partial Translation of Itard's Report on the Wild Child of Aveyron

Carol Solomon

INTRODUCTION

In the fall of 1799, a boy about eleven or twelve years old was captured near the woods of Aveyron, France. He had been seen in the vicinity for several years prior to his capture. Apparently abandoned at a very young age, he had survived on his own in the forest for at least four or five years. It was hoped
5   that an examination of this feral child might throw some light on man's "essential" nature, a topic of great interest in an age influenced by Rousseau. The child was therefore sent to Paris to be examined by a noted doctor of the day, Citizen Pinel. A young doctor, Jean Marc Gaspard Itard, was also in Paris at this time and saw the child. Itard describes the boy Pinel examined:

10   ... his senses had fallen into such a state of inertia ... that he was inferior even to some of our domestic animals. His unstable, expressionless eyes wandered vaguely from object to object, ... and he could not distinguish between objects and mere pictures of objects. His ears were insensible to both the loudest noises and the most moving music, and he was completely mute, uttering only a single guttural
15   sound. He was indifferent both to the odor of perfume and to the rank stench of his own excrement. ...

   As for his intellect, the child was incapable of attending to anything except the objects of his immediate needs, and therefore had developed none of the attributes which require attention, such as memory, judgment, and the ability to imitate
20   others. Even when attempting to satisfy his immediate needs, he was unable to open a door or to climb on a chair to reach food being held high above his head. ...

   His emotions would change rapidly from the deepest apathy to the wildest laughter without apparent motive. He was insensible to any kind of moral influence. His

25

only pleasures were the taste of certain foods; his intelligence appeared to be nothing more than a few incoherent "ideas" related to his own needs; his whole existence was at the level of an animal.

Based on these observations, Pinel supposed the boy to be a congenital idiot and recommended confining him to an institution. Fortunately for the child, Itard disagreed with Pinel's diagnosis and was able to convince the au-

30 thorities to place the treatment and education of the wild child entirely in his care. Itard believed, first of all, that society had some responsibility to this creature whom it had forcibly removed from a free and innocent life, and he did not consider that responsibility fulfilled by sending the boy to die of boredom in an asylum. Secondly, Itard had some hope that the child was teachable

35 because he had survived those years alone and indeed had learned enough to satisfy his immediate needs in a hostile environment. The fact that his forest environment had not required him to develop finer sensibilities did not mean that he was by nature incapable of such development.

With this in mind, Itard planned the boy's educational program, always

40 attempting to conceive of the child not as an adolescent, but as a ten- or twelve-month-old infant. Itard has left a detailed record of his work with this child, whom he named Victor, in a report titled *De l'éducation d'un homme sauvage, ou des premiers développemens* [sic] *physiques et moraux du jeune sauvage de l'Aveyron* (Itard, 1801). Itard organized Victor's education under the follow-

45 ing five goals. He wanted the child to:

1. develop a broader range of physical and emotional feelings;
2. become more attached to life in human society;
3. develop a need for social contact that went beyond using others to fulfill his physical wants;

50 4. learn to speak;
5. develop his intellectual capacities.

EDUCATION OF THE WILD CHILD

Attachment to Human Society

In order to accomplish the second goal, having the child form an attachment to his new life in human society, Itard placed Victor in the care of Mme. Guérin, who treated him with great kindness. Itard surmised that the child's life in the

55 wild had consisted of four activities: eating, sleeping, roaming outdoors, and doing nothing. At any rate, these were the only activities the boy seemed to enjoy, so Itard proposed to associate them with Victor's new life. Accordingly, at the beginning of the child's training, Itard and Mme. Guérin patiently accepted Victor's indolence, regularly put him to bed early, continually supplied

60 him with his favorite foods, and accompanied him on frequent lengthy outdoor walks.

Itard noticed that the child delighted in snowfalls, rainstorms and other sudden weather changes, as well as in full moonlight. Victor could also amuse himself quietly for hours, by tossing bits of debris into a pond. These pleasures Itard continued to encourage and to associate with the child's new life. On the other hand, Itard gradually decreased the time allotted for activities related to eating, sleeping, and roaming outdoors, because he believed these activities took time away from the development of the boy's higher mental faculties. Itard considered his first goal achieved when Victor appeared to be happier in his new life even though he walked less far and less frequently, ate less often, and spent less time in bed.

Development of Physical and Emotional Feelings

Itard's first goal involved developing a range of feelings in the child. He had noticed that, in Victor's early months in civilization, the boy did not attend to the sound of pistol shots fired behind his back. Yet Victor was not deaf, since he would quickly turn around at the sound of a walnut being cracked. According to Itard, other signs of the boy's undeveloped sensibilities included the fact that he had never wept despite his early mistreatment in the institution, he was able to remove hot potatoes from the fire without haste or apparent injury, and snuff placed in his nose did not cause him to sneeze.

Itard believed that he had to train Victor's senses to distinguish among these various stimulants before he could begin to train the intellectual faculty of attention. He began by surrounding the child with physical warmth: warm house, warm clothes, warm baths, warm foods. Soon he noticed that the boy became sensitive to cold; Victor would test the temperature of his bath water and would refuse to enter if it were too cool. And while he had previously scorned clothing, he would now dress himself if left in a cold room. From these results Itard concluded that the program of applied "warmth" improved the child's senses of taste and touch, but not his senses of hearing and smell.

In addition to sensual stimulation, Itard attempted to develop and extend Victor's range of emotions. The two emotions the boy expressed at this point were joy and anger. Itard would only rarely provoke him deliberately to anger. On the other hand, he would frequently attempt to amuse and excite the child. The boy was delighted with such things as the use of a mirror to reflect sunlight, a small boat floating in his bathwater, and the slow dripping of water into his bath. All of these things Itard supplied him with frequently to encourage the expression of joy.

Developing a Need for Social Contact

The third goal was to expand Victor's intellect by increasing his social contacts, thus helping him to develop new needs. Itard's own description of his progress toward this goal follows.

If this child's progress toward civilization and my success in developing his intellect have been so slow and difficult to date, I must attribute this to the many

obstacles I have encountered in attempting to achieve this goal. I have shown him all sorts of games and toys. Many times I have spent whole hours together trying to teach him to play with them, yet I am forced to admit that these objects are still
105   far from giving him pleasure. Indeed, they seem to irritate him so much that he hides or destroys them as soon as he can. Once he hid our game of nine-pins in a nightstand, and when he was alone in his room he even had the courage to throw them in the fireplace. We found him happily warming himself by the blaze!

Nevertheless, I occasionally succeeded by devising some games revolving around
110   his favorite foods. One such game, which I often played with him at the end of our dinners in the city, involved chestnuts. I placed several small silver cups upside down and in an asymmetrical arrangement before him. Under one of the cups I placed a chestnut. Now sure that I had his attention, I would lift one cup after the other, all except the cup which hid the chestnut. After having shown him which cups
115   hid nothing, I made signs to him to search for himself. The first cup he would search was precisely the one which hid the small reward for his attention.

At this point the game required but a feeble effort of memory. But slowly I made it more complicated. Thus, after having hidden another chestnut in a similar manner under a cup, I would move the cups about on the table slowly so that his eyes
120   could follow the movements of the cup which hid the precious treasure. Then I hid chestnuts under three of the silver cups, and even though his attention was divided among three objects, he was able to follow their respective movements and always selected the correct cups.

But I had still not attained my goal. His attention to this game was merely the
125   result of his gluttony. To render it less animal-like, I removed the chestnuts and all foods from the game. I would only hide small inedible objects under the silver cups. The result was satisfactory; the exercise became a simple game played for amusement, and was not without certain advantages in promoting the child's attention and judgment.

130   I have found it impossible to interest him in other games designed for children of his age, excepting games like the one just described. I am certain that, had I been able to interest him in such games, I could have used them with great success in his education. My certainty in this matter is based on observations of the powerful influence of children's games on an infant's developing mind, as well as
135   the influence I have noted of the pleasures of sweets and other edibles on a child.

I tried everything I could to awaken in this child a taste for such sweets, offering him the cakes that all other children find irresistible. I hoped to be able to use these sweets as a new means of reward, punishment, encouragement and instruction. But his aversion to all sweets and delicate foods was insurmountable. I then
140   thought I should try highly spiced foods, as his taste had probably been blunted by eating very coarse foods in the forest. I succeeded no better, however. When he was most hungry and thirsty I offered him strong liquors and highly spiced foods in vain.

I finally despaired of developing his taste for different foods and decided to make
145   the most of the few foods he liked. I attempted to accompany them with all sorts of extra attention designed to increase his pleasure in them. For this reason I have often taken him to dine with me in the city. On those days I would see that all of his favorite dishes were served. The first time this occurred, he went into such a paroxysm of joy as to appear almost in a frenzy. Doubtless he thought he wouldn't
150   eat as well later, because he left with a stolen plate of lentils.

I congratulated myself on this occasion. I had just discovered a pleasure for him; I had only to repeat it several times and it would become a necessity. I did this, and even more. I preceded these excursions with certain preparations which he could easily notice. I would enter his room about four o'clock, my hat on my
155 head and his shirt in my hand. Soon these actions became a signal for him that we were about to leave. As soon as I appeared, I was understood; he dressed quickly and followed me happily.

I do not offer this as proof of superior intelligence since one could easily point out that even a dog would do as much. But even in admitting such a parallel, we
160 are recognizing a great improvement. Those who saw the wild child of Aveyron upon his arrival in Paris knew him to be much less discerning than a dog.

It was impossible for us to walk when we went out for dinner. I would either have had to run full speed alongside of him or to use a great deal of punishment to keep him walking quietly alongside of me. Therefore, we went by carriage.
165 This new pleasure also served to endear these excursions to him. Before long these feast days became real necessities for him. When too long a time would pass between such excursions he would become sad, restless, and nervous.

How much happier he was when we would take our excursions in the country-side. Not long ago I took him to the countryhouse of Citizen Lachabeaussière in
170 Montmorency Valley. His great joy at the sight of the hills and woods of this de-lightful valley was both curious and touching. He spent two days at this country house where, under the influence of these hills and woods, he appeared more wild and impatient than ever. In this midst of the kindest attention and care he would do nothing but attempt to escape. This idea controlled him completely. Even when
175 he sat down to eat, he would continually rise from the table to run to the windows. If they were open he would escape to the park, and if they were closed he would gaze outdoors toward the countryside to which he was so irresistibly drawn by his still-recent habits, and perhaps even by the memory of a free, happier life. So I resolved never to tempt him so greatly again. But in order not to sever him entirely
180 from the beloved countryside, we continued to take him for walks in some neigh-boring gardens. These well-tended, carefully manicured gardens had little in com-mon with the wild countrysides of nature. . . .

Development of Speech

Itard's fourth goal was teaching this child to speak. Itard reasoned that the boy had heard very few sounds while in the forest and had exercised his ears only
185 for self-preservation. Thus, the child's ears were not attuned to the subtle vari-ations in sounds which comprise a human language, and he appeared deaf. Yet Itard noted that the quietest cracking of a walnut, the slightest turn of the key in the child's door, were heard immediately. Itard hoped that as Victor grew more accustomed to human language, his ability to hear it would improve. He
190 also expected that the ability to hear the language and the attempt to imitate people speaking would lead to language production.

At first Itard merely observed the boy closely to discover what sounds he did hear. Although, as mentioned before, Victor did not seem to notice the sound of a pistol, Itard noted that the child had learned to distinguish the
195 guttural cry of the deaf and dumb children who also lived in the institution.

He would quickly leave the room if he heard this sound, which signaled their approach. Itard also noted that Victor would invariably turn his head toward any speaker who pronounced the syllable "oh." Itard then selected the name *Victor,* which in the French pronunciation ends with the vowel sound *o,* so

200   that Victor would look toward any person who called his name.

Having noticed some slight progress in Victor's hearing, Itard was disappointed that the boy still did not attempt to speak. Further training was obviously necessary. Reasoning that the sound first heard might be the sound first pronounced, Itard also hoped to make use of a coincidence—the vowel sound

205   *o* is also the French word for water, *eau.* Thus, when Victor was thirsty, Itard would hold out a glass of water, pronouncing the word *eau.* Then another person would pronounce *eau* and Itard would give this person the glass of water. Rather than imitate the speaker, however, Victor merely became wildly frantic as his need for water was ignored. Reduced to this state he was obviously un-

210   able to speak. Itard did not torment the child further and instead gave him the water.

He then carried out the same process more successfully with a glass of milk, *lait* (pronounced "lay"). On the fourth day of this instruction Victor pronounced the word *lait*—his first articulate sound. Itard was greatly pleased;

215   yet he noted that Victor only pronounced the word when he actually saw the milk. No matter how much Victor wanted the milk, he only said *lait* when he received milk; he did not use the word to express his desire for milk. Believing this to be a misuse of language, Itard was greatly disappointed. Because Victor used the word only as a sign of possession, Itard attached no further impor-

220   tance to his pronunciation of *lait.* He decided instead to watch and wait while attempting to develop some other method of teaching Victor to speak. (Note: you may wish to review the segment of Skinner's article in Unit 5 which deals briefly with language development in normal children.)

Development of Intellectual Capacities

Itard's fifth goal was to force Victor to use his intelligence to obtain certain

225   of his physical needs and then to have him learn to apply this developing intelligence to other tasks. Itard's own description follows.

I will not describe here in detail the methods used to force the savage of Aveyron to exercise his mind to satisfy his physical needs. It is sufficient to say that we simply placed ever larger, ever new obstacles between him and the objects which

230   he needed. He could only surmount these obstacles by exercising his intellect, his memory, his judgment and all his senses. And so all the faculties useful to his instruction were developed. I had only to find the simplest way to use them well.

I could hardly count on his sense of hearing for his instruction, as the young savage appeared very like a deaf-mute in this respect. So I attempted to teach him

235   using methods developed for the deaf-and-dumb by Citizen Sicard. I began by drawing on a blackboard the outlines of simple objects with obvious shapes: a key, scissors and a hammer. Whenever I knew I was being watched, I would repeatedly

place each of these objects on its outline. And when I felt sure that I had made him understand the meaning of this relationship, I asked him to bring each thing to
240   me in turn by pointing to its drawing. This got no results. I asked many times, and was always unsuccessful. Either he obstinately refused to bring me anything or he brought me all three objects at once. I'm sure that this was simply a result of his laziness as he would not make three trips when he could accomplish all in one.

    I then decided to find a method which would require him to attend to each object.
245   I had noticed, over the past few months, that he had a very decided taste for setting things in order. He would even get out of bed to put a piece of furniture or utensil back in place had it been accidentally moved. He was even more particular about places for things which hung on the walls. . . . I only needed to find a like arrangement for the objects I wanted him to pay attention to.

250   I suspended each object by a nail under its outline and left them there for some time. When I finally removed them and gave them to Victor, they were quickly replaced in order. I did this over and over again, and always with successful results. I could not yet attribute these results to his discrimination, however. The task could simply be done by memory. To test this, I changed the order of the drawings, and,
255   indeed, Victor replaced the objects in their old order. In fact, nothing was so simple for him as memorizing a new order, and nothing so difficult as reasoning it out. He memorized each new arrangement. . . .

    Finally I managed to fatigue his memory by increasing the number of objects and drawings, and frequently rearranging them. At last he was unable to memorize each
260   new arrangement of the several objects; he was forced to compare each object to its drawing. I had no doubt that he was making this comparison as I watched young Victor look over the objects in turn, select one, and search for the drawing to which it belonged. Even so, I attempted to prove this by inverting the drawings. Victor correctly replaced the objects, inverting them also.

265   My hopes were raised by this success. I even believed that all difficulties had been conquered. Yet at this point a new, insurmountable problem arose which forced me to renounce this teaching method. In instructing deaf-and-dumb children, ordinarily this first discrimination is followed by a second, more difficult one. Having learned the relationship of an object and its drawing, the name of the object is
270   written on the drawing, and finally the drawing is erased, leaving only the letters of the name. The deaf-mute views this as a change in drawing; the letters continue to be the sign of the object. This was not the case with Victor. In spite of frequent repetitions and a prolonged exposure to the object hanging under its name, he could not learn this new task. . . .

275   Another method more fitted to the still-undeveloped senses of our savage had to be found; a method in which each problem surmounted prepared the child to surmount yet a more difficult problem. In this spirit, I developed this new plan.

    I pasted three pieces of paper, each obviously distinct in shape and color, on a two-foot square board. The paper cut-outs were a red circle, a blue triangle and a
280   black square. Three pieces of cardboard identical in color and shape were also made. Each was hung over its pasted cut-out "match" by a nail, and left there for several days. I then removed the cardboard forms and gave them to Victor, and he easily replaced them. I assured myself that these results were achieved by a true comparison by inverting the board and thus changing the order of the figures.

285   After a few days, I substituted a new board. On this new board I pasted cut-

outs of those three figures, only now all the same color. When using the first board
my pupil could solve this problem by using both shape and color; using this second
board he had only one guide—shape. Very shortly afterward, I gave him a third
board in which the three cut-outs had identical shapes but different colors. I got the
290   same results on all tests, not counting mistakes due to inattention. The ease with
which he solved these problems led me to present others to him. I added to and
changed these last two boards. To the shape-board I added less obviously different
figures, like a parallelogram next to the square. To the color-board I added a grey-
blue figure next to the sky-blue one. Here he made some errors and showed some
295   hesitancy, but these difficulties disappeared with a few days' work.

  These results encouraged me to attempt new, ever more difficult variations. . . .
For the colored cut-out shapes pasted on the board, I substituted line drawings of
the shapes on which I merely indicated the colors with irregularly torn bits of
colored paper. These new problems were but a game to this child—this was the
300   result I had hoped for in devising this system of obvious comparisons. The time had
come to replace it by another more advanced problem which, if given earlier,
would have presented insurmountable difficulties. . . .

  I had the twenty-four letters of the alphabet printed in capitals, each letter on one
two-inch square piece of cardboard. I had an equal number of square impressions
305   of that size cut in a board, so that each square impression would hold one cardboard letter in place without paste, allowing the letters to be easily removed and
rearranged as necessary. Finally, I had metal letters of the same size made. My
student was to compare the metal letters to the cardboard ones which were in
place on the board, and then was to place each metal letter in the square which
310   held its matching cardboard letter.

  Mme. Guérin tried this with Victor first, during my absence. When I returned I
was quite surprised to learn from her that Victor had successfully discriminated all
the letters and arranged them correctly. I had him do it again immediately, and
again he did it correctly. Amazed by this sudden success, I was yet at a loss to un-
315   derstand how he did it. It was only several days later that his method became clear
to me. In order to make his work easier, he had himself devised a little "trick"
which he used to solve this problem without straining his faculties of memory or
judgment. As soon as the board was placed in his hands, he himself would remove
the metal letters which were in place over the cardboard cut-outs. In removing the
320   metal letters, he would be careful to keep them in order in his hand, so that when
all were removed, the last letter of the arrangement would be on top of the pile in
his hand. He would then begin "matching" with this top letter, always starting at
the end of the board and moving now from right to left. Nor was this his only
trick: he was able to further perfect this method. Frequently the pile of letters in
325   his hand would collapse and fall in disorder on the floor. He would have to replace
them by the tedious process of true matching. His solution was simple. The twenty-
four letters were arranged on the board in four rows of six letters each. He would
simply remove and replace one short row at a time!

  I do not know if his reasoning was as I have reconstructed it, but he executed
330   the problem exactly as I have described. It was indeed a solution—by-rote, but his
invention of this rote method may have been as great a credit to his intelligence as a
careful classification would have been a credit to his powers of discrimination. It
was not difficult to get him to do this problem correctly, simply by giving him the

metal letters all out of order before giving him the board. Finally, despite frequent
335 rearrangements of the letters, despite difficult placements of the *G* beside the *C* and
the *E* next to the *F,* and so on, his discrimination was perfect.

In teaching Victor the alphabet I hoped to prepare him to use the letters to express his needs as he could not by speech. But I was so far from expecting this kind
of use to occur in the near future that it was curiosity rather than hope of success
340 which prompted my next experiment.

One lunchtime while he was impatiently waiting for his daily glass of milk, I took
out his board on which I had previously placed the four letters *L A I T.** Mme.
Guérin approached me, looked at the letters and gave me a full glass of milk, as we
had planned. I pretended that I would keep this glass and drink it myself. A moment
345 later I approached Victor and gave him the four letters which I lifted from the
board. I pointed to these letters with one hand, while in the other I held the pitcher
of milk. The letters were immediately replaced on the board, but they were inverted
to spell *TIAL* instead of *LAIT.* I indicated the corrections that Victor should make
by pointing at each letter and then pointing to where it ought to be placed. As soon
350 as he made these corrections I gave him the milk.

It is hard to believe, but five or six similar lessons were apparently enough not
only to teach him to methodically arrange these four letters for the word milk, but
also to teach him that a relationship existed between this letter-game and one of his
own needs. At least, after what happened about a week later I dared to hope that he
355 at last understood the relationship between the word and the thing itself. At that time
we were preparing as usual to take him for the evening to the observatory. We saw
Victor, on his own initiative, take the four letters and put them in his pocket. As
soon as we arrived at Citizen Lemeri's, where Victor daily has a glass of milk, he
took the letters out of his pocket and laid them on the table to spell the word
360 *L A I T.*

In planning this book, I had originally intended it to end with a summary of all
the individual achievements previously described under each separate goal. I altered
this plan because I believe that the combination of these separate achievements does
not equal this final accomplishment. I am describing it simply and exactly, without
365 additional speculation, so that it can stand as a striking sign of the stage at which
we have arrived, and as a guaranty of future success. In the meantime, all of my observations and writings point to the conclusion that this child, known as the Savage
of Aveyron, is endowed with the full use of all of his senses, that he has shown evidence of the faculties of memory and attention; that he can discern, compare and
370 judge objects, and apply all of these faculties to his education. We must remember,
too, that all of these improvements have occurred in the short space of nine months
at the beginning of which the child was thought incapable of attending to anything.
So we must conclude at this point that his education is possible, perhaps even guaranteed, by this early success. . . .

ITARD'S SECOND REPORT

375 In 1806 Itard published a second report on Victor's progress. After five years
of careful teaching, Victor did not quite achieve as much as Itard had hoped,

---

* Lait is the French word for milk.

but he did continue to make progress. The bulk of this second report is devoted
to the child's progress in the use of language.

Despite Itard's continued efforts, Victor never learned to speak, but he did
380 learn to write. Itard analyzed writing as an imitative behavior, so he began to
teach it by having Victor imitate him as he lifted an arm, moved a leg, rose
from the table, etc. As Victor became adept at imitating these gross movements, Itard progressed to finer movements and finally to drawing a line on
the blackboard. Victor drew an identical parallel line. The actual writing les-
385 sons then began. Victor would first copy a word that Itard wrote, then he
would reproduce a word from memory, and finally he would ask for something by writing the word.

In order for Victor to reach this last stage of expressing his desires through
writing, Itard had to backtrack and rethink his methods of language teaching.
390 Despite the singular success of the $L\ A\ I\ T$ experiment, Itard noted that Victor
almost never used the metal letters to form a word until the actual object was
placed before him. He concluded that Victor still did not connect use of the
sign or word with the possibility of satisfying his needs. Patiently, he began
again.

395   This time Itard used cards with the names of small objects ("book,"
"knife," "key," etc.) written on them. First, he trained Victor to discriminate
these words, so that if Itard wrote one of the words on a blackboard, Victor
could select the matching card. Then Itard placed the objects on a shelf, each
beside its namecard. After Victor studied this arrangement, Itard reversed a
400 few cards and Victor replaced them. Then Itard removed all the cards, and
Victor again replaced them. Then Itard placed the cards at one end of the
room and the objects at the other, and asked Victor to bring him an object by
showing Victor its card. At first Victor had to keep his eye on the card as he
crossed the room or he would forget what was asked for, but finally a mere
405 glance at the card was sufficient for him to bring the correct object, even from
another room.

All of these exercises were carried out using the same group of objects.
At one point, Itard hid the book always used in these lessons and then asked
as usual for a book. Despite the fact that books of all sorts surrounded him,
410 Victor searched and searched for *the* book and finally gave up in confusion.
Itard quickly recognized that Victor had not forgotten or misread the card,
but that he had instead applied its meaning too strictly. For Victor the card
referred only to the particular book that had been used in the lessons.

Itard then gave Victor an armful of books including one nearly identical
415 to the original. Victor quickly selected this one and gave it back to Itard. Itard
proceeded to show Victor the similarities among various books. He also taught
Victor to generalize among the other objects used in these lessons by demonstrating their common uses. For example, Itard might use several knives in
cutting bread and then ask Victor for each knife using the same card.

420   Itard enlarged Victor's vocabulary carefully. The first words taught were

nouns referring to small, concrete objects that could easily be carried about in their lessons. He next taught Victor words like *tree* and *room,* whose referents were concrete, yet not easily pointed to in *toto.* Then he taught more abstract concepts including adjectives like *big* and *small.* Finally he introduced verbs.

425   After five years, Victor could communicate some of his needs through writing and could read the written words of others. Nevertheless, he never grew to a normal adulthood, despite Itard's inspired and patient teaching.

REFERENCES

Itard, Jean Marc Gaspard. *De l'Éducation d'un Homme Sauvage, ou des Premiers Développemens Physiques et Moraux du Jeune Sauvage de l'Aveyron.* Paris: Goujon fils, 1801.

UNIT

22

Concepts

Content

Mechner, F. "Science Education and Behavioral Technology." In R. Glaser, ed., *Teaching Machines and Programed Learning, II*. Washington, D.C.: National Education Association, 1965, pp. 441–508.

This unit presents the final section of the Mechner article in which he discusses the problems of concept formation and transfer of training, and illustrates his points with samples from several teaching programs.

Objectives

Students will explain Mechner's definition of concept formation and will closely analyze samples of teaching materials that establish various concepts. They will then select a concept and devise an instructional strategy. Students will also discuss the relationship of task analysis to transfer of training, and of a variety of examples to generalization. Finally, students will decide whether each of four tasks is best taught by backward chaining.

Instructions

1. Read the objectives, then read the article.
2. Answer the questions. Various questions will refer back to specified portions of the article.
3. Check your answers before seeing your instructor.

Science Education and Behavioral Technology
(Second Part)
Francis Mechner

IV. SCIENCE PROGRAMMING

So far, we have discussed the terminal populations and the terminal behavior specifications, or objectives, of science teaching.* This section will be devoted to the problems of establishing the specified terminal behavior in the student.

A. The Teaching of Concepts and Chains

It can safely be said that most of the behavior discussed in the previous section falls into the gross categories of concept formation and chaining, in the sense in which psychologists such as Hull (1920), Skinner (1938), Piaget (1929), Keller, and Schoenfeld (1950) understand the terms. In this section, therefore, we shall discuss the nature of concepts and chains, and how these are taught.

1. What Is a Concept?

To a psychologist, conceptual behavior involves generalizing within classes and discriminating between classes (Hull, 1920; Keller and Schoenfeld, 1950). We discriminate between things when we make different responses to different things. We generalize among things when we make the same response to different things. When we make the response "triangle" to any three-sided figure and the response "quadrilateral" to any four-sided figure, we are discriminating between triangles and quadrilaterals, and we are generalizing among triangles and among quadrilaterals. In general, when we make the same response to some members of a set and different responses to other members of the set, then we are both discriminating and generalizing among members of the set, and a psychologist would say that we have a "concept." When we make the response "triangle" to different kinds of three-sided figures, but not to other kinds of figures, we are said to "have the concept" of "triangle." When a child makes the response "horse" to small and large horses, to live horses and to horses in pictures, and to horses of different colors and breeds, then he is generalizing within the class of horses. But we cannot say that he has the concept of horse unless he *does not* make the response "horse" to other things, like dogs, cats, cows, and automobiles. In other words, he must not only generalize

F. Mechner, "Science Education and Behavioral Technology," in *Teaching Machines and Programmed Learning, II,* ed. R. Glaser (Washington, D.C.: National Education Association, 1965), pp. 441–508. Reprinted by permission of the Association for Educational Communication & Technology.

* Editors' note: See Unit 12.

within the class of horses, but he must also discriminate between the class of horses and other classes.

2. How Are Concepts Taught?

The basic procedure may be summarized by saying that it involves teaching the student to generalize within classes, and to discriminate between classes. The student must learn to make the same response to all members falling within a class, and to make different responses to members of different classes.

A psychologist teaching a child who does not yet know colors the concepts "red" and "blue" might proceed as follows: He might choose objects around the room, some red, some blue, and some of other colors. First, he might show the child a set of three objects, two of them red, and one not red. Each time, he would ask, "Which one is not red?" thereby asking the child to discriminate the different, non-red one. He would repeat this with blue objects. Once these discriminations are established, he might start showing the child pairs of colored objects, asking each time, "Which one is red?" or "Which one is blue?" Then, he would increase the number of non-red and non-blue objects in each set until only one of four or five objects is red or blue. In choosing the objects, he would be careful to include large ones and small ones, distant and near ones, coarse and smooth ones, dark and light ones, whole objects and parts of many-colored objects. This would prevent attributes other than redness and blueness from becoming associated with the responses "red" and "blue" through inadvertent selection.

With the properties of the objects varied, the child would learn to generalize among objects having in common no characteristics other than their color. Once the child says "red" only to red objects, and never to non-red objects, and says "blue" only to blue objects, he may be said to have acquired the concepts of redness and blueness. The method outlined above can, of course, be modified to include the simultaneous teaching of any number of color-names.

As a further illustration, we shall now apply this method of analysis to three medical concepts which are related to each other: the electrocardiographic patterns of ischemia, injury, and infarction. Note that we are not analyzing or attempting to teach the concepts of "ischemia," "injury," or "infarction." The concepts being analyzed are only the electrocardiographic patterns of ischemia, injury, and infarction as these are seen on Lead 1 of the electrocardiogram. It is assumed that the doctor for whom the instruction is intended already has the concepts of ischemia, injury, and infarction: He knows that the heart muscle tissue is said to be ischemic when it has a deficit of oxygenated blood, that it is said to be injured when this deficit has produced some damage which is still reversible, and that it is said to be infarcted when it is dead. These concepts are prerequisite, and are not being taught in the situation illustrated in Fig. 22.1.

Each of the three rectangles surrounds a set of tracings that are examples of one of the three types of patterns. When an individual can discriminate between

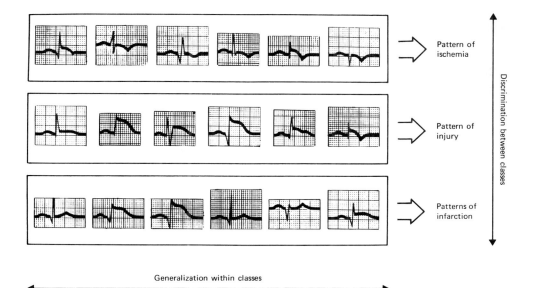

Fig. 22.1. Each of the three boxes surrounds a set of tracings that have something in common. The tracings in the top box all show the pattern of ischemia; the tracings in the center box all show the pattern of injury; and the tracings in the bottom box all show the pattern of infarction. The student has learned the three concepts when he has learned to generalize among the tracings within each box, and to discriminate between tracings in different boxes. To have a concept is to generalize within classes and to discriminate between classes.

tracings shown to him at random on the basis of whether they show the pattern of ischemia, injury, or infarction, and can generalize among patterns of ischemia, patterns of injury, and patterns of infarction, then we would say that he has those three concepts.

This method of concept analysis may be extended to any concept in science. Here are some additional examples: (1) Each tracing could be replaced with a disease syndrome, and the concepts could be, for example, hyperthyroidism and hypothyroidism. (2) Each tracing could be replaced with a description of a clinical case, complete with history, just the way a physician would see it. The concept would be the appropriate diagnosis. (3) Each tracing could be replaced with a set of chemical data and observations; the concepts could be "alcohol," "aldehyde," "ketone," and "organic acid."

3. What Is a Chain?

In spite of the large number of concepts in science that yield to this form of analysis, there is nevertheless another important category of knowledge which is not merely a matter of concept formation.

Here are examples of forms of knowledge that cannot be analyzed merely as concepts:

1. Figuring out the appropriate power rating of a resistor to put in a circuit.
2. Going through a sequential decision process in trouble shooting.
3. Dissecting a frog.
4. Doing a qualitative chemical analysis.
5. Explaining a procedure in a technical report.

These examples all have something in common: Each one involves a sequence of actions, not just a single discrimination or generalization. They all involve sequences of discriminations and generalizations. In short, they involve sequences of concepts. In the terminology of behavior theory, a form of behavior which involves a sequence of actions in which each action depends upon the outcome of the last action is called a chain. Some other examples of chains are:

1. Reciting a poem.
2. Tying a shoelace.
3. Solving a mathematics problem.
4. Writing a program for a computer.

Let us now examine in greater detail the thought process which the medical diagnostician must go through in arriving at the response "pattern of infarction" on the basis of one of the tracings in the oval. It turns out that this thought process, rapid though it may be for the experienced diagnostician, is really a brief "chain." The elements of this chain must be made explicit when diagnostic skill is being taught. The chain involved in this reasoning process is shown in Fig. 22.2.

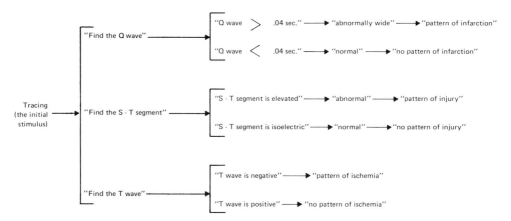

Fig. 22.2. *All phrases in quotes are responses. They are statements which the student makes silently, to himself, in reasoning his way to the correct diagnosis.*

This diagram makes explicit the thought process which the student must be taught when he learns to decide whether a Lead 1 tracing shows ischemia, injury, or infarction. It is not exactly the same diagram a behavior analyst would make in analyzing the decision process, but it does illustrate the general idea underlying this technique of analysis. The diagram makes explicit each response link in the reasoning chain. In the terminology of behavioral analysis, a phrase like "Find the T wave" becomes "Discriminate the T wave from other portions of the tracing." The phrase "Find the T wave" is the one the student would learn to think to himself as he goes through the diagnostic reasoning process.

Note that the first decision point, after the arrow leading away from the word "tracing," represents a so-called "and" junction. This means that all three paths leading away from that point must be followed in succession. The next decision point (after "Find the Q wave," "Find the S-T segment," etc.) is an "or" junction, in that the diagnostician makes a discrimination here according to what he sees, and continues along only one of the alternative paths. Figure 22.2 does not attempt to make the distinction between "and" and "or" junctions, although these are important in analyzing reasoning processes and behavioral chains. The reason for presenting this analysis is only to illustrate a technique for making explicit the detailed sequence of responses and decisions that the student must learn to make.

In constructing the analysis of the reasoning process or decision process, as in Fig. 22.2, the behavior analyst makes some decisions which will have an ultimate effect on the size of the steps in the first draft version of the instructional program. For example, had the behavior analyst had a lower opinion of his target population, or had he been writing for college students instead of doctors, he might have inserted an intermediate response after "Find the Q wave." The intermediate response might have been "Determine whether the Q wave is wider or narrower than one subdivision of the graph." This intermediate step would have an impact on the construction of Frame 3 in the program beginning on page 277, and would probably have increased the total length of the program by one or two frames.

In analyzing concepts, also, the behavior analyst makes decisions which take into account the sophistication and learning ability of his target population. For example, in constructing Fig. 22.1, the behavior analyst made a judgment concerning the level of this target population when he decided to present six examples each of patterns of ischemia, injury, and infarction. Had he been preparing the analysis for, say, nurses, he might have included eight or ten examples of each, or he might have taught the physiological aspects of the three concepts first. Usually, the estimates made by the behavior analyst at this stage in the development of an instructional program have to be corrected later on when the actual frames of the program are being tested on the target population. If the program proves too easy or too repetitive, examples are sometimes eliminated. The main point being made here is that the behavior analyst, prior to writing any frames of the instructional program, makes some initial guesses concerning the ability of the target population. These guesses function as first approximations, to be corrected and adjusted during the testing phase.

Once these behavioral analyses have been completed, the behavior analyst must decide in which order to teach the behavioral elements that have been identified. In the case of a concept, he must decide in which order to teach the discriminations and generalizations, and also how many of them to teach at one time. In the case of a chain, he must decide at which end of the chain to begin, in what order to teach the various links, and how many links to teach at one time. When the behavioral analysis consists of both chains and concepts, he must arrange these in the optimal teaching sequence.

Behavior theory is able to provide answers to most questions of this type. The answers are sometimes easy and obvious, on the basis of voluminous and directly relevant experimental evidence. For example, learning theory suggests strongly that the last links in a chain should be taught before the early links, that discriminations are best taught by random alternation of examples, and that related concepts should be taught concurrently. At other times, the answers are less obvious, and must be arrived at by judging the relative importance of different features of the teaching problem, or by extrapolating the results of experiments that are only indirectly relevant. In still other cases, behavior theory cannot provide any answers at all, even when all available experimental data are stretched to their limit. For example, learning theory provides few guidelines for deciding how many concepts to teach concurrently when there are too many (say, 26) for it to be possible to take them all at one time. In most cases of practical importance, however, behavior theory provides sufficient guidelines. A behavior analyst who knows the behavior literature well, and has experience in analyzing complex behavior, is usually able to make educated guesses that turn out to be right or almost right most of the time, and is rarely driven to the position of having to "flip a coin."

4. The Relationship of the Frames of a Program to the Behavioral Analysis

Let us now examine how the behavioral analysis presented in Figs. 22.1 and 22.2 for diagnosing the Lead 1 tracing is translated into a sequence of teaching frames.

QUESTIONS	ANSWERS

1 *The diagram below, taken from the Lead 1 tracing of a normal subject, shows the standard deflections of the electrocardiogram.*

Label the five deflections, using the conventional letters P, Q, R, S, and T:

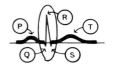

  Circle the QRS complex.
  The T wave is ☐ positive
  ☐ negative

positive

FRAME 1   The QRS complex is discriminated from other portions of the tracing.

The T wave is discriminated from other portions of the tracing.

The positivity of the T wave is discriminated from the possible negativity of the T wave.

2 *The Q, R, and S waves are defined as follows:*

The Q wave is the negative (downward) deflection which initiates the QRS complex.

The R wave is the positive (upward) deflection of the QRS complex.

The S wave is the negative deflection immediately following the R wave.

In each QRS complex below, label the Q, R, and S waves if they are present:

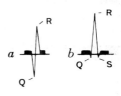

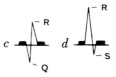

(example)   a   b   c   d

FRAME 2   The student generalizes among different types of Q waves, R waves, and S waves.

The student discriminates between Q waves, R waves, and S waves.

Thus, the concepts of the Q wave, the R wave, and the S wave are formed.

3   *A Q wave wider than one standard division, i.e.,*
longer than 0.04 seconds in duration, is considered
abnormal.

Under each diagram, indicate whether the Q wave is
normal or abnormal:

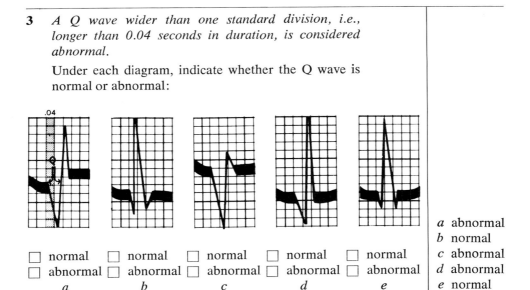

					a abnormal
					b normal
☐ normal	☐ normal	☐ normal	☐ normal	☐ normal	c abnormal
☐ abnormal	☐ abnormal	☐ abnormal	☐ abnormal	☐ abnormal	d abnormal
a	*b*	*c*	*d*	*e*	e normal

FRAME 3   Again, the student discriminates the Q wave from other portions of the
tracing, thus strengthening his concept of the Q wave.

The student discriminates between Q waves wider than .04 sec. and Q
waves narrower than .04 sec.

Two links of the chain are formed:

"Q wave wider than .04 sec." ———→ "abnormal"
"Q wave narrower than .04 sec." ———→ "normal"

4   *The S-T segment begins at the end of the QRS complex and ends at the beginning of the T wave. An
elevated S-T segment is abnormal.*

For each diagram below, indicate whether the S-T
segment is normal or abnormal:

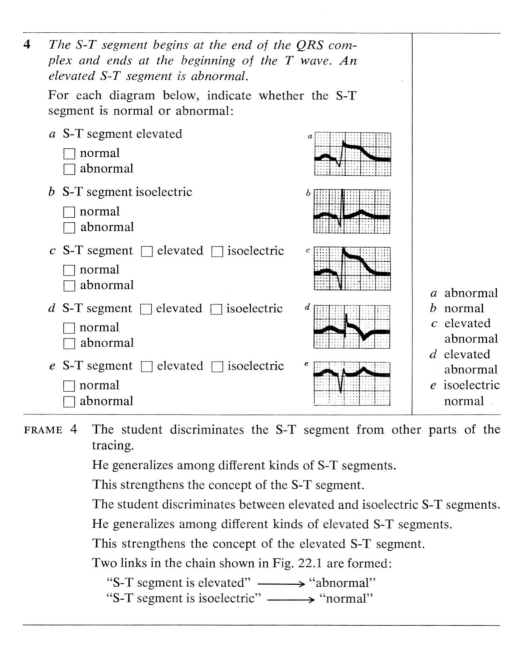

a S-T segment elevated

☐ normal
☐ abnormal

b S-T segment isoelectric

☐ normal
☐ abnormal

c S-T segment ☐ elevated ☐ isoelectric

☐ normal
☐ abnormal

d S-T segment ☐ elevated ☐ isoelectric

☐ normal
☐ abnormal

e S-T segment ☐ elevated ☐ isoelectric

☐ normal
☐ abnormal

a abnormal
b normal
c elevated
    abnormal
d elevated
    abnormal
e isoelectric
    normal

FRAME 4   The student discriminates the S-T segment from other parts of the
tracing.

He generalizes among different kinds of S-T segments.

This strengthens the concept of the S-T segment.

The student discriminates between elevated and isoelectric S-T segments.

He generalizes among different kinds of elevated S-T segments.

This strengthens the concept of the elevated S-T segment.

Two links in the chain shown in Fig. 22.1 are formed:

"S-T segment is elevated" ⟶ "abnormal"
"S-T segment is isoelectric" ⟶ "normal"

5 Referring to the diagrams in the panel below, check the correct box:

a. An elevated S-T segment suggests
☐ ischemia ☐ injury ☐ infarction.
b. A negative T wave suggests
☐ ischemia ☐ injury ☐ infarction.
c. An abnormally wide Q wave suggests
☐ ischemia ☐ injury ☐ infarction.

a injury
b ischemia
c infarction

These diagrams show the ECG changes which, in various combinations, may be observed in myocardial infarction.

Normal Pattern   Pattern of Ischemia   Pattern of Injury   Pattern of Infarction

FRAME 5 a. The student discriminates between an elevated S-T segment and the normal S-T segment.

The chain link:

"elevated S-T segment" ⟶ "injury"

is strengthened, this time with omission of the auxiliary mediating link:

"elevated S-T segment" ⟶ "abnormal"

b. The student discriminates between a negative and a normal T wave. The chain link:

"negative T wave" ⟶ "ischemia"

is strengthened.

c. The student discriminates between an abnormally wide Q wave and a normal Q wave.

The chain link:

"abnormally wide Q wave" ⟶ "infarction"

is strengthened, this time with omission of the auxiliary mediating link:

"abnormally wide Q wave" ⟶ "abnormal"

. . .

5. Applications of Behavioral Analysis to Other Problems in Science Teaching

Experience suggests that all diagnostic problems in medicine, trouble-shooting procedures in engineering, and problem-solving procedures in a variety of contexts are susceptible to this form of analysis. It is always possible to break the process down into a series of decisions. Suppose we are dealing with medical diagnosis. At each decision point the physician "asks a question." Asking a question can mean any of the following:

1. Requesting a laboratory test.
2. Asking the patient a verbal question.
3. Looking up an aspect of the patient's history.
4. Looking at the electrocardiogram, etc.

To each of these "questions," the physician can receive a range of answers. Each of the possible "answers" is treated by the behavior analyst as a stimulus to which the student learns to make the appropriate kind of response. The stimulus "triggers" the doctor's next response, which may be another question, or an observation, or a diagnosis. Thus the entire diagnostic process is analyzed as a decision process consisting of stimuli, and responses to these stimuli. The foregoing analysis for the diagnosis of the Lead 1 tracing was an example of the analysis of a decision process in terms of "concepts" and "chains." To reformulate what appears to be a simple, old-fashioned decision process into esoteric behavioristic terminology like "concepts" and "chains" is not merely an idle exercise in academic psychology. The application of concept formation theory and chaining theory to this type of decision process *brings the decision process within the domain of instructional technology.* Once the reformulation in terms of concepts and chains is accomplished, we are able to apply learning theory to the development of the instructional program. Learning theory does not tell us how to teach decision processes as such. But it does tell us how to go about teaching concepts and chains. Since a decision process turns out to be nothing other than a network of concepts and chains, we are able to teach any decision process. The general schema for translating any decision process into a network of concepts and chains is illustrated in Fig. 22.3. . . . This schema also applies to trouble shooting, computer programming, or any other kind of problem solving.

Each of the ovals represents a class of conditions among which generalization is to occur, in the sense that the same response is appropriate to all members of the set. Thus, all of Fig. 22.1 (patterns of ischemia, injury, and infarction) could be included in one of the brackets, say the center bracket, which contains three ovals. Each of the S's would correspond to one of the tracings shown in Fig. 22.1, and the responses R_6, R_7, and R_8 in Fig. 22.3 would correspond to the diagnosis "pattern of ischemia," "pattern of injury," and "pattern of infarction."

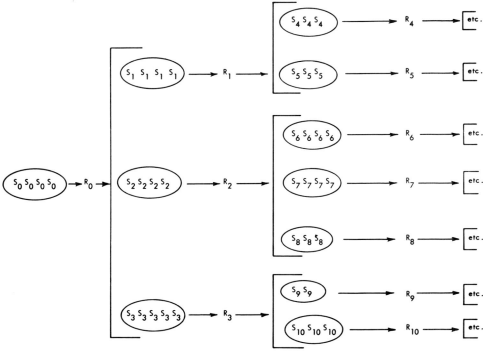

Figure 22.3

The techniques of behavioral analysis illustrated above are fundamental to any mode of teaching or interpersonal communication. They are applicable to the construction of lectures, to individual tutoring, to the writing of textbooks, to film-making, and to ordinary conversation. Even great works of art, in music, poetry, and literature, can be shown to be consistent with certain principles of concept formation and chaining (Mechner, 1961).

Programmed instruction, in the sense of a sequence of printed frames which require the student to write in a response, for which he receives immediate feedback, is only one particular technique for presenting the outcome of a behavioral analysis of knowledge. Small steps, active response, and immediate feedback, in and of themselves, are not very useful concepts. They enhance instruction only when the "small steps" are relevant to the behavioral structure of the knowledge being taught, and when the "active response" is actually a building block of the behavioral repertoire which is being established. Small steps and active response are useful when the nature of the steps and of the responses is in accord with a sound behavioral analysis of the material.

Teaching a student to generalize within a class and to discriminate between that class and other classes is generally a straightforward process, and poses technical problems only insofar as the properties to be generalized and discriminated are very subtle. When the concept is very difficult, such as, for instance, the concepts "early Mozart" and "late Mozart" for a tone-deaf individual, it may be necessary to administer some preliminary discrimination and generalization training. The tone-deaf individual might first have to learn pitch and interval discrimination, and acquire various harmonic and melodic concepts. Even though the concept is a difficult one and may take a very long time to teach, the basic concept formation process still applies.

The chief problem in teaching advanced or complex concepts is not so much the procedure as the definition of the classes. The definition of classes becomes particularly problematical where there is disagreement among the "experts" or where the semantics are imprecise. The reason it would be difficult to teach the concept of "good rhythm in prose writing" is that it is difficult to develop a sufficient number of good rhythm examples and bad rhythm examples on which different experts would agree. Once the classes have been adequately defined, however, and a sufficient number of examples are available, the remainder of the teaching process poses few problems.

With this formulation of concept formation, it becomes possible to consider the problems of teaching some of the concepts discussed in Section III B on Terminal Behavior Specifications. The approach described in the foregoing analysis of concept formation implies a method of teaching which is related to what is sometimes called the "case method." Difficult and critical training tasks are frequently taught by this method. Other names given to the "case" method are "simulator training" and "field training." Much sales training and military training is done by this method.

In some places, the "case" method is also used in academic settings, especially on the graduate training level. "Original research projects" and "term projects" are illustrations of reasonably unsystematic applications of the case method in the academic sphere. The "case" method has also appeared in some textbooks. The most brilliant book of this type in the science field is Conant's *Harvard Case Histories in Experimental Science* (1948). The two volumes of this book lead the reader through a series of six case studies taken from the history of science. In each one, the reader is given a detailed account of the historic development of the concept, the false hypotheses and their fates, the experimental efforts of all the investigators who tackled the problem over years and sometimes centuries, and the eventual stabilization of our views on the issue. In reading through these specific cases, the reader develops a concept of how scientists work. His concept increases in richness and generality with each successive case. Another example of this approach is Herrnstein and Boring's *A Source Book in the History of Psychology* (1965).

The question may well be asked at this point whether training programs that utilize the case method are *ipso facto* examples of programmed instruction. This is not an important question. The significant fact is that these methods apply one very important principle of behavior theory—the principle that general concepts are built up in the behavior repertoire through a series of specific instances. To apply this principle is a good beginning, but a beginning is all that it is. Behavior theory has a great deal more than this to contribute. For example, behavor theory suggests that at every point in the learning process the student must emit relevant responses. Also, behavior theory suggests that the cases or specific instances should be arranged in order of systematically increasing complexity and generality.

6. Examples of Frequently Neglected Scientific Concepts

The application of concept formation procedures to the teaching of complex scientific skills can be illustrated in connection with the problem of teaching a science student to apply mathematics to the solution of problems he will encounter. The first step is certainly to teach him mathematics. He must learn arithmetic, elementary algebra, set theory, probability theory, calculus, statistics, etc. But an equally important step is to teach him which branch of mathematics to use, when. This vital step is usually omitted from the curriculum, with the result that few of us are able to use our mathematics in practical situations, even though we may have a fairly good mastery of the techniques proper.

 This second step, deciding which branch of mathematics to use when, is a straightforward example of concept formation. The programmer can begin his behavioral analysis by developing an extensive table, as shown in Table 22.1.

The columns of the table would contain specific problems to which the branch of mathematics named on top is applicable.

TABLE 22.1

Differential equations	Arithmetic	Algebra	Probability theory	Statistics	etc.
1. heat transmission	1. division	1. coin problems	1. card problems	1. sampling problems	
2. movement in which friction, viscosity, acceleration, and mass must be considered	2. multiplication	2. compound interest problems	2. balls-in-urns problems	2. distribution	
	3. subtraction	3. projectile trajectory problems	3. genetics problems	3. reliability	
	4. addition	etc.	etc.	4. confidence limits problems	
3. electrical circuits involving capacitance, inductance	5. decimals			etc.	
4. analysis of the rates of chemical reactions	etc.				

Once this table is available, the programmer can proceed with the construction of the program, following essentially the formula described in the earlier example where the psychologist was teaching the concepts "red" and "blue."

A second example of concept formation in the development of complex scientific skills may be found in the teaching of inferential reasoning skills and "statistical intuition." Each one of the five terminal behavior examples given in Section III B 4(b) refers to a major domain of concepts.

Consider question 1: Out of fifty tubes you tested, three were defective. What would you guess is the probability that 10% of all tubes in the batch are defective? Give your answer in ten seconds.

The domain of the examples might be defined as follows by the psychologist in developing his classes: "Out of x tubes tested, y were defective. What is the probability that $z\%$ of all tubes in the batch are defective?"

The response required of the student is the probability statement. He could be required to state into which of the following ten classes the probability falls: .001–.002; .002–.004; .004–.008; .008–.016; .016–.032; etc.

It may well be that thousands of combinations of x, y, and z would be needed in an instructional program to teach the student to estimate the probability accurately if he is given the values of x, y, and z. This teaching process must be repeated for a variety of statements like the one above.

It might be noted that this procedure is not very different from "giving the student extensive experience." It is different only in that the experience is planned and controlled, with immediate feedback being provided after each response. In every other sense it is, of course, exactly like giving the student very extensive experience.

Thus, a thoroughgoing application of behavioral science to the teaching of abstract concepts demands the presentation to the student of a series of specific cases arranged in a systematic order of gradually increasing complexity and abstraction. Each case should require the student to make an active response which builds toward the type of behavior specified as the behavioral objective. This is the key to the teaching of high-level conceptual skills.

B. Behavioral Analysis Applied to the Teaching of Experimental Science

As was stated earlier, interest in the application of behavioral technology to the teaching of experimental science has grown considerably during recent years. This trend must be distinguished from numerous attempts to develop science programs, in the sense of programs which teach "the facts," or the current state of theoretical knowledge, with little reference to the empirical bases of the knowledge.

One good example of research and development effort in the area of experimental science teaching is the UNESCO-sponsored science teaching project in São Paulo, Brazil discussed earlier (Mechner, 1964). While the project is concerned primarily with the teaching of experimental physics, its findings have implications for the teaching of science in general.

One portion of the course being developed in São Paulo has as its objective to teach students to describe, in experimental terms, the properties that light shares with particles and the properties that light shares with waves. The teaching materials for this course consist of programmed textbooks in which the students write their answers, a set of kit materials which the students use to perform experiments in conjunction with the text, a set of optional film loops which show experiments, and a set of optional concept films.

This project generated some significant advances in the application of behavioral technology to science teaching. Here are some of them:

1. The Systematic Extension of Concept Formation Principles to Science Teaching

Applied to science teaching, the definition of the concept which states that a concept involves "generalization within a class and discrimination between that class and other classes" becomes: "generalization within a class of observations or experiments, and discrimination between that class and other classes of observations and experiments." One immediate corollary of this definition is that concept formation in science teaching requires that the student make observations and perform experiments. This conclusion is in accord with the views of many modern science teachers and curriculum reform groups. In the case of the UNESCO project, the application of this definition to the subject matter of the physics of light resulted in a syllabus similar to that suggested long ago by the Physical Science Study Committee (17).

A second corollary of this definition is that one single experiment or observation is not enough for the formation of a concept, for two reasons: (1) It is not possible to generalize from one instance, and (2) In order to form a discrimination, the student needs at least one instance and one non-instance of the concept in question.

2. Techniques for Applying Behavioral Analysis to the Design of Laboratory Work

Objections which are often leveled at the "cookbook" approach to laboratory teaching are circumvented by isolating six distinct aspects of laboratory instruction, each of which requires a separate teaching approach. The six aspects are:

a) Guiding the student through the steps of a procedure without any intent of *teaching* the procedure, as when the student is instructed to assemble a piece of equipment.

b) Teaching the student a procedure which he must learn to follow by heart, without prompts.

c) Teaching the student the reasons underlying the procedure.

d) Using the outcome of the experiment to provide one of the observations which are to be generalized with, and discriminated from, other observations in the formation of a concept.

e) Teaching incidental subconcepts within a single experiment.

f) Teaching the student to conceive, design, and carry out his own experiments.

This separation of categories of possible alternative objectives allows the techniques of behavioral analysis to be applied fruitfully to laboratory teaching.

C. The Problem of Generality and Transfer of Training

Another way of formulating this colossal problem is as follows: How do you know when you have built a sufficient variety of specific cases into the program, and what is "variety" anyway? How do you determine whether two specific examples are, in fact, "different"? How do you know that all your specific cases are not just a lot of variations of one basic case?

In psychological terms, this is the problem of generalization gradients. For some stimulus dimensions, there is no ambiguity about the intervals along the scale. When it comes to specifying "degree of difference" between two examples involving scientific inference, say, one in physics and one in biology, anyone would be hard pressed to quantify the degree of difference. We are reduced, in such a case, to leave the decision to "programming art" or impressionistic judgment. It is up to the programmer's ingenuity to find as wide a range of examples as possible. The wider the range he is able to cover in his program, the more general the resulting concept will be, and the greater the eventual transfer of training.

To illustrate the problem more concretely, let us return to the task of teaching "patience" and "perseverance." Suppose you sat the student down at the edge of a stream with his fishing rod. You are sitting a few yards upstream, hidden behind a bush, and you release a hungry fish into the stream whenever you want to reinforce your student. You gradually increase the time interval between fish according to a carefully worked out schedule. The student becomes more and more patient. But does he? The truth is that he becomes a more and more patient *fisherman*. But he does not, because of that experience alone, become a more and more patient person. In order to develop generalized patience, exposure to a wide variety of patience-building situations would be required. The wider the range and diversity of situations in which such training is given, the greater the likelihood that the training will generalize to the types of situations in which a scientist functions. We have, as yet, very little experience with this type of personality training in man, but we can be quite confident that a carefully worked out program of this sort would produce definite changes in the individual's capacity to tolerate delays.

In the area of perseverance training, there is again the problem of the generality of the perseverance which is established. If you manipulated a pinball machine at which your student is working in such a way that his payoffs gradually decreased in frequency, you would soon have an inveterate gambler on your hands. Skinner describes this procedure in his *Science and Human Behavior* (1953). This student would have enormous perseverance at the pinball machine. This perseverance might even transfer to a one-armed bandit or a gambling table. But would it carry over to threading a needle? Or to getting a paper published? Probably not. In order to develop generalized perseverance, it would be necessary to administer perseverance training in a wide variety of situations.

One serious practical problem in developing effective programs of this sort is to invent a set of training situations that is sufficiently varied, that can be managed in a school, and that can be administered economically. Clearly, it is unfeasible to lead the student from the fishing pond to the gambling casino every day. This problem will pose a major challenge to the programmer and the behavioral engineer. Actually, it is the type of problem which the programmer faces all the time, whether he realizes it or not. The problem of transfer of training is not unique to the teaching of patience and perseverance. The problem exists whether we are teaching salesmanship or English grammar. A good instructional program varies the range of examples and applications as much as is possible and practical within the economic and administrative constraints that are prescribed on the basis of overall considerations. A program to teach salesmen how to converse with their clients includes a wide variety of client's voices: deep voices and shrill ones; mellow voices and harsh ones; fast speech and slow speech. The trick is to vary the trainee's experience in the training situation as much as is feasible within the limitations imposed by the medium. The program stops short of taking the student into live client situations, rigged into a programmed series of interviews, because this would be too expensive. The amount of transfer actually achieved by the program may be far from complete, and may even be inadequate, but it may still provide ample justification for the investment of training time that is required. A similar argument will have to be accepted in the case of personality training for scientists. We can surely develop a wide assortment of patience exercises that can be conveniently administered in the classroom with an inexpensive set of materials. While such training may not encompass the complete range of situations the student may ever encounter, it may produce enough transfer to make it worth his time.

These principles apply to all of the concept formation tasks described earlier, including:

1. Deductive reasoning skill.
2. Scientific inference skill.
3. Skill in generating hypotheses.
4. Discriminating fruitful from non-fruitful hypotheses.
5. Skill in testing hypotheses.
6. Formulating problems so that they can be solved by the scientific method.

All of these skills must be developed inductively through a long series of specific cases of gradually increasing complexity. It will not be surprising if it turns out that thousands of hours of training may be involved in developing some of these skills to any high degree.

To sum up, we can say that behavioral technology has not yet addressed itself to the problems of science teaching in any significant way. Programs that have been written have barely begun to scratch the surface of science teaching, and that has been teaching only in the area of subject matter. Even there, the most important steps have not yet been taken.

Once behavioral technology addresses itself to the task of science teaching in a serious and concerted manner, some striking results may be expected.

D. Case Studies in Science Programming

The purpose of this section is to show some examples of science programs that have met with at least moderate success. The examples chosen do not address the most interesting ones of the science teaching problems discussed in Section III B. They do, however, illustrate some of the techniques that have proven useful to present-day practitioners of the technology. For each example presented, the underlying behavioral analysis is discussed.

Case I: Teaching an Empirical Law by Experimental Induction

In Section III B 3 of this article the point was made that science educators are becoming increasingly conscious of the need to teach science students the empirical or experimental basis of laws and principles, in addition to the principles themselves.

The sample presented below teaches Ohm's Law by experimental induction with the aid of a laboratory kit. The kit includes electric batteries, wire, light bulbs, and a switch. At the point in the program where the sample starts, the student has already learned from the program how an incandescent light bulb works, about electron flow, conductors, insulators, resistance, voltage, switches, and symbolic circuit representation. In reading through the frames, note the progression from manipulations of the physical equipment, to specific observations, and then to generalizations.

QUESTIONS	ANSWERS
211 DRAW the circuit diagram of the circuit you have just built.	
212 Throw the switch to position 1, then to position 2. What happens to the light bulbs in each case? _____ _____	In position 1, one bulb glows brightly. In position 2, both bulbs glow dimly. (or equivalent response)
213 Suppose each light bulb has a resistance of 10 ohms. How much resistance would two light bulbs in series have? _____	20 ohms (10 ohms + 10 ohms = 20 ohms)

214

How can you tell by looking at a bulb how much current is in it? _____

The brighter a bulb is, the more current there is in it.

215

Is a bulb brighter when the electrons go through both bulbs in series, or when they go through just one bulb? _____

A bulb is brighter when the electrons go through just one bulb.

216

What can you conclude about the relationship between the number of light bulbs in series and the amount of current in the circuit? ___ ___ ___ ___ ___

The more light bulbs, the less current.

or

The fewer light bulbs, the more current.

217

What can you conclude about the relationship between the amount of resistance in the circuit and the amount of current? ___ ___ ___ ___ ___

The more resistance in the circuit, the less current.

or

The less resistance in the circuit, the more current.

218

The ohm is the unit of ___ ___ ___ ___.

resistance

The ampere is the unit of ___ ___ ___ ___.

current

219

The more _____ _____s (unit) in a circuit, the fewer _____ _s (unit) will flow.

ohms

amperes

In the next 25 frames, the student learns that voltages add when dry cells are placed in series, and that voltage is measured in volts. Then the student interchanges the light bulbs and dry cells in his or her circuit.

244

DRAW the diagram of the circuit you have just built.

245

In which circuit is there more voltage?

☐ in the circuit with two dry cells in series and one light bulb

☐ in the circuit with two light bulbs in series and one dry cell

in the circuit with two dry cells in series and one light bulb

---

246

Try the switch in both positions.

What do you observe? _____

When the circuit has two dry cells in series, the bulb is brighter than when the circuit has only one dry cell.

(or equivalent response)

247

You observed that the bulb glowed more brightly when there were two dry cells in series. What does this tell you about the effect of voltage on current?

_____

The more voltage, the more current.

(or equivalent response)

248

When you increased the voltage, the current:

☐ increased

☐ remained the same

☐ decreased

increased

249

When you increased the resistance, the current:

☐ increased

☐ remained the same

☐ decreased

decreased

250

In your experiments you observed that:

1. the higher the _____, the higher the current.

voltage

2. the higher the _____, the lower the current.

resistance

251	
WRITE this observation in the form of an equation: $$\text{current} = \frac{(?)}{(?)}$$	$$\text{current} = \frac{\text{voltage}}{\text{resistance}}$$
252	
Now WRITE the equation again, from memory, using the proper units in place of current, resistance, and voltage.	$$\text{amperes} = \frac{\text{volts}}{\text{ohms}}$$

In Frame 217, the student is ready to state the general relationship between resistance in a circuit and the amount of current flowing through that circuit. The student arrives at this statement by generalizing from his own empirical observations. Similarly, in Frame 247, he arrives at the relationship between voltage and current. In Frames 248–252 he combines these two statements into a single statement and translates it into mathematical form. This sample is another illustration of the technique of advancing from the concrete to the abstract in the teaching of concepts.

. . .

REFERENCES

Conant, J. B., editor. *Harvard Case Histories in Experimental Science.* Cambridge, Mass.: Harvard University Press, 1948.

Ferster, C. B., and B. F. Skinner. *Schedules of Reinforcement.* New York: Appleton-Century-Crofts, 1957.

Herrnstein, R. J., and E. G. Boring. *A Source Book in the History of Psychology.* Cambridge, Mass.: Harvard University Press.

Hull, C. L. "Quantitative Aspects of the Evolution of Concepts: An Experimental Study." *Psychological Monographs* 28:1–25; Whole No. 123, 1920.

Keller, F. S., and W. N. Schoenfeld. *Principles of Psychology.* New York: Appleton-Century-Crofts, 1950.

Margulies, S. *Some General Rules of Frame Construction.* New York: Basic Systems, 1963.

Mechner, F. "A Notation System for the Description of Behavioral Procedures." *Journal of the Experimental Analysis of Behavior* 2:133–50; April 1959.

Mechner, F. *Programming for Automated Instruction, III.* New York: Basic Systems, 1961.

Mechner, F. *Behavioral Technology and Medical Education.* Paper presented at Rochester Conference on Programmed Instruction in Medical Education, June 26, 1964.

Mechner, F., and D. A. Cook. *Behavioral Technology and Manpower Development.* Background paper prepared for the Directorate of Scientific Affairs, Organization for Economic Cooperation and Development, 1963.

Mechner, F., D. A. Cook, and S. Margulies. *Introduction to Programmed Instruction.* New York: Basic Systems, 1964.

Moore, O. K., and A. R. Anderson. *Early Reading and Writing.* 15 min., 16mm, sound, color. Basic Education, Hamden, Connecticut, 1960.

Piaget, J. *The Child's Conception of the World.* New York: Harcourt, 1929.

Skinner, B. F. *The Behavior of Organisms: An Experimental Analysis.* New York: Appleton-Century-Crofts, 1938.

Skinner, B. F. *Science and Human Behavior.* New York: Macmillan Co., 1953.

Skinner, B. F. "A Case History in Scientific Method." *American Psychologist* 11:221–33; May 1956.

Zacharias, J. "The Age of Science." *The Nation's Children.* (Edited by Eli Ginzberg.) New York: Columbia University Press, 1960. Vol. 2, Development and Education, pp. 93–115.

QUESTIONS

1. In nontechnical terms, explain what Mechner means by generalization within a class and discrimination between classes.

Answer the following four questions by referring to the electrocardiogram program in the Mechner article.

2. Apply the blackout procedure to the first five frames of this program. What is the result?

3. Both frame 2 and frame 3 require the student to discriminate the Q wave. What prompts a correct discrimination of the Q wave in frame 2? This prompt is removed in frame 3. Will frame 3 probably be answered correctly by the doctors for whom the program is intended? Why or why not?

4. Frame 4 introduces discrimination of the S-T segment. Does section *a* of frame 4 require discrimination of this segment? Does section *c* of frame 4 require this discrimination?

5. Mechner states, in his discussion of the shortcomings of the case method of concept teaching, that concept formation requires more than the mere presentation of a series of examples in a systematic order from most to least obvious. The frames you have just read introduce the concepts of Q wave and S-T segment by presenting a series of examples. Would Mechner have the same criticism for the concept teaching embodied in these frames as he does for the case method? Explain your answer.

Mechner describes a process that might be used to teach a child the concept red. Review that description, then answer these three questions. (The description is on p. 272.)

6. If you were using this method to teach the concept red, would you begin with three objects that were identical except for color and then gradually introduce objects that differ in many respects, including color? Or would you simply start with three objects that differ in many ways, including color? Explain your choice.

7. This concept could be taught by beginning with one red and one nonred object. The child would be asked, "Which object is red?" Why is Mechner's method better than this method?

8. In a variation of the method described in question 7, the teacher could begin instruction by pointing to the red object to cue the correct response. Gradually the pointing fades out. What takes the place of this pointing cue in Mechner's method? Which cue do you prefer? Why?

The following five questions refer to section 2 of part B, "Behavioral Analysis Applied to the Teaching of Experimental Science," pp. 286–287.

9. Task b requires the student to learn a particular procedure—let's say setting up some lab equipment without using a manual or notes. Assume this procedure requires several very delicate motor responses which could not be assumed in the typical beginning student. In addition to learning to perform these responses, the order of the setup must be memorized. Using the task taxonomy from Unit 14, how would you classify this task?

10. Task c requires that the student learn the reasons underlying this procedure. Task c could be stated behaviorally as: When performing the procedure, the student can answer the instructor's questions about the reasons for various steps. How would you classify this task?

11. Task d could be stated behaviorally in relation to the Ohm's Law program as: The student builds a circuit following directions and is then directed to move the switch from position 1 to position 2 and observe the brightness of the bulbs. The student uses these observations and some prior learning to relate the concepts of resistance and amount of current. How would you classify this task?

12. Many educators hope that what is learned in one situation will transfer to another similar situation. Assuming that good instructional strategies were developed for each of the three tasks described above, which do you expect will provide the most transfer to similar tasks?

13. When you are planning an instructional strategy for a task for which maximum transfer is desirable, is your task analysis affected? If so, how?

14. Mechner points out that his scheduled-fish-releasing program to establish patience would train a patient fisherman. What is necessary to develop more generalized patience?

15. Suppose you want to train a patient scientist and have developed a feasible, graduated, and varied series of situations that build patience, none of which is very similar to a practicing scientist's situation. Would you expect generalization to the scientist's situation? Explain your answer.

Answer the following three questions by referring to the program teaching Ohm's Law in the Mechner article.

16. Look at frame 216. Describe what the student has done previously that allows him or her to answer this frame correctly.

17. How does the behavior called for in frame 216 relate to the behavior called for in frame 217?

18. Many programs that attempt to teach the induction of general rules from specific instances fail because of poorly designed contingencies for responding to the specific instances. In this program, could a student answer frame 217 correctly without having manipulated the circuit?

19. Mechner uses several examples to teach the concept "how concepts are taught." Select a concept from your project work, if there is one, and devise a rationale and tactics to establish your concept. If your project work does not include concepts, select one from your outline of terminal tasks prepared for Unit 13.

20. An uncritical acceptance of Mechner's categorization of any sequential task as a "chain" for which "learning theory suggests strongly that last links . . . be taught before the early links" may lead to inappropriate teaching sequences. Mechner's theory is derived from animal training, where chains must be built backward because the primary reinforcement follows the final step and all other links in the chain derive their reinforcing value from the stimulus associated or paired with the primary reinforcement. This is not always the case for humans. However, certain tasks, like a golf shot, are chains of behavior in which the final step is more highly reinforcing than the earlier steps and is also simpler than the earlier steps. In these cases, teaching the chain backwards may be advantageous. Do Mechner's examples of chains benefit from being taught backwards? Consider each separately and offer a rationale for your answer. Ask yourself what the reinforcers are, where they occur, and what is the relationship of the final step to the earlier steps for the following: (a) reciting a poem; (b) tying a shoelace; (c) solving a mathematical problem; (d) writing a computer program.

UNIT

23

Sesame Street

Content

The popular educational television program, *Sesame Street,* is examined for its application of the learning principles taught in this course. The quotations used in question 2 are from: Lesser, G. S. "Learning, Teaching and Television Production for Children: The Experience of *Sesame Street.*" *Harvard Educational Review* 42 (1972): 232–272. Reprinted by permission.

Objectives

Students will:

1. Infer the teaching objective of some of the skits in the program.
2. Point out instances in the program where attention-getting devices make the student interact with the educational task, and other instances where they distract the student from the critical content.
3. Determine how (or whether) the various instructional principles are represented in *Sesame Street.* A list of seven principles is provided.
4. Find examples of gradual progression and of simple (rote) repetition. State whether they are appropriate to the objectives.

Instructions

1. Read over the objectives and the questions, then review the program. Consult a TV schedule for time and channel in your local viewing area. You may find it helpful to take notes.
2. There are no suggested answers for these questions, so you may want to watch and discuss the program with another student.

QUESTIONS

1. Recall two or three skits from the program and infer the teaching objectives behind them.

2. Animation, music, camera techniques, and humor are among the devices used in *Sesame Street* to make the child attend to and interact with the educational task. But there is a danger in their use. If these "attention grabbers" are not well integrated with the skit's teaching objectives, the child may ignore the educational task while attending to the "attention grabbers." Gerald Lesser describes such a situation in "Learning, Teaching, and Television Production for Children: The Experience of *Sesame Street*."

   > For example, a child may concentrate on the quality of a voice and miss what the speaker is saying. In evaluating the appeal of stories read on television, Lauren Bacall's voice "sounded funny" to many children, and they concentrated on this voice quality instead of the story itself. These children may have been engaging in significant incidental learning about variations in vocal patterns, but their attention had been diverted from the intended focus.

   Lesser also describes an instance where the "attention grabber" (humor, in this case) is well integrated with the teaching objectives:

   > For example, a series of short animated films is designed to teach counting backwards from ten. In these films, an identical situation—a countdown to a rocket blast-off—results in a variety of comic endings. The launch director counts off the seconds in a solemn voice as surrounding dignitaries wait expectantly. The numbers appear at the top of the screen as the countdown progresses. In every film but one, something catastrophic happens to embarrass the launch director. . . . The naturally suspenseful situation of the rocket countdown is enhanced by the additional suspense of waiting for a particular form of disastrous payoff, with the child's attention being drawn to the number sequence.

   Watch for both types of uses in *Sesame Street*. Describe one example of each, if it occurs.

3. Determine how (or whether) and how well the various instructional principles are represented in *Sesame Street*. Consider especially:
   a) variation of exemplars in forming an abstraction or concept,
   b) adapting to individual differences,
   c) gradual progression,
   d) relevant and irrelevant cueing (the blackout problem),
   e) emission and reinforcement of active responses,
   f) other.

4. In most programs examined in this course, there is little rote repetition; items in a gradual progression vary at least a little from previous items to extend the concept involved rather than strengthen a single association. In other rare cases, rote recitation is a behavioral objective (e.g., the new recruit learns his serial number).
   a) In *Sesame Street* describe examples of progressive variation and of simple repetition (if they occur).
   b) If they occur, are they appropriate to the objectives? For each type, are special programming considerations met?

UNIT

24

Project, Part II

In the preceding six units you evaluated a variety of teaching materials and you should now have a better understanding of response contingency and gradual progression, two concepts important in all good lesson design. The best way to learn more about these concepts is to begin implementing them in your own lesson materials.

In Unit 17 you formulated behavioral objectives and wrote a general description of the appropriate gradual progression for achieving those objectives. Now you are ready to begin writing the lesson materials to teach these objectives.

As you have learned, the format of a lesson is greatly influenced by the lesson objectives and the task analysis. Devise a lesson format suitable to your objectives and with which you feel comfortable. Previous students have designed games, TV scripts, and classroom management procedures, as well as traditional lessons teaching verbal content. As you write, apply the critical procedures you have acquired to evaluate your work.

Peer evaluation of your lesson materials will be most helpful. If this is impossible, plan to set aside your completed project work for a week and then review it objectively. If the blackout technique is appropriate for your lesson format, do it. If not, find another way of identifying the behaviors that allow a correct answer to be achieved. If behaviors other than the desired behavior result in correct answers, think of possible improvements. Finally, reevaluate your use of gradual progression. Final evaluation and revision of your materials will be called for in Unit 29.

UNIT

25

Mimosa Cottage

Content

Lent, J. R., J. LeBlanc, and J. Spradlin. "Designing a Rehabilitative Culture for Moderately Retarded, Adolescent Girls." In R. Ulrich, T. Stachnik, and T. Mabry, eds., *Control of Human Behavior,* Vol. 2. Glenview, Ill.: Scott, Foresman, 1970, pp. 121–135.

This article describes the design of a complete subculture in an institution for mentally retarded girls. The designed subculture teaches behaviors that will permit the students to return to the larger outside community. The token reinforcement system, the selection of appropriate reinforcers, and the shaping of desired behaviors are described.

Objectives

The student will describe the operation of a token system, the restructuring of the environment to facilitate transfer, the reasons underlying selection of reinforcers, and the shaping of a desired behavior.

Instructions

Read the objectives, then read the article and answer the questions. Confer with your instructor when you've completed the unit.

INTRODUCTION TO MIMOSA COTTAGE

This article, which describes a rather unusual teaching problem, should expand your understanding of the use of learning principles in instruction. Lent, LeBlanc, and

Spradlin consciously apply principles of the experimental analysis of behavior to the problem of preparing moderately retarded adolescent girls for a return to the community. You may want to compare this reading with Unit 21 in which Itard's work with the feral child Victor is described. Itard intuitively applied some of these same principles to an extremely unusual and difficult situation.

The goal of Lent, LeBlanc, and Spradlin, as well as of Itard, is integration of the learner into the "real world" community. Both articles speak directly to the problem of transfer of training also discussed by Mechner in Unit 22. While it is unlikely that you as a curriculum writer will face such severe challenges, you will always face the problem of planning for effective transfer of training to real-world situations. The need for such planning is more obvious in unusual cases, but in no learning situation should effective transfer simply be assumed.

Designing a Rehabilitative Culture for Moderately Retarded, Adolescent Girls

James R. Lent, Judith LeBlanc, and Joseph E. Spradlin

The primary purpose of the program is to train fifteen- to twenty-one-year-old moderately retarded girls for life outside an institution. There are two general ways in which this has been approached. First, some of the girls are able to return to their parents if their behavior is modified in ways which are more acceptable to the family. Secondly, some of the girls are able to make a semi-independent adjustment. Essentially, this means preparing the child for useful employment and providing for close supervision of nonwork hours by persons other than the natural family.

The secondary purpose of the program is to train the girls to make a smoother adjustment to institutional life. This does not mean, however, institutional traditions are accepted. Rather, the standards of the community are deemed as appropriate to institution life.

Casual observation, as well as published studies, seems to indicate that in order for a person to be accepted in a community he must meet at least minimal criteria in four skill areas—personal, social, educational, and occupational. These skill areas have served as guidelines for developing both a generalized reinforcement system and specific training programs in the project to be described.

ENVIRONMENTAL SETTING

The experimental population consisted of 27 fifteen- to twenty-one-year-old moderately retarded girls with IQs ranging from approximately 25 to 55. The girls were

J. R. Lent, J. LeBlanc, and J. Spradlin, "Designing a Rehabilitative Culture for Moderately Retarded Adolescent Girls," in *Control of Human Behavior,* Vol. 2, ed. by R. Ulrich, T. Stachnik, and T. Mabry (Glenview, Ill.: Scott, Foresman, 1970), pp. 121–135. Reprinted by permission.

all assigned to the third floor of a "typical three-story institutional building, which was built in 1931 to house adult epileptics" (see Fig. 25.1). The third floor of this building will hereafter be called Mimosa C cottage.

The living space on Mimosa C cottage had not been modified to accommodate an adolescent female population or appropriate training goals. Conditions seemed overcrowded and the environment sterile. Also, the environment provided few opportunities to learn community-required behavior or to transfer skills learned in the ward to the community. Since these conditions are common to many institution settings, it seemed worthwhile to attempt to demonstrate that the rearrangement of internal space based on a careful analysis of program goals could transfer a typical institution building into a functional living and training area.

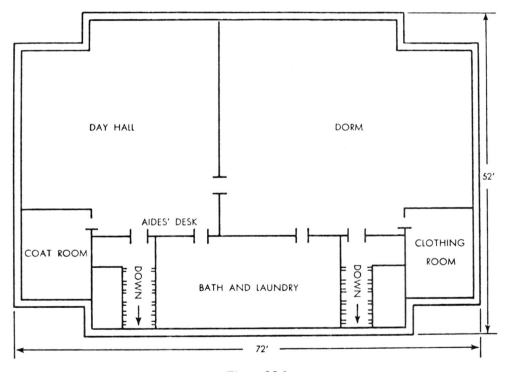

Figure 25.1

Modification of the Physical Environmental Setting

It has long been recognized that the more similar two sets of stimuli are, the more likely that behavior learned in the presence of one set will be transferred to a second. Yet, a close analysis of the physical environment of the cottage indicated that there was little similarity between the physical environment of the ward and that found in community homes. These observations led to the environmental modification to be described.

It was necessary for training purposes to have a kitchen, dining, and living room area that was similar in size and equipment to middle-class homes in the community. Also needed was space for sewing, ironing, dancing, playing games, having parties, and an office area for demonstration assistants hired by the project. Figure 25.2 depicts the modified cottage area. The modifications included: (1) The south wall of the area marked "Coat Room" was removed so that a kitchen, dining, and living room area could extend from the east wall, in a line, into the dormitory area. (2) The bathroom and laundry area was divided by a wall so that half of the area could be used for washing and drying clothing and for instruction in ironing. (3) The west end of the dormitory area was walled off to become a storage area. Cabinets and coat racks were built to provide the storage space lost by previous modifications. (4) The area designated "Clothing Room" became office space. (5) Bunk beds were purchased to provide the needed additional floor space. Dressers were purchased so that each girl would have a specific area in which to keep her personal belongings. Furniture and appliances were purchased for the living area. (6) A moveable observation booth was built so it could be moved on wheels to any location on the top floor.

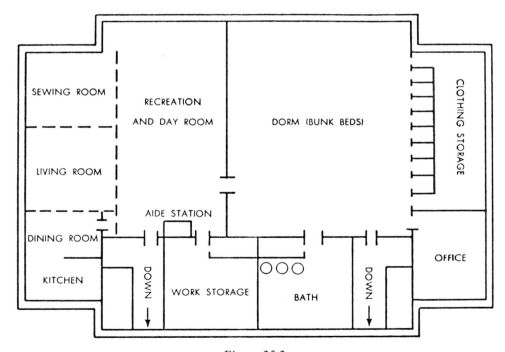

Figure 25.2

The changes in the physical environment described above were made prior to the initiation of the behavior modification program.

Modification in the Social Environmental Setting

Before the modification program was initiated, one hospital aide per eight-hour shift was assigned to Mimosa C cottage. The aides were charged with the responsibility of housekeeping chores, keeping records, care of clothing, administering medication, and managing the behavior of twenty-seven girls. The training program for aides had primarily developed quasi-nursing skills, rather than skills of behavioral management. The heavy work load, in addition to the general lack of behavioral training, resulted in a rather typical institutional ward for moderately retarded girls. The girls received little attention from the aides unless there was some disturbance or crisis. Almost no effort was directed toward training, and behavior was likely to be controlled by threats, prohibitions, and restrictions rather than through any systematic application of behavioral principles. Insofar as the aides' primary interaction with the girls was directive, the particular role that the aide played was not one which was appropriate for imitation by the girls.

The psychiatric aides employed by the hospital (one per eight-hour shift) were retained, and registered nurses with supervisory responsibility were available, one each eight-hour shift. These nurses, however, had responsibility for four other cottages in addition to Mimosa cottage. Two demonstration assistants, selected primarily on the basis of ability, interest, and personal appearance, were hired from project funds. The aim of the personnel selection was to obtain demonstration assistants who could readily learn simple reinforcement principles, who were sensitive to community norms for behavior, and who could serve as appropriate imitative models for the girls on the cottage. Ultimately these two demonstration assistants were assigned, across a thirteen-hour per day period, to work directly with the girls as behavioral modifiers.

After selection, the demonstration assistants participated in an intensive formal training program which consisted of: (1) reading and responding to a set of materials which described and illustrated operant conditioning principles, (2) shaping the behavior of an animal in a Skinner Box, (3) learning to systematically observe and record behaviors of the girls, and (4) learning how to use operant principles while working with groups of girls. The study program was required to introduce the demonstration assistants to the principles and vocabulary of operant conditioning. Shaping of an animal in a Skinner Box was invaluable experience in the application of contingent reinforcement without the use of verbal directions, one of the most important but most difficult to train principles for the behavioral manager to learn. Behavioral observation and recording was taught so the demonstration assistants could also serve as observers to collect the data on the training projects.

During the training period for the demonstration assistants, the aides and nurses assigned to the cottage were also meeting with the cottage director and cottage supervisor to receive a somewhat less intensive training in behavioral principles. The purpose of training both the aides and assistants was to develop knowledge of reinforcement principles and behavioral observation skills, and to encourage them to exhibit behavior appropriate for imitation by the girls on the cottage.

IMPLEMENTING A GENERAL REINFORCEMENT SYSTEM

Prior to the initiation of the actual program, baseline data on the personal and social skills of the girls were gathered. The specific procedures for collecting this data will be described later under the section entitled, "Evaluation of Behavioral Change."

Once baseline data were collected, the first step in developing a training program involved establishing a generalized reinforcement system. A token system similar to the one described by Girardeau and Spradlin (1964) was put into effect.

At this point, it may be well to discuss a question that frequently comes up. This question is, could you make the same changes by just introducing social reinforcement? We doubt it for several reasons. First, the presence of tokens is a significant change in the environment, signaling to both the girls and staff that the procedures in the cottage have changed. No such explicit stimulus is present when one seeks merely to change behavior and contingencies through social reinforcement. Second, the presence or absence of tokens for a specific individual provides a gross record of the frequency with which that individual is coming into contact with the imposed contingencies. Moreover, the overall number of tokens given allows the supervisor to determine the amount of reinforcement delivered. Of course, presence of tokens does not mean that the contingencies have been appropriate. But absence of tokens means that the procedures have not been followed. No such record of either individual contact with the culture or staff cooperation exists in the usual social reinforcement system. Third, it seems inconceivable to us that tokens which are redeemable for nutrients, trips downtown, telephone calls home, and dates with a boyfriend are not superior to smiles, nods, and comments such as "That's good." In fact, it is our speculation that staff association with tokens which provide such back-up reinforcers greatly enhances the effectiveness of social reinforcement delivered by the staff.

The token system initiated on the demonstration cottage differs from that described by Girardeau and Spradlin (1964) in several ways. First, the metal planchets used initially were bulky and inconvenient; therefore, a checkmark system of reinforcement was initiated. Each girl was given four 3 × 5 oak tag-cards joined by a string. A grid network of small squares was printed on each side of each card. Points given on one side of the card were redeemable in money, and those on the other side were redeemable in activities. A given number of squares were designated for each of several areas—personal appearance, performance in serving programs, etc. These categories provided an additional stimulus for the staff to attend to and reinforce performance in these areas. The cards were collected once each week and the amount of money points and activity points were recorded in the "bank book." This system, while much more abstract than that described by Girardeau and Spradlin (1964), was easily learned by the girls.

Second, reinforcement and punishment contingencies were, for the most part, made explicit to the girls (see Tables 25.1 and 25.2). The contingencies were printed and posted on the cottage bulletin board. Many of the children had to learn by experience since they could not read, i.e., when points were given to, or taken

TABLE 25.1

Ways to earn points

Reinforcement categories	Category breakdown	No. points earned
Ironing:	Dress	8
	Full skirt	7
	Straight skirt	7
	Blouse	6
Sewing:	Button	5
	Hem of full skirt	7
	Hem of straight skirt	8–10
	Embroidering	6–8
	Machine sewing	6–8
Hair set:	Setting hair for resident on immediate floor	5
	Setting hair for resident on lower floor	10
Hair washed :		3–5
Letter writing:	Off campus: to friends and relatives	8
	On campus: to residents on the lower floor or pen pals on male cottage	10
Errands:	For psychiatric aide or demonstration assistant	6–10
Cottage work:	Assigned work area	8–10
Social activities:	Cooperative behavior in activities	8–10
Personal effects:	Neat dressers	3–5
	Clothing in bins and dresser drawers clean and neatly folded	3–5
Check station		
Morning:	Beds	4
	Dresser	4
	Shoes	2
	Socks	2
	Bins	4
	Teeth	2
	Hair	4
Evening:	Legs shaved	3
	Nails manicured	3
	Hair well groomed	3
	Dress appropriate	3
	Shoes polished	3

away from a girl, she was told the reason. This system also increased the probability that staff persons would administer the contingencies and hastened the modification of selected behavior. When positive reinforcement is administered, the interaction between staff person and child is pleasant and affectionate. On the other hand, when a cost contingency is enforced, the interaction is depersonalized. The adult main-

TABLE 25.2

Costly behavior

Categories	No. points cost
Disrespectful attitude toward aide	20
Disrespectful attitude toward peers	5
Inappropriate verbal behavior	5
Disobedient behavior	5
Neglect of cottage work-assignment	10
Failure to complete cottage work-assignment satisfactorily	20
Stealing	20
Lying	20
Tantrum behavior	10
Personal effects in disarray (bed drawer, bin, rack, etc.)	15
Wearing dirty clothes	5
Wearing other girls' clothing	10
Inappropriate night wear in day hall	5
Sitting on the front steps of the cottage	5
Turning television volume above the designated mark	10
Crossing line into aide area or kitchen area	5
Sitting in front of the television on the floor	5
Entering demonstration assistants' office without knocking and asking to talk to person desired	10
Refusing to take medicine when aide calls	10
Not cleaning up game or sewing when finished	5

tains a neutral expression and simply states the rules of the program, then stands ready to apply the contingency. GC, a nineteen-year-old resident, had a typical reaction to the system: During the second week of the project's operation on Mimosa C, GC began an argument with another girl about a work assignment. She was shouting, screaming, and threatening harm to the other girl when the psychiatric aide approached and said, "GC, if you want to shout and scream and argue, you may; but it will cost ten points." GC looked at the aide momentarily, then resumed her argument with the other girl. The aide then said, "Get me your point cards, G" (points already earned are blacked out with a magic marker). The girl then went to her dresser where her point cards were kept, shouting, "I don't give a damn if you take all my lousy points!" However, she returned in a moment, without the cards, saying, "Well, I've thought about it and it ain't worth it!" The aide, skeptical of the system up to this point, was now convinced it was not necessary to scold and shout at the girls to influence their behavior. In point of fact, such behavior on the part of adults often serves a reinforcing function, especially among children who are deprived of any interaction with adults.

The third way in which the system differs from the Girardeau and Spradlin

TABLE 25.3

Privilege list

Categories		No. points cost
Scheduled activities on campus:	Movies	20
	Canteen (45 min.)	10
	Swimming	20
	Programs	10
	Record dance	20
	Band dance	25
	Sports activities	20
Cottage activities:	Phone call to boyfriend	50
	Phone call home	50
	Picture of boyfriend	50
	Picture to send home	50
	Picture with boyfriend	50
	Late TV	30
	Parties	15
	Date	15
Other activities on campus:	Walks	5
	Parties on other cottages	10
	Canteen (15 min.)	5
Off-campus activities:	Downtown restaurant	100
	Picnic	50
	Dinner at bowling alley	100
	Roller skating	75
	Downtown swimming	100
	Trip to another town	100
	Shopping downtown	50
	Church downtown	20
	Walk downtown	20
	Recreation downtown	20
	Drive-in movie	100
	Car ride for coke	50
	Dari-Queen	15
	Shopping L & N	15
	Movie downtown	120
Dates:	Dinner on campus	25
	Church	10
	Movie	20
	Canteen	10
	Dance	20
	Swimming	20
	Drive-in movie	100
	Skating	100

method is that many of the back-up reinforcers have powerful training properties (see Table 25.3). The aim of this miniature culture was to develop behavior which is directed toward return to the community. Going downtown shopping is a back-up reinforcer, but it is also a way of developing community-oriented behavior.

Fourth, there is a direct and continuing relationship between the reinforcement system, the training programs, and the end goals of the project. (1) End goals were determined by observing in the community those behaviors which seemed most generally useful. (2) These observations were incorporated into a behavioral check list which was used in gathering baseline data. (3) Categories of the check list were used to determine which training programs were needed to effect the desired behavior changes. (4) These categories of response (and training) appeared on the reinforcement cards carried by each girl.

THE DEVELOPMENT OF TRAINING PROGRAMS

When target behaviors had been selected, it became a relatively easy task to determine what training programs were needed. The following programs were developed for use with the Mimosa C children.

Hair care: The aim of this program was to teach girls to set and style their own hair and to maintain it at all times in an acceptable manner. A local beautician instructs the girls in these skills.

Complexion care: Teenage complexion problems were managed in a once-a-week program. Proper diet, hygiene, and cosmetic care relieved some girls of acne. Some girls had to be made aware that a bad complexion can be a social handicap. As with many of the programs, liberal use of mirrors and Polaroid photography have proved very useful.

Fingernail care: This is another area of personal appearance usually ignored in institutions for the retarded. Initially, all subjects had dirty, poorly cut, and/or bitten nails. Polaroid pictures of weekly progress aided in developing and maintaining this skill.

Walking: One of our earliest discoveries was that many institutionalized children can be identified as retarded by observing them walk. A close analysis of the girls' walking behavior and careful programing resulted in our being able to modify the behavior during the training sessions. Generalization to other stimulus conditions, however, is quite another matter. In this we have been only moderately successful.

Sewing: Detailed instructions for teaching hand and machine sewing were written, as well as criteria for judging responses in all areas. Baseline performance was established for each child, the training program implemented, and then the baseline check list administered again to assess progress. Several girls made such clothing items as skirts, blouses, and dresses, while others only mastered mending and stitching.

Ironing: As with all training programs for this group, the relatively casual techniques used to instruct the normal and even educable level retarded were not adequate. It was necessary to break the task into very small components and arrange them sequentially for teaching, and also for data gathering purposes. The Mimosa C girls now do all their own ironing, even though some are not as accomplished as would be desired.

Clothing selection: A color movie of models wearing outfits of various combinations was shown as a pretest. The girls were asked questions about the appropriateness of the models' dress to provide pretest data. They were then systematically taught in a manner similar to programed instruction, to select clothes that match in color, style, and pattern, and which were appropriate to the season and the occasion.

Dancing: Dancing and the related social skills were taught to the girls and to boys from other cottages who were invited for the training sessions. A party following the instruction period was held for those students who accrued sufficient reinforcer points during the training session. This program served as an "ice-breaker" for many of the girls who are now having dates on the cottage and the hospital grounds.

Sex education: Frank explanations were given concerning basic sex-hygiene facts, and equally frank discussions of the implications of promiscuity were held in small groups for all girls. For some of the girls who were working and/or living in the community, I.U.D.'s (intrauterine device) were prescribed. The parents of these children were solidly in favor of the instruction and the implantation of the birth control devices.

Leisure time activities: One of the marked observations that can be made about a typical cottage for moderately retarded persons is the general lack of activity of the patients. They do not initiate or maintain leisure-time activities. Games and activities were made available to the girls on the demonstration cottage and they were instructed in their use. Initially, points were given for merely participating. Later, the reinforcement value of playing the games and the subsequent interaction with peers and adults was sufficient to maintain their participation. Games were chosen which had absolute carry-over value to the community. That is, they cost little or nothing and were stimulating enough to maintain over a long period of time. Solitaire, hearts, canasta, dominoes, and jigsaw puzzles remained the favorites. The Mimosa C girls watch television now only occasionally, instead of continuously.

Social behavior: Cooperation and politeness were typically taught in the context of evening games and activities. However, preliminary observations indicated this approach was not totally adequate and that a more intensive program is necessary.

Town orientation: Going from place to place in the community in a purposeful manner is a critical skill. Children must be able to select the appropriate type of store for a given purchase, find the store, negotiate the purchase, and return to the cottage. Tight control typified the initial instruction, and gradually children were trained to go about the community independently. For instance, under supervision, the child was sent to a store only two blocks from the campus. The next trip was taken without supervision, but in company with other girls. During this trip, a

demonstration assistant observed from a discreet distance. On the following expedi-
tion, the girls made the trip without supervision. This process was repeated using
destinations which were successively more distant.

Cooking: Classes were held for four girls each at breakfast and supper times.
The children in these classes learned to plan menus, shop for food, and prepare
meals. The meals were prepared in the model living area of the cottage. They ate
the meals in the model dining room next to the kitchen. Many of the skills learned
are occupationally useful, as well as socially critical.

Housecleaning: The ability to clean a house thoroughly and independently is
regarded as a most valuable skill for these girls. It was discovered, however, that
the watch-and-do method was not sufficient. It was necessary to write a program
similar to the ones used to teach sewing and ironing before success was experienced.
The first training sessions were held in the model living area on the cottage. Succeeding sessions were held in a variety of local homes to insure generalization of
the cleaning skills from one environment to another.

Education: Programed instruction techniques similar to those reported by Birnbrauer, *et al.* (1965) and Bijou, Birnbrauer, Kidder, and Tague (1966) are employed to give girls basic academic preparation, and to teach skills specific to
occupations. Persons with IQs between 25 and 55 are most often considered non-
educable. However, it has been demonstrated that many are capable of acquiring a
functional basic reading vocabulary, as well as learning to count and in some cases
make change. Traditional educational techniques have not enjoyed this measure of
success. Programing with its emphasis on identifying the smallest components of the
learning task, sequential presentation, and positive reinforcement of correct responding seems a more promising approach.

Attempts to Transfer Girls from the Miniature Culture to the Community

Since one of the primary aims of the program was to train the girls in skills necessary for community adjustment, the staff was extremely cognizant of opportunities
for placing the girls in community situations. Two major official channels for community transition were used. The first channel was a downtown sheltered workshop
in the local community which was sponsored by VRA. The second channel was the
Vocational Rehabilitation Center in Topeka. However, opportunities were quite
varied and occurred at unexpected times such as when a local nursing home needed
extra personnel or when a mother needed aid in babysitting or ironing. Opportunities
for the girls to participate in community activities occurred on such occasions as
when an interested minister of the downtown churches suggested that some of the
girls visit his church. Once the opportunities were available to engage in some type
of community activity, the girls were initially well supervised. If the opportunity
involved a job, a member of the staff went with the girl to observe and train her
in the specific work situation. Moreover, the staff person discussed with the employer
procedures for maintaining adequate performance by the girl, such as when it was

appropriate to socially reward the girl and when it was not. The employer's work supervisor was instructed not to tolerate inferior work habits or personal habits because the girl is retarded. He was also told that a member of the demonstration staff would aid him in modifying the behavior if the girl involved was not adequately performing.

Such on-the-job supervision procedures allowed for gradual, rather than abrupt, shifts of control of the child's behavior from cottage contingencies to those provided in the community environment.

Evaluation of the Effectiveness of the Miniature Culture

Immediately preceding the initiation of training on the demonstration cottage, observations made on the basis of a check list were used to evaluate the behavior of the girls on the cottage. The procedure followed was to have the two observers simultaneously record all behaviors on the list for the same one-fourth of the group (seven girls). The observers were given instructions to record a behavior only once a session for each girl, regardless of its frequency during the three-hour observation periods. During this period, they also kept notes on those behavioral definitions which made observer agreement difficult, and those which were too difficult to observe for any other reason. From these observations and notes, the categories to be observed were revised. After the revision, the same procedure of observing simultaneously and keeping notes was again followed. From this second set of observations and notes, certain categories were removed from the list. Following this, the actual baseline observations, according to the list shown in Table 25.4, were begun in October 1965, and lasted six weeks. No girl was observed fewer than eight times, and none more than twelve times.

TABLE 25.4

Behavior observed	t Value df = 7	Number of changes in:			No. who stayed at 0 level	Sign test prob. level
		Desired direction	Undesired direction	No change		
Clothing	10.85†					
Dress inapprop. to occ.		12	8	1	1	> .25
Clothes dirty		13	5	3	3	.10
Clothes unpressed		21	0	0	0	< .01
Clothes do not fit		12	2	7	7	.05
Clothes not matched		4	2	15	15	> .25
Socks dirty		2	2	17	17	> .25
Shoes dirty		12	1	8	8	.01
Clothes hung improperly		14	3	4	4	< .05
Physical cleanliness	3.45*					
Hair dirty		10	4	7	7	.25
Face dirty		4	0	17	17	.25
Hands dirty		2	0	19	19	> .25
Elbows dirty		3	1	17	17	> .25

TABLE 25.4 (Cont.)

Behavior observed	t Value df = 7	Number of changes in: Desired direction	Undesired direction	No change	No. who stayed at 0 level	Sign test prob. level
Physical grooming	10.07†					
Hair not parted		21	0	0	0	< .01
Hair style not approp.		20	0	1	1	< .01
Hair not combed		16	3	2	0	.01
Eyebrow pencil inapprop.		3	0	18	18	.25
Lipstick not approp.		8	3	10	10	.25
Fingernails untrimmed		4	0	17	17	.25
Fingernails bitten		6	3	12	12	> .25
Walking	22.19†					
Head not up		21	0	0	0	< .01
Back not straight		18	1	2	2	< .01
Stomach not in		16	2	3	3	< .01
Toes not forward		15	3	3	3	.01
Shuffling		18	3	0	0	< .01
Heavy walk		17	2	2	1	< .01
Sitting	3.05*					
Legs not together		6	15	0	0	.10
Back not straight		19	2	0	0	< .01
Sprawls		15	6	0	0	.10
Verbal behavior	1.73					
Inapprop. adult title		6	11	4	4	> .25
Swears		2	4	15	15	> .25
Screams		4	0	17	17	.25
Giggles		10	5	6	5	> .25
Talks too loudly		6	13	2	2	.25
Talks to self		11	3	7	7	.10
Meaningless verbalization		6	1	14	14	.25
Rude		0	0	21	21	—
Social behavior	1.01					
Inactive (over 15 min.)		4	11	6	6	.25
Throws items		1	0	20	20	> .25
Punches/pokes others		5	7	9	9	> .25
Touches others		12	1	8	8	.01
Vulgar hand gestures		1	0	20	20	> .25
Mouth hanging open		15	4	2	1	.05
Picks nose		10	2	9	9	.05
Chews gum; mouth open		5	0	16	16	.10

* p ≤ .05
† p ≤ .001

Follow-up data were collected approximately one year after the collection of baseline data on the personal and social skills of the girls. These data were collected to evaluate the combined effects of both the general reinforcement system as well as the specific training projects. The same procedures were used in collecting follow-up data as were used in collecting the baseline data. However, different observers collected the data. Both the pre- and post-baseline observers were trained by the program supervisor.

Twenty-one of the twenty-seven girls were residents on the cottage during both baseline and follow-up observations. Thus, the data presented are based on twenty-one Ss. Each of the twenty-one Ss was observed on no less than eight occasions. Two types of analyses of the data were conducted. The first type involved collapsing the items under each of the seven categories and comparing the number of occasions of inappropriate behavior within each category on baseline and follow-up sessions for the total group. A test for differences between means of related samples (Peatman, 1963) was used to calculate the significance of difference. The resulting ± values indicated significant group improvements in clothing, physical cleanliness, physical grooming, walking, and sitting. The ± value for verbal behavior and social behavior were not significant.

In order to obtain a better understanding of the nature and extent of the changes, sign tests were made of the individual items of the check list. If the proportion of time a S was observed engaged in an appropriate behavior decreased from baseline to follow-up, she was assigned a "+" (desirable), and if the proportion increased, she was assigned a "−" (undesirable). If there were no change, the S was excluded from the analyses for that item. The results of the sign test of the individual items of the check list indicated that seventeen items showed significant changes in the desired direction (see columns 2, 3, 4, 5, and 6 of Table 25.4 and Fig. 25.3). Since large numbers of the girls showed zero occurrence of maladaptive behavior on some items in both baseline and follow-up observations, the failure to show significant differences on these items is not surprising. This does not mean that these items should be overlooked. For example, only four girls screamed during the baseline condition; however, none screamed during the follow-up test. Moreover, the fact that thirteen girls increased in loud talking while only six decreased, indicates that if loud talking is in fact a drawback to rehabilitation, the program is inadequate with regard to this item and should be changed.

In summary, comparison of the baseline and follow-up observations indicates that the overall cottage system and its specific projects have been generally effective in improving such personal skills as care of clothing, physical cleanliness, physical grooming, walking, and sitting. The baseline and follow-up, however, provided no evidence of improvement in the general categories of verbal behavior or social behavior. This does not mean that there has been no change in these behaviors; nevertheless, it does dictate a closer evaluation of training procedures, evaluation procedures, and the relationship between the training and evaluation procedures.

The observation data suggests improvement in many areas. However, the overall evaluation of the miniature culture must include information concerning flow of girls toward the community. On July 1, 1965, there were twenty-seven girls on Mimosa C. Of those twenty-seven girls, seventeen remained on the cottage as of September 1, 1967. Of the ten who left the cottage, four returned to the community, four were transferred to higher level cottages, one was transferred to a lower level

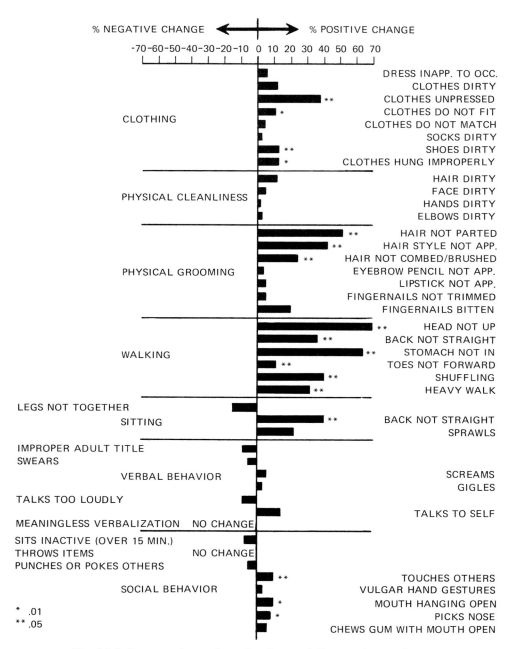

Fig. 25.3. Percent change from baseline to follow-up for total group.

cottage, and one was transferred to an intensive-care cottage. In other words, eight of ten transfers suggested behavioral improvement.

An illustrative case: Our most successful graduate thus far has been EH. Her case is illustrative of the procedures used in preparing children for life outside the institution. EH is a nineteen-year-old girl who has been institutionalized for ten years. Her parents were judged unfit to provide care for her and her siblings. She was made a court ward and subsequently institutionalized.

A recent administration of the WISC indicated a full scale IQ of 48. At the time when the project was begun on Mimosa C, she was observed to be a plain-looking girl who was somewhat overweight. Some of her work tasks were performed adequately, but only when she "wanted to." She exhibited her tantrum behavior whenever she was asked to perform an unattractive task or when she was frustrated by peers or adults. Her educational attainments were unmeasurable on standardized tests, but she could count by one's to sixty, could write her name, and read a few common words.

EH was included in the programs relating to personal appearance and personal hygiene. As her habits and skills improved, she began to take pride in her appearance. In many ways, she learned to maintain herself in an independent manner; she could sew and mend, style and set her own hair, and select and buy attractive clothing which was within her budget. Programed instruction techniques were employed to teach her the basic academic skills needed to get along in the community. She learned to tell time, to make change, read menus and words that were functional to work in the home and community. Her work assignments at the hospital were made increasingly difficult, and finally, she was given a training placement in the community. After placement, problems occurred which could not be solved by instruction in a group. Intensive individual instruction to correct observed deficiencies were initiated. Attempts were made to modify her social behavior. As a substitute for temper tantrums following frustration, she was trained to ask clarifying questions to help her understand the directive. Phrases such as, "I'm sorry, I don't understand," "Could you tell me again, please," and "I don't know how to do that yet," were practiced and role played. She was also encouraged to smile more often.

Many things learned in the context of training programs on the cottage did not transfer to similar but different community settings. To generalize the skills involved in planning menus, buying food, and preparing and eating meals, it was necessary to give her individual training in the home of a research assistant. Since she had a severe articulation disorder, our efforts in speech therapy were also intensified. Since the city of Parsons does not have public transportation, she had to learn to phone for a taxi and to budget for this expenditure.

Finally, EH was placed as a nurse's aide in a local nursing home, and a local family agreed to take EH into their home. She was working full time and living away from the institution. At this time (eight months later) EH has received two raises in pay and her duties at the nursing home have increased in difficulty many times. Her problems of adjustment in the community have not become less difficult, but they have become more normal. For instance, her foster father is worried because she has started to date a local boy (of normal intelligence). It was explained to the father that this is a problem shared by many parents and has little to do with mental retardation.

DISCUSSION

No doubt the current report has raised several questions for the reader. Some of these may be directed toward the design; some may be directed toward the ethics of the culture. We shall attempt to address some of the more frequently occurring questions.

The first question is, "Did the changes in the cottage culture have anything to do with the reported changes in the behavior? Couldn't time alone produce these changes?" The writers are tempted to respond, "We don't know; we did not have an appropriate control group." However, this is not entirely true. There are scores of wards for moderately retarded females in institutions all over the United States and there is little evidence children are improved in any respect by such placement. In fact, there is evidence to the contrary. Cain and Levine (1961) compared trainable retarded children who stayed at home with those who were placed in institutions on the basis of social competency scores. Those who remained at home, whether they attended school or not, showed significant increases in social competency. Those who were residents of institutions, and were in school or not in school, showed significant decreases in social competency scores. Studies by Schlanger (1954) and Lyle (1959) also indicate that the direction of behavior change in institutions is down—not up. Tizzard (1960) suggests that this finding is not a phenomenon of United States institutions for the retarded. In surveying the situation in Great Britain, he concludes that institutionalization has a crippling effect on retarded children.

A second question is, "Which of the specific changes resulted in the behavior change reported?" Perhaps reinforcement or appropriate models are irrelevant. To this question we must answer that we do not know the extent to which any one change in the culture produced changes in the behavior of the girls. This question stems in part from a confusion between research and engineering endeavors. The aim of this program was not to test whether reinforcement works, or whether people imitate models. The laboratory data on these matters is quite clear. The issue was: "Could a culture be developed based on established learning principles, which would in turn establish and maintain community-related behavior?" Rather than isolate variables as one does in a laboratory, our aim was to combine every variable which we had reason to believe would change behavior in the desired direction.

A third design question was, "Couldn't the changes simply be the result of a Hawthorne effect?" This question usually implies that the Hawthorne effect is, in fact, unreal. It seems more likely that the Hawthorne effect is a real but transitory effect, due to the fact that social reinforcement contingencies are changed by some manipulation of the environment. Management changes the lighting and then shows increased interest in the personnel and production, and in a sense temporarily reinforces productive behavior. Every attempt is made in the design of a culture to enhance such effects and, if possible, maintain them.

A fourth question which arises is, "Is a set of behavioral principles enough to bring about the behavioral changes reported?" The answer is, "No." One can use the same behavioral principles to prepare a child for the community, or to prepare a child to vegetate in an institution. The principles of behavior, like the principles of any scientific field, know no ethics.

An ethical question which arises is, "Are you sure you selected the appropriate goals for these girls?" Our answer is, simply, "We selected behavioral goals on which most members of our community could agree." For example, most members would agree that it is better for an adolescent girl to know how to cook and sew than not to know how to cook and sew. Most members would agree that it is better to say, "Please," when requesting something than not to say, "Please."

A practical question is, "But isn't it extremely hard to train an aide or demonstration assistant to interact with the girls in a natural and spontaneous manner when so much of their behavior is prescribed?" When an aide or demonstration assistant initially starts reinforcing on a schedule, rather than "naturally," their behavior appears somewhat mechanistic and stilted. However, as time goes on, they come to respond quite "naturally" and "spontaneously" when the child is engaging in appropriate behavior. Moreover, the effectiveness of positive reinforcement procedures increases the frequency of "affectionate, happy" responses. The staff person is "affectionate" and "happy" because the child is performing in an acceptable manner—thus the staff person is reinforced and the child is "happy" and "affectionate" because the staff adult-behavior is quiet, systematic, and thus predictable, as well as associated primarily with positive reinforcement.

Another ethical question which comes up is, "Isn't it wrong to pay a girl to do something she already should be doing for nothing? For example, a girl should not have to be paid to comb her hair." This question overlooks certain behavior facts and demonstrates a strong tendency of the person, who asks the question, to resort to aversive techniques to control behavior. The first fact is that if the behavior does not already occur, positive reinforcement is probably the most effective way of establishing it; and second, that once it is established, one may maintain it on natural reinforcers—thus "doing it for pay" is a transition step to "doing it for no pay." Moreover, if you exclude positive reinforcement to establish and maintain behavior, then you are left with aversive techniques. Personally, we think it is more ethical to pay a girl for combing her hair than to punish her because she has not. Certainly the former procedure is more effective since it leads to a happy child who combs her hair.

Questions regarding cost occur. The first question usually takes the form of, "How much does the project cost above the regular services provided by the hospital?" The answer is: The program is expensive, costing approximately $35,000 per year above the cost of regular hospital treatment. The next question is, "In view of the high cost, is it practical?" If this project is successful in returning girls to the community, at least a part of the cost will be saved by the taxpayer. For example, if we can be sure that a girl who was returned to the community will be self-support-ing, the tax saving over her life span in an institution will approximate $100,000. A third cost-question is, "Couldn't the same effects be obtained with a less costly program?" We cannot answer this question with certainty. However, it is likely that systems will be developed which will apply the same principles and achieve the same end as this prototype culture but with much less cost. Already, various aspects of the reinforcement and training system are being implemented in cottages at Parsons with no increase in staff personnel.

REFERENCES

Ayllon, T., and N. H. Azrin. "Reinforcement and Instructions with Mental Patients." *Journal of the Experimental Analysis of Behavior* 7(1964):327–331.

Bandura, A., and R. H. Walters. *Social Learning and Personality Development.* New York: Holt, Rinehart and Winston, 1963.

Birnbrauer, J. S., S. W. Bijou, M. M. Wolf, and J. D. Kidder. "Programmed Instruction in the Classroom." In L. P. Ullmann and L. Krasner, eds., *Case Studies in Behavior Modification.* New York: Holt, Rinehart and Winston, 1965, pp. 358–363.

Cain, L. F., and S. Levine. *A Study of the Effects of Community and Institutional School Classes for Trainable Mentally Retarded Children.* San Francisco: San Francisco State College, 1961.

Ellis, N. R., C. D. Barnett, and M. Pryer. "Operant Conditioning in Mental Defectives: An Exploratory Study." *Journal of the Experimental Analysis of Behavior* 3(1960):63–69.

Girardeau, F. L., and J. E. Spradlin. "Token Rewards in a Cottage Program." *Mental Retardation* 2(1964):345–352.

Hollis, J. H. "Development of Perceptual Motor Skills in a Profoundly Retarded Child: Part I. Prosthesis." *American Journal of Mental Deficiency* 71(1967):941–952.

Lindsley, O. R. "Operant Conditioning Methods Applied to Research in Chronic Schizo-phrenia." *Psychiatric Research Reports* (American Psychiatric Association), 1956, pp. 118–139.

Lyle, J. G. "The Effect of an Institution Environment upon the Verbal Development of Imbecile Children." *Journal of Mental Deficiency Research* 3(1959):122–128.

Peatman, J. G. *Introduction to Applied Statistics.* New York: Harper & Row, 1963.

Schlanger, B. B. "Environmental Influence on Verbal Output of Mentally Retarded Children." *Journal of Speech and Hearing Disorders* 19(1954):339–345.

Sherman, J. A. "Use of Reinforcement and Imitation to Reinstate Verbal Behavior in Mute Psychotics." *Journal of Abnormal Psychology* 70(1965):155–164.

Spradlin, J. E., F. L. Girardeau, and E. Corte. "Fixed Ratio and Fixed Interval Behavior of Severely and Profoundly Retarded Subjects." *Journal of Experimental Child Psychology* 2(1966):340–353.

Tate, B. G., and G. S. Baroff. "Training the Mentally Retarded in the Production of a Complex Product: A Demonstration of Work Potential." *Exceptional Children* 33 (1967):405–410.

Tizzard, J. "Residential Care of Mentally Handicapped Children." *British Medical Journal* 1(1960):1041–1046.

Tizzard, J., and N. O'Connor. *The Social Problem of Mental Deficiency*. New York: Pergamon Press, 1956.

Wolf, M. M., T. R. Risley, and H. L. Mees. "Application of Operant Conditioning Procedures to the Behavior Problems of an Autistic Child." *Behavior Research and Therapy* 1(1964):305–312.

QUESTIONS

1. Briefly describe the token system used at Mimosa Cottage. How was reinforcement delivered, by whom, and for what?

2. Points could be exchanged for money or for certain activities designated as "privileges." These activities were the kind people would generally agree indicate community-oriented, normal behavior.

   a) Why were these kinds of activities chosen?

   b) Any reinforcement system to program behavior change must also consider the problem of maintaining desired behavior. When a successful graduate of Mimosa Cottage leaves the point system of reinforcement for desired behavior patterns, why wouldn't she revert to old behavior patterns?

3. Lent *et al.* made certain changes in the physical environment of Mimosa Cottage. What was the general direction of these changes? Why did they make the changes?

4. When EH graduated into the community at large, the authors discovered that some of the skills she had learned at Mimosa Cottage were not being used in her new environment. How did they deal with this problem? What might this problem indicate about the changes you have just described?

5. In developing their training programs, Lent *et al.* frequently found that casual watch-and-do teaching methods were insufficient. In those cases they had to analyze the task to be taught, then devise an instructional sequence that would lead gradually to the terminal behavior. Select one of their training goals, like town orientation, and describe the desired terminal behavior, the task analysis, and the sequence of contingencies used to establish the terminal behavior.

UNIT

26

Comparison of Two Music Programs

Content

Barnes, R. A. *Fundamentals of Music: A Program for Self-Instruction.* New York: McGraw-Hill, 1964, pp. x, xi, xiii, 76, 78–84, 98–99.

Clough J. *Scales, Intervals, Keys and Triads: A Programed Book of Elementary Music Theory.* New York: Norton, 1964, pp. 4, 7–12, 22–23.

Selections from these two music programs introduce the concepts of intervals and major scales. The preface of each program describes its development and intended users.

Objectives

See instructions.

Instructions

In this unit, questions are placed *before* the readings. Use the questions to direct your reading of the following selection. There are two sets of questions: the first set asks for a comparison of the two programs' prefaces; the second set asks for a comparison of teaching material. Answer the first set of questions after reading the two prefaces, then go on to the next set of questions and the lesson material.

QUESTIONS

The Prefaces

Read over these questions, then read the following set of materials, which includes both authors' prefaces and a chapter introduction from Barnes' book. Then answer these questions.

1. While detailed objectives are not listed in either case, evaluate how the aims of each book rate as behavioral objectives. Does either author identify the kind of behavior to be demonstrated by the student?
2. How well has each author described the learner's entering behavior?
3. Compare the two in terms of adequacy of specification of students used in the pilot run and the outcomes one could expect as based on their data.

Fundamentals of Music

Robert A. Barnes

PREFACE

This book, which contains information on music fundamentals and normally takes four to six hours to complete, is designed to alleviate some of these difficulties, which concern both the instructor and the student. While it was originally developed to enhance the music learning of future elementary teachers, it has received increasing acceptance by teachers of general music classes in the junior and senior high school; beginning instrumental students in band, orchestra, and piano; students in remedial music-theory classes in college; and by individuals who wish to engage in a home-study program in music.

A Program for Self-instruction

If you have leafed through the pages of this book, you have probably noticed that it does not have a traditional format. It is a programmed text—a rather recent development in education. Programmed books offer to the student several advantages not offered by conventional textbooks.

Briefly, the content of this book, the fundamentals of music, has been broken down into small, logical steps which lead you slowly, easily, and systematically to a place at which you are able to answer some rather complicated questions about music. This book consists of a series of short statements and questions. You are asked to respond in some way to every pertinent idea presented. At first, some of

R. A. Barnes, *Fundamentals of Music: A Program for Self-Instruction* (New York: McGraw-Hill, 1964), pp. x, xi, xiii, 76, 78–84, 98–99. Copyright © 1964 by McGraw-Hill, Inc. Used with permission of McGraw-Hill Book Company.

the questions may appear to be extremely simple. Don't, however, be misled by this. Answer each one as carefully and as accurately as you can. When you have answered the question, you will then learn whether or not your response is correct. This system will help you to learn in several ways:

1. *You will not only learn the material, but you will know that you have learned it.* You can be sure that you are on the right track, because each time you answer you are informed immediately whether your answer is right or wrong.

2. *You will not have a chance to daydream.* Perhaps you have had the experience, while reading a book, of suddenly realizing that you have no idea what the last page was about. Your mind can not wander while reading this book, for you will participate actively in the learning process by frequently writing short answers.

3. *You will not have to spend time reading or studying material you already know.* Unlike other textbooks, you will be asked a criterion question at the beginning of each chapter. If you answer the question correctly, you merely skip to the next chapter.

4. *You may work at your own rate of speed.* In learning through this system, you take as much time as you need—moving slowly in difficult parts and as fast as you like in the easier sections.

. . .

INTRODUCTION TO CHAPTER FIVE

In this chapter you will be introduced to the concept of half steps and whole steps, and you will learn how to write these on a staff. If you would like to try a few before you start, answer the following questions. If you cannot answer the questions, turn the page now.

Criterion Questions

1. Write on the staff a note which is one whole step above each note given.

2. Write on the staff a note which is one half step above each note given.

Check your answers on the next page after you have completed both questions.

Scales, Intervals, Keys and Triads:
A Self-Instruction Program

John Clough

PREFACE

To the Classroom Teacher

This program may be used in high school or college courses in elementary music theory. It is intended to provide a foundation for subsequent work in one of the standard textbooks, and to serve equally well the needs of teachers who prefer not to use a text.

Most students will require 6–12 hours to complete the program. Thus, in some courses it will be convenient to assign completion of the entire program within a prescribed period at the beginning of the course, say two or three weeks. Or it may be assigned in sections, provided that each set is done in its proper turn. (One exception: sets 10 and 11, and the frames in set 12 relating to them, may be deferred until the end of the program, or omitted altogether, if desired.) Following completion of the program a test composed of items similar to those in sets 12 and 24 should be given.

The program has been revised on the basis of trials in classes at the Conservatory of Music, Oberlin College. All sections of the program have been tested by at least one hundred and fifty students; some sections have been tested by more than four hundred students over a period of four years.

It can be reported that this program has done an effective job of teaching its subject matter. However, those who adopt it should be cautioned not to expect miraculous extensions of learning to areas not really covered in the program. For example: a student who has completed the program should know that five sharps is the key signature of B major or G♯ minor. But the ability to identify the key of a given passage in an actual composition is not dealt with in the program, since it ultimately involves a judgment based on aural, not visual facts. The teaching of this skill (not to mention countless others) properly belongs to the classroom teacher.

To the Private Teacher

Few private teachers are able to devote sufficient time to basic theory. Many are keenly aware of their students' lack of knowledge of key signatures and other fundamentals. A self-instruction program in theory therefore seems a logical adjunct to private applied study. A good plan might be to assign the student one part of the

J. Clough, *Scales, Intervals, Keys and Triads: A Programmed Book of Elementary Music Theory* (New York: Norton, 1964), pp. 4, 7–12, 22, 23. Reprinted by permission of W. W. Norton & Company, Inc. Copyright © 1964, 1962 by John Clough.

program at a time and, following his completion of each part, to discuss with him its applications in a piece he is currently studying.

This program was written with high school age and older students in mind, but it may also be undertaken by musically and intellectually gifted students of junior high school age.

THE TEACHING MATERIAL

We have chosen from each program brief selections that teach similar concepts so that you may compare the different treatments. The concepts of semitones or half steps, whole tones or whole steps, and the major scale are introduced.

For those with no musical background: a scale consists of eight notes and begins and ends on the same note. That is, a scale that begins at middle C ends at C above middle C. A major scale is defined as having a semitone or half step between notes three and four and notes seven and eight, and whole tones or whole steps between all other notes. Therefore, in order to teach the concept of a major scale, one must first teach the concepts of half steps and whole steps. (We can ignore the question of the aural difference between a half step and whole step because these programs are designed to teach only theory.)

An examination of the table of contents preceding each selection reveals that both authors have followed this order in teaching the major scale. You might also note that very little else in their subject-matter organization is similar. For example, Barnes teaches key signatures when he teaches the major scale, while Clough introduces key signatures a full chapter after the major scale. Be sure to locate each selection within the appropriate table of contents to get some idea of each text's organization.

Each selection is taken from the beginning of its particular chapter or set. Read the questions below, then read the selection from each program. Do not work through the programs, just read the answers to get a quick picture of how each author handles his material. Then answer these questions.

QUESTIONS (continued from p. 321)

4. Do a blackout on each program. Which is better programed?
5. Look at the frame-by-frame responses each program requires of the student. Write several behavioral objectives for each program, based on these responses.
6. Compare the behavioral objectives you have derived for both programs and briefly discuss their differences.
7. Do you think the behavior that you have just described for both programs represents each author's objectives?
8. Look at the major-scale selection from each program. We noted above that the concept of a major scale is dependent upon certain other concepts. You have done a

blackout on these selections. Does either program appear to have built on established behavior when introducing this concept? Explain your answer.

FUNDAMENTALS OF MUSIC:
A PROGRAM FOR SELF-INSTRUCTION
Robert A. Barnes

TABLE OF CONTENTS

CHAPTER FIVE

Intervals: Whole Steps; Half Steps

We have already said that the keys on a piano keyboard are one half step apart. In other words, the distance or interval from C to C♯ on this

---

* Editors' note: The following selections are taken from Chapters 5 and 6.

half

keyboard is a half step. Knowing this, we can also figure that the interval between F and F♯ is also a _____ step.

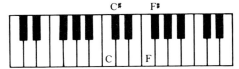

The interval from any key on the keyboard to its nearest neighbor is a *half step.* The interval from key number 2 to key number 1 is a half

half
step

step. The interval from key number 2 to key number 3 is a _____
_____.

half step

The interval from any key on the keyboard to its closest neighbor, *either above or below,* is always one _____ _____.

is

The closest neighbor is always one half step away. The nearest neighbor *below* G♯ is G. The interval between G♯ and G, then _____ [is/ is not] one half step.

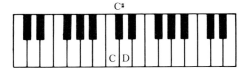

yes

The interval from C to C♯ is a half step. Is the interval from C♯ to D also a half step? _____ [yes/no]

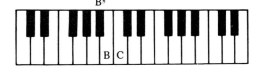

C
C

The nearest neighbor to B, on the lower side, is B♭. The nearest neighbor to B, on the upper side, is _____. There is one half step between B and its upper neighbor which is _____.

F

There is one half step between E and its upper neighbor which is _____.

half steps

If there is an interval of *one* half step between D and D♯, then there must be *two* h_____ s_____ between D and E.

two

If there is an interval of *one* half step between G and G♯, there must be _____ [number] half steps between G and A.

. . .

one

Now, from what we know about arithmetic, we might guess that two half steps will be equal to _____ [number] whole step(s).

one

The interval from F to G is two half steps or _____ [number] whole step(s).

one

The interval from G to A is _____ [number] whole step(s).

half

The interval from C♯ to D is one _____ step.

. . .

half   Try one more. The interval from B to C is one _____ step.*

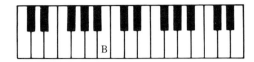

half   Try a few this way now. The interval between the arrows is one
            _____ step.

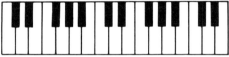

. . .

C   Looking at the keyboard, we can see that there is always a black key
            between the white keys *except* between E and F and between B and
            _____.*

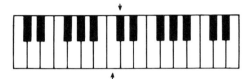

F, C   We will always find a black key between the white keys, except between
            E and _____ and between B and _____.

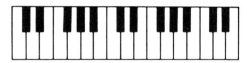

[Later in Chapter 5 students are asked to identify the interval between two
notes without use of a piano keyboard diagram. At the end of the chapter, students
are given a note on a staff and must write another note one semitone higher or
lower.

In Chapter 6 Barnes introduces the major scale. Only the first two pages of this
chapter are included in this selection, so you will not see Barnes' complete development of this concept. However, from these two pages you should get a sense of his
use of gradual progression.]

---

* Editors' note: In an earlier chapter the names of the keys were taught.

CHAPTER SIX

Major Scales and Key Signatures

C
  This is a C scale. It begins on C and ends on _____.

D, D
  This is a _____ scale. It begins on D and ends on _____.

F, F
  This F scale begins on _____ and ends on _____.

8
  Scale step number 1 is C. Scale step number _____ is also C.

Scales form the basis for most of our music. You will learn about two kinds of scales—*major* scales and *minor* scales. We will save the *minor*

major
  scales until later. Right now we will talk about the _____ scales.

Major scales are distinguished from other kinds of scales by the arrangement of half steps and whole steps within the scale. From what you know of whole and half steps, it is easy to see that there is a whole step between each of the notes in this scale *except* between numbers 3

4, 8
  and _____ and 7 and _____.

half
  A major scale always has h_____ steps between numbers 3 and 4 of the scale and between numbers 7 and 8 of the scale.

This C scale (*a*) is a *major* scale with half steps between 3 and 4 and

is not

between 7 and 8. This F scale (*b*) _____ [is/is not] a major scale. (Notice where the half steps come.)

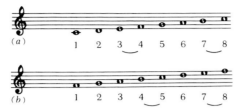

4

In order to have a *major* scale, the half steps must come between numbers 3 and _____ and between numbers 7 and 8.

8

Now, if we wish to make the *F scale* at (*a*) into an *F major scale,* all we do is place a flat in front of note B and we have a *major* scale with half steps between 3 and 4 and between 7 and _____ [see (*b*)].

Scales, Intervals, Keys and Triads: A Programmed Book of Elementary Music Theory

John Clough

TABLE OF CONTENTS

INTRODUCTION

The following illustrations, based on diagrams in *Rudiments of Music* by John Castellini, will serve as a guide to note and key names.

---

* Editors' note: The following selections are taken from sets 1 and 4.

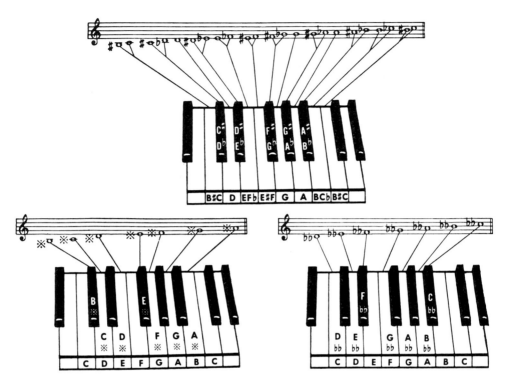

SET ONE

The Semitone

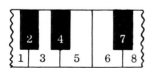

1

This diagram is a section of a piano keyboard. Complete the numbering of keys from the lowest to the highest.

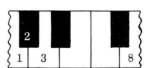

2

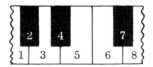

Two keys with consecutive numbers are *adjacent*. Key no. 2 and key no. 3 are adjacent. Key no. 2 and key no. 1 are _____.

adjacent

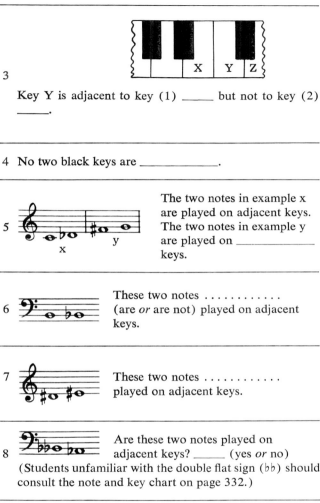

3

(1) **X**
(2) **Z**

Key Y is adjacent to key (1) _____ but not to key (2) _____.

---

adjacent

4 No two black keys are _____.

---

adjacent

5

The two notes in example x are played on adjacent keys. The two notes in example y are played on _____ keys.

---

are

6

These two notes . . . . (are *or* are not) played on adjacent keys.

---

are not

7

These two notes . . . . played on adjacent keys.

---

yes

8

Are these two notes played on adjacent keys? _____ (yes *or* no)
(Students unfamiliar with the double flat sign (♭♭) should consult the note and key chart on page 332.)

---

one semitone

9

The distance between these notes played on adjacent keys is one *semitone*. The two notes shown are played on adjacent keys. The distance between them is _____ _____.

---

adjacent keys

10 *Half step* and *half tone* are synonyms for *semitone*, but only the word *semitone* will be used in this book. The distance between two notes played on _____ _____ is one semitone.

is

11

The distance between these notes
. . . . (is *or* is not) one
semitone.

is

12

The distance between these notes
. . . . one semitone.

no

13

Are these notes one semitone
apart? _____

one semitone

14

These notes are . . . . apart.

lower

15

The first note is one semitone
_____ (higher *or* lower)
than the second note.

lower

16

The first note is one semitone
_____ than the second note.

one
semitone higher

17

The first note is _____
_____ _____ than
the second note.

(Students unfamiliar with the double sharp sign (x)
should consult the note and key chart on page 332.)

one
semitone higher

18

The second note is _____
_____ _____ than
the first note.

or

19 Write a note which lies one semitone higher than the given note.
*(There is more than one correct
answer.)*

Write
here
↓

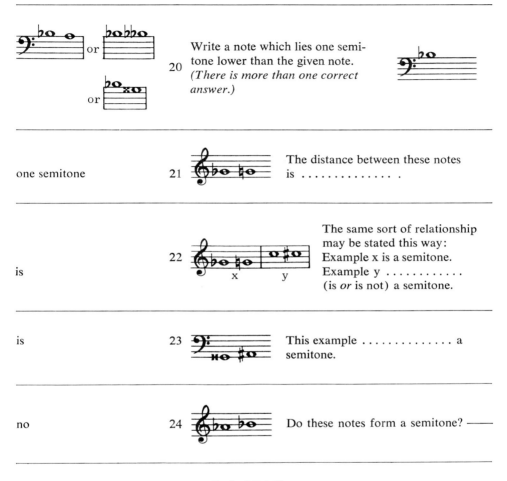

20   Write a note which lies one semi-tone lower than the given note. (*There is more than one correct answer.*)

---

one semitone

21   The distance between these notes is . . . .

---

is

22   The same sort of relationship may be stated this way: Example x is a semitone. Example y . . . . (is *or* is not) a semitone.

---

is

23   This example . . . . a semitone.

---

no

24   Do these notes form a semitone? ———

End of Set One.

[Clough's Set Two teaches students to distinguish two particular kinds of semitones, the diatonic semitone (DST) and the chromatic semitone (CST). In a CST, both notes are written on the same line or space, so one note must be sharped or flatted. In a DST, one note is written on a line and the other on a space, so both or neither may be sharped or flatted.

Clough's Set Three teaches the concept of a whole tone using a format similar to Set One.

The following selection is from Clough's Set Four, which teaches the concept of a major scale. As with Barnes, only the first two pages from this Set appear, but they should be sufficient to give you a sense of Clough's progression.]

SET FOUR

The Major Scale

1

(s)cales

Shown above are two different s_____.

2

whole tone

In this scale the distance between notes 1 and 2 is
a . . . .

---

whole tone

3 The distance between notes 2 and 3 is a . . . .

2–3

4 In discussing scales we will use 1–2 as an abbreviation
for "the distance between notes 1 and 2." "The distance
between notes 2 and 3" would be abbreviated
. . . .

DST

5 In the above scale 3–4 is a . . . .
(DST *or* CST *or* whole tone)

---

whole tone

6 4–5 is a . . . .

---

(1) whole tone
(2) whole tone
(3) DST

7 5–6 is a (1) . . . .
6–7 is a (2) . . . .
7–8 is a (3) . . . .

3–4

8 This scale has DST's at _____ and 7–8, and whole tones
everywhere else.

9

3–4 (and) 7–8

This scale has DST's at _____ and _____, and whole
tones everywhere else.

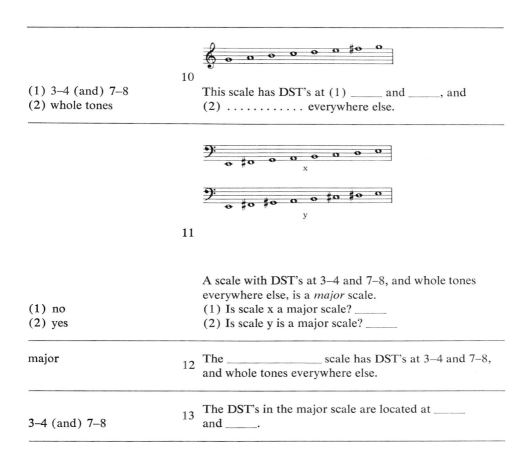

10

(1) 3–4 (and) 7–8
(2) whole tones

This scale has DST's at (1) _____ and _____, and
(2) . . . . everywhere else.

11

A scale with DST's at 3–4 and 7–8, and whole tones
everywhere else, is a *major* scale.

(1) no
(2) yes

(1) Is scale x a major scale? _____
(2) Is scale y is a major scale? _____

major

12   The _____ scale has DST's at 3–4 and 7–8,
and whole tones everywhere else.

13   The DST's in the major scale are located at _____
and _____.

3–4 (and) 7–8

PART
V
The Uses of Tests

The tests discussed in the following three units are not criterion referenced tests. Unit 27 presents methods of assessing the effectiveness of tests that adapt to individual differences, such as those used in the Individually Prescribed Instruction model examined in Unit 3 (pretests, posttests, CETs, etc.).

Unit 28 describes a very different kind of testing—the testing of instructional materials in order to improve their instructional design. In Unit 29 you will be asked to submit your own materials to similar tests and to revise the materials if necessary.

UNIT

27

Variables in
Adaptive Decisions

Content

Holland, J. G. "Variables in Adaptive Decisions in Individualized Instruction."
Pittsburgh: University of Pittsburgh, Learning Research and Development Center,
1975. (a selection.)

The selection from this article presents three quantitative measures for evaluating adaptive decisions in individualized materials. Use of the measures on samples
of curriculum materials is also described.

Objectives

Students describe the difference between a good teaching item and a good diagnostic
test item. They list the three functions of tests designed to adapt to individual differences in subject-matter knowledge, and describe how each measure of an adaptive
test is derived from one particular function. Students also calculate a consequence
ratio, a predictive-validity ratio, and a discriminability ratio for various adaptive
programs. They describe the general relationship of test time and predictive validity.
Finally, they discuss what a consumer of individualized materials should know and
do before buying.

Instructions

1. Read the objectives and use them to guide your reading.

2. Read the selection from the article.
3. Answer the questions, referring back to the selection as necessary.
4. Check your work, then discuss your responses with your instructor.

Variables in Adaptive Decisions in Individualized Instruction
James G. Holland

The present study attempts to elucidate some quantitative measures to assess the adequacy of adaptive decisions in individualized materials. The primary purpose of this effort is to sharpen the curriculum developer's ability to generate better adaptive materials by sharpening his judgment of the quality of the diagnostic portions of his material in meeting the objectives of adaptive instruction. Despite the heavy emphasis over the past decade on prescribing materials adaptive to individual needs by diagnosing these needs through criterion-referenced tests (Glaser, 1963), the principles involved in preparing good adaptive materials have been left implicit.

The measures described here are derived from the rationale for adapting and from an attempt to formulate rather direct, simple indices of the important variables. The general strategy adopted is similar to that followed in developing the black-out ratio (Holland, 1967) as a measure for programmed teaching items. The resulting measures should do for diagnostic items what the black-out ratio does for teaching items. They should provide a basis for research in adaptive decisions while giving clear guidelines to the developer of adaptive materials. Effort was made to develop measures which (1) assess the adequacy of diagnostic items in meeting the aims of adaptation, (2) are simple and easy to apply, (3) discriminate among programs which differ in the adequacy of adaptive decisions, and (4) are objective in that different persons using the measures will obtain the same results.

"Individualization" or "adaptive education" have become vogue terms which have occasionally been used to describe quite different things (cf. Cronbach, 1971). To some the terms connote the unstructured curriculum of the open classroom; and for others, they can mean individual choice of objectives. In this paper, the terms are taken to mean that individual differences in needs are diagnosed in an attempt to present each student with only those teaching materials he needs to reach proficiency in the terminal objectives of the course. Hence, the course objectives are the same for all students, but the student who is able to pass many diagnostic items skips much unnecessary teaching material, while the student who misses many diagnostic items gets additional material, sometimes identified as remedial.

Thus, adaptive materials have two separate components: test items which diagnose the student's need, and teaching materials which fill that need. In Individually

---

J. G. Holland, "Variables in Adaptive Decisions in Individualized Instruction" (Pittsburgh: University of Pittsburgh, Learning Research and Development Center, 1975). Reprinted by permission.

Prescribed Instruction (IPI) and most other adaptive materials, the two different types of items are clearly designated by the developer.

The present paper addresses criteria for diagnostic items used in adapting, not criteria used for developing the teaching items. There is already a set of well-established principles as to how teaching materials should be designed and by what criteria they might be judged. Teaching items have a quite different function, and a different, even incompatible, basis for evaluating their worth than diagnostic items. Generally, whether or not the teaching material is in the old familiar formats of early programmed instruction, the principles embodied in its design are programming principles. Usually, the student's tasks follow some form of gradual progression. (Although in individualized materials, some effort is made to tailor this progression to the individual.) Individual teaching items are expected to evoke the desired, to-be-learned behavior before the student reaches a correct answer. Thus, the items should provide a low black-out ratio (Holland, 1967). It is anticipated that when the student reaches a particular level, he will be able to give the required performance since his answer insures he has performed adequately. Hence, good teaching material generally has a low error rate. The teaching item does not trap the student into errors or attempt to diagnose his deficiencies. Instead, its purpose is to evoke the new behavior so that it may be reinforced and established.

By way of contrast, individualization requires a quite different type of item. Test items serve a diagnostic function. They serve to differentially predict; different performance on a diagnostic item is used to recommend different learning materials. Therefore, considerations in test design are appropriate for these diagnostic items. First, to be useful, a diagnostic item must discriminate among individuals. A zero error-rate item would be worthless. A good diagnostic item reveals differences in performance with some students answering correctly and others making one or more types of errors. Thus, a good diagnostic item meets criteria incompatible with those met by good teaching items. It is for the special properties of the diagnostic process that new measures are here proposed and demonstrated.

THE MEASURES

Adaptive materials characteristically (1) save the student's time and effort by letting him skip unneeded teaching material, (2) test each student to determine his needs, and (3) reflect individual differences among the students. These considerations suggest three important measures for the merit of adaptive tests. One reflects the potential savings in the student's time compared with the cost to him in time for the diagnosis. Another reflects the validity of prediction of the need for the learning material, and a third reflects the discriminability of the test. Simple indices of these three factors are proposed in the form of three ratios. The three indices will be called consequence ratio, predictive-validity ratio, and discriminability ratio.

Consequence Ratio

Adaptive tests are designed to give the student the teaching material he needs without wasting his time (and patience) with material he does not need. But testing itself comes at a cost in student time. It would be inefficient to spend a lot of time testing to enable a student to skip only a short teaching sequence. The appropriate index is a ratio of teaching time to total time. The total time is the combination of teaching time and testing time. If a unit of teaching material requires 30 minutes to complete but is preceded by a 30 minute pretest that would enable a passing student to skip the material, then the cost to the student of being tested is as great as the savings he stands to gain by passing the pretest. The consequence ratio for this test would be the 30 minute teaching period divided by the one-hour total (30 minute teaching plus 30 minute testing) or .50. Clearly, no matter what other merits this test may have, it would be unacceptable since the passing student can only break even. If, on the other hand, a 1-minute test could be used to prescribe this same 30-minute teaching unit, the cost is small compared to the potential gain in passing and the consequence ratio is 0.97. If other necessary conditions are met, this would be a very worthy instance of adapting.

The phrase "consequence ratio" is used to avoid implying anything about the merit of the teaching material that follows. The consequence of a test being evaluated might even include further testing; for example, placement tests place the student in units which may include test items that permit "looping" past subsections of the unit. The size of the consequence is everything in the catchment area under the test in question. It should be apparent that it is the *potential* consequence which is of concern here. That some students skip the material does not change the potential consequence of failing the test; it is, rather, the point. The consequence ratio addresses itself to the size of the cost in time (or amount of material) saved compared with the total amount of time (the test plus the consequence).

Predictive-Validity Ratio

The validity of a diagnostic item is the extent to which the item correctly predicts the need or lack of need for some teaching material before a posttest is taken to measure the same competence. The adequacy of such a prediction can be measured simply by giving first the diagnostic test and then the criterion (or posttest) *without* giving any instruction between the two tests. Poor performance on the diagnostic test predicts poor performance on the criterion test unless instruction is received. Likewise, good performance on the diagnostic test predicts good performance on the criterion test even when instruction is omitted.

In form, this procedure may sound to the reader like a reliability measure because it involves prediction by one test of performance on another parallel test. However, because performance on the criterion test is the targeted performance, validity seems conceptually correct.

When no instruction is provided between tests, the diagnostic test predicts correctly or "hits" when comparable material is answered correctly both on the initial and subsequent tests or when comparable material is answered incorrectly on both (see Table 27.1). A student passing a diagnostic test is expected to be able to skip the teaching material and pass the criterion test while one who fails the diagnostic test needs the teaching material and without it should fail the criterion test. Failures

TABLE 27.1

Sample decision table

		criterion test	
		pass	fail
diagnostic test	pass	hit	miss
	fail	miss	hit

$$\text{Predictive-Validity Ratio} = \frac{\text{hits}}{\text{hits} + \text{misses}} = \frac{\text{hits}}{\text{total decisions}}$$

of prediction, or "misses," occur when the student is correct on the diagnostic test but incorrect on the criterion test or incorrect on the diagnostic test but correct on the criterion test.

With the test and retest procedure, with no intervening instruction, the predictive-validity measure is based on the ratio of hits to total number of decisions. If everyone who passed a diagnostic test also passed the criterion test and all who failed the diagnostic test also failed the criterion test, then the ratio of number of hits to total number of decisions would be 1.0. If, on the other hand, tosses of a coin were used as the diagnostic test, these chance decisions would lead to half or a 0.5 ratio of hits to total number of decisions. Most tests will fall between these two extremes; for example, with a ratio of 0.75, one quarter of the students either were unnecessarily assigned teaching material or directed to skip material they in fact need. Such a low value for the validity ratio would presumably be acceptable to the developer or the user only if the consequence were very large compared with the time needed to complete the test. Ordinarily, one should expect validity ratios close to 0.90 or better.

Discriminability Ratio

In an exploratory effort applying the consequence ratio and the predictive-validity ratio to several sets of curriculum material, the need for this third measure became apparent. There are instances in which virtually all students answer diagnostic items correctly and others in which all answer incorrectly. In either case, all students receive the same prescriptions; therefore, the programs are not adaptive because the tests detect no individual differences to accommodate.

The discriminability measure is the ratio of the number who either passed or failed, whichever is smaller, to the total number taking the test. The discriminability ratio, then, varies from 0.0 to 0.50. It is zero if either all students pass or all fail; half passing would give a ratio of 0.50; one quarter passing (or one quarter failing) would give a ratio of 0.25.

It is clear that when there is no discriminability, that is, when the ratio is 0.0, the materials are not adaptive to individual differences because the test reveals no differences. Beyond this, there is no absolute minimum acceptable value; but a ratio as low as 0.10 would presumably be useful only if the test is highly valid and the consequence very large. Ordinarily a ratio of approximately 0.25 would be adequate if both validity and consequence are at least fairly large.

Use of the Measures

These three indices are quantitative measures of three variables involved in goodness of adaptive decisions. Adequacy on each of the variables is a necessary condition to meet the rationale of adaptive instruction. Excellence in any one is not a sufficient condition. Complete inadequacy for validity, consequence, or discriminability renders the diagnostic procedure worthless for individualization regardless of the value of the other two. On the other hand, there are no fixed, all-purpose values that can be regarded as acceptable. The ideals are clear, as are the values indicating extreme failure. Between these extremes experience with the measures will be required.

It must be clearly understood that these measures do not evaluate the overall usefulness of any set of curriculum material. The technique for such evaluation is well known and involves measurement on criterion measures *after* the students have used prescribed teaching material. The present three measures in no way evaluate the teaching material. They are, rather, measures of the adaptive characteristics of the program and not measures of characteristics of the teaching material. Neither are they measures of the achievement to be expected from using the materials. It is possible for the adaptive testing to be excellent and for the curriculum to fail to teach. It is even possible for the adapting characteristics to be poor and the overall usefulness of the material to be very good; although, in this case, the overall worth of the curriculum material would probably be improved by correcting the deficiencies in the diagnostic testing and adapting procedures.

PROGRAMMED REVIEWS OF MATHEMATICS
(Flexer and Flexer, 1967)

This is a program in remedial mathematics for college students who have had the typical mathematics background required of entering college students but who are now beginning a science course requiring use of math. Flexer and Flexer indicate that many students are unprepared to handle the mathematics in a typical basic science course. They prepared six short, remedial books each of which can usually be completed in one to three hours. Each book has a placement test to diagnose the student's need for remedial work in the area of mathematics covered by the book.

The Flexer and Flexer program is useful for the present study for several reasons. First, the problem they address seems especially likely to provide important advantages of adapting to individual differences. All of the students supposedly have learned all of the mathematics covered, but the experience of college science teachers is that a sizable percentage of their students lack the basic mathematics necessary for lab work. Abraham Flexer was motivated by the desire to avoid spending weeks of class time in a biology course teaching math to those students who need it and thereby depriving those who do not of the opportunity to proceed with the intended contents of the course.

Second, the present author was well acquainted with this program because it was developed as a project of an organization directed by him (the Harvard Committee on Programmed Instruction). To the author's knowledge, Flexer and Flexer were aware of the requirements of good adaptive test materials. They knew the need for correctly assessing the individual's need as efficiently as possible and the need to discriminate between students who did and did not need special work in math. In short, this program was chosen because it should be exemplary on all three variables.

Each of the six programs is published in a separate booklet and includes a considerable amount of data from the several test-runs of the material at Harvard University and Emmanuel College in biology, chemistry, psychology, and sociology courses. Much of the data is concerned with the teaching material and the gains produced by the course, which are, of course, the proper emphasis for program evaluation. They also include ample data on teaching times and at least enough data to estimate the consequence ratio for the program as they tested it. Discrimination ratios are also reported as the percentage of each class which passed each test item and hence was excused from using that portion of the program. Unfortunately, they did not test for the validity of the test items.

To obtain estimates of validity for the present study, a group of undergraduate psychology students were administered the test materials for one logarithm unit and for the three fraction units. The tests used were not the single items on which the programs were originally evaluated, but instead, were the tests provided in the introduction of the books which contained from five to eight items per decision for the four decisions evaluated. The criterion for a pass in each case allowed for one incorrect answer in each set.

Surprisingly, this was not the form of test used by Flexer and Flexer in their testing of the program. They tested the whole class at the beginning of the term with a placement test having a single item for each separate diagnostic decision. They gave no reason in the published version for changing from the single item to the several item test. Perhaps it was an effort to increase the validity or perhaps it was on the advice of the publisher who may have felt that a slightly longer test would have better face validity and thus be better for marketing. Nevertheless, it seemed the proper course to apply the measures of the adequacy of adapting to the final published long test form.

This decision led to a serendipitous result. The outcome for the longer test is considerably different than for the shorter test. Changing the test in a way that superficially would seem likely to improve it, instead, when empirically evaluated, is shown to have seriously flawed a previously excellent program.

In the first effort to apply the measures, 28 students took the eight-item pretest for the logarithm unit (the first of three decisions for the logarithm book) and one week later repeated this test without, of course, having used the program. Similarly,

10 students took the three pretests for the three parts of the fractions program (the lengths of these were four, five, and six items) and retook the tests one week later. For all sets of tests, records were kept of the time required for each student to complete each test. In calculating the consequence ratio, the published times for the programmed materials were used. Tables 27.2 and 27.3 indicate the results of these evaluations. Both show reasonably high validity ratios (0.93 for logarithms and 0.83 for fractions) and fair consequence ratios (0.88 for logarithms and 0.82 for fractions). Surprisingly, however, the tests for both programs showed poor discrimination. Of the 28 students taking the logarithm test, 26 failed and only 2 passed for a discriminability ratio of only 0.07. Of the 30 decisions in the fractions program, only 5 were passed for a discriminability ratio of 0.17. These discriminability ratios were far from the values indicated by Flexer and Flexer for the percentage passing the various tests with one item per decision. Unlike the present results with the longer tests in which the bulk of the students failed, they found most single item tests were passed (62 percent for the fractions tests yielding a 0.38 discrimination index). The combination of the validity data measured in the present study which was unavailable in the Flexer and Flexer data and the consequence ratio and discriminability from Flexer and Flexer's data suggest that this program is excellent in its overall adapting characteristics. However, the very low discriminability obtained in this study indicates that the recommended long form of the test has largely ruined the adaptive feature of the program.

To determine whether or not the unexplained change in the tests had this effect, the fraction tests were administered to another set of ten psychology students. It was possible to identify a single test item in each of the three fraction tests which was like that used in the original single item test. Using these items, an evaluation was made for both the single item and the longer test form with the same subjects. It can be seen in Table 27.4A that the results with the long form of the tests replicate the first set of data reported in Table 27.2. For the long tests a good validity ratio (0.83) and a good consequence ratio (0.83) is to little avail in view of the poor discrimination ratio (0.17) caused by the bulk of the outcomes being failures. On the other hand, as shown in Table 27.4B, using the single-item test, as Flexer and Flexer did originally, provided very good discriminability (0.40), (quite close to their reported 0.38 ratio) with many passes. The single-item test also, of course, increased the consequence ratio to an excellent 0.96. However, as one might expect, the short test does have a lower validity ratio (0.73).

These results dramatically illustrate the merit of gathering the data needed for these three indices of the goodness of adapting. An originally tested version adapted fairly well to individual differences with excellent discriminability and a sizable gain for passing the diagnostic test. Flexer and Flexer may have had some indication that the predictive validity was low, although in combination with the good values for the other two variables the original form was useful and acceptable. It may have seemed prudent and safe to lengthen the test somewhat to increase its validity. Surprisingly, this created a serious deficiency in the program which apparently went undetected. An adequate level is necessary on all three measures. Each is necessary, no two of

TABLE 27.2

Flexer and Flexer, logarithms

Validity and discriminability

(1 Decision × 28 Subjects = 28 Total decisions)

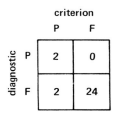

$$\text{Validity} = \frac{\text{Hits}}{\text{Hits and misses}} = \frac{26}{28} = .93$$

$$\text{Discriminability} = \frac{\text{Passes}}{\text{Passes and failures}} = \frac{2}{28} = .07$$

Consequence

$$\frac{\text{Teaching time in minutes}}{\text{Teaching time and testing time}} = \frac{67}{76} = .88$$

TABLE 27.3

Flexer and Flexer, fractions
First evaluation—long form tests

Validity and discriminability

(3 Decisions × 10 Subjects = 30 Total decisions)

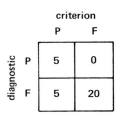

$$\text{Validity} = \frac{\text{Hits}}{\text{Hits and misses}} = \frac{25}{30} = .83$$

$$\text{Discriminability} = \frac{\text{Passes}}{\text{Passes and failures}} = \frac{5}{30} = .17$$

Consequence

$$\frac{\text{Teaching time in minutes}}{\text{Teaching time and testing time}} = \frac{150}{184} = .82$$

TABLE 27.4

Flexer and Flexer, fractions
Second evaluation

A. Long-form tests

Validity and discriminability

(3 Decisions × 10 Subjects = 30 Total decisions)

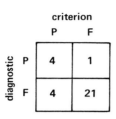

criterion
P   F

diagnostic

P   4   1

F   4   21

$$\text{Validity} = \frac{\text{Hits}}{\text{Hits and misses}} = \frac{25}{30} = .83$$

$$\text{Discriminability} = \frac{\text{Passes}}{\text{Passes and failures}} = \frac{5}{30} = .17$$

Consequence

$$\frac{\text{Teaching time in minutes}}{\text{Teaching time and testing time}} = \frac{150}{181} = .83$$

B. Single-item tests

Validity and discriminability

(3 Decisions × 10 Subjects = 30 Total decisions)

criterion
P   F

diagnostic

P   15   3

F   5   7

$$\text{Validity} = \frac{\text{Hits}}{\text{Hits and misses}} = \frac{22}{30} = .73$$

$$\text{Discriminability} = \frac{\text{Failures}}{\text{Passes and failures}} = \frac{12}{30} = .40$$

Consequence

$$\frac{\text{Teaching time in minutes}}{\text{Teaching time and testing time}} = \frac{150}{156} = .96$$

---

them sufficient. Moreover, a step taken to improve one could cause deterioration in another. Lengthening a test could reasonably be expected to improve validity, but it will also take more student time and a high validity can be obtained by using pre- and posttests which almost all will fail (or everyone will pass), but such a test has low discriminability.

REFERENCES

Cronbach, L. J. "How Can Instruction Be Adapted to Individual Differences?" In R. A. Weisgerber, ed., *Perspectives in Individualized Learning*. Itasca, Ill.: Peacock, 1971, pp. 167–182.

Flexer, R. J., and A. S. Flexer. *Programmed Reviews of Mathematics*. New York: Harper & Row, 1967.

Glaser, R. "Instructional Technology and the Measurement of Learning Outcomes: Some Questions." *American Psychologist* 17(1963):519–521.

Holland, J. G. "A Quantitative Measure for Programmed Instruction." *American Educational Research Journal* 4(1967):87–101.

A NOTE ON THE PARAMETERS OF ADAPTING

As you may have noted, this course does not have formal adaptive features. When the course was first developed, there was an attempt to adapt by having students try to answer the unit questions before reading the source material. However, very few students were able to do this successfully. Although the three measures covered in this unit had not been formally developed, the authors believed that requiring unit "pretests" that almost all students would fail was a waste of student time. The formal request that students attempt the unit questions first was dropped.

Since that first course tryout, measures of an adaptive feature's discriminability, predictive validity, and consequence ratio have been developed and tested. The work on developing these measures has shown some of the parameters of such adapting. There certainly exist subject matters and disciplines which are entirely new to the typical learner as well as materials that require the student to take a new look at familiar territory. Given subject matter of this kind, pretests that have a high predictive-validity ratio will probably have low discriminability. That is, if most students could pass a posttest on unfamiliar material only after some form of instruction, a predictively valid pretest that would indicate this need would also have low discriminability.

It is possible, with unfamiliar material, to have highly discriminable pretests, but usually at the expense of predictive validity. For example, assume that the to-be-learned behavior is *not* in the typical novice's repertoire, and assume also that the posttest accurately represents this to-be-learned behavior. If the pretests are high on discriminability (i.e., 50 percent of the typical novices pass and 50 percent fail the pretest), most of those who pass the pretest must be misses in terms of the test's predictive validity. That is, in spite of having passed the pretest, if given the post-test without intervening instruction, they would fail. (Remember that we are assuming the posttest accurately tests the to-be-learned behavior and that most entering students do not possess this behavior.)

When pretests lack discriminability, the major consequence to the student is wasted time. When the pretests are not valid, the consequences can be far more serious. In the example described above, in which we assume that the posttest really measures the to-be-learned behavior, pretests that inaccurately predict that the student can skip some instructional material may result in serious student difficulties with later material, and perhaps in ultimate student failure. Thus, in certain situations, the potential dangers of adapting may outweigh the potential advantages.

Accurate adapting can be most useful when there is a large amount of material to be covered, some of which typical students may be familiar with. For example, it would seem reasonable to adapt a curriculum like the *Job Corps Advanced General Education Program* which prepares adults to take and pass the General Educational Development (GED) test for a high-school diploma. It may be less reasonable to adapt a first-year high-school algebra or biology course. The three measures discussed earlier can be useful in making decisions about whether to adapt, as well as in making decisions about how to improve a given adaptive feature.

QUESTIONS

1. The term "adaptive" has been used to describe many kinds of educational situations. Briefly describe the kind of individualized materials for which measures of discriminability, predictive validity, and consequence are applicable.

2. The function of a good teaching item is to evoke the desired, to-be-learned behavior. Briefly explain how using the blackout technique on a particular item and obtaining a measure of errors on that same item can be used to evaluate the effectiveness of that teaching item.

3. A low error rate on a teaching item is desirable. Why is a low error rate on a diagnostic test item not desirable?

4. What are three functions of good adaptive tests?

5. a) What is the rationale for the consequence ratio?

   b) What is the general formula for calculating the consequence ratio?

   c) What number indicates a perfect consequence ratio?

6. In the second evaluation of the Flexer and Flexer Fractions Program (See Table 27.4 of the Holland article) the calculated consequence ratio for the long-form test is .83. For the short-form test the consequence ratio is improved to .96. What is responsible for this improvement?

7. Calculate a consequence ratio for the *Job Corps Advanced General Education Program Unit II-2*. There are six lessons in this unit, requiring (according to the Teacher's Manual) a total of 510 minutes of teaching time. The unit screening or diagnostic

test takes an average of 14 minutes to complete. What is the consequence ratio? Is this an adequate value for a consequence ratio?

8. a) What is the rationale for the predictive-validity ratio?

   b) The general formula for calculating the predictive-validity ratio is:

$$\frac{\text{hits}}{\text{hits} + \text{misses}}$$

   What is a hit? Include both types of hits in your answer. What is a miss? Include both types. Do not simply reproduce the table, give a verbal description.

   c) What number indicates a perfect validity ratio?

9. In calculating a predictive-validity ratio, subjects first receive the diagnostic test and then the criterion test, without any intervening teaching material. Why do they not receive the teaching material?

10. Refer to Table 27.1 in the Holland selection as you use the following hypothetical information to fill out this decision table:

Criterion Test

Ten subjects took a diagnostic test for Unit X. Five subjects passed and five subjects failed the diagnostic test. The next day these same ten subjects took the criterion test for Unit X without, of course, having used any of the teaching material.

If the diagnostic test had perfect predictive validity, the five subjects who passed the diagnostic test would also pass the criterion test. In fact, however, only four of the five passed the criterion test. The four who passed the diagnostic test and passed the criterion test are "hits" in terms of the diagnostic test's predictive validity. Fill in the appropriate cell of the decision table with that number. The one subject who passed the diagnostic test and failed the criterion test is a "miss." Again, fill in the appropriate cell.

There were five subjects who failed the diagnostic test. Two of these five passed the criterion test, and three failed the criterion test. Fill in these numbers in the appropriate cells also.

11. Calculate the predictive-validity ratio for the decision table you filled in for question 10. Is this value an acceptable predictive-validity ratio?

12. Look at Table 27.4 of the Holland selection. This table gives real data for the two versions of the Flexer and Flexer Fractions Program (second evaluation). The long-form test has a predictive validity of .83 and a consequence ratio of .83. Using the short-form test, the validity decreases to .73, but the consequence ratio improves to .96. Describe the general relationship suggested by these figures between predictive validity and the consequence ratio.

13. a) What is the rationale for the discriminability ratio?

b) How is the discriminability ratio calculated?

c) What value represents a perfect discriminability ratio?

14. Results of a diagnostic test given to twenty-five students were ten passes and fifteen failures. Calculate the discriminability ratio. Is this an adequate value for discriminability?

15. Suppose you were in the market for some individualized instructional materials and a publisher was trying to sell you Program Z. You don't want to buy the whole program in order to experimentally test its adaptive feature, yet you want to be sure that it really is adaptive. What information would you ask for from the publisher and the developer? How would you use this information?

UNIT

28

The Use of Data in Revision

Content

This unit presents an adaptation and summary of a section of an article by Murray Sidman and Lawrence Stoddard, "Programming Perception and Learning for Retarded Children," which was published in the *International Review of Research in Mental Retardation, Vol. 2.* (New York: Academic Press, 1966.) This adaptation describes a tryout-and-revision cycle that resulted in improved teaching materials.

Objectives

Students will discuss the various changes in Sidman and Stoddard's teaching programs and will describe how tryout data prompted each change. They will also explain the value of small-group tryouts and will plot an error-by-item graph on three subjects.

Instructions

Use the objectives to direct your reading of the adaptation, then answer the questions. Check your answers and confer with the instructor.

Tryout-and-Revision Cycles

INTRODUCTION

Lessons written by even the most experienced designers are improved when the lessons are used by the target population and revised according to data derived from this tryout. The necessity for tryout-and-revision cycles is implied in a programming principle mentioned in the first unit of this book: Let the student write the program.

> When the student has trouble with part of a program, the programmer must correct this. The student's answers reveal ambiguities in items; they reveal gaps in the program and erroneous assumptions as to the student's background. The answers will show when the program is progressing too rapidly, when additional prompts are necessary, or when the programmer should try new techniques. When unexpected errors are made, they indicate deficiencies *not* in the student but in the program. (Holland, 1960, p. 284.)

Certainly the data from a tryout can tell the designer all of those things, but the tryout data is most useful when the lesson is well constructed to begin with. Describing the principle as "letting the student write the program" is, thus, a little misleading. The designer must spend a considerable amount of time formulating the lesson before a tryout will produce good data, i.e., data that will clearly indicate the need for particular revisions. A basically well-constructed lesson used by a suitable target population will produce a pattern of errors for which there is a relatively limited number of explanations. The designer will find this data very suggestive of appropriate revisions. However, if the lesson is poorly constructed, if the task analysis is completely incorrect, or if the lesson was used by students it was not intended for, the tryout data will be difficult to interpret. For one thing, the designer frequently will be unable to find any consistent error pattern in the data. In addition, possible explanations for an error made on a poorly designed item are almost limitless in number.

Thus it is very important that lessons be adequately drafted *before* the first tryout. As a designer you should attempt to make sure you have a satisfactory task analysis and a well-designed test for terminal behavior, as well as standards for evaluating that test. You should also check your lessons for a blackout problem before submitting the lesson material to a small-group tryout.

Assuming you have done these things, what can be learned from small-group-tryout data? Sidman and Stoddard (1966) describe a striking example of lesson improvement based on tryout data. Asked to develop a method of testing the visual acuity of retarded, nonverbal children, Sidman and Stoddard devised the following task, which does not require the children to respond to verbal directions or to verbally describe what they see. Normal adults can discriminate a circle from an ellipse whose vertical axis is nine-tenths of its horizontal axis. Yet, to a person with poor visual acuity, that ellipse would be indiscriminable from a circle. The smallest perceived difference between a circle and an ellipse may be described as an individual's difference threshold. The difference threshold varies from individual to individual according to visual acuity and is easily measured objectively. Based on this information, Sidman and Stoddard developed the test described in the Skinner article in Unit 5. Seven ellipses and one circle were projected onto an eight-key matrix, as illustrated in Fig. 28.1.

At first the ellipses were very flat (A), but they systematically became more and more like circles (D). The child was taught to select the circle. The point at

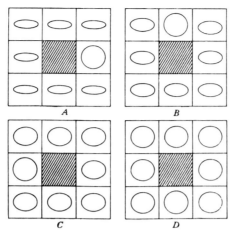

Fig. 28.1. A program to test visual acuity. Early in the program ellipses are very differ-ent from the circle (A), and as the program progresses the ellipses more and more closely approximate the circle (D). The person whose vision is tested is to select the circle as long as possible.

which the child was no longer able to discriminate the circle from the ellipses pro-vided an objective measure of the child's difference threshold and, thus, of the individual's visual acuity.

Having devised this test, Sidman and Stoddard were now faced with the prob-lem of teaching retarded, nonverbal children to select a circle and ignore an ellipse. Obviously the children could not simply be told to "pick the circle." The history of this program's development illustrates most of the points mentioned earlier in the Holland quotation—they could see from their tryout data when the program was progressing too rapidly, when additional prompting was necessary, and when they should try a new approach. However, since most designers will be producing lessons that rely on language to communicate task directions, perhaps we should first defend our selection of a nonverbal program to illustrate this important tryout-and-revision process.

When relying on verbal or written directions to communicate what is expected of the learner in performing a particular task, we frequently make the incorrect assumption that because the same words are read or heard by both the learner and the designer, the learner understands what the designer means by those words. Yet, in fact, if the designer tells the child, "pick the circle," and the child proceeds to select the ellipse, we do not know from this response whether the child cannot learn to discriminate a circle from an ellipse because of poor vision or whether the child is applying the word "circle" to the forms that the designer calls ellipses. In verbal lessons, because of the formal identity of the words read by learner and designer, the designer is often tempted to interpret such response data as meaning that the learner understands the task but is unable to perform it. Given this interpretation, the designer is unlikely to make effective use of the data in revising the lesson.

Although it is possible, of course, to interpret errors in tryout data on verbal programs as due to a communication problem, the temptation to blame the learner is very strong when the directions are given in "plain English" that anyone "ought" to understand. Yet the most fruitful way to use tryout data for revision is to assume that, in Keller's words (Unit 2), "the student is always right."

The description of the Sidman and Stoddard nonverbal program serves two purposes. First, the designers are as concerned with programming task directions as they are with programming the task itself. In fact, in this task, the directions comprise the task. Therefore this lesson clearly illustrates the kind of careful programming and attention to learner response that is also important, but more difficult to discern, in lessons with verbal task directions. Second, the development of Sidman and Stoddard's final excellent program is an example of how helpful tryout data can be when developers are willing to interpret learner errors as a programming problem rather than as a learner deficiency. This attitude may be initially less rewarding for a lesson designer, but it has the greater payoff in terms of producing a well-designed, effective lesson.

DEVELOPMENT OF THE SIDMAN AND STODDARD PROGRAM

Preliminary Work

Sidman and Stoddard used the eight-key matrix described earlier (Fig. 28.1) to teach the initial circle-ellipse discrimination also. The terminal task for this initial discrimination was the selection of the single circle from seven very flat ellipses. This task is illustrated in panel A of Fig. 28.1. Their goal was the development of a nonverbal program that would achieve this discrimination in normal children at least as young as two and one-half years.

They did their preliminary work with the forty-year-old microcephalic idiot described by Skinner in Unit 5. Although not a child, C.M. was so severely retarded (IQ less than 20) and had such an extremely small behavioral repertoire that he seemed representative of the most difficult retarded children the developers were likely to reach.

C.M. quickly learned to pick up and eat M&M's from the automatic dispenser associated with the eight-key matrix. He also learned, by imitating the experimenter, to press the one lighted key of the matrix. Pressing the lighted key operated the M&M dispenser automatically and also rang a chime. Soon C.M. was able to press the lighted key entirely on his own. Of course the position of the correct key changed for each trial. Sidman and Stoddard wanted to find out if C.M. could see well enough to attend to any form projected on a key, so after pressing the lighted key was established, a form was projected on the bright key. In this preliminary work, the forms were a circle, a square, or an X. At first the forms were redundant cues; that is, C.M. needed only to continue selecting the bright key and could ignore the forms. Gradually, however, the brightness of the other seven keys was increased. At some point in this fading process all keys appeared equally bright to C.M. but the correct key could be distinguished by a form projected on it. If C.M. could see the form and learn to attend to it, he could continue to select the correct key even after all keys were equally bright. C.M. was able to learn this discrimination, indicating that his vision was sufficient to attempt to teach him the circle-ellipse discrimination. Sidman and Stoddard would later return to this early fading program to improve their circle-ellipse program, but at this point they thought of this preliminary work as specific to their need to minimally assess C.M.'s vision.

The First Teaching Program

Figure 28.2 presents a schematic illustration of the fading process over the 72 slides of the first circle-ellipse teaching program. At first the correct key was brightly lit *and* had a circle projected on it. Gradually, the other seven keys were brightened and, at the same time, the ellipses projected on the keys became more apparent. Sidman and Stoddard describe this first program:

> At the beginning of this program C.M. was able to base his selection on brightness alone; then we gradually changed the basis for his discrimination so that he could select the key with a distinct figure out of several keys with relatively indistinct figures *and* with dimmer backgrounds; finally these criteria were gradually faded out until the only remaining basis for choice was the actual shape of the forms, i.e., the circle and the ellipse. By changing the criteria in very small steps, we expected to help our subject understand what was being asked of him. The fading program was our way of telling C.M. what we wanted him to do; the candy was our way of telling him he was doing it correctly. (Sidman and Stoddard, 1966, p. 160)

Sidman and Stoddard were able to use the record of C.M.'s performance to improve the circle-ellipse teaching program because of several factors. The first program was initially well constructed and well planned. Also, C.M. and all subsequent subjects used the program under very controlled conditions—distractions were few and the equipment reliably delivered reinforcements immediately after each correct response. In addition, a cumulative recorder kept very accurate records of each response. Finally, Sidman and Stoddard's method of dealing with errors proved to be most useful in providing good data for revision.

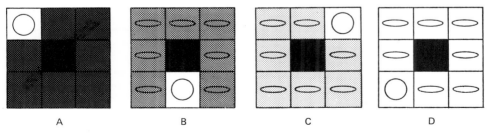

Fig. 28.2. Schematic illustration of widely spaced steps in the fading process. The correct key always had the circle on a bright background. The incorrect keys were dark at first (A), and gradually became brighter (B, C, D). As the incorrect keys became brighter, the contrast between the ellipses and the background also increased.

The tryout data were recorded as follows. The paper of the cumulative recorder unrolled continuously and a pen connected with the operation of the circle-ellipse slide tray traced a continuous line on this paper. When the learner made a correct choice the slide tray advanced to the next slide and the pen simultaneously moved vertically up a step. During periods of nonresponding the pen moved horizontally across the paper. When the learner selected an incorrect key, the chime did not ring, the M&M was not delivered, and the slide did not change. As far as the learner was concerned, nothing changed after an error. On the cumulative record, the error was marked by an oblique downward line after which the pen reset to the same horizontal. When repeated errors were made on the same slide, each error was indicated by one oblique line. Thus, four lines on the same horizontal indicated four errors on the same slide. When the learner selected the correct key after one or more errors, the chime rang, the M&M was dispensed, and the slide changed. However, the slide tray moved backward after an error to show the previous slide. On the cumulative record this correct choice after an error is represented by a vertical downward line with the pen resetting at a lower horizontal. Using this method, the record of a perfect performance resembles the side view of a staircase, with risers indicating correct choices and the length of the tread corresponding to the learner's interresponse times.

Figure 28.3 presents part of the record of C.M.'s performance on the first circle-ellipse discrimination program. The numbers along the vertical axis correspond to particular slides in the series. The numbered dots on the record indicate

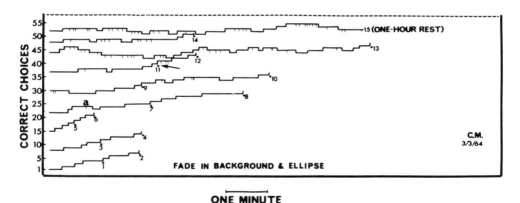

Fig. 28.3. The performance of a severely retarded subject on the first circle-ellipse program. The numbered dots indicate the last slide of each successive brightness increment. a indicates the subject's first error, followed by the reversal of the slide tray after he corrected his error. Each of the small marks, like the one at a, indicates an incorrect choice. The arrow shows the end of the first slide tray. Although C.M. made three errors on the first slide of the new tray (after the arrows), there was no backup from the first slide of the tray. An apparatus failure prevented the backup on one occasion in fading increment 14.

the end of each stage in the fading sequence. At each dot the brightness of the seven incorrect keys increased by one increment.

This method of dealing with errors allowed Sidman and Stoddard to distinguish between two kinds of errors, both represented in C.M.'s record in Fig. 28.3. C.M.'s first error is at slide 24, marked by the small letter *a* on the record. The next slide presented was slide 23. C.M. did not make an error on slide 23 when it originally appeared; nor did he make an error on it for its second presentation. When slide 24 was presented again, C.M. selected the correct key on his first attempt. Sidman and Stoddard interpret this type of error as due to such trivial factors as momentary inattention.

However, the designers noticed a different, more serious kind of error at slide 46 (Fig. 28.3). C.M. had selected the correct key on the first choice for slides 42, 43, 44, and 45 (the steps before brightness increment number 12 on the record). At slide 46 he made two errors before selecting the circle. When returned to slide 45, he again made two errors before choosing the circle, so his next slide was slide 44. On this slide he made one error before selecting the circle, and then on the second presentation of slide 43 he made six errors before selecting the correct key. Remember that C.M. had just gone through these same slides without error. Sidman and Stoddard called this an instance of "errors creating errors," and interpret the record as follows:

> When he made his first error on slide 46, he was presumably using the criteria for selection that had been successful up to that point. However, the error showed these criteria to be wrong. Therefore, when slide 45 appeared again, he changed his basis for choice, and where he had previously been correct he was now wrong. He then continued to have trouble throughout brightness increment 13, oscillating up and down, occasionally recovering his performance, but always meeting the same troublesome obstruction on slide 46. Eventually he passed through this difficult region but continued to have trouble when we increased the brightness of the incorrect keys a bit more (increment 14) and he made little progress through 15 (before the one-hour rest).
>
> The processes involved here are thoroughly normal. Whoever our subject may be, retardate, normal student or psychotic patient, if he finds himself inadequately instructed he will oscillate between alternative modes of action. Unless he happens by chance to hit upon a correct solution, he will show no further progress. (Sidman and Stoddard, 1966, p. 165)

Thus, whenever the backup procedure revealed learners making errors on slides that they had previously passed through without error, a problem spot in the program was pinpointed. From C.M.'s record, Sidman and Stoddard knew they had to do something about brightness level 13.

As you may remember from Unit 5, C.M. was eventually successful on this initial circle-ellipse discrimination and went on to demonstrate previously unsuspected visual acuity in the second-phase program, in which the ellipses gradually transform into circles. From C.M.'s success Sidman and Stoddard knew they were on the track of an effective teaching program, but his many problems also told them this first version needed revision.

The Second Teaching Program

Using C.M.'s record (Fig. 28.3) as their guide, Sidman and Stoddard revised the first teaching program. C.M. had very few problems with brightness levels 1 through 8, so the designers decided to shorten this section of the program. This is a very important modification. Lessons frequently tend to get longer with each revision, since tryout data make trouble spots obvious but do not so clearly indicate sections that are too easy or repetitive. However, there is a virtue in brevity. Sidman and Stoddard continued to shorten the program wherever the learner records indicated few problems with the fading sequence. If this shortened version gave the next try-out group problems, the developers were prepared to add slides until an optimal sequence could be found.

Since C.M. had considerable trouble with brightness level 13, the designers decided to add an intermediate brightness increment at that point. And, in addition to this intermediate brightness increment, Sidman and Stoddard added more "practice" slides to brightness levels 16 and above, thus lengthening the overall program to eighty slides. The extra practice slides were added because the designers expected repetition with reward to help learners in the more difficult parts of the program, in which the brightness cue was effectively useless. They gave up this idea as a result of tryout data on the second program.

Seven children used the second program, only three of whom learned the criterion discrimination. Children could earn over eighty M&M's in the program and Sidman and Stoddard had several indications that the program's ineffectiveness was due in part to the decreasing effectiveness of M&M's, a satiation effect. Several children moved quickly through the first half of the program (the shortened half) and then became too restless to continue to the end. The children who did continue made many errors on the latter half of the program, but the designers noted that these errors usually came on subsequent slides of a new brightness increment. If the size of the brightness increment had been the problem, errors would be more likely to cluster around the first slide of each increment. To check the possibility of a satiation effect, Sidman and Stoddard had one hyperactive autistic child work through the program before breakfast. The child successfully completed the program, earning and eating eighty-two M&M's on the way.

The Third Teaching Program

Since satiation seemed to be a problem, and since none of the children had trouble with the shortened first half of the second program, the designers drastically cut the program from eighty to twenty-four slides. They removed all "practice" slides, so each of the twenty-four slides represented a new brightness increment. Figure 28.4 is the record of a hyperactive autistic three-year-old who successfully completed this third version of the program.

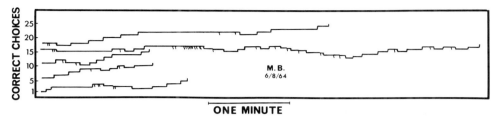

Fig. 28.4. The performance of an autistic child, age 3 years and 3 months, on the third circle-ellipse program.

The record is typical of the eighteen children who used this third version. Notice that errors group around slides 15–17. At that point the brightness cue becomes very difficult to use. All children over four (with one exception) were able to complete this program with few problems. However, three of the seven children younger than four were not able to complete it. Sidman and Stoddard still had not achieved their goal of a program effective with very young children, but they had created a short program that seemed to do as good a job as an earlier program that was three times as long.

Unsure of what to do next, the designers decided to try shortening the program even further. They removed five slides from the first half of the program, so the incorrect keys became bright much more quickly. However, this fourth version appeared to be somewhat less effective than the third version, particularly with very young children.

At this point Sidman and Stoddard had revised the program extensively based on tryout data and still had not achieved their goal, so they decided to reevaluate their entire procedure. Such a reevaluation is a good idea whenever an apparently good lesson is *not* improved by a tryout-and-revision cycle. Sidman and Stoddard recalled their preliminary work with C.M. in which the correct key was bright with a form projected on it, while the brightness of the incorrect keys was gradually increased, but no forms were projected on them. This fading process was designed to learn whether C.M. could attend to form. In all the training programs, however, a different fading procedure was used, i.e., the ellipses were faded onto the incorrect keys while their brightness level was increased. In comparing the two fading programs, Sidman and Stoddard began to find an explanation for the continual problems children had with the later programs at the point when the brightness cue became difficult to use:

> Although the ellipse faded in gradually [in the later programs] it was clearly visible to the children long before its background brightness equalled that of the circle. Because of this the children could continue to use the brightness cue long after the ellipse was clearly available to them. The children needed to look only for the bright key; they did not even have to observe the circle. Since it was possible for them to ignore the forms, we can assume many children did. The circle and ellipses were present, but irrelevant. We were, in fact, *teaching* the children to ignore them.

When the background fading eventually made it impossible for them to use brightness, many of the children could already have learned *not* to pay any attention to
the forms. Separating the background fading and the ellipse fading eliminated this
deficiency in our program. (Sidman and Stoddard, 1966, p. 179)

Sidman and Stoddard looked at C.M.'s record again in the light of this reasoning. After learning to attend to *form* in the preliminary work, C.M. began the new
program, in which he only needed to attend to *brightness*. In the preliminary program, the transfer from a brightness discrimination to a form discrimination had
occurred easily, but in the teaching program C.M. had major problems when the
brightness cue became difficult to use. Perhaps this problem area was a result of a
learned inattention to form which he was able to overcome because of the preliminary work.

The Fifth Teaching Program

Sidman and Stoddard decided, based on this reasoning, to divide the circle-ellipse
discrimination program into two parts. The first part, called background fading,
corresponded to C.M.'s preliminary work. At first the correct key was bright with
a circle projected on it. Over eight slides the brightness of the other seven keys increased to equal that of the correct key. No forms were projected on the seven
incorrect keys. (See Fig. 28.5.)

In this first part of the fifth teaching program control of responding passed from
brightness to form, although the learner had to attend only to presence or absence
of a form and not to any particular feature of the form.

The second part was called ellipse fading. Over nine slides ellipses appeared
on the seven incorrect keys, at first merely as faint lines but gradually becoming as
dark as the circle. (See Fig. 28.6.)

In this second part of the program, control of responding passed from "pick the
key with a form" to "pick the circle and ignore the ellipses." Note, however, that no
verbal instructions were ever given to the children.

Both stages of the total fading program consisted of only seventeen slides. The
final three slides were repetitions of the criterion circle-ellipse discrimination, so the

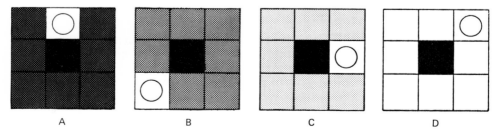

A   B   C   D

*Fig. 28.5. Schematic illustration of a few steps in the background-fading portion of pro-
gram 5. The correct key always had the circle on a bright background. The incorrect
keys were dark at first (A) and gradually became brighter (B, C, D).*

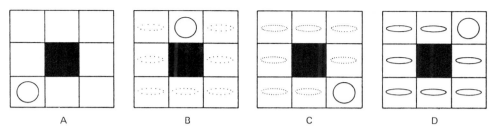

A   B   C   D

Fig. 28.6. Schematic illustration of a few steps in the ellipse-fading portion of program 5. The ellipses appeared gradually on the bright backgrounds of the incorrect keys. (The ellipses were not actually dotted; they were drawn that way here for convenience in reproduction.)

total program contained twenty slides. Six children used this fifth teaching program, five successfully. The records of these five children are shown in Fig. 28.7. The youngest child, T.E.S., was two years and nine months old. Four of the children made errors on slide 13, although none made as many as C.M. had on slide 46 of the first program. The one child who did not make an error on slide 13 made a revealing comment: "Oh, no! All of 'em! Wait a minute, there's one?" (Sidman and Stoddard, 1966, p. 181). He then selected the circle. This comment and the other children's errors indicated that the ellipses seemed to suddenly appear at slide 13, so Sidman and Stoddard added an intermediate fading slide between slide 12 and 13.

With this addition the program was tested with forty children. It was very successful with children over four years old, as were most of the previous versions.

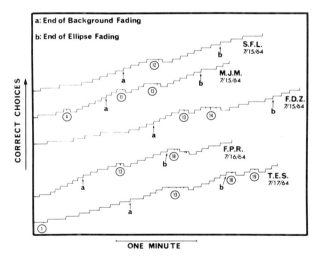

Fig. 28.7. The performance of five normal children on the fifth circle-ellipse program. The arrows at (a) *indicate the end of background fading; the arrows at* (b) *indicate the end of ellipse fading. The encircled numbers are the slides on which the children made "first-time" errors.*

However, unlike the other versions, this version was also successful with children under four. Through cycles of tryout and revision Sidman and Stoddard had achieved a program of less than twenty slides that was far more effective than their first teaching program of nearly eighty slides.

GENERAL TRYOUT-AND-REVISION METHODOLOGY

Small-Group Tryout

Several principles of methodology can be abstracted from the Sidman and Stoddard tryout-and-revision cycle which are useful for all kinds of lessons. Sidman and Stoddard did preliminary work and tested their first program using only one subject. Subsequent versions were tested on five to eighteen subjects. Only version six, about which they were fairly confident, was tested with a relatively large number of subjects—forty. A seventh, slightly changed version, was tested with thirty children.

Using a single subject or a very small group of subjects may be especially important in paper-and-pencil lessons—when fewer copies of the lesson are produced it remains economically feasible to make extensive changes. At all stages of the tryout-and-revision cycle it is very important *not* to reproduce an insufficiently tested lesson in so large a volume that future revisions are economically precluded!

Single-subject or small-group tryouts have another advantage. To obtain maximum information about the lesson itself the designer must be able to insure that controlled conditions are maintained, even though the lesson eventually will be used in all sorts of uncontrolled situations. Once the designer is sure the lesson is effective on its own, tryouts that more nearly approximate "uncontrolled" use conditions will provide information necessary to revise the lesson so as to improve its marketability, appearance, ease of learner and teacher use, implementation, etc. While these concerns are undeniably important, they are beyond the scope of this book.

Recording the Data

Since Sidman and Stoddard used a cumulative recorder, each subject's performance data was recorded in immediately usable graph form. In addition, their backup-after-errors procedure allowed them to discriminate between two kinds of errors. Paper-and-pencil lessons are not usually attached to a cumulative recorder, nor can the backup procedure be easily adapted to this format. The designer of paper-and-pencil lessons must devise an appropriate way of displaying tryout data and must find another way of discriminating serious from not-so-serious learner errors.

A simple error-by-item graph is a very informative method of displaying tryout data from paper-and-pencil lessons. Figure 28.8 presents such a graph with tryout data for three subjects. In an error-by-item graph, item numbers lie along the horizontal axis and cumulative errors along the vertical axis. Each individual's progress through the lesson is plotted separately. It is most useful to represent each subject by a different color felt-tip pen. In Fig. 28.8, subject A's first error was on item

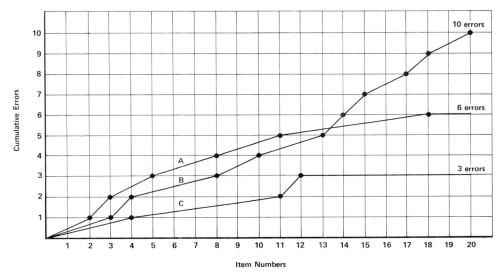

Fig. 28.8. An error-by-item graph with data for three subjects.

number 2, second error on item 3, third error on item 5, fourth error on item 8, fifth error on item 11, and last error on item 18. Subject B made a total of ten errors and subject C a total of only three errors.

When real tryout data is plotted in this way, both problem areas in the program and atypical subjects become apparent. For example, the graph in Fig. 28.9 is from an early version of a lesson teaching children to discriminate final consonant sounds. The lesson consists of 161 items; ten subjects' performances are recorded. Although much detail is lost when the graph is reduced to this scale (about one-fifth of normal size), we can still detect two obvious problem areas in the program. In Fig. 28.9 these areas are circled and labeled A and B. Problem area A (items 23–31) teaches the discrimination of the final consonant sounds in words like WI*N*-WI*NG* and LI*ME*-LI*NE*. Problem area B (items 111–116) consists of items like HA*VE*-HA*LF*. Designers of this program might add more items, devise a new form of prompting, or improve the gradual progression in teaching these sounds.

Another method of analyzing problem areas when the data are plotted as in Fig. 28.9 is to divide the lesson items into several equal sections and count the total number of errors in each section. When the items in Fig. 28.9 are divided into three sections of approximately fifty items each, we note that the ten subjects made a total of 103 errors in the first third of the program, 63 errors in the second third, and 90 errors in the last third. Using this analysis, the designers might compare items in the first and third thirds with items in the middle third in order to alert themselves to further revision possibilities. Of course, divisions into any number of sections are possible, but not always profitable.

The error-by-item graph will also reveal atypical subjects—two such subjects are visible in the Fig. 28.9 graph. The uppermost line represents a subject who

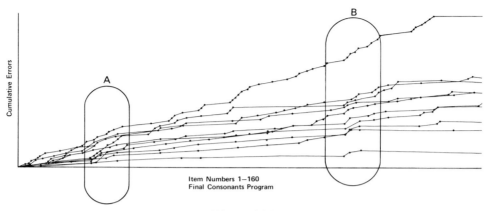

Figure 28.9

missed a total of 58 items, almost one-third of the program. The bottom line represents a subject who made only 6 errors over 161 items. The other eight children
made between 15 and 35 errors. While the designers might not want to ignore the
data of atypical subjects, they may wish to differentially weight this information
when revising the program.

The Student Is Always Right

This is the most important principle illustrated in Sidman and Stoddard's program
development. It is also the one tryout-and-revision principle for which it is impossible to prescribe a simple methodology. Obviously, Sidman and Stoddard would
not have developed a very effective program if they had decided their subjects were
too dumb and too blind to perform according to the designers' original expectations.
But it is more difficult to describe how the designers learned where to start in
developing a program for that special population, and how to discover the variables
(like the early appearance of the ellipses) that might control or disrupt an individual's performance. This kind of sensitivity, essential for lesson designers, is best
acquired through experience. The last unit of the book further elaborates on this
principle.

REFERENCES

Holland, J. G. "Teaching Machines: An Application of Principles from the Laboratory."
Journal of the Experimental Analysis of Behavior 3(1960):275–287.

Sidman, M., and L. T. Stoddard. "Programming Perception and Learning for Retarded
Children." In N. R. Ellis, ed., *International Review of Research in Mental Retardation,
Vol. 2.* New York: Academic Press, 1966, pp. 151–208.

QUESTIONS

1. What should a designer do before the first tryout so as to be sure of obtaining the most useful information?

2. Describe the major difference between the fading process in Sidman and Stoddard's first teaching program and the fading process used in the fifth teaching program.

3. Teaching programs 1–4 were certainly not total failures, so why did Sidman and Stoddard make such a radical change for program 5?

4. Sidman and Stoddard concluded that the fading sequence in programs 1–4 may actually have taught some children to ignore the ellipses that were vital to the criterion discrimination. Explain how they thought the sequence could have this effect, and describe the tryout data that led them to this interpretation.

5. Why did the designers cut the number of slides from eighty to twenty-four for the third teaching program rather than deal with the satiation problem by trying intermittent reinforcement or tokens?

6. What are two advantages of a single-subject or small-group tryout?

7. Given the following data for a twenty-item lesson, produce an error-by-item graph: Subject A makes errors on items 8, 9, 11, and 15. Subject B makes errors on items 4, 7, and 8. Subject C makes errors on items 9 and 12. Subject D makes an error on item 10.

8. Circle the problem area(s) on your graph.

UNIT

29

Project, Part III

At this point, your lesson material is ready for a first tryout. Unit 28 described the kind of complete tryout-and-revision cycle with subjects from the appropriate population which is maximally useful to the designer. All lessons intended for wide distribution should undergo a similar process.

However, within the confines of this course, you will probably only have time for one tryout and revision. Finding appropriate subjects may be a difficult problem. If you can find only one appropriate subject, by all means, try out your material with this single subject. However, you may be forced to use inappropriate or atypical subjects. Such subjects might be asked to do the lesson "as if" they were the intended group. You could then treat the data as described in Unit 28. Alternately, you may also obtain useful information from atypical subjects by being present for the tryout and asking for their comments and discussion as they do the lesson. This information, while not as useful as "real" tryout data, will tell you if the lesson can be understood by someone other than the designer.

Once your lesson has been tested in some way, you may find it helpful to discuss your interpretation of the tryout data with your peers. Finally, revise the lesson based on your interpretation of the tryout data.

PART

VI

People to People

The articles in these last two units describe two very different instructional situations. Koch, a poet, teaches urban grade-school children to write poetry. Ferster, a psychologist, describes a clinician's work with an autistic child. In both situations, the teacher devises and implements instructional strategies on the spot in response to perceived learner needs. Sensitivity to the needs of a learner is often viewed as a "gift," a touch that a teacher either does or doesn't have. The authors of this text believe that such sensitivity can be learned, given the appropriate instructional conditions. This course is designed to provide a basis in behavior theory and practical experience in instructional design, both appropriate prerequisites to developing on-the-spot sensitivity. While Koch obviously developed his skills by another route, Ferster describes the contribution of formal training in behavior theory to skilled practical teaching.

UNIT

30

Wishes, Lies and Dreams

Content

Koch, K. *Wishes, Lies and Dreams: Teaching Children to Write Poetry.* New York: Chelsea House, 1970. (a selection)

This unit presents a selection from a book by Kenneth Koch, a poet, which describes his success in teaching children to write poetry. Koch probably does not think in terms of curriculum-design principles, but he has thought out his objectives and has developed teaching techniques that exemplify the principles described in this course.

Objectives

Students will describe Koch's objectives and his teaching process in behavioral terms.

Instructions

1. Read the selection from Koch's book.
2. Answer the questions, referring to the selection as necessary.
3. Check your work and confer with your instructor.

Teaching Children to Write Poetry
Kenneth Koch

The Dawn of Me

I was born nowhere
And I live in a tree
I never leave my tree
It is very crowded
I am stacked up right against a bird
But I won't leave my tree
Everything is dark
No light!
I hear the bird sing
I wish I could sing
My eyes, they open
And all around my house
The Sea
Slowly I get down in the water
The cool blue water
Oh and the space
I laugh swim and cry for joy
This is my home
    For Ever

Jeff Morley, Fifth Grade, P.S. 61

Last winter and the spring before that I taught poetry writing to children at P.S. 61 on East 12th Street between Avenue B and Avenue C in Manhattan. I was sponsored first by the Academy of American Poets, then by the Teachers' and Writers' Collaborative.* I was a special teacher, who, like an art teacher, took classes at certain times. I could vary these arrangements thanks to the sympathetic cooperation of Jacob Silverman, the principal, who helped me to see any class I liked, even on short notice. Unlike other special teachers, I asked the regular teacher to stay in the room while I was there; I needed her help and I wanted to teach her as well as the children. I usually went to the school two or three afternoons a week

K. Koch, *Wishes, Lies and Dreams: Teaching Children to Write Poetry* (New York: Chelsea House, 1970). Reprinted by permission of International Creative Management and Kenneth Koch. Copyright © 1970 by Kenneth Koch.

* Poetry teaching at P.S. 61 has been continued by Ron Padgett. I have also gone back a few times this year. In the summer of 1968, along with David Shapiro, I taught writing to children at Muse, the neighborhood museum in the Bedford-Stuyvesant section of Brooklyn, and some of what I say here is based on that experience, particularly the last part of Section III.

and taught three forty-minute classes. Toward the end I taught more often, because I had become so interested and because I knew I was going to write about it and wanted as much experience as possible. My interest in the whole subject originally was largely due to Emily Dennis and to her inspiring ways of teaching art to children at the Metropolitan Museum.

I was curious to see what could be done for children's poetry. I knew some things about teaching adults to write, for I had taught writing classes for a number of years at Columbia and the New School. But I didn't know about children. Adult writers had read a lot, wanted to be writers, and were driven by all the usual forces writers are driven by. I knew how to talk to them, how to inspire them, how to criticize their work. What to say to an eight-year-old with no commitment to literature?

One thing that encouraged me was how playful and inventive children's talk sometimes was. They said true things in fresh and surprising ways. Another was how much they enjoyed making works of art—drawings, paintings, and collages. I was aware of the breakthrough in teaching children art some forty years ago. I had seen how my daughter and other children profited from the new ways of helping them discover and use their natural talents. That hadn't happened yet in poetry. Some children's poetry was marvelous, but most seemed uncomfortably imitative of adult poetry or else childishly cute. It seemed restricted somehow, and it obviously lacked the happy, creative energy of children's art. I wanted to find, if I could, a way for children to get as much from poetry as they did from painting.

I. IDEAS FOR POEMS

My adult writing courses had relied on what I somewhat humorously (for its grade-school sound) called "assignments." Every week I asked the writers in the workshop to imitate a particular poet, write on a certain theme, use certain forms and techniques: imitations of Pound's *Cantos,* poems based on dreams, prose poems, sestinas, translations. The object was to give them experiences which would teach them something new and indicate new possibilities for their writing. Usually I found these adult writers had too narrow a conception of poetry; these "assignments" could broaden it. This system also made for good class discussions of student work: everyone had faced the same problem (translating, for example) and was interested in the solutions.

I thought this would also work with children, though because of their age, lack of writing experience, and different motivation, I would have to find other assignments. I would also have to go easy on the word "assignment," which wasn't funny in grade school. In this book I refer to assignments, poetry ideas, and themes; in class what I said was "What shall we write about today?" Or "Let's do a Noise Poem." My first poetry idea, a Class Collaboration, was successful, but after that it was a few weeks before I began to find other good ones. Another new problem was how to get the grade-school students excited about poetry. My adult students already were; but these children didn't think of themselves as writers, and poetry to most of them seemed something difficult and remote. Finding the right ideas for poems would help, as would working out the best way to proceed in class. I also needed poems to read to them that would give them ideas, inspire them, make them want to write.

I know all this now, but I sensed it only vaguely the first time I found myself facing a class. It was a mixed group of fifth and sixth graders. I was afraid that nothing would happen. I felt the main thing I had to do was to get them started writing, writing anything, in a way that would be pleasant and exciting for them. Once that happened, I thought, other good things might follow.

I asked the class to write a poem together, everybody contributing one line. The way I conceived of the poem, it was easy to write, had rules like a game, and included the pleasures without the anxieties of competitiveness. No one had to worry about failing to write a good poem because everyone was only writing one line; and I specifically asked the children not to put their names on their line. Everyone was to write the line on a sheet of paper and turn it in; then I would read them all as a poem. I suggested we make some rules about what should be in every line; this would help give the final poem unity, and it would help the children find something to say. I gave an example, putting a color in every line, then asked them for others. We ended up with the regulations that every line should contain a color, a comic-strip character, and a city or country; also the line should begin with the words "I wish."

I collected the lines, shuffled them, and read them aloud as one poem. Some lines obeyed the rules and some didn't; but enough were funny and imaginative to make the whole experience a good one—

> I wish I was Dick Tracy in a black suit in England
> I wish that I were a supergirl with a red cape; the city of Mexico will be where I
>   live.
> I wish that I were Veronica in South America. I wish that I could see the blue
>   sky . . .

The children were enormously excited by writing the lines and even more by hearing them read as a poem. They were talking, waving, blushing, laughing, and bouncing up and down. "Feelings at P.S. 61," the title they chose, was not a great poem, but it made them feel like poets and it made them want to write more.

I had trouble finding my next good assignment. I had found out how to get the children started but didn't yet know how to provide them with anything substantial in the way of themes or techniques. I didn't know what they needed. I tried a few ideas that worked well with adults, such as writing in the style of other poets, but they were too difficult and in other ways inappropriate. Fortunately for me, Mrs. Wiener, the fourth grade teacher, asked me to suggest some poetry ideas for her to give her class. (I wasn't seeing them regularly at that time—only the sixth graders.) Remembering the success of the Collaborations, I suggested she try a poem in which every line began with "I wish." It had worked well for class poems and maybe it would work too for individual poems, without the other requirements. I asked her to tell the children that their wishes could be real or crazy, and not to use rhyme.

A few days later she brought me their poems, and I was very happy. The poems were beautiful, imaginative, lyrical, funny, touching. They brought in feelings I hadn't seen in the children's poetry before. They reminded me of my own childhood and of how much I had forgotten about it. They were all innocence, elation, and intelligence. They were unified poems: it made sense where they started and where they stopped. And they had a lovely music—

> I wish I had a pony with a tail like hair
> I wish I had a boyfriend with blue eyes and black hair
>   I would be so glad . . .

Milagros Diaz, 4 *

> Sometimes I wish I had my own kitten
> Sometimes I wish I owned a puppy
> Sometimes I wish we had a color T.V.
> Sometimes I wish for a room of my own.
> And I wish all my sisters would disappear.
> And I wish we didn't have to go to school.
> And I wish my little sister would find her nightgown.
> And I wish even if she didn't she wouldn't wear mine.

Erin Harold, 4

It seemed I had stumbled onto a marvelous idea for children's poems. I realized its qualities as I read over their work. I don't mean to say the idea wrote the poems: the children did. The idea helped them to find that they could do it, by giving them a form that would give their poem unity and that was easy and natural for them to use: beginning every line with "I wish." With such a form, they could relax after every line and always be starting up afresh. They could also play variations on it, as Erin Harold does in her change from "Sometimes" to "And." Just as important, it gave them something to write about which really interested them: the private world of their wishes. One of the main problems children have as writers is not knowing what to write about. Once they have a subject they like, but may have temporarily forgotten about, like wishing, they find a great deal to say. The subject was good, too, because it encouraged them to be imaginative and free. There are no limits to what one can wish: to fly, to be smothered in diamonds, to burn down the school. And wishes, moreover, are a part of what poetry is always about.

I mentioned that I had told Mrs. Wiener to ask the children not to use rhyme. I said that to all my classes as soon as I had them start writing. Rhyme is wonderful, but children generally aren't able to use it skillfully enough to make good poetry. It gets in their way. The effort of finding rhymes stops the free flow of their feelings and associations, and poetry gives way to sing-song. There are formal devices which are more natural to children, more inspiring, easier to use. The one I suggested

---

* Here, as elsewhere in this introduction, the number following the child's name indicates the grade he or she was in when the poem was written.

most frequently was some kind of repetition: the same word or words ("I wish") or the same kind of thing (a comparison) in every line.

Once I understood why the Wish Poem worked so well, I had a much clearer idea of what to look for. A poetry idea should be easy to understand, it should be immediately interesting, and it should bring something new into the children's poems. This could be new subject matter, new sense awareness, new experience of language or poetic form. I looked for other techniques or themes that were, like wishes, a natural and customary part of poetry. I thought of comparisons and then of sounds, and I had the children write a poem about each. As in the Wish Poems, I suggested a repetitive form to help give their poems unity: putting a comparison or a sound in every line. Devoting whole poems to comparisons and sounds gave the children a chance to try out all kinds, and to be as free and as extravagant as they liked. There was no theme or argument with which the sounds or comparisons had to be in accord: they could be experimented with for the pleasures they gave in themselves. In teaching painting an equivalent might be having children paint pictures which were only contrasting stripes or gobs of color.

In presenting these poetry ideas to the children I encouraged them to take chances. I said people were aware of many resemblances which were beautiful and interesting but which they didn't talk about because they seemed too far-fetched and too silly. But I asked them specifically to look for strange comparisons—if the grass seemed to them like an Easter egg they should say so. I suggested they compare something big to something small, something in school to something out of school, something unreal to something real, something human to something not human. I wanted to rouse them out of the timidity I felt they had about being "crazy" or "silly" in front of an adult in school. There is no danger of children writing merely nonsensical poems if one does this; the truth they find in freely associating is a greater pleasure to them—

A breeze is like the sky is coming to you . . .

Iris Torres, 4

The sea is like a blue velvet coat . . .

Argentina Wilkinson, 4

The flag is as red, white, and blue as the sun's reflection . . .

Marion Mackles, 3

Children often need help in starting to feel free and imaginative about a particular theme. Examples can give them courage. I asked my fourth graders to look at the sky (it was overcast) and to tell me what thing in the schoolroom it most resembled. Someone's dress, the geography book—but best of all was the blackboard which, covered with erased chalksmear, did look very much like it. Such question games make for an excited atmosphere and start the children thinking like poets. For the Noise Poem I used another kind of classroom example. I made some noises and asked the children what they sounded like. I crumpled up a piece of paper. "It sounds like paper." "Rain on the roof." "Somebody typing." I hit the chair with a ruler and asked what word that was like. Someone said "hit." What else? "Tap." I said close your eyes and listen again and tell me which of those two words it sounds more like, hit or tap. "It sounds more like tap." I asked them to close their eyes again and listen for words it sounded like which had nothing to do with tap. "Hat, snap, trap, glad, badger." With the primary graders* I asked, How does a bee go? "Buzz." What sounds like a bee but doesn't mean anything like buzz? "Fuzz, does, buzzard, cousin." The children were quick to get these answers and quick to be swept up into associating words and sounds—

A clink is like a drink of pink water . . .

Alan Constant, 5

A yoyo sounds like a bearing rubbing in a machine . . .

Roberto Marcilla, 6

Before they had experimented with the medium of poetry in this way, what the children wrote tended to be a little narrow and limited in its means—but not afterwards. Their writing quickly became richer and more colorful.

After the Comparison Poem and the Noise Poem, I asked my students to write a Dream Poem. I wanted them to get the feeling of including the unconscious parts of their experience in their poetry. I emphasized that dreams didn't usually make sense, so their poems needn't either. Wishes and dreams are easy to doctor up so they conform to rational adult expectations, but then all their poetry is gone.

Their Dream Poems contained a surprising number of noises, and also comparisons and wishes—

I had a dream of a speeding car going beep beep while a train went choo choo . . .

Ruben Luyando, 4

I dream I'm standing on the floor and diamonds snow on me.
I dream I know all the Bob Dylan songs my brother knows . . .

Annie Clayton, 4

My students, it was clear, weren't forgetting things from one poem to the next; they had been able to write more vivid poems about their dreams because of the other poems they had recently written.

[Koch describes several other kinds of assignments and warm-up exercises, as well as a method of introducing adult poetry to the children.]

. . .

There are other barriers besides rhyme and meter that can keep children from writing freely and enjoying it. One is feeling they have to spell everything correctly.

---

* At P.S. 61 some first and second grade classes are combined in one primary grade.

Stopping to worry about spelling a word can cut off a fine flow of ideas. So can having to avoid words one can't spell. Punctuation can also be an interference, as can neatness. Good poetic ideas often come as fast as one can write; in the rush to get them down there may be no time for commas or for respecting a margin. All these matters can be attended to after the poem is written.

Another barrier is a child's believing that poetry is difficult and remote. Poetry should be talked about in as simple a way as possible and certainly without such bewildering rhetorical terms as *alliteration, simile,* and *onomatopoeia.* There are easy, colloquial ways to say all these: words beginning with the same sound, comparisons using *like* or *as,* words that sound like what they mean. Poetry is a mystery, but it is a mystery children can participate in and master, and they shouldn't be kept away from it by hard words.

Again on the subject of language, the various poetry ideas should be presented in words children actually use. I don't think the Wish Poems would have been so successful if I had asked my students to start every line with "I desire." Nor would "My seeming self" and "My true self" have worked well in place of "I Seem To Be/ But Really I Am." One should be on the lookout, too, for words and phrases which tell the child what to say and take him away from important parts of his experience: I think "make-believe" and "imaginary" are such words. When I told a teacher at another school about the "I wish" assignment, she said that she had done almost the same thing but it hadn't turned out as well. She had had her students write poems in which every line began with "Love is." I never heard a child say "love is" in my life, and so I wasn't surprised that they hadn't responded wholeheartedly.

One bar to free feeling and writing is the fear of writing a bad poem and of being criticized or ridiculed for it. There is also the oppression of being known as not one of the "best." I didn't single out any poems as being best or worst. When I read poems aloud I didn't say whose they were, and I made sure that everyone's work was read every so often. If I praised a line or an image I put the stress on the kind of line or image it was and how exciting it might be for others to try something like that too. That way, I felt, the talent in the room was being used for the benefit of everyone.

The teacher shouldn't correct a child's poems either. If a word or line is unclear, it is fine to ask the child what he meant, but not to change it in order to make it meet one's own standards. The child's poem should be all his own. And of course one shouldn't use a child's poetry to analyze his personal problems. Aside from the scientific folly of so doing, it is sure to make children inhibited about what they write.

. . .

The way of teaching I have described worked as well with so-called deprived or disadvantaged children as it had with others. The children I worked with who had problems in reading and writing were those in "N.E." * classes at P.S. 61 and

---

* N.E. stands for "non-English speaking," a rather misleading administrative term. Children I taught in such classes could all speak English, and all except one or two "language learners" could write it, though often with some difficulty in grammar and spelling.

some of the students in the writing workshops at Muse. The reason I say "so-called" is because the words *deprived* and *disadvantaged* may be thought to apply to the children's imaginations and their power to create things, and they do not. The tragedy—and for a teacher, the hope and the opportunity—is not that these children lack imagination, but that it has been repressed and depressed, among other places at school, where their difficulties with writing and reading are sometimes a complete bar to their doing anything creative or interesting. They needn't be. Degree of literacy certainly makes a difference in a child's ability to write easily and confidently, but it does not form his imagination. The power to see the world in a strong, fresh and beautiful way is a possession of all children. And the desire to express that vision is a strong creative and educational force. If there is a barrier in its way—in this case it was writing—the teacher has to find a way to break that barrier down, or to circumvent it.

Since writing was the problem, I had them say their poems out loud. So that they would excite and inspire each other as much as possible, I had them compose their poems together. When we did these spoken collaboration poems, I would sit with from six to fifteen students around a table or in a circle of chairs. I would propose a theme, such as Wishes or Lies, and they would make up lines, which I would write down. When we thought we had enough, we stopped, and I read the poem back to them. Often in the course of composition I read it back too, to reinspire the students and to show them where we were. I usually called on them in order, though occasionally I yielded to the irrepressible inspiration of someone who couldn't wait to tell me his line. I found writing—or even typing—better than using a tape recorder. The time it takes to write or type a line gives the children a chance to work a little more on their ideas. And when the work is read back, it sounds more like a poem because all the incidental noise (laughter, shouted comments) is left out.

These collaborations almost always made the children want to make up, and usually to write, poems of their own. Composing a poem together is inspiring: the timid are given courage by braver colleagues; and ideas too good to belong to any one child are transformed, elaborated on, and topped. Lies are particularly exciting in this regard, but Wishes, comparisons, Noises, I used To/But Now, and some other themes can also become exhilaratingly competitive—

> I wish I was an apple
> I wish I was a steel apple
> I wish I was a steel apple so when people bit me their teeth would fall out . . .

So a subject is built up, starting with something rather plain and becoming deeper and more interesting in its elaboration. The teacher can help this process along by interposing questions: Any special kind of apple? Why? Are there any other fruits anyone would like to be? Hands. Shouts. "I want to be an orange!" (spoken with an air of great discovery and a feeling of creative power). How big an orange? "I want to be an orange as big as the school!" More hands. "I wish school was a big orange and New York City was a fruit store and my block was a pineapple!" Excited by this atmosphere, and often having stored up ideas of their own which they are eager to express, children are willing to face even the uncertainties of writing.

It's understandable that children with reading and writing difficulties might be shy of being natural and spontaneous in school. Often what they say is "corrected" for what's wrong in it before what's good in it is acknowledged. That makes it not much fun to talk. To help them be poets, I did just the opposite. I immediately praised whatever it was that was imaginative or funny or anything in what they said, and let the mistakes fall where they would. If I didn't understand something I would ask, but I made it clear I wanted to know the exact word or meaning so I could get more out of the line. Once children sense a playful, encouraging, and esthetic (rather than corrective) attitude in the teacher, they become less shy and more willing to take risks.

The speed with which "non-writing" children can become excited about writing poetry was made very clear to me in working with Mrs. Magnani's fourth grade "N.E." class. Ron Padgett came with me the first time I visited this class, and he, Mrs. Magnani, and I each worked with about twelve students. We had decided to do a Lie Poem Collaboration. Lying, for all its bad points in daily living, is a very quick way to the world of the imagination. It is also a competitive pastime. Like the Mississippi riverboat men in *Huckleberry Finn,* the children at P.S. 61 were eager to do each other one better, to tell an even bigger, more astonishing untruth: I live on the moon; I live half the year on the moon and half on the sun; I live on all the planets: January on Jupiter, March on Mars, December on the Planet of the Apes. Different kinds of lies could also please and astonish: I am ten years older than my teacher; I like school. These fourth graders, with just the slightest encouragement from us, began to create strange realities with great gusto. When we read the group poems back to them, they were very excited. At all three tables they demanded to write Lie Poems of their own.

Once the students began to write down their individual poems, there was terrible chaos, since they were bursting with untruthful inspiration, eager to write, and unable to spell half the words they wanted to use. All the time they were writing, there would be a few students, frantically excited, shouting at me at the head of the table. I couldn't tell them, as I had told children in other classes (and even there not always with success), just to write the word any way they could, that spelling didn't matter, I would understand it anyway. They knew perfectly well they couldn't write it at all, and I knew I wouldn't be able to tell January from an elephant if I didn't show them how the words were spelled. Showing turned out to be better than telling. I had paper in front of me, and when they asked me a word, I wrote it down—rather, I printed it—as fast as I could. Telling them how to spell all the words would have taken forever, since no one could hear anything I said. It is tiring to work at the center of an inspired mob, and also rather heady. The noise and the activity had other values for the children: they were part of an excitement which enabled them to forget their "illiteracy" long enough to write poetry.

Another cause of the high spirits of this class was my asking them to put some of their lies in Spanish. I thought their knowledge of a second language was clearly an advantage, and I wanted them to know it. They liked using Spanish, and they also enjoyed translating for me when I didn't know what they had written. The mere fact that a word or phrase was in Spanish made it interesting and amusing to them. They all spoke English, but English was the language of school, whereas Spanish was a kind of secret. Very few could write Spanish, in fact, so those who could helped the others to spell Spanish words as I was helping everyone to spell English ones.

After this beginning in which the children had spoken and written Lie Poems they were excited about poetry, and though spelling problems remained they went on liking to write it. They wrote a good deal. Like everyone else's poetry, theirs became richer and freer as a result of the poems they listened to and those they wrote themselves—

In spring I play
I eat in spring
I do my work in spring
I'm good in spring
I'm doing my things in spring
Spring, Spring, you're mine
Spring is the color of a rose
If I was spring
Spring, Spring I'm calling you
Spring, Spring play with me
Spring, Spring I love you.

Maria Mesen, 4

The third eye can see inside me
The third eye can see the hosts
The third eye can see Puerto Rico
The third eye can see my voice
The third eye can see my bones
The third eye can see the wind . . .

Robert Melendez, 4

As in groups of good readers and writers, some children with writing problems are more inclined toward poetry than others; and some who can hardly write are more imaginative poets than many who write without mistakes. What seemed most important was that, of the children I taught, every one had the capacity to write poetry well enough to enjoy it himself and usually well enough to give pleasure to others, whether it was entire poems or surprising and beautiful images, lines, or combinations of words.

The educational advantages of a creative intellectual and emotional activity which children enjoy are clear. Writing poetry makes children feel happy, capable, and creative. It makes them feel more open to understanding and appreciating what others have written (literature). It even makes them want to know how to spell and say things correctly (grammar). Once Mrs. Magnani's students were excited about words, they were dying to know how to spell them. Learning becomes part of an activity they enjoy—when my fifth graders were writing their Poems Using Spanish Words they were eager to know more words than I had written on the board; one girl left the room to borrow a dictionary. Of all these advantages, the main one is how writing poetry makes children feel: creative; original; responsive, yet in command.

QUESTIONS

1. In teaching poetry in the classroom, Koch seeks something in addition to the usual outcome. What new behaviors does he want to establish in the students? In other words, what are his objectives?

2. In the second half of this selection, Koch describes teaching "disadvantaged" children to write poetry. In a brief essay, describe this process in behavioral terms. You may find these questions helpful in writing your essay:

   a) How does Koch analyze his task?

   b) What reinforcers does he select and *why*?

   c) Why is there a gradual progression in complexity of student response?

   d) Why is an errorless learning approach important in teaching this task?

3. What barriers to writing poetry did Koch find? How did he deal with each? Why is this errorless approach so important to Koch?

4. One of the learning principles stressed in this course is "let the student write the program." With this in mind, discuss how Koch formed and changed his ideas on teaching poetry.

UNIT

31

The Value of a Functional Analysis

Content

Ferster, C. B. "Perspectives in Psychology: XXV Transition from Animal Labora-tory to Clinic." *The Psychological Record 17* (1967): 145–150.

This article presents a sensitive functional analysis of a complex interaction be-tween a clinical therapist and autistic child. The value of this analysis in teaching clinical skills is described.

Objectives

Using the article as a model, students will do a functional analysis of a complex educational interaction between a student and a spelling lesson.

Instructions

Read the article. A description of a child's work in a spelling lesson follows the article. Read this description and do a functional analysis of the interaction.

Perspectives in Psychology: XXV Transition from Animal Laboratory to Clinic

C. B. Ferster

This paper describes my experiences at the Linwood Children's Center, a day care and residential treatment center for autistic and schizophrenic children. Since the experience I bring to Linwood comes mainly from laboratory experiments with animals, the Linwood project (Ferster, 1968; Ferster and Simons, 1966) represents one kind of transition from laboratory knowledge to clinical treatment. At Linwood we are looking to the laboratory to find more effective treatments and better teaching methods.

The bridge between my general knowledge about behavior and practical knowledge about children began when I observed Linwood's clinical staff, particularly the director, Miss Simons, who is an especially gifted therapist. One incident was an interaction between Miss Simons and Karen, a four-year-old autistic girl. Karen had been in day care at Linwood for about two weeks during which she spent most of her time clutching a plastic doll and crying. Let me read my original notes to give you the flavor of Miss Simons' style and the kind of events which I saw and recorded.

"Jeanne Simons placed Karen on a rocking horse where she stayed without crying as long as Miss Simons rocked the horse and sang to her. After a few minutes Miss Simons stopped rocking the horse for brief periods but kept on singing. She carefully sensed how long she could stop rocking the horse without losing control of Karen. The return to rocking always followed some behavior other than crying. In general Miss Simons stopped rocking the horse whenever she judged that Karen's behavior was strongly maintained by some current factor, such as playing with the handles of the rocking horse. Next, Miss Simons took the plastic doll from Karen's hands, set it on a nearby table, and quickly moved the table next to Karen who promptly picked up the doll. One would guess that under other circumstances taking the doll away from Karen would lead to screaming. Although Karen was without the doll only for a few seconds, this situation provided the basis for the reinforcement of a specific constructive piece of behavior—reaching for the doll. This was the first time that Miss Simons required some behavior of Karen.

"Now Karen moved the rocking horse slightly, and Miss Simons' singing usually occurred contingent on the rocking. When Karen sat quietly, Miss Simons simply watched, smiled, and hummed gently. When Karen rocked, Miss Simons sang in rhythm to the movements of the horse. Then the episode with the doll was repeated, but this time the movements were a little slower and Karen was without her doll for

C. B. Ferster, "Perspectives in Psychology: XXV Transition from Animal Laboratory to Clinic." *The Psychological Record* 17(1967):145–150. Reprinted by permission of the publisher and author.

a few seconds longer. When Karen returned to rocking, Miss Simons sang in rhythm. Soon Karen placed the doll on the table herself. This probably occurred because the behavior controlled by the rocking horse was becoming prepotent over that controlled by the doll. Also, it was difficult for Karen both to clutch the doll and to hold the handles of the rocking horse. Karen continued rocking without the doll for over a minute as Miss Simons sang along. The magnitude and rhythm of the rocking were quite vigorous.

"Next Miss Simons kept silent for brief periods while Karen rocked. Technically this was intermittent reinforcement of the rocking. At this point Karen turned to the doll, possibly because she was less inclined to rock the horse when Miss Simons did not sing. But in picking up the doll Karen dropped it to the floor, perhaps accidentally, and for the first time during the episode, she began to cry. Miss Simons asked, "Do you want to pick up your doll? I'll help you," and extended her hands to Karen. When Karen touched Miss Simons' hand, Miss Simons clasped Karen's hands and helped her from the rocking horse. When Karen did not lift her foot over the saddle, Miss Simons simply held her there until she made some movement. When Karen did not move, Miss Simons prompted the behavior by moving the foot partially over the saddle and allowed Karen to complete the final part of the action. Miss Simons then held Karen in the vicinity of the doll until Karen picked it up, and once more she offered her hands as she said, "Do you want to get up?" Karen lifted her hands in the gesture which many children characteristically use as a mand for being picked up, but Miss Simons simply continued to hold her hands out until Karen touched them.[1] Back on the horse, Karen now rocked without Miss Simons' singing. Once again, she dropped her doll and the same episode was repeated. This time Miss Simons supported the behavior slightly less than she had on the previous occasion.

"Next Miss Simons placed the doll on a couch about fifteen feet away. Karen stopped rocking for a few seconds while she looked at the doll, but then began to rock again, and after about a minute Miss Simons picked up the doll, attracted Karen's attention by tapping it, and sang in rhythm to the tapping. Karen made some sounds and began rocking the horse in the same rhythm, possibly in response to the tapping. At this point Miss Simons returned the doll. Karen had been away from it over a minute without crying. However, the next time Miss Simons took the doll away and placed it on the couch, Karen began to cry even though she continued to rock. Miss Simons sang in rhythm to the rocking and the crying stopped. At this point Miss Simons herself took Karen off the horse, and they walked over to the sofa where Karen picked up the doll and sat on Miss Simons' lap. A minute later Karen indicated some disposition to get on the horse again by tugging on Miss Simons. Miss Simons did not take her to the horse, but instead picked her up and hummed to her as she carried her about. Several times Miss Simons picked up Karen, smiled, and sang to her, but she did not place her on the horse."

The whole interchange lasted about thirty minutes during which several hundred

---

[1] The term *mand* implies that some action be taken by the listener as, for example, in command, demand, countermand, etc.

reinforcements altered Karen's repertoire substantially. In contrast to food reinforcement, in the usual animal experiment, very simple features of the child's environment were manipulated very skillfully and rapidly in a symphony of action.
Even though these behavioral processes were the same ones that I knew from animal
and human laboratory experience, I discovered many new ways to control and influence the behavior of these children as I observed this and similar episodes.
Although I saw applications of every principle of behavior I knew, there was a content here that could not come solely from laboratory experience. I could make a
functional analysis of the interaction, but I could not have designed it.

Note the unusual way in which Miss Simons weakened the doll's compulsive
control of Karen. She waited until Karen's behavior was strongly controlled by other
reinforcers so that she could remove the doll for brief periods. She very slowly
lengthened the intervals during which Karen was without the doll by pacing them
with the development of these other behaviors. At no point during the intervention
was the frequency of crying decreased in the way that we carry out extinction in an
animal experiment. With my limited experience with children I might have kept
Karen on the horse until her crying stopped before I handed her the doll or lifted
her off. When Karen dropped her doll and began to cry, Miss Simons reacted immediately and used the doll itself as the reinforcer for generating a small increment in
the child's repertoire. Instead of simply carrying out extinction Miss Simons identified the operant reinforcer maintaining crying and began to apply this reinforcer
differentially in favor of behaviors, other than crying, which she judged to be more
useful for the child. The weakened control by the doll and the extinction of the crying were by-products of the reinforcement of other behaviors. In the meantime, the
amount of crying and emotional states were kept small enough so they did not disrupt the new emerging repertoire.

It was not practical to interact with Karen on the rocking horse all day, so Miss
Simons anticipated the next step by decreasing the frequency of performances on
the rocking horse at the same time that she supported Karen's behavior in another
way. For example, when they were sitting on the couch, Miss Simons did not reinforce Karen's gesturing toward the rocking horse. Instead, she picked her up and
interacted with her via body contact and singing. I don't know what Miss Simons
would have done if Karen had struggled in her arms and continued gesturing toward
the horse. I suspect that Miss Simons already had gauged the probability of this
when she shifted the reinforcer. In many other instances it appeared at first glance
that primitive behavior was being reinforced. But after more observation I discovered that extinction was being carried out in a new way.

Another example is a boy who teased Miss Simons by pulling her hair. When
Miss Simons continued to give him her full attention, I wondered why she didn't
simply withdraw, since it was so clear to me that the annoying behavior was reinforced by her attention. But when I looked more closely I saw that Miss Simons was
holding the boy's wrist close to her hair so he couldn't really pull it. Furthermore
she released her grip on him only when his performance shifted in a direction that
she wished to reinforce. This was another example of decreasing the frequency of a

performance by finding another that would be prepotent over the one that was annoying. In this case the reinforcement was negative, the removal of the restraint she applied.

Miss Simons was amazed at how closely she was able to see herself in the notes describing her interaction with Karen. "Charles," she said, "I don't see how you can understand therapy, it takes years of training to do this." But I did have clinical experience even though it was with infra-human organisms. In my animal experiments I dealt with each subject as an individual. During the course of the experiment the conditions were changed continuously in pace with the subject's performance. I learned the fine grain of my organism's behavior, and as an experimenter I responded to the details of it. Rarely was an animal too deviant to work with. I always looked for the factor responsible for each animal's uniqueness and tried to take it into account. Each pigeon differed in how much grain was necessary for reinforcement to maintain an adequate amount of behavior. The height of the key or lever had to be adjusted for the size of the animal, and the transition from one schedule of reinforcement to another was always a unique affair, carefully adjusted to the animal's current performance, even though the general form of the final performance was common to all of the animals. Each animal was different in many ways and the goal of the experiment was to find a common factor beyond the individual characteristics of each subject.

The observations that I made were not solely for my benefit. Miss Simons' amazement at my close description of her encounter with Karen came partly because of the difficulty she had in conveying her procedures to other people. Despite Miss Simons' consummate skill with the children, other staff members fell far short of the mark, and they did not learn simply by watching her. Nor was she able to instruct them verbally. Terms such as "keep your antennas out" or "watch for the health in the child," often eloquent descriptions for those of us who appreciated a fine-grain analysis of behavior, did not help the staff in actual procedures with the children.

Perhaps a quotation from a recent talk by Miss Simons will suggest the impact a technical language about behavior has had on her work. "I think I can explain little step-by-step procedures now so that people don't just look blindly at me with awe. I'm not even sure intuition is so mysterious. I think it's having eyes all over the place and seeing the tiny little things that children are doing and then suddenly the child reacts to it. And I am able to see the tiny little steps and explain much better what I am doing with the children so the magic is out of Linwood—which I think is wonderful." Now she has an objective language that is simple and concise enough for everyone to understand. To supplement Linwood's magic there is a training program in the experimental analysis of behavior. It is a key part of the project. The course is designed to make more inventive and effective therapists and we constantly experiment with ways to improve it. The main emphasis is on a detailed technical analysis of animal behavior, because we have found that facility and skill in the fine grain technical description of animal behavior makes it possible for therapists to systematically observe the details of the complex natural environment.

The DRO, differential reinforcement of other behavior, is an example of animal data and procedures which influenced almost every therapist who took the training course at Linwood. In the context of DRO, they understood how Miss Simons weakens primitive behavior by positively reinforcing other performances.

The functional analysis of her interactions with the children also changed Miss Simons' practices. As she became more self-conscious about her own activities, she saw more clearly which parts of her complex interchange with the child were having particular effects and, accordingly, refined her activities and increased the frequency of effective contingencies. Small, hour-by-hour increments in the child's repertoire became reinforcers for her as she learned to observe the fine grain of the interaction with a child.

Another consequence that came from learning a systematic language about behavior was an increased ability to design new ways of activating the child's environment. Reinforcement theory and a technical analysis of verbal behavior have led to new procedures in the schoolroom never before used at Linwood. For example, children are now taking part in classroom educational activities who have never done so before. Part of the reason for this has been the use of chains or sequences of behavior so that a child goes on to the next activity such as writing when he demonstrates that he can read a short text perfectly.

In summary, I want to describe how the clinical staff at Linwood and I have modified each other's behavior. In general we have found less benefit from literal methods from the animal laboratory than we have from a systematic and objective description of behavior. A systematic language about behavior allows the clinic to use its own special knowledge and experience more effectively.

At first the Linwood clinicians feared conditioning because they thought of the usual laboratory situation where the *experimenter* determined the behavior to be developed. When they thought of applying operant conditioning to children, it appeared arbitrary, immoral, and at the expense of the child's development. They discovered, however, that they, with their intimate clinical knowledge of the child, still decided what behaviors were to be developed. Principles of conditioning simply aided them in working more effectively.

From my point of view as an experimental psychologist, the reverse lend-lease has provided "grist for my mill." The phenomena I dealt with in the animal laboratory now are a design in an actual fabric and I find many theoretical challenges in our frequent discussions and observations of the children.

QUESTIONS

1. Because of his knowledge of the experimental analysis of behavior, Ferster was able to analyze a very complex clinical interaction. As a result of this functional analysis, Miss Simons was better able to teach her methods to new clinicians and she was also able to improve her own clinical interactions.

    When you watch a student working through a lesson, you are watching a complex educational interaction. Your knowledge of the experimental analysis of behavior should help you analyze that interaction. You should be able to see what is really happening, i.e., what behaviors are probably reinforced by the lesson, what behaviors the designer intended to reinforce, what reinforcers are maintaining the student's work in the lesson, etc. As a result of this functional analysis, you should be able to evaluate and, if necessary, improve the lessons. For your final exercise, you will produce a functional analysis of a complex educational interaction. However, you need not go beyond the analysis to suggest improvements in the lesson design.

Assume that this is a lesson from a spelling program for ten-year-olds. However, the objective of this program is not to teach the spelling of particular words, but, rather to teach the alternative spellings that exist for certain sounds. This particular lesson teaches that the phoneme [k] can be spelled with the letter *K*, the letter *C*, or the letter combination *CK*. One terminal objective for the program is: given a written word that contains a target phoneme, the child locates the phoneme in the word and lists other spellings for that phoneme. Only words in the reading vocabulary of an average ten-year-old are used in the program.

The program is presented by computer. The child sits before a touch-sensitive screen. (See Unit 16 for a detailed description of this instrument.) Information appears on the screen. In addition, there is an audio component that permits verbal delivery of directions, confirmations, and error messages. The child interacts with the display on the screen by touching relevant parts of it. In the following description of the interactions, words which appear on the display screen are in upper case, LIKE THIS. All audio messages are presented in quotation marks, "like this." And all descriptions of the child's responses are italicized *like this*.

The Spelling Program

"Look at this list of words."

CARRY	KEEP
CREEP	KING
CHECK	BLACK

"Each of these words has a [k] sound in it. Read each word out loud and touch the letter or letters that spell the [k] sound in that word."

1. *The child touches the C in CARRY.*
   "Good, the letter *C* spells the [k] sound in that word."

2. *The child touches the C in CREEP.*
   "Good, the letter *C* spells the [k] sound in that word."

3. *The child touches the first C in CHECK.*
   "No, that letter does not spell the [k] sound in that word."

4. *The child touches the second C in CHECK.*
   "No, that letter does not spell the [k] sound in that word."

5. *The child touches the C in CREEP.*
   "You already did that one. Try another one."

6. *The child touches the K in KEEP.*
   "Good, the letter *K* spells the [k] sound in that word."

7. *The child touches the K in KING.*
   "Good, the letter *K* spells the [k] sound in that word."

8. *The child touches the B in BLACK.*
   "No, that letter does not spell the [k] sound in that word."

9. *The child touches the K in BLACK.*
   "No, that letter does not spell the [k] sound in that word."

10. *The child doesn't respond for 15 seconds.*
    "You haven't done them all yet. Try another one."

11. *The child touches the C in BLACK.*
    "No, that letter does not spell the [k] sound in that word."

12. *The child doesn't respond for 15 seconds for a second time.*
    "There are three spelling patterns for the [k] sound in this list of words: *C, K,* and *CK.** Look for these spelling patterns in this new list of words. . . ."

A new list of [k]-sound words appears. The child continues to work through lists of [k]-sound words in this manner until all three spellings for the [k] sound are identified correctly. This is the terminal behavior as described by the objective.

The terminal objective is achieved in many cases, but the lessons tend to be long and unpopular. One obvious problem is that the children make too many errors, so a new format is designed to correct this.

The New Format

"Look at this list of words."

CARRY	CREEP
CHECK	KEEP
KING	BLACK

"Each of these words has a [k] sound. The [k] sound is spelled differently in different words. Count the number of ways the [k] sound is spelled in the words on this list. Press the number that tells how many ways the [k] sound is spelled."

   2   3

The child presses the number 2.
"No, try again."

The child presses the number 3.
"Yes, the [k] sound is spelled three ways: with a *K,C,* or *CK.**"

In this new format, also, a new set of words appears and the child works in a similar manner until the correct number of spelling patterns is selected on the first try. Children who work through this new format proceed quickly and make few errors. However, tests reveal that they do not usually achieve the desired terminal objective.

---

* These letters appear on the screen as they are pronounced.

The following questions should help you start your analysis of these two educational interactions. Do not restrict yourself to simple answers; instead, try to explain these interactions as Ferster explained the interaction between Miss Simons and Karen. Questions to think about:

1. Is there something in the first lesson which could lead the child to make that mistake at response 3?

2. Does a mistake on response 3 throw any light on possible controlling factors of the child's earlier responses?

3. Why would the child select the letter *B* as a possible spelling for a [k] sound? (See response 8.)

4. How might the child finally learn the *CK* letter combination in the first format?

5. In the new format, why might the terminal objective not be achieved if the student can select the correct number of spellings for a phoneme?

6. Why is the new format *not* an improvement over the first format?

A Final Note

Congratulations on finishing this course! If you have worked through all thirty-one units satisfactorily, you should be prepared to use behavioral principles in designing effective instructional materials, just as previous successful students have done. In fact, the second author of this book was introduced to instructional design by using an earlier experimental version of this course.

But, of course, developing a sensitivity to students' instructional needs requires careful laboratory or field observation. We hope that you will become skilled in identifying the reasons for a student's responses and will have a sense of what to do to improve teaching materials. We believe you have a good basic foundation from your work in this course. It now takes experience, so go to it. Teach.

Answers

In this section, suggested answers for the unit questions are provided. Always write your complete response to the questions *before* checking the suggested answers.

Unit 1

1. a) immediate reinforcement for correct responding;
   b) behavior is learned only when it is emitted and reinforced;
   c) gradual progression to establish complex repertoires;
   d) another form of gradual progression, the gradual withdrawal of stimulus support called fading;
   e) control of student's observing and echoic behavior;
   f) establishing an abstraction through the use of many varied examples;
   g) let the student write the program—unexpected errors indicate deficiencies in the program rather than the student—tailor the learning material to fit the student.

2. Behavior is learned only when it is emitted and reinforced. Laxness in answering could easily become general laxness in performing the task involved in the item. While much of the task to be learned is covert, as in reading or thinking, requiring an overt answer insures that the desired covert behavior has taken place. Also, when students are active, you insure their attention .

3. a) abstraction—Holland describes a method for teaching shape discriminations by presenting a sample and matches to the sample which start out being identical, but gradually differ in all other respects but shape.
   b) gradual progression—In *shaping* a pigeon to turn a circle, you would first reinforce small movements of the head in an appropriate direction, then head move-

ments when accompanied by movements of the feet, then a few steps in the right direction, then half a circle, and finally the pigeon would have to turn a complete circle before being reinforced. In the *fading* method described in the article, the student first answers questions using a fully labeled diagram, then an initialed diagram, then an unlabeled diagram, and finally answers the questions with no diagram at all.

    c) control of observing behavior—The environment must be arranged to require some response from the student, and this response will be correct only if the student has observed the relevant material. The application described in the article is a teaching machine and a programmed text.

    d) immediate reinforcement—A teaching machine provides the correct answer immediately after the student's response.

4. The following points should be covered in this answer:

    a) begin with a behavior already in the student's repertoire;

    b) allow the behavior to be emitted, then reinforce it;

    c) gradually progress to more complex behavior, always reinforcing correct responses; or

    d) gradually "fade" or withdraw stimulus support for the response;

    e) if establishing an abstraction, give a variety of examples.

5. a) Behavior is learned only when it is emitted and reinforced. When students make errors, they are not emitting the prescribed behavior. They have definitely not learned the prescribed behavior, and may even be learning something else. The behavior that resulted in wrong answers may have been accidentally reinforced.

    b) With too many errors, students are reinforced too infrequently; thus, working might decrease or cease altogether. Students frequently show frustration under these conditions.

Unit 2

1. a) The instruction is individualized.

    b) Students advance at their own speed.

    c) There is clear specification of terminal skills for each unit.

    d) Mastery is demanded at every level of training for every student.

    e) Lectures are used as supplementary motivating devices rather than as the primary information-imparting device.

    f) Monitors are successful graduates of earlier courses.

    g) Student activity in learning is maximal.

    h) Students may work where they like.

2. Immediate results of tests; lectures and demonstrations open only to those who have achieved a certain entry behavior; personal interaction with proctors; wall chart of test results; frequent feedback. (Other pleasant features that do not, in fact, serve to reinforce behavior because they are not contingent upon a student action are such things as lack of time constraints, freedom to work where and when one prefers.)

3. Repeated testing; immediate scoring; tutoring; enhancement of the personal-social aspect of learning.

Unit 3

1. An overview of IPI:

   a)   *Theoretical Bases*   *Procedures*

   1. The individual learns, not the group.

   Instructional plans are prepared for the individual, not the group.

   2. The type of planning and "programming" used in programmed instruction can be used to develop a program for schools.

   The curriculum sequence ignores grade lines.

   Students progress at their own rate.

   b) *Steps in the development of the curriculum:*

   1. Objectives to be achieved were spelled out in terms of desired pupil behaviors.

   2. The objectives were ordered in a logical sequence.

   3. Material was made self-instructional as far as possible.

   4. Diagnosis and placement tests were developed to place students appropriately.

   5. Students progress at their own rate; advancement is based on individual work habits and ability.

   6. Students actually practice the desired behaviors.

   7. Students receive immediate feedback through self-scoring and use of teacher aides.

   8. Pupil performance is the basis for revision of learning materials.

2. First, the placement test directs students to a particular unit. Then a unit pretest on each objective taught in the unit allows the development of a prescription for work in unit objectives not yet mastered. The unit posttest and curriculum-embedded tests within each unit indicate whether the student has achieved the objectives of that unit.

3. a) Students' worksheets are scored almost immediately after completion.

   b) Emphasis is on providing students with activities that require performance of the actual, to-be-learned behavior.

   c) For each subject-matter area, objectives are arranged so that mastery of previous units facilitates mastery of subsequent units.

   d) Newly developed material is tried out with a small sample of children and then revised, if necessary. After the materials are made part of the course, changes are made at the suggestion of the teachers who observe children's difficulties with the material.

Unit 4

1. A behavioral contingency is a situation in which an environmental change is dependent upon behavior. An example would be, if the pigeon pecks the disc, the food mechanism operates.

2. a) Leigh should complete each day's math assignment and each problem should be answered correctly.

   b) If a problem was answered correctly, Leigh received one token. If a page of math work was completed, Leigh received two tokens. (Tokens could be exchanged for desired activities.)

   c) Leigh's teacher checked the math homework at the end of each school day.

3. The desired behavior was doing her reading assignment quietly at her desk without sobbing. The effective contingencies were, if Kirman worked quietly the teacher smiled at her or praised her, and if Kirman sobbed, the teacher and students ignored her. The teacher observed Kirman's behavior directly in deciding when to reinforce.

4. Since during baseline the class had already had at least one day with less than forty outbursts per half-day session, establishing this as one criterion assured that the class would frequently be able to "win" recess.

   It is important to establish a "reachable" criterion because the behavior must oc-cur to be reinforced. If the criterion is unreachable, the class would never receive reinforcement. If this class had not been able to "win" recess the resultant restless-ness would be likely to lead to even more outbursts, which would make achieving criterion even more unlikely.

5. Both begin with the specification of the desired change in behavior. (Programmed in-struction begins with the specification of behavioral objectives.)

   Both design contingencies of reinforcement—the behavior and its consequences are specified. (In programmed instruction, these contingencies are the program itself. If the student reads certain material, his or her answer will be confirmed.)

   Both provide for observation of the desired behavior. (In programmed instruction, the student must emit an overt response.)

Unit 5

1. A response will be reinforced only if it is emitted under certain conditions. The three terms are:

   a) the occasion for behavior, or the discriminative stimulus;

   b) the behavior;

   c) the reinforcing stimulus.

2. Modifying existing behavior to establish a new form of behavior.

3. Bringing behavior under stimulus control—this particular program teaches discrim-ination of the occasion for behavior.

4. Bringing behavior under stimulus control.

5. Maintaining behavior under infrequent reinforcement.

6. Modifying existing behavior to establish new forms.

7. Modifying existing behavior to establish new forms.

8. The main points to be covered are:

   a) break the complex behavior into simpler steps or sequence the objectives from simple to complex;

b) begin with a step that is in the learner's current repertoire;

c) as each response is learned, move on to the next, more complex, response.

Unit 6

1. a) Keller created two personnel classes, proctors and assistants, in addition to the instructors. The effect of the proctor is increased personal contact between the learner and someone who knows the material, with increased information exchange both ways.

b) Much classroom time was devoted to reading of the texts.

c) Lectures and demonstrations were used as reinforcers for completing a certain amount of reading and passing a test on it.

d) A list of study questions accompanied each reading assignment—to insure that the student attended to the critical parts of the readings.

e) Tests were frequent to allow for a high rate of responding from the student.

f) After the proctor corrected the examination, he or she discussed it with the student. This provided immediate reinforcement for correct answers, an opportunity for the student to defend or explain doubtful answers, and an opportunity to have wrong answers explained to a student.

2. *Adapting the organism to the environment* (to reduce emotional behavior). Craig allowed three days for the children to get used to the reinforcing device before the experiment began. Observers wore dark glasses.

The immediacy with which reinforcement follows a response. (A conditioned reinforcer may have to be used if the unconditioned reinforcer cannot be presented immediately after the response.) In Craig's procedure, a flash of light (a conditioned reinforcer) followed immediately after an observed sample of "attending" behavior. In simple conditioning (as distinct from shaping), a first response must occur although this operant level may be low.

Desirability of the reinforcer. Craig determined what would reinforce the children. She used candy and a variety of toys and privileges.

Magazine training to establish stimuli that can act immediately as reinforcer when there is a time delay between the behavior and the already established (possibly unconditioned) reinforcer. Although not described in Helen Craig's article, presumably she found the verbal instruction that M&M's would be given for each flash of light to be sufficient to establish the light as an immediate reinforcer.

Reference: Holland and Skinner, Sets 11 and 13.
          Whaley and Malott, Chapter 2.
          Ferster *et al.,* 1975 ed., Chapter 3, part 1.

3. Positive reinforcement is the presentation of a positive stimulus immediately following a response. Negative reinforcement is a termination or removal of a negative or aversive stimulus immediately following a response. They both increase the probability of the response that immediately precedes reinforcement. Craig used positive reinforcement.

4. Check in all nine cells. With the teaching machine, confirmation of correct answer is assumed to be a reinforcer.

5. a) By trying the reinforcer and observing whether or not the behavior preceding the reinforcement increases in rate. A reinforcement is defined in terms of its effect on behavior.

   b) The rate of "attending" or appropriate visual orientation increased.

   c) This answer is open ended. The important point is that something is classed as a reinforcer on the basis of its effect in increasing behavior, not in terms of it being "pleasing" or otherwise "self-evident" as a reinforcer.

Unit 7

1. *Differential reinforcement*—writing outside the allowed limits produces a different colored line by means of specially treated paper and ink.

   Successive approximation—in early items of the program the child is required to complete letters by following dotted lines. Later this cue is faded out and the child must complete letters freehand.

2. Reinforcement given regardless of what the organism is doing is an accidental reinforcing contingency, for whatever behavior preceded the reinforcement will be more likely to occur again. Superstitious behavior, e.g., a bowler making movements as if he still controlled the ball after it has left his hand, is an example of the effects of accidental reinforcing contingencies.

3. In accidental contingencies, regardless of what the teacher intends to reinforce, whatever the child is doing at the time of reinforcement increases in strength. In this case, looking "attentive" rather than being attentive may be reinforced. The point is best understood if one calls this an example of superstitious behavior.

4. a) Temper tantrums were extinguished when not reinforced.

   b) The child was deprived of food and then food was used as a reinforcer.

   c) A progression of tasks was arranged, from touching glasses to wearing them.

Unit 8

1. By noting whether the organism responds differently to the two stimuli after conditioning.

2. Parts: (a) a discriminative stimulus (S^D); (b) a response; and (c) a reinforcer.

   Example: a pigeon is reinforced for pecking at a key when it is lighted but not when it is dark, answering the ring of a telephone will be followed by hearing a voice, or any other example of stimulus control.

   Reference: Holland and Skinner, Set 21.
   Ferster *et al.,* Chapter 14, part 1.
   Reynolds, Chapter 4.
   Whaley and Malott, Chapter 8.

3. S^D R   Reinforcement
   held note—touch toes—praise or a smile

   Note: The S^D is actually the held note although the teacher intended it to be a C.

4. a) Simple shapes were presented at first, then more complex shapes.

   b) The number of choices was increased.

c) Rotation was introduced, at first only a slight degree of rotation, later an increasing degree.

d) Window position of the correct match was gradually moved farther from the position just under the sample stimulus.

e) Mirror images were faded in by transforming an obviously incorrect choice into one increasingly like the mirror image of the stimulus.

f) The mirror image was at first presented next to the correct match, then later presented at increasing distances from the correct match.

g) An increasing number of mirror images was added to the choices.

5. The error rate is quite low. The program was designed so the likelihood of a correct answer was high.

6. By presenting different colors, different shapes, different degrees of rotation of both the sample and the match.

   Note: A general statement like the following is not a complete or sufficient answer. "By gradually introducing a number of irrelevant stimuli until the learner is able to disregard all but the crucial characteristics."

7. (a) We expect little difficulty with minor differences in size; (b) not much difficulty with most changes in type font—unless extreme (e.g., italic); but (c) we expect sizeable problems in reading handwriting. This is an example of stimulus generalization.

Unit 9

1. Presentation of an S^D is a reinforcer for the behavior just completed as well as a signal for the next behavior.

2. a) *immediate reinforcement*—provided by advance of the tape. After the program, when the child has learned to discriminate the [s] sound, correct production of the sound is reinforced by the child's hearing the properly made sound.

   b) *gradual progression*—the discrimination tasks are arranged in order of difficulty. Within each task the examples are arranged in order of difficulty. As an added clue to make the early part of the program easier, the narrator emphasized the [s] sound.

   c) *variety of examples*—a large number of words are presented and all the phonetic contexts in which the sound can occur in English are presented.

3. Gradual elimination of the speaker's emphasis on the [s] sound, which might become the only basis for responding if not faded out. Also, the [s] sound is presented in all its phonetic contexts, thus precluding the possibility that the combination of [s] with certain neighboring sounds will become an S^D, or that a certain position of [s] in a word will become an S^D.

4. Articulation of speech sounds is an example of a continuous repertoire in which small variations in the method of producing a sound will result in small, finely graded variations in the sounds produced. After training in discriminating these slight variations, the automatic differential reinforcement produced by the student's own speech shapes correct production. Improving the ability to discriminate sounds increases the

probability of automatic differential reinforcement to shape sound production, making the production more closely approximate correct articulation.

5. a) The learner must discriminate subtle differences between letters;
   b) the learner must discriminate between correct and incorrect forms as produced by the learner himself;
   c) stimuli resulting from the response (the letters themselves and the muscle feedback) become differential reinforcers.

6. Immediate reinforcement for selecting the correct note is rather easy for a teacher to arrange. Immediate reinforcement of the response that produces the correct note is more difficult to arrange. So discrimination is somewhat easier to teach than production. And, once discrimination is established, the sounds produced are automatically differentially reinforced.

Unit 10

1. Looking or attending behaviors are often reinforced because they produce a discriminative stimulus for some other response. Examples of chains that start with looking: copying letters, stopping at a traffic light.

2. Your answer should consider the following:
   a) Select reinforcers or establish conditioned ones. Reinforcers most commonly mentioned are food and praise. Since the child is nonverbal, the semantic content of praise will be ineffective but the emotional content of the tone of voice may work.
   b) Task analysis of walking behavior. Components which may be mentioned are creeping, crawling (on hands and knees), reaching and pulling self up, kneeling (supported), standing (supported), walking (unsupported).
   c) Alter environment to make desired response more likely. To start: an open space, free from distractors and obstacles, with a nonabrasive, resilient surface. Later: add low furniture and large toys for support.
   d) Gradual progression through steps in the task analysis. Keep each step in the behavior analysis small. Use supports first, then withdraw them.

3. Person A probably was exposed to someone who shaped and reinforced discrimination and production of tones. He can now differentially reinforce and shape his own behavior. Person B never learned to make the discriminations and so cannot be differentially reinforced for producing correct tones.

4. The child's behavior may be shaped inadvertently by the parent who ignores the child's speaking in a normal voice and attends to loud tones only. The parents' behavior is to some extent controlled by the child. The child's loud tones are an aversive stimulus for the parent. Attending to the child when he speaks in a loud voice is negatively reinforced by termination of the noise (the aversive stimulus).

5. Simple visual matching (without any audio information) is sufficient to perform the task correctly. There is nothing contingent upon saying the word. A deaf child could perform this task.

Unit 11

1. Answers should include the following: the teacher/designer can
   a) select appropriate learning experiences;

b) communicate to students what is expected of them;

c) set criteria and evaluate student progress.

2. *Inferred*   *Observed*

understand	list
comprehend	check
appreciate	paint
grasp	design
remember	write
recognize	label
enjoy	compare
etc.	identify
	recite
	etc.

3. The answer must include the following two points:

a) "understanding" or "appreciation" must be demonstrated by some behavior on the part of the student;

b) behavioral objectives are not restricted to rote memory kinds of learning. Other, more complex tasks can also be described behaviorally.

4. Sample correct answer:

a) Having heard a lecture on the plot of *Hamlet* and how it fits in the Elizabethan revenge-tragedy genre, the student will write an essay in class time on this subject, using his or her lectures notes.

5. Any variation that has the student performing the relevant behavior is acceptable. For example, "The student will explain the technique ...."; "The student will write an essay describing the technique ...."; or "The student will demonstrate the etching technique. ...."

6. "The student will solve linear algebraic equations." Other acceptable answers are possible, of course.

7. "Given a list of events, the student will check those that were major causes of the Great Depression." Or any answer relating to the subject which describes *observable* behavior.

8. "The student will mix a burnt orange color ... ," or "After the demonstration on mixing a burnt orange color ... the student will list the approximate amounts of each contributing color." Or any other variation in which the student performs an observable action.

9. "The student will translate Spanish sentences from the second-year high-school Spanish reader into standard English." All variations describing observable student behavior are acceptable.

10. The answer should specify both how "neat" (e.g., no tucks or puckers) and the time allotted for the task.

11. The answer should specify how "correct" the English should be (e.g., "no more than two punctuation errors, two pronoun errors, and no spelling errors"). It may also include a time period for the writing and minimum length of the essay.

12. Include the number of parts to be named.

13. No criterion. Include time period for recitation and specifications for acceptable

level of performance (e.g., "minor words may be paraphrased or transposed so long as the flow of the recitation is not halted and the sense of the passage is not changed.")

14. No observable student behavior, no criterion. Sample acceptable alternative: "The student will list at least four modern artists who were greatly influenced by Picasso's cubist period."

15. This objective is adequate.

16. Insufficient criterion. Answer should include some specifications for workmanship.

17. Insufficient criterion. Answer should include some content specifications (e.g., "The essay should cover the three major points in Chapter 1").

18. No observable student behavior, no criterion. Sample acceptable answer: "The student will carry out the titration process within fifteen minutes, following the steps demonstrated earlier. The titration must be stopped before the liquid turns purple."

19. No observable student behavior, insufficient criterion. Sample acceptable answer: "Through use of the card catalog, the student will locate a specified book in the library within fifteen minutes."

20. This objective is adequate.

21. No observable student behavior, no criterion. Sample acceptable answer: "In the two-hour examination period, the student will explain in an essay the complex economic issues involved in the formation of the Common Market. No notes will be permitted. The essay should include a description of the five major points covered in the text and the student's own evaluation of the relative importance of each."

22. No observable student behavior, no criterion. Sample acceptable answer: "When asked what happens when measuring units are of all different kinds, the student will describe an example of the kinds of problems which might occur. The example may be taken from the filmstrip on measuring units, but it must be restated in the student's own words."

Unit 12

1. A wide variety of answers is possible, of course. Here is a passable example of each answer.

   Cooking—functional categories:
   a) ordinary person cooking for self and family;
   b) professional restaurant chef and caterer;
   c) gourmet chef and cookbook writer;
   d) nutritional specialist for hospitals and other institutions.

   Cooking—substantive categories:
   a) skills commonly called for in following recipes, like creaming, beating, etc.;
   b) knowledge of various typical food combinations from other geographic areas;
   c) knowledge of chemical and physical changes that take place in the various cooking processes, like baking, rising, broiling, etc.;

d) knowledge of the nutritional value of various foods and of the needs of the human body.

Cooking matrix

	Recipe skills	Food com- binations	Chemical changes	Nutritional values
Ordinary person	high	low	low	medium
Chef	high	high	medium	medium
Gourmet	high	high	high	medium
Nutritionist	low	low	high	high

Automobiles—functional categories:
a) ordinary driver;
b) gas station attendant;
c) skilled mechanic;
d) engine designer.

Automobiles—substantive categories:
a) manual dexterity;
b) combustion system;
c) hydraulic system (brakes);
d) electricity and electronics (starter, lights, battery, generator, etc.);
e) human engineering and automotive design.

Auto matrix

	Manual dexterity	Combustion system	Hydraulic system	Electricity and electronics	Human engi- neering and automotive design
Driver	low	low	low	medium	medium
Gas station attendant	high	medium	medium	medium	low
Mechanic	high	high	high	high	low
Designer	medium	medium	medium	medium	high

2. Following are examples of student answers to question 2, both good and poor, with comments. Use them as guidelines for your own evaluation.

A. *Formal Descriptive and Analytic Systems*

a) *Applying mathematics*

If a tank holds 20 gallons and two hoses feed water into the tank at the rates of 1 gallon per minute and 2½ gallons per minute, how long will it take the empty tank to fill? (Good)

Solve ten word problems. (Acceptable)

The student will convert any given amount of English currency into its equivalent in American currency within one minute. (This student followed Mager's principles for stating behavioral objectives, which is good but not essential for this exercise.)

b) *Pure mathematics*

Factor the following quadratic equation: $3x^2 - 3x - 6$. (Poor; it is an example of *applying* mathematics.)

How is the formula for square roots related to the area of a square? (Good)

Derive corollaries from theorems. (Acceptable)

The student will answer a 100 item multiple choice exam concerning logic with the aid of any classroom materials. The criterion will be 80% correct. (Acceptable)

c) *Descriptive mathematics*

The student must construct a regression analysis of the dependent and independent variables to see if they are related linearly. (Good)

Describe the data below by constructing a graph. (Good)

d) *Deciding which branch of math to use in particular applications*

Solve the given problem using first geometry then trigonometry. Choose the better method and explain why this method is preferred. (Good)

Is the following a problem in plane or solid geometry? (Acceptable but rather similar to Mechner's own example.)

Which distribution would you use to solve this probability problem: t, X^2, or F? (Good)

B. *Current Body of Scientific Knowledge*

State Newton's three laws of motion. (Good)

Blue eye color is carried by recessive genes; brown eye color by dominant genes. What are all the possible eye colors and gene combinations for children of one blue-eyed and one brown-eyed parent? (Good)

C. *Experimental and Theoretical Bases of Scientific Knowledge*

The existence of "black holes" or quasars cannot be fully explained by our current energy theory. Why not? (Good)

What physical changes take place in a plant that is denied light? (Not acceptable; what Mechner is aiming at here is that the learner understand the experimental basis for a theory, why the theory is held. This answer would be acceptable if it asked how one could find out what changes take place or what theory encompasses the data.)

Describe the process of carbon-14 dating. (Not acceptable; the criticism of the preceding example applies here too.)

D. *Scientific Method and Research Skills*

   a) *Deductive reasoning skills*

      Given: All birds can fly.
              A hummingbird can fly.

      What can you conclude?

      a) A hummingbird is a bird.
      b) All birds are hummingbirds.
      c) Some birds are hummingbirds.
      d) None of the above. (Good)

      Given data about the parts of a plant, describe how photosynthesis takes place. (Not as appropriate here as it would be under B.)

      Given a problem the student will make an argument using both inductive and deductive reasoning skills. (Poor; too vague)

      Given the archeological remains of a group of people, what can you conclude about their society—eating habits, dress, state of technology, etc? (Good)

   b) *Inferential reasoning skills*

      The student will make logical inferences on fifty problems presented him at the conclusion of the course. He will do this within 30 minutes. (Poor; it does not specify the essential information—precisely what will a student be doing while making "logical inferences"?)

      A scientist used fifty rats in an experiment with a serum for a particular virus. The control group of twenty-five rats was checked and 65% showed adverse effects of the virus. The experimental group given the vaccine was checked. After checking ten, the scientist discovered that only one showed signs of the virus. What tentative conclusions could he make? (Good)

      You have tested a drug with adverse side effects but with the potential for curing a certain disease. Will you advocate the commercial production of this drug and in what instances would you prescribe it? (Not appropriate as phrased; it could be improved by asking for a guess at the probability of side effects versus the probability of a cure.)

   c) *Skill in generating hypotheses*

      (Mechner doesn't give examples here but instead describes the process and requirements for writing terminal behaviors for this skill: "The terminal behavior test for this skill would require the learner to generate and test, at a certain minimal rate, hypotheses about a universe. . . . The programmer, in developing the terminal behavior specifications, would have to (1) make the behavior overt . . . , (2) circumscribe the universe for the hypotheses, and (3) circumscribe the range of data against which the hypotheses are tested. . . .")

      Given the information that substance A is present in the blood of hospitalized schizophrenics in significantly higher levels than in the normal population, give as many hypotheses to explain this condition as you can think of.

(Passable; but it doesn't call for any kind of testing of the hypotheses even at a minimal level.)

The student will backward chain from the conclusions presented him to the hypothesis that "gave birth" to the conclusions. (Not acceptable; it does not meet Mechner's requirements.)

On the final exam the student will generate five hypotheses concerning bacteriology which have not been investigated thus far. The hypotheses must be testable and represent valid research areas. (Acceptable)

d) *Skill in selecting "fruitful" hypotheses*

(Mechner gives no examples, but does state the general form for the terminal behavior: "Which of the following hypotheses is the most promising on the basis of present knowledge?")

Given limited funding and a specific goal, which of several hypotheses would you experimentally pursue in order to reach the goal in the shortest time with the least expenditure of funds and concurrently generate solutions to other goals? (Good)

Given the information that substance A is present in the blood of hospitalized schizophrenics in significantly higher levels than in the normal population, which hypothesis is most likely in view of present knowledge:

1. Substance A is an indication of a physical cause of schizophrenia.
2. A steady diet of hospital food leads to high blood level of substance A.
3. Substance A is a physical byproduct of emotional imbalance. (Good)

Which of the following alternatives seems most promising as a solution to the problem? (Not acceptable; not specific enough.)

The student will outline the steps in discriminating between alternative hypotheses before starting to test them. (Passable, but the terminal behavior should in addition require the student to do some discriminating himself.)

e) *Skill in testing hypotheses and selecting experiments to perform*

(Again Mechner gives no examples but does state the general form for the terminal behavior: "Given what you know now, which variables would you manipulate at this point, and in which way?")

Having chosen one hypothesis which you believe to be most worth exploring, what steps would you go through in testing it. (Not acceptable; this amounts to no more than a restatement of Mechner's general statement of form.)

In theory a certain metal should withstand a certain amount of stress before it will collapse. What tests should be done before incorporating this metal into a commercial airplane. (Good)

The durability of a paint seems to be affected by the pigment/vehicle ratio. What methods would you use to show the relationship between durability and this ratio. (Good)

f) *Skill in formulating problems so they can be solved by the scientific method*

Which makes the best building material—aluminum, steel, or wood?

The student must define "best" and defend his hypothesis both economically and structurally. (Good; this follows the form of Mechner's examples.)

How would you go about finding an answer to the following question: What is the effect of light on the reproduction of single-celled organisms? (Passable, but should be more elaborated as to the form of the student response.)

The student will operationally define the general empirical questions presented him in the test following the course. (Not acceptable; merely a general restatement of Mechner's statement.)

The student will be given ten statements of empirical questions and will choose those which are sufficiently elaborated for an experiment to be conducted. (Acceptable)

E. *Generalized Traits Useful in Scientific Activity*

(Mechner is not explicit about the distinction he makes between *patience* and *perseverance*. Some students interpret patience as being passive and perseverance as active. Other students make no distinction.)

a) *Patience*

Place the student in a long line of people waiting for some reinforcement at the end and observe his frustration at inordinate delays. (Good)

Game-hunting is another example of a real-life contingency in which patience is required. (Good)

The student will make fewer than five complaints or negative statements while solving a problem designed to take an exorbitant amount of time. (Good)

b) *Perseverance*

The learner is given a set of multicolored blocks which must be stacked so that all of them show red on one side, blue on another side, etc. The task involves a lengthy trial-and-error period. The learner must accomplish this task in whatever time he must take. (Good)

The student will work continuously at an unsolvable problem until told to stop. (Good)

Given a problem in bacteriology, the student will spend six weeks in the laboratory working on a solution. A ratio of the number of different tests applied to the problem and the amount of time spent in the lab will be a measure of the student's perseverance. A minimum ratio will be 5 tests to 60 hours. (Good)

c) *Scientific curiosity*

Willingness to consider fields of inquiry which might contradict or refute "established truths" in your own field. (Good)

How frequently does the student explore new, previously unintroduced material? (Good)

Spend the next hour doing whatever you want with the materials in the lab. (Good)

Unit 13

Guidelines for evaluating your answers

If you have chosen an outline different from Mechner's, your functional categories will probably still include at least three of his: the consumer of the product or service; the skilled worker in the chosen area; the worker in the area at a higher level of skill, competence, and originality. Of course, more than three categories are possible.

Next look at your substantive or behavioral categories. They should include something like: (1) basic skills, (2) current body of knowledge, (3) theoretical—or perhaps historical—bases of knowledge, (4) method and skills, (5) a category of general traits useful to the given activity. These may be arranged in a hierarchy of increasing complexity. A hierarchical arrangement may not be possible for all topics, however.

Several examples of student answers preceded by critical comments follow.

Example 1: Spanish Language Education. Example 1 is good. All terminal objectives are stated behaviorally. The subject area is fairly well organized, but comprehension of spoken Spanish is not adequately considered.

A. Gross Categorization of Terminal Behavior

    1. Functional categories: How much Spanish is needed for the following (and in what areas):

    a) Tourist. Would need only basic applied Spanish. An understanding of *what* he's saying is much more important than why it makes sense in Spanish. For that reason, grammar need not be emphasized as much as knowledge of specific phrases (or numbers) and some pronunciation.

    b) Person interested in Spanish literature. Would need much grammar, vocabulary, and sentence construction with little or no need for pronunciation.

    c) Residents in Spanish-speaking areas of the United States. Would need more extensive applied Spanish than a tourist with some emphasis on pronunciation.

    d) Spanish instructor in the United States. Should have extensive knowledge in all areas.

    e) Semi-permanent or permanent resident of a Spanish-speaking country. Needs mastery of pronunciation, grammar, vocabulary, history, customs, etc.

    2. Behavioral categories

    a) Formal descriptive and analytic systems

    b) Current body of Spanish history

    c) Spanish method and sound

    d) Generalized traits useful in learning a foreign language

B. Terminal Behavior Specifications in the Four Substantive Categories

    1. Formal Descriptive and Analytic Systems. The Spanish language can be used for two purposes: as a means of communicating your own feelings and purposes to a Spanish-speaking person, and also as a means to gain understanding of that person and the culture from which he comes. (To understand and to be understood.) Broad skill categories may be as follows:

    a) Exercises in applying basic Spanish

(1) Ask how much the wallet costs.

(2) Ask if this is the street of the Thieves Market.

b) Pure Spanish

(1) Conjugate the following irregular verbs: *ir, dar,* and *ser.*

(2) Substitute the following words in the appropriate positions in the sentence above.

c) Descriptive Spanish

(1) Write a plot summary of *One Hundred Years of Solitude* (in Spanish).

(2) Describe the conditions in Cuba before Castro came to power.

d) Exercises in deciding which Spanish verb or noun to use in particular applications

(1) Complete the following sentences using *ser* or *estar* where appropriate.

(2) How would you say, "I like Jane" (as a friend)? How do you say, "I like the city of Toledo"?

2. Current Body of Spanish History. An understanding of the background of the Spanish people is very important in understanding the conditions which exist today. Comprehension of current Spanish thought can occur only after comprehension of the Spanish people's past. That understanding may be demonstrated by answering the following.

Explain why the Catholic Church had virtually no difficulty in persuading the Indians of Central America to adopt its doctrines. Name at least three factors the Church and the religions of the Indians had in common.

3. Spanish Method and Sound

a) Skill in generalizing basic grammar rules to unfamiliar dialogue. Translate the following from English to Spanish using correct positioning of all parts of speech.

b) Skill in Spanish pronunciation. Pronounce the following cognates, first in English, then in Spanish. Be sure to make a clear distinction between the two languages.

c) Skill in deciding which word to use (vocabulary). Complete the following sentences, choosing the appropriate word from the list above.

d) Distinctive vocabulary. From the following list of phrases and words, state in which Spanish-speaking country one would most likely hear them. Include their meanings.

4. Generalized Traits Useful in Learning a Foreign Language

a) Perseverance. Can be judged by how well a student has memorized a difficult dialogue. He needs only to recite it.

b) Curiosity (as to how other people live and think). Can be judged by how completely cultural assignments are completed.

Example 2: Writing. Example 2 is a passable answer; it is well organized but the terminal behaviors are not stated in behavioral terms. The answer would be improved by stating exactly how a student demonstrates when, for example, he or she is "able to recognize faulty organization in writing."

1. Occupational or functional categories:

   reader
   critic
   scholar
   casual writer
   artist
   commercial writer
   research writer

2. Behavioral categories:

   knowledge of past writings
   knowledge of how to write
   knowledge of how to criticize
   knowledge of linguistics
   knowledge of how to research
   criticizing sources
   finding material
   organizing material
   analyzing material

3. Personality:

   perseverance
   intuitiveness
   love of art
   logic

Terminal behaviors:

   a) knowledge of past writings: the knowledge of the form of writing used by 18th century prose writers.
   b) knowledge of how to write: being able to compose paragraphs.
   c) knowledge of how to criticize: being able to recognize faulty organization in writing.
   d) knowledge of linguistics: being able to recognize strategic use of connotation.
   e) knowledge of how to research: being able to use the resource materials in the library.
   f) criticizing sources: being able to discover the background of a writer.
   g) finding material: being able to find books and other materials pertinent to chosen topic.
   h) organizing material: being able to put the research together into a whole.
   i) analyzing material: being able to approach research and comment on it.
   j) perseverance: being able to complete a lengthy paper.
   k) intuitiveness: being able to write a short story with creativity.
   l) love of art: being able to read unrequired pieces of literature for enjoyment.

m) logic: being able to formulate and recognize logical conclusions in writing being done or being read.

Unit 14

1. Task A) S^D—"pencil" or "penthil" as pronounced by the tape recorder;
response—pressing button one or button two;
reinforcement—M&M is dispensed.

   Task B) S^D—teacher's pronunciation of the word;
response—pronouncing the word;
reinforcement—teacher praise.
(Note: In Unit 9 we discussed a slightly different three-term contingency for pronunciation in which the pronunciation is automatically differentially reinforced to the extent that the self-produced sound matches the sample. This contingency operates properly only if the student can discriminate correct and incorrect pronunciations.)

   Task C) S^D—long slender object used for writing;
response—"pencil";
reinforcement—teacher says "right".

2. This is a discrimination task. The appropriate gradual progression involves highlighting the differences among the stimuli. In this case, the correct sound might be stressed slightly more than the incorrect sound, and the incorrect sound should be very grossly different from the correct sound. Gradually, these differences in stress are faded out.

3. This is response learning. Shaping is the appropriate gradual progression. At first, reinforce any approximation to the correct [th] sound, then require closer and closer approximation for reinforcement.

4. This is paired-associate learning. The teacher could hold up the pencil and prompt the correct response, perhaps by saying the name first. Then prompts are removed. If there is only one pair to be learned, spaced practice and rest sessions are not necessary, nor can the pairs be introduced gradually. If names for many similar objects must be learned, gradual progression may be accomplished by gradually introducing new pairs while reviewing old ones.

5. a) the children can discriminate the different letter sounds as they are pronounced;

   b) the children can discriminate the different written letters;

   c) the children can write or print each letter;

   d) the children can associate a letter name with the proper letter form.

6. This answer will vary according to the topic chosen. On a test for verbal repertoire the student restates or paraphrases the topical material and on a test for concepts the student judges new examples of the subject matter. On a test for a verbal repertoire in music the student might write an essay describing the characteristics of Mozart's music, while on a concept test the student might identify whether or not previously untaught selections of classical music were composed by Mozart.

7. After completing the Mechner program most college students could identify behavioral contingencies, because the program used many examples from everyday

life. Most college students should have prior mastery of the concepts in those examples.

8. This is an association task; therefore, gradually introducing the associations would be a good instructional procedure. Learners could be given two metric names and their definitions and, with these definitions in front of them, could answer a series of questions like, "Write the name of the foot with two unstressed syllables followed by one stressed syllable," and "Describe the meter of the iambic foot".

Then, without using the definitions, the learner could pair each name with its metrical description. Finally, the learner could produce the description, given the name. Additional terms and definitions are next added, with continued review of the previously learned pairs.

9. This task involves developing a verbal repertoire. The student could be given a short passage to read which describes various poets' uses of poetic meter. After reading this passage, students would answer some questions paraphrased from the language of the reading. This would be followed by another short reading with more paraphrased questions until a variety of examples has been presented.

10. This is an example of concept learning. Begin with two very obviously different meters and with samples of poetry which clearly and distinctly illustrate each meter. The students should respond to each example with the name of the particular meter. Gradually, less and less obvious examples of each type should be introduced. Also, a new meter should be introduced after the first two are well established. In this situation, an instance of one meter is also a noninstance of another meter, so no other method of introducing nonexamples need be developed.

11. Chains of behavior with animals are usually built backwards because S^D's and conditioned reinforcers are established through their relationship to the final primary reinforcer. Each stimulus in the chain must become a conditioned reinforcer for the immediately preceding response, and an S^D for the next response. The last response to be performed in the chain is followed by the primary reinforcer. Human response chains are not always built backwards, for an instructor can use already established conditioned reinforcers, like praise, to shape responses in any order.

12. If discrimination is taught before production the student's own productions are then automatically differentially reinforced.

13. Dancers must discriminate good from poor movements before using the mirror to shape their own movements.

14. The terminal objective should describe the student selecting the better-written paragraph (or the poorly written paragraph). The terminal objective for this task should *not* require that the student write a paragraph.

This task could best be classified as an example of concept formation, because the goal involves the ability of students to identify a paragraph as good or poor even if they have never seen that particular paragraph before. Basically, you want them to form the concept of a well-written paragraph.

The instructional strategy appropriate for concept formation involves the presentation of examples and nonexamples of the concept to which the student responds appropriately. The examples should vary in all aspects that are irrelevant to the concept. The students' responses should indicate that they have attended to the relevant aspects of each example and nonexample.

15. Their responses are controlled by internal kinesthetic stimuli, i.e., the "feel" of good form. This transfer is accomplished by first shaping the response using the mirror and then glancing away from the mirror while performing the response, until internal kinesthetic stimuli control the response. At this point, the mirror is no longer necessary.

16. To test for the association, bring in Trigger and ask the child what the horse's name is. To test for formation of the concept "horse," bring in some cows and several new varieties of horses and have the child select the horses.

17. In a paired-associate task the learner can already discriminate the stimuli. In a multiple-discrimination task the learner cannot recognize the differences among the stimuli.

18. Either a sufficient variety in examples and nonexamples is lacking or correct responses can be made without attention to the relevant aspects of the example or nonexamples.

19. Acceptable answers will vary somewhat. Here is one example.

Task analysis:

a) discriminate the various sounds of American English,
b) produce the phonetic symbols,
c) associate sound and symbol.

We can assume that the first skill is largely part of the entering behavior of the target population, although some of the more subtle discriminations are probably not. Neither of the other two skills can be assumed in the entering behavior of the target population.

The S-discrimination program by Holland and Matthews provides a detailed description of ways to teach aural discrimination. These methods could be modified to teach the relevant discriminations for this task.

The Skinner and Kracower writing problem from Unit 7 is one way of teaching symbol production. With adults, however, a less time-consuming method might involve teaching symbol discrimination first, so that the learner's own symbol production could be automatically differentially reinforced.

One teaching method would involve combining these two tasks through the use of fading. The symbol could be presented visually and aurally at first and learners would copy the symbol. Then the visual symbol would slowly fade out, until the learner was producing the symbol in response to the sound alone.

Symbols should be introduced a few at a time, and practice periods alternated with rest periods until the whole list is learned.

At the beginning of instruction, single sounds would be transcribed, then words, phrases, sentences, and paragraphs, until the learner can transcribe at conversational speed.

Unit 15

1. "What behaviors must be in the learner's repertoire before he can successfully perform this task?"

2. a) The student must be able to discriminate among the letter shapes.

   b) The student must be able to pronounce the letter names.

3. a) Make a detailed description of all the steps involved in the skilled performance of the objective.

   b) For each step or component of the terminal task, ask what simpler behaviors the learner would have to possess in order to be able to perform this step—these simpler behaviors are the prerequisites of the component behavior.

   c) Analyze each prerequisite behavior for simpler behaviors until you reach the probable entering behavior of the learner.

4. There are at least two methods of validation.

   a) The order of the tasks is varied for different groups of learners. If the hypothesized hierarchy is correct, the group using that sequence should reach mastery quicker than the groups using the scrambled sequence.

   b) People who can do the terminal task are tested on the prerequisite tasks. In a true hierarchy, mastery of the terminal task should reliably predict mastery of the prerequisite tasks.

5. a) blue

   b) orange, green, red, purple

   c) brown, blue

   d) no

6. See the chart for Units 3 and 4, Fig. 15.2 of the article.

Unit 16

1. The learner is exposed to some stimuli and interacts with the stimuli. That interaction is then evaluated and reinforced.

2. a) The learner is exposed to stimuli: the stimuli were slide pictures of various objects to be classified, projected on a screen.

   b) The learner interacts with the stimuli: the learner touched the pictures of all objects that were similar in some way (color, shape, size, function, etc.).

   c) Interaction is evaluated and reinforced: the objects were projected on a touch-sensitive screen that transmitted information about the area touched to a computer. The computer was programmed to evaluate these responses. When all objects of a given set were touched, a light flashed (reinforcement). If the set was not completed, ten seconds after the last touch the child heard, "You didn't find all of them. Try again." When the objects had been classified in all possible ways, a bell sounded and a marble was delivered (reinforcement).

3. a) A metal plate overlaid with a paper disk was placed on a phonographic turntable. The paper disk had a patterned series of holes cut in it. A metal contact swept over the disk, much as a phonograph needle sweeps over a record, except that contact was only completed through the patterned series of holes. Each completed contact resulted in the presentation of an auditory stimulus. Thus, the auditory stimulus was presented in a rhythmic pattern determined by the pattern of holes cut in the paper disk.

b) The learner strikes a key in synchrony with the auditory stimulus.

c) The paper disk had a second series of holes swept by a different metal contact. Each hole in this second series corresponded to a hole in the stimulus series, but was a bit longer. If the child struck the key during the time of the sweeper contact (which was synchronized with the stimulus presentation) a bell and light reinforced the response. If the key was pressed when the sweeper was not making contact, no reinforcement was delivered.

4. The second set of holes in the paper disk (those which sense the response) can be varied in length. The longer the hole in the paper disk, the longer the sweeper is in contact with the metal plate. A key strike during this contact period will be reinforced. Thus, by varying the length of the response-sensing holes, the time period allowed for a response can also be varied. Beginning with long holes and gradually shortening the holes results in a gradual raising of the response contingency.

5. These response contingencies possibly could be managed by an individual tutor, but management would be very difficult since we are dealing in fractions of seconds for the later response contingencies.

6. a) The stimuli (both sample and matches) are presented, one set at a time, on slides or photocells.

b) The learner interacts by pressing the sample and match windows. Pressing the windows operates appropriate electrical switches.

c) When the correct match window is pressed, the stimuli (slides) change, a gong sounds, and a light flashes. When an incorrect match window is pressed, a bottom shutter covers the matches. The learner must then press the sample window again to open this shutter.

7. This instrument is designed to teach visual discrimination and not to shape motor responses. We assume that learners can already adequately perform the motor responses that operate this instrument. The instrument does allow a gradual progression in the complexity of the stimuli presented (both sample and matches). The slides may be ordered from obvious examples of the to-be-learned characteristic to subtle examples and then presented in that order. In addition, there can be a progression in number of matches presented.

8. When a teaching program is instrumented, the whole package can be reproduced and transported. The effectiveness of the program does not depend upon the inspiration of a particular teacher.

Unit 18

1. No.

2. Yes.

3. a) Reading "* is the equivalent of plus," transcribing "4*3" to "4 plus 3" and adding correctly is the precursory behavior required for the right answer to frame A.

b) Correctly adding 4 and 3 is the only behavior required for the right answer to frame B.

4. "* is the equivalent of plus" should be circled.

5. Nothing should be circled.

6. To answer frame B correctly, the student never need notice that the * sign indicates addition. He or she needs only to solve a simple problem in which addition is indicated in the normal, presumably familiar, form.

7. Information vital to achieving the behavioral objective should be made contingent upon the answer and should not black out.

8. Because the student could have answered frame B simply by adding 4 and 3, and not attending to the symbol *. This subsequent frame builds on use of the symbol *, but we can't assume from a correct answer to frame B that use of this symbol has occurred.

9. The contingency for a correct response is, "Copy the underlined word into the blank, making sure the letters fit."

10. If the Gaul frame is typical, it is not surprising that active responding had little effect on posttest results. The active responding required by the Gaul frame had no relationship to the critical content of the frame, which is presumably what the posttest is testing. Only when reading the critical content of the frame serves as a contingency for the correct response would we expect to see a difference in posttest results according to whether or not the student made the active response.

11. Both cases require students to learn all the material presented, or at least all that they judge to be significant. This requires an enormous amount of time and also requires discriminations that students, who are new to the material, aren't necessarily competent to make.

12. It provides an objective measure of the degree to which material is programmed, i.e., the degree to which the correct answer is contingent on the appropriate preceding behavior.

    (Note: The "black-out" version is *not* considered an "improved" version. Rather, it suggests the need to rewrite in order to improve the contingent relationships.)

13. By its effect on error rate. Test the blackout version and the normal version to demonstrate that the error rate on the program has not been influenced to a *statistically significant* extent. If error rate is affected, the blackout must be revised and retested until no effect is found.

14. Throw out the program and start over, or rewrite it. You do not assume that what remains after blackout constitutes an adequate program.

    You don't automatically discard it from your program but examine it in light of the behavioral objectives to determine whether the material is truly superfluous. Much of it will be essential so you must rewrite the frames, making sure that a response to the frame is contingent upon the essential material.

15. *Plants* should be circled.

16. $\dfrac{\text{number of words blacked out}}{\text{total number of words}} = \dfrac{8}{10} = .80$

17. No, it probably would not be answered correctly, because there are many pairs of words which "fit" the frame and make some kind of sense, and not enough information is given in the frame to enable the learner to select the correct pair of words. The frame is undetermined.

18. a) Nothing blacks out.

b) Yes, it is more likely to be answered correctly because the basis for a correct answer is present in the frame itself. The student must think through the problem:

Plants do not eat food.
A rose bush is a plant.
A rose bush does not eat food.

and

Plants make their own food.
A maple tree is a plant.
A maple tree gets its food by making it.

19. a) A low error rate is necessary because it indicates that learners are doing the behavior to be learned. They are meeting the response contingency and being reinforced, and therefore they are learning.

b) A low error rate is not a sufficient condition, however, because it can be achieved by a response contingency in which merely trivial responses unrelated to the desired terminal behavior can result in correct answers.

20. Apply the blackout technique and watch for "hints" in a repeated grammatical format, etc.

Poor answer: "Plants need soil, sunlight, and water to grow. Plants need _____, _____, and _____ to grow."

Acceptable answer: "Plants need soil, sunlight and water in order to grow. What things must a rose bush and a maple tree have to grow? _____ _____."

Unit 19

Sample Program 1
Intended users—sixth graders

THE WHEEL AND AXLE

1. A *wheel and axle* ▉▉▉▉▉▉▉▉ A w __ __ __ __ and a __ __ __ ▉▉▉
   ▉▉▉▉▉
   (wheel, axle)

2. ▉▉▉▉▉▉▉ wheel and _____ ▉▉▉▉▉▉▉▉
   (axle)

3. ▉▉▉▉▉▉▉▉ _____ and axle.
   (wheel)

4.
   ▉▉▉▉▉▉▉▉▉ wheel and axle.
   "A" is the wheel. "B" is the _____.
   (axle)

5. ▬▬▬▬▬▬▬▬▬▬

▬▬▬▬▬▬▬▬▬ the wheel is (smaller/larger) than ▬▬▬▬
▬▬▬ the axle. ▬▬▬▬▬▬▬▬▬▬
▬▬▬▬▬▬▬▬▬▬

(larger)

6 ▬▬▬▬▬▬▬▬▬▬▬▬ when the wheel turns the axle also t ___ ___ ___ ___.

(turns)

7. When you turn the _____ knob to open a door, ▬▬▬▬▬▬
   ▬▬

(door)

8. When you exert a force ▬▬▬▬▬▬▬▬▬ The shaft exerts
   a _____ ▬▬▬▬▬▬▬▬
   ▬▬▬▬▬▬

(force)

9. When you turn the knob one revolution, the shaft turns one revolution. How many times does the shaft turn when you turn the knob three times? _____

(three)

Sample program 2
Intended users—tenth graders

THE SPANISH-AMERICAN WAR

1. Spanish misrule in Cuba led to repeated attempts by C_____ patriots to
   ▬▬▬▬▬▬▬▬▬

(Cuban)

2. ▬▬▬▬ Great Britain and France joined * in guaranteeing Spanish authority in
   Cuba. Millard Fillmore refused to join them * in guaranteeing _____
   authority in Cuba.

(Spanish)

* Note: The circled parts of frame 2 are not response-contingent for that frame. However, they are needed for correct responses to frames 3 and 4. This is the programming error described by Margulies as the "everything is learned" technique, but blackout is not sensitive to this error.

3. Two European countries which supported Spanish authority in Cuba were _____
   _____ and _____.

(Great Britain and France)

4. ▬▬▬▬▬▬▬▬▬ Millard Fillmore (did, did not) guarantee Spanish
   authority in Cuba.   (did not)

Sample program 3

Intended users—tenth graders. For this program apply the blackout technique to non–response-contingent sections of the reading as well as of the questions.

████████

████████████ two satellites. ██ They were ██ discovered in 1877 by Asaph Hall. The outer satellite* ██████████████████████ revolves around ██████ in about 31 hours. The inner satellite,* ████████ whips around ████████ in a little more than seven hours, ████████████████████████████ ████████████████████████████████

Answer the following questions based on the passage you've just read. You may refer back to the passage.

1. ████████ has _____ satellites, ████████████████████

(two)

2. ████████████████ the outer satellite, takes (more/fewer) hours to revolve around ████████ than does ████████████ the inner satellite.

(more)

3. ██ ████████████ 7 x 3 or _____ ████████████████

(21)

4. The satellites were discovered by _____ in the year _____.

(Asaph Hall, 1877)

* Note: An acceptable alternative involves retaining the names of the satellites and blacking out references to "inner" and "outer."

Sample program 4

Intended users—college students

ONOMATOPOEIA!

1. An onomatopoetic word ██ ██ ████████████████████████████████ a/an _____ word.

(onomatopoetic)

2. ████████████████████████████ The sound of the word imitates the sound ████████ ████████████████████████████████ the sound of a word _____ the sound ██

(imitates)

3.* An onomatopoetic word sounds like what it means. "Hiss" is an example ████████ ████████████████████████████████ "Crash," "bang," and "ding-dong" are other examples. Underline other words from this list that are onomatopoetic:

MOTHER	BUS	BUZZ
ZING	WHAP	HURT
SING	THUD	SCREECH

(zing, whap, thud, buzz, screech)

4. Now you think of some words that are onomatopoetic. Write them down here: _____

_____

(check your list with the instructor)

* Note: In frame 3, blacking out the words which are not onomatopoetic would definitely affect error rate.

Sample program 5

Intended users—beginning readers. These children have already learned that they are to underline the word or words that describe the picture.*

CAN   CAT

trip.
tree.

..[Mary] (dog.)
[Joey] (log.)

_____

* Although beginning readers might have to read every word in order to decide which is the illustrated word, a correct response does not indicate that the blacked out words have been read *correctly*.

** The third frame presents an example of redundant cues. The children could answer correctly once they have decided that the picture is of Mary rather than Joey, *or* once they have decided that it is a dog, not a log. Either set of these redundant cues could black out.

Sample program 6
Intended users—college students

HALLMARKS ON ENGLISH SILVER

1. ▆▆▆▆▆▆▆▆▆▆▆▆▆▆▆▆▆▆▆▆▆▆▆▆▆▆▆▆▆▆▆▆▆▆▆▆
   ▆▆▆▆▆▆▆▆▆▆▆▆ The hallmark is a m ___ ___ ___ ▆▆▆▆▆▆▆▆▆▆▆▆▆
   ▆▆▆▆▆▆▆▆▆▆▆▆▆▆▆▆▆▆▆▆▆▆▆▆
   (mark)

2. The hallmark, or town mark ▆▆▆▆▆▆▆▆▆▆▆▆ denotes the t ___ ___ ___
   ▆▆▆▆▆▆▆▆▆▆▆
   (town)

3. ▆▆▆▆▆▆▆▆▆▆▆▆▆▆▆▆▆▆▆▆▆▆▆▆▆▆▆▆▆▆▆▆▆▆▆▆
   ▆▆▆▆▆▆▆▆▆▆▆▆▆▆▆▆▆▆▆▆▆▆▆▆ h_____mark ▆▆▆
   ▆▆▆▆▆▆▆▆▆▆▆

   ■■■■■■■■■

   (hall)

4. ▆▆▆▆▆▆▆ assay offices ▆▆▆▆▆▆▆ Each _____ office ▆▆▆▆
   ▆▆▆▆▆▆
   (assay)

5. ▆▆▆▆▆▆▆▆▆▆▆▆▆▆▆▆▆▆▆▆▆▆▆▆▆▆▆▆▆▆▆▆▆▆▆▆
   ▆▆▆▆ the a ___ ___ ___ ___ ▆▆▆▆▆
   (assay)

6. A 1 ___ ___ ___ ___ ___ of the alphabet ▆▆▆▆▆▆▆▆▆▆▆▆▆▆
   ▆▆▆▆▆▆
   (letter)

7. ▆▆▆▆▆▆▆▆▆▆▆▆▆▆▆▆▆▆▆▆▆▆▆▆▆▆▆▆▆▆▆▆▆▆▆▆
   the sterling standard. ▆▆▆▆▆▆▆▆▆▆▆▆▆▆▆▆▆▆▆▆▆▆
   ▆▆▆▆▆▆▆▆▆ the _____ standard.
   (sterling)

8. ▆▆▆▆▆▆▆▆▆▆▆ the standard mark. The s_____ mark
   ▆▆▆▆▆▆▆▆▆▆▆▆▆▆
   (standard)

9. All assay offices ▮▮▮▮▮▮▮▮▮▮▮▮▮▮▮▮▮▮▮▮▮▮▮▮▮▮
   ▮▮▮▮▮▮▮▮ all _____ offices ▮▮▮▮▮▮▮▮▮▮▮▮▮▮▮▮▮▮▮

(assay)

10. A fourth _____ ▮▮▮▮▮▮▮▮▮▮▮▮▮▮▮ This mark ▮▮▮▮▮▮
    ▮▮▮▮▮▮▮▮▮▮▮▮▮▮▮▮▮▮▮▮

(mark)

11. ▮▮▮▮▮▮▮▮▮▮▮▮▮▮▮▮▮▮▮▮▮▮▮▮▮▮▮▮▮▮▮▮▮▮▮

A   B

"A" is the London hallmark.
"B" is the standard mark.
Which mark shows where this piece of silver was tested? _____
Which mark shows that the silver meets the sterling standard? _____

("A", "B")

Sample program 7
Intended users—college students

BEHAVIORAL CONTINGENCIES

Francis Mechner

1. Your being born *was not* a "response-event" for you. That is, it was not an action you initiated.

   Your throwing your rattle out of your crib, however, *was* an action initiated by you. It *was* a "response-event" for you.

   Underline each sentence below that describes a response-event for the person or animal named in the sentence:

   a) Clara dyed her hair red.

b) Herman died of old age.

c) The dog has fleas.

d) The cat meowed.

(a, d)

Note: Frame 1 of Sample program 7 also has somewhat redundant cues. Response-event is both defined and illustrated. In our judgment, however, blacking out one set of these cues would probably increase the error rate.

2. When you hit someone, it (is/is not) your action. It (is/is not) your response-event. When the other person hits you back, it (is/is not) your response-event.

   Underline each sentence below that describes a response-event for the person or animal named in the sentence:

   a) Philip ran fast.

   b) Gregory was run over.

   c) Alice cheated on the exam.

   d) Mary was reprimanded for cheating.

   e) The canary lost all its feathers.

   f) The parrot said "Polly wants a cracker."

(is, is, is not,
a, c, f)

3. The sentence, "The officer gave Mr. Smith a summons," *describes* the officer's giving the ticket, but merely *implies* Mr. Smith's speeding or going through the red light. Does the sentence describe a response-event for Mr. Smith? (yes/no)

   Underline the sentences below that describe, not merely imply, response-events for *you:*

   a) You solved a hard math example.

   b) Your teacher gave you a good grade in math.

   c) You are a doctor.

   d) You are studying to be a doctor.

(no, a, d)

4. ▬▬▬▬▬▬▬▬▬▬▬▬▬▬▬▬▬▬▬▬▬▬▬▬▬▬▬▬▬▬▬
   ▬▬▬▬▬▬▬▬▬▬▬▬▬▬▬▬▬▬▬▬▬▬▬▬▬▬▬▬▬▬▬
   ▬▬▬▬▬▬▬▬▬▬▬▬▬

   ▬▬▬▬▬▬▬▬▬▬▬▬▬▬▬▬▬▬▬▬▬▬▬▬▬▬▬▬▬▬▬

   ▬▬▬▬▬▬▬▬ only people or animals can initiate response-events. Underline the response events below:

   a) The hurricane struck here yesterday. (for the hurricane)

   b) Tom struck Harry. (for Tom)

   c) Tom struck Harry. (for Harry)

   d) The clock struck ten. (for the clock)

(b)

5. Complete the definition of the term "response-event" below. Your definition should include the word "action." A response-event is _____.

(any action initiated
by a living creature—
or equivalent response)

Unit 20

1. One can tell what it teaches from the tests and objectives for lessons included in the Teacher's Manual. One can tell how well it teaches from the data provided in the "Guide to Performance of the Program" section of the Teacher's Manual.

2. The blackout ratio is low. The material is well programmed.

3. The information that is needed to answer frame 14 is provided in frame 13. But frame 13 can be answered without reading this material. Students reach frame 14 without having responded to the information needed to answer frame 14.

4. Some different forms of response: composing answers, drawing and labeling diagrams.

5. The purpose of changing the position of the blank in frames 6 and 8 is to bring the correct response under control of both stimulus words, nucleus and atom.

6. The necessary scientific concepts are atom, electrons, nucleus, energy levels, and energy. (Nonscientific but also necessary concepts would include "traveling" and "farthest.") Scientific concepts that are taught in this program before the rule is taught are nucleus, atom, electron, and energy levels.

7. Such a student probably couldn't answer frame 25 without working the previous frames, but could answer it after having worked them. This indicates that some form of gradual progression in complexity of student response occurs in the program.

8. In frames 20 and 21 learners are given some verbal information and a diagram, and use both to decide which electron is traveling in the electron level nearest the nucleus and to count electron levels. These frames ensure that students have observed the symbol for electrons and the position in the diagram of electron levels. In frame 22 they count electron levels in a diagram, but without the supporting verbal description of energy levels. In frame 23, given a brief verbal stimulus implying location, students produce the words "nucleus" and "electrons" (previously learned behavior). With that self-produced cue and the stimulus "_____ergy levels," they produce the letters *en*. In frame 23, given the stimulus "level," they produce the whole word, "energy." Finally, in frame 25 they are given an unlabeled diagram with three energy levels. Asked what the atom has three of, students respond with the full term, "energy levels," under stimulus control of the diagram only.

9. The students draw the symbols representing electrons in the proper place on a diagram; describe in their own words one property of electrons—their small size; tell what part of the atom electrons move about; describe the path of electrons; count the number of electrons shown in a diagram; respond with the word "electrons" when given a definition; label the electrons on a diagram.

10. Chemistry 1A is a poorly designed program because the student can answer the frames correctly using only trivial cues. The "program" has a very high blackout ratio, and there is no progression in complexity of student response.

    Chemistry 1B is also a bad program, because the responses are not cued enough.

Students would make many errors on this program, so appropriate behavior would not be developed. In essence, the program doesn't teach, it tests.

11. All the frames should be revised. Only frame 36 does not black out, and it accomplishes objective (a). However, objective (a) describes elementary behavior upon which other responses should build, so frame 36 is too late in this short segment of program to be the frame that accomplishes objective (a). Frame 36 should either become the first frame in the revised program, or it should itself be revised to accomplish a later objective. There is no single correct revision. Show your revised frames to your fellow students and to your instructor and discuss them thoroughly. The response called for in each objective should be the contingency for a correct answer to one frame.

12. The subjects who have been through a complete version of a program are no longer typical of the population for whom the program is intended. Since all revised versions should be tested on a typical population, old subjects are "spoiled."

Unit 21

a) *Itard determining what things or activities could be used as reinforcers or punishers:*

55–61—pleasurable activities;
62–65—pleasurable activities;
84–86—warmth and cold become positive and negative reinforcers;
110–116—chestnuts are reinforcers;
126—conditioned new reinforcer in silver cup game;
139–143—aversion to sweets and spicy foods;
144–152—excursion is a conditioned reinforcer;
164–166—carriage and excursion are conditioned reinforcers;
168–174—natural beauty is a powerful reinforcer, Itard arranges to use a manicured version of it;
245–249—ordered arrangements as a reinforcer;
346–350—milk reinforces placing letters in order.

b) *Identifying a need for discrimination training:*

10–26—first description of Victor;
73–75—apparent deafness is lack of discrimination;
77–79—no sensitivity to temperature or tobacco;
183–189—apparent deafness is lack of discrimination;
267–274—could not discriminate the letters;
395–398—discriminate the word.

c) *Identifying a need for gradual progression and examples of gradual progression used by Itard:*

39–41—think of Victor as an infant;
101–105—other games probably too difficult;
109–129—progression in the cup game;
228–230—"ever larger ... obstacles;"
230–232—progress from tasks revolving around physical needs to more abstract tasks;
275–277—need for progression in discrimination training;
277–302—progression in the discrimination of shapes and colors;
296–302—fading the colors, new task requires finer shape discriminations;

334–336—difficult discriminations come last;

380–384—progression in imitation;

385–387—progression in language use;

395–406—discriminations established first, then associations established by gradually increasing the distance between sign and object;

420–424—progression in vocabulary.

d) *Task analysis, both good and poor:*

65–68—certain activities are not conducive to higher mental development: good task analysis;

80–82—discrimination training must precede development of faculty of attention: good task analysis;

97–98—developing needs will develop the intellect: good task analysis;

102–108—games too difficult: faulty task analysis;

124–129—removing food from game develops a less self-interested attention: good task analysis;

189–191—language production results from discrimination and imitation: incomplete task analysis;

202–221—Itard attempts to teach language through imitation of a sound Victor is known to discriminate: incomplete task analysis;

230–232—develop intellect with tasks revolving around physical needs, then use the intellect in more abstract tasks: good task analysis;

233–243—this teaching method too complex for Victor: faulty task analysis;

258–261—increase number of objects to force discrimination: good task analysis;

286–289—identifying solution cues: good task analysis;

307–310—matching shape task: faulty task analysis because metal letters were not presented in random order;

332–336—metal letters mixed-up: good task analysis;

346–350—association learning task: good task analysis for association learning;

380–384—writing is an imitative behavior: good task analysis;

390–393—language use still improper: new task analysis needed;

395–398—discriminations established before associations: good task analysis;

407–413—only one example used: faulty task analysis for establishing an abstraction;

415–419—several examples used to establish abstractions: good task analysis;

420–424—use of concrete reference first, then more abstract concepts: good task analysis.

e) *Establishing an abstraction:*

414–424—generalization based on uses of objects; vocabulary taught.

f) *Identifying contingencies for responding, both appropriate and inappropriate:*

212–220—word pronounced only in the presence of the object: inappropriate contingencies;

253–257—memorizing the order: inappropriate contingency;

258–261—increase number of objects: appropriate contingencies;

263–264—assuring the appropriate contingencies;

314–328—rote-solution method: inappropriate contingencies;

390–392—letters used to form word only in the presence of the object: inappropriate contingencies.

Unit 22

1. By generalization within a class, Mechner means that a person learns to identify many different objects as members of a particular class and responds similarly to these different objects. For example, lettuce, ice cream, and ham are foods and may be eaten. By discrimination between classes Mechner means that the person learns to respond differently to objects in different classes. He eats lettuce, but does not eat grass.

2. Very little, if any, of this program blacks out.

3. A correct discrimination of the Q wave in frame 2 is prompted by an example and a verbal description. Frame 3 will probably be answered correctly even though the prompts have been removed, because the discrimination behavior called for in frame 3 has been established in frame 2.

4. Section *a* of frame 4 does not require discrimination of the S-T segment. The student is told the S-T segment is elevated, and that an elevated S-T segment is abnormal. He or she need not look at the diagram at all to answer section *a*. Section *c* of frame 4 does require discrimination of the S-T segment in the diagram of the electrocardiogram.

5. No, he would not have the same criticism, because in these frames the learner *responds* to each example presented; whereas the case method has no response provisions.

6. It is better to begin with three objects identical except for color. Then the cue (find the nonred, *different* object) is unambiguous in directing the child to attend to color. Suppose, instead of three objects identical except for color, a child were given a red ball, red triangle, and a blue cube. When asked to select the one which was not red (i.e., *different*), he might select the ball because it alone has no corners.

7. Using Mechner's method, a child who already has developed the concept of difference is likely to be correct the first time he or she responds to the three objects. Using the other method, the child initially is as likely to respond to the nonred object. Responding to nonred objects when asked, "Which object is red?" is an error. In this teaching method, errors are likely to occur and will have to be extinguished.

8. In Mechner's method, given objects that are identical except for color and of which all except one are red, a child directed to find the one that is not red must use color to achieve a correct answer. The cue in Mechner's method is the concept of difference. A child who has this concept and bases responses on it will be correct, just as a child who selects the object pointed to will be correct.

   In general, a cue such as Mechner's, which requires attention to the to-be-learned characteristic in order to achieve a correct answer, is preferable to a cue like pointing which allows a correct response without requiring such attention. The pointing method of concept teaching is analogous to verbal programs with very high black-out ratios; in both cases a correct answer may be achieved by behavior unrelated to the to-be-learned behavior.

9. response-chain learning

10. establishment of a verbal repertoire

11. principle applying and strategy learning

12. Instruction for task d would provide the most transfer, and instruction for task b the least.

13. Yes. The task must contain the important aspects of the various situations to which transfer is desired. Often this means principle applying and strategy learning must be the objectives.

14. Exposure to a wide variety of patience-building situations.

15. You could not expect complete transfer since the training situation is very different from the situation in which the behavior will be practiced. If there is a large variety in the tasks, however, some transfer to very different situations may occur.

16. The student has constructed a circuit in which he or she has tried one bulb and then two bulbs in series. The student has noted that the two-bulb arrangement is dimmer than the one-bulb arrangement, and that dimmer bulbs mean less current is in the circuit.

17. In answering frame 216 the student uses his or her recent specific experience with light bulbs. In frame 217 the student must translate this specific experience with light bulbs into a more general concept, "resistance."

18. No.

19. Obviously there will be great variety in this answer. Discuss your rationale and tactics with your instructor and with other students in the course.

20. The answers to this question are not settled and it may generate some good discussion. The following answers, compiled from various student replies, could serve as the basis for a discussion.

    a) reciting a poem—The reinforcement is completing the recitation, so the end lines might be considered more reinforcing than the earlier ones. On the other hand, the last lines are no easier to recite than the earlier ones. Moreover, reciting the end lines does not depend on reciting all earlier ones, as the reciter can skip over or forget lines and still get to the end. This might be more accurately called a serial memory task rather than a "chain." Backward chaining would probably not be beneficial here.

    b) tying a shoelace—The reinforcement is completing a functional bow. The final step of pulling the loops seems relatively simple compared to intermediate steps, and more highly reinforcing. Successful completion of the bow depends upon proper execution of all preceding steps. This is indeed a chain of motor responses and would probably benefit from being taught backwards.

    c) solving a math problem—The reinforcement is getting an answer. In practice, any answer, even a wrong one, may be reinforcing before the correct answer is known. A wrong answer may be the result of either an incorrect computation or an incorrect ordering of the steps in the problem. In either case, as with reciting the poem, reinforcement may occur even if the steps have been incorrectly executed. This is more properly classified as an algorithm and would not necessarily benefit from being taught backwards.

    d) writing a program for a computer—The reinforcement is achieving a program (sequence of commands to the computer) that will run and yield the desired data. The final step is simpler than the early ones in that it involves fewer options, while at the start of writing a program one has a very large number of possible approaches to the desired end. The commands must follow each other logically and be executed in order. This could be better classified as an instance of principle-applying rather than as a "chain." To the extent that the intermediate steps can be discriminated as correct, writing a program would not need to be backward chained. If intermediate discriminations of correct elements can not be reliably made, then backward chaining is needed.

Unit 25

1. Each girl was given 3x5 oak tag cards with a grid network of squares printed on each side. Points given on one side of the card were redeemable for money, on the other side for certain activities. Certain blocks of squares were designated for certain behavioral areas—personal appearance, peer relations, etc. When the staff observed the performance of designated desired behaviors, the staff member placed the appropriate number of checks in the squares of the card. When designated undesired behaviors were observed, the relevant number of checks was blacked out with a felt-tip pen. The cards were collected once a week and money and activity points recorded in a "bank book."

2. a) The primary purpose of this program was to train students to live outside the institution. The privilege activities functioned both as reinforcers and as training situations for noninstitutional living.

   b) The student will maintain new desirable behavior patterns if the desirable behavior has natural reinforcing consequences that can take over the point system's function.

3. The changes were designed to make the cottage more closely resemble the typical home environment the girls were expected to return to. The changes included installing a kitchen, dining room, laundry area, and sewing room. The purpose of the changes was to make the place where the girls learned such skills as cooking, setting the table, ironing, etc., as similar as possible to the place where they would eventually be expected to practice these skills. In this way, Lent *et al.* hoped to facilitate transfer of these skills to the normal community.

4. Lent *et al.* arranged individual training for EH, at the home of a research assistant, in such skills as planning menus, buying food, and preparing and eating meals. The need for this additional training could indicate that even the remodeled environment of Mimosa Cottage was too unlike a typical home to allow for successful transfer; or that when successful transfer is desired, training should not be restricted to only one environment; or that the training program at Mimosa Cottage had been deficient. (Of these three possibilities, only the first involves the physical changes described in question 3.)

5. Town orientation is the training program described most completely in the article. In this program, the terminal behavior was described as going from place to place in a purposeful manner. This behavior was analyzed into several components: a) select the appropriate type of store for a particular purchase, b) find the store,

c) conclude the purchase, d) return to the Cottage. The sequence of contingencies involved a gradual progression from trips under close supervision to nearby stores, to group trips without direct supervision to nearby stores, to unsupervised trips to nearby stores. This progression was repeated for more distant stores.

Unit 26

1. Barnes' chapter introduction mentions the kinds of things to be taught in that particular chapter, one of which is stated in somewhat behavioral terms. Clough nowhere specifies what behavior the students will acquire.

2. Barnes includes criterion tests for each chapter (see his preface), thus permitting different entry points into the program. Clough states briefly the assumed entering behaviors but gives no criteria for them.

3. In neither program is the pilot testing adequately described. Barnes merely says that his program was originally developed for elementary teachers and specifies some others who have found it useful. Clough tells us that he did have two trial runs, that all sections of the program have been tested by at least 150 students and some parts by more than 400. From this data he has derived information on the average time required to complete the program.

4. Clough's is better programed. Here is a blackout version of the first page from each selection:

Barnes—blackout

the distance or interval from C to C♯ on this keyboard is a half step. Knowing this, we can also figure that the interval between F and F♯ is also a

half   _____ step.

The interval from any key on the keyboard to its nearest neighbor is a *half step*. The interval from key number 2 to key number 1 is a half step. The interval from key number 2 to key number 3 is a

half step   _____ _____.

half
step

The interval from any key on the keyboard to its closest neighbor,  is always one _____
_____.

is

The closest neighbor is always one half step away. The nearest neighbor *below* G♯ is G. The interval between G♯ and G, then _____ [is/is not] one half step.

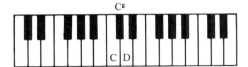

yes

The interval from C to C♯ is a half step. Is the interval from C♯ to D also a half step? _____ [yes/no]

Clough—blackout

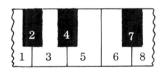

1

This diagram is a section of a piano keyboard. Complete the numbering of keys from the lowest to the highest.

2

adjacent

Two keys with consecutive numbers are *adjacent*. Key no. 2 and key no. 3 are adjacent. Key no. 2 and key no. 1 are _____.

3

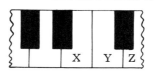

(1) X
(2) Z

Key Y is adjacent to key (1) _____ but not to key (2) _____.

adjacent

4   No two black keys are _____.

5

The two notes in example x are played on adjacent keys. The two notes in example y are played on _____ keys.

adjacent

are

6

These two notes . . . . (are *or* are not) played on adjacent keys.

5. *Barnes: Chapter Five*

Given the information that the interval between two piano keys is a half step, identify the interval between certain piano keys.

Identify by name the neighbors of various piano keys.

Given "h_____ s_____"—fill in the blanks with the words "half steps."

Count the number of half steps between various piano keys.

Given two half steps, say they equal one whole step.

Identify various intervals on a piano keyboard as half or whole steps.

Given a keyboard, note where the black keys are.

Clough: Set One

Given a partially numbered piano keyboard, complete the numbering.

Identify adjacent keys on a piano keyboard.

Note that no two black keys are adjacent.

Given two notes on a staff, say whether they are played on adjacent keys.

Given that the distance between notes played on adjacent keys is a semitone, state that the distance between notes played on adjacent keys is a semitone.

Given two notes on a staff, identify the distance between them as a semitone or not a semitone.

Given two notes on a staff a semitone apart, say whether one is higher or lower than the other.

Given one note on a staff, write another note one semitone higher or lower.

6. Clough's objectives represent somewhat more varied and certainly more complex behavior than do Barnes' objectives. In addition, Clough's objectives form a better progression. By numbering the keyboard, the student responds actively to the concept of adjacent keys. Then the concept of a semitone is built on this concept of adjacent keys. In Barnes, adjacent keys are immediately identified as half steps and the progression is from identifying adjacent keys (half steps) given a keyboard diagram to identifying them without a keyboard diagram. Barnes' progression encourages memorization rather than an enlargement of the students' understanding of the concept.

7. It appears that Clough has done what he intended to do with this program. Frame 9 (Set One) is probably an exception to this, as it can be answered by copying the italicized word—Clough surely would prefer some other behavior. Barnes has been less successful at achieving his objectives.

8. Clough appears to build on established behavior. For example, in frame 11 of Set Four, identification of a major scale is dependent upon the concepts of semitones and whole tones established earlier.

   While Barnes talks about the relationship of half steps and whole steps to the major scale, all of his questions could be answered by someone who had not worked through the earlier chapters teaching these concepts. Therefore, Barnes does not build on established behavior when teaching this concept.

Unit 27

1. These measures are applicable to adaptive materials that diagnose differences among students in order to present each student with only those teaching materials needed to reach proficiency in the terminal objectives of the course.

2. Applying the blackout technique to an item will reveal what portion of the item a correct response is contingent on. The correct response should be contingent on the desired behavior. A measure of the error rate on that item reveals whether or not the desired behavior is actually occurring.

3. The diagnostic test item is supposed to reveal differences in student performance; if there are few errors on an item, few differences are revealed.

4. a) The student saves time by skipping unnecessary teaching materials.

   b) The student is tested to determine what teaching materials are needed to reach criterion performance.

   c) Differences in students' needs are revealed.

5. a) One objective of utilizing adaptive materials is to save the student's time. But since testing also uses student time, it would be inefficient to spend a lot of time testing to enable a student to skip a short teaching sequence.

   b) $\dfrac{\text{teaching time}}{\text{teaching time} + \text{testing time}}$

   c) .99+

6. The testing time has been shortened.

7. $\dfrac{\text{teaching time}}{\text{teaching time} + \text{testing time}} = \dfrac{510}{524} = .97$

This is a very good consequence ratio.

8. a) The diagnostic test should predict whether the student needs some teaching material in order to perform acceptably on the criterion test. The predictive-validity ratio is a measure of how well this function is achieved.

   b) A hit is when the diagnostic test correctly predicts a pass or a fail on the criterion test, without any intervening teaching material. A miss is either when the diagnostic test predicts passage of the criterion test, but the subject fails the criterion test (without intervening teaching material, of course); or when the diagnostic test predicts failure of the criterion test and the subject, in fact, passes the test (again without teaching material).

   c) A perfect validity ratio is 1.0.

9. It is not the teaching material which is evaluated by the predictive-validity ratio, but only the adaptive features of the material. Poor performance on the diagnostic test should predict poor performance on the criterion test *if no intervening teaching occurs*. This prediction can only be tested by giving the criterion test after the diagnostic test, without giving the intervening teaching material.

10.

Criterion Test

		P	F
Diagnostic Test	P	4	1
	F	2	3

11. $\dfrac{\text{hits}}{\text{hits} + \text{misses}} = \dfrac{7}{10} = .70$

This is ordinarily not an acceptable validity ratio.

12. The shorter the test, the better the consequence ratio. But, the shorter the test, the less reliable and valid the test itself is likely to be. Longer tests tend to be more valid than shorter tests, so longer tests tend to give better validity ratios. Longer tests also tend to give poorer consequence ratios.

13. a) If all students pass, or all fail, the diagnostic test, the material is not adaptive, since it reveals no differences to adapt to.

    b) It is the ratio of the number of students who either passed or failed, whichever is the smaller number, to the total number taking the test.

    c) 0.50

14. $\dfrac{10}{25} = .40$

This is a high discriminability ratio.

15. You would ask for the pretests and posttests, and use them to establish a predictive-validity ratio. You would select some subjects from the target population and administer the pretests. Then the same subjects would take the posttests at least one day later. From this data, hits and misses are derived and a validity ratio is calculated.

You also ask for approximate or average lesson times. Testing times you have established yourself from the pretest administrations. With this time data you calculate a consequence ratio.

You may also ask the publisher how many students passed and failed the pretests when the materials were tested, or you may again use the number of passes and fails from your own pretest administrations. From this data a discriminability ratio may be calculated.

Unit 28

1. The designer should have a good lesson to begin with, since good lessons will provide the most useful data. Before the tryout the designer should rethink the task analysis, prepare a test for terminal behavior and standards for evaluating that test, and have the lesson material checked for a blackout problem.

2. In the first teaching program there was a single fading sequence. The fading sequence began with the correct key bright with a circle projected on it and the incorrect keys dark. Gradually the incorrect keys became bright while, at the same time, the ellipses on the keys became more apparent. In the fifth teaching program there were two fading sequences. In background fading the correct key was bright with a circle, and the incorrect keys went from dark to equally bright, but with no forms projected on them. In the second stage, ellipse fading, faint ellipses appeared on the incorrect keys and gradually became as apparent as the circle.

3. Programs 1–4 were successful with most children over four years old, but Sidman and Stoddard's goal was a program that would be successful with children as young as two and one-half years. The revisions done on programs 1–3 did not seem to be accomplishing this goal although the revised programs usually allowed older children to progress more smoothly. When several revisions based on data do not bring a designer closer to the goal, it is time to reanalyze the task in preparation for a more drastic revision.

4. In the fading sequence for programs 1–4, the brightness of the incorrect keys increased and the ellipses became more apparent at the same time. However, the ellipses were clearly present while the brightness cue was still easy to use, so children could select the correct key by attending only to brightness and ignoring the ellipses.

In the tryouts for programs 1–4, serious errors occurred at the point where the brightness cue became difficult to use (slide 46 for C.M. in Fig. 28.3 and slide 15 for M.B. in Fig. 28.4.) Repeated errors on slides that a child had previously passed through successfully indicated that the fading program was not adequate in instructing the child to attend to form. Thus a different fading sequence was in order.

5. The designers had shortened the first half of the second teaching program and the tryout indicated that this short first half was successful. Also, children who used the long second teaching program made few errors on the first slides of a new brightness increment after increment 15, but they did make errors on subsequent slides. This pattern indicated that the fading sequence after increment 15 was not too difficult and suggested elimination of the practice slides.

6. First, inadequately tested versions of the lesson are not reproduced in large volume so extensive revisions are economically feasible. Second, the small-group tryout can be conducted under carefully controlled conditions so the designer has some security that the tryout data reflect variables arranged by the lesson rather than accidental implementation conditions.

7 and 8.

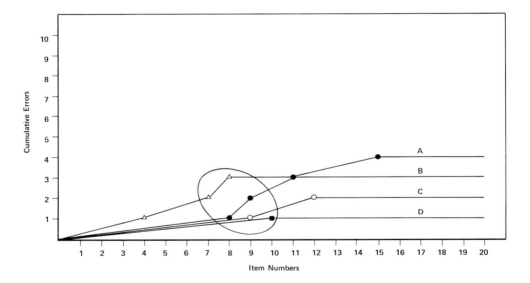

Unit 30

1. Koch not only wants the students to produce poems, he also wants them to be turned on to poetry. In fact, the affective and productive objectives go together, since writing good poetry is enjoyable.

2. As Koch analyzes his task, the problem is to remove the children's writing barrier so that their fresh vision of the world may be expressed. The barrier was removed by having them orally collaborate on a poem which Koch wrote down. The child who orally contributed a line was reinforced by the pleasure of expressing his or her own vision, by the response of fellow students, by Koch's response, and by the writing and reading of the line as part of a complete poem. By requiring only a line of poetry before reinforcement rather than a complete poem, Koch established a criterion that the children could meet. He also ignored all errors and reinforced, by positive comments, all funny and imaginative contributions. This approach encouraged the chil-

dren to have fun with words and did not discourage the idiosyncratic productions vital to good poetry. Most importantly, the approach got the students to actually *produce* some poetry. Only after some production has happened can the reinforcement that naturally accompanies production become effective. Once the child was reinforced for producing a line of poetry, he or she was frequently ready to try longer poems, and sometimes was even willing to try writing the poem independently, thus delaying reinforcement even longer.

3. rhyme and meter—he had the children use repetition and other more natural poetic devices;

belief that poetry is remote and difficult—he used colloquial language in explaining all poetic devices;

imposed adult language—he introduced all poetry ideas in words that the children actually used;

fear of criticism—he ignored errors, never singled out poetry as best or worst, read everyone's work aloud every so often, praised the work rather than the child, never corrected a child's poem or changed it to meet his standards.

This liberal use of positive reinforcement was important because Koch also had affective objectives in mind. He wanted the actual writing to be an enjoyable experience. Errorless learning promotes positive responses to the subject matter (see Unit 5).

4. Koch had developed some effective procedures in teaching poetry to college students and modified these procedures to suit grade-school students. After a tryout period, he built on those procedures that worked and discarded those that proved ineffective. By carefully analyzing the good points of effective assignments, he was able to create new lessons. Koch always acted on the assumption that the children could write poetry if he could only develop appropriate "assignments."

Unit 31

1. In the first format, the child makes the first mistake on the word CHECK. The mistake itself is very revealing of certain deficiencies in the program. The child selects the initial letter *C* of CHECK. The initial letter *C* has been the correct choice twice earlier. A child who was pronouncing the word CHECK and listening for the position of the [k] sound is unlikely to select the first letter as the one which spells the final sound. So this mistake reveals that the child is not, at this point, listening for the [k] sound and looking for the appropriate letter to spell it. Rather, this response is probably a function of the earlier reinforced responses of selecting the initial letter *C*.

Does any earlier answer reliably indicate that the child has attended to sound-symbol correspondence? The correct first response is not a function of any prior reinforcements *that we have seen*. Thus it may be the function of attention to sound-symbol correspondence. If so, following it with a second correct initial *C* functioned to change the basis for the child's responding from sound-symbol correspondence to looking for an initial *C*. Of course, the first response may also have been a function of a previously learned rote performance in which the child presses every letter in order. In that case, the child simply lucks out when the first letter is also the correct choice.

The child has a lot of problems with CHECK. When the first C is rejected, the child changes the criterion used to make the next selection or response. From the record we have, however, we cannot be sure of what the new criterion is. The child may have noted that the [k] sound in CHECK is at the end of the word and selected the second C based on a combination of prior history of reinforcement for selecting C's *and* attention to the [k] sound. Or the child may simply have selected another letter C without regard to sound. At any rate, after learning that the second C is wrong, the child retreats to a previously correct choice, possibly in an effort to reconfirm the old criterion of selecting an initial C. The program's message gives no help in this regard.

Response 6 (K in KEEP) is the first non-C that the child selects, so we know that the criterion of selecting an initial C has changed. The child may have made this choice of an initial K based on sound-symbol correspondence. However, selecting the B in BLACK (response 8) indicates that, at that later point, the criterion is probably selecting the initial letter. We cannot be sure that that criterion is not also operating in response 6 as well.

The criterion for response 9 (K in BLACK) is again ambiguous. It may be sound-symbol correspondence, or it may be selecting the letter K, a previously reinforced response.

A child might finally learn the three spelling patterns, including the CK pattern, simply because they are all eventually presented on the screen, whether or not the child has associated each spelling pattern with a phoneme. In other words, the child can learn the CK spelling pattern without first attending to sound-symbol correspondence; and once the child has learned to identify the pattern by sight, it is a simple matter to continue to select the CK pattern when it appears in later word lists on the basis of visual identification rather than by sounding out the word.

In the new format, the child has a fifty-fifty chance of selecting the correct number on the first try, even if the word list is totally ignored. In other words, this format evokes behavior that is functionally like guessing whether a flip of the coin will turn up heads or tails. There is no assurance at all that the word list will be read, let alone attention given to sound-symbol correspondence within words on the list.

This new format is not an improvement over the first format. The first format is ineffective because there are too many illegitimate bases for correct responses and not enough use of gradual progression to shape the child's attention to relevant features of the stimuli which should be controlling the response. These same problems are inherent in the new format. In fact, in the new format there is one overriding illegitimate basis for a correct response—guessing. When a difficult problem can be easily solved by guessing and the penalty for a wrong guess is small, why should a child actually try to count the ways the [k] sound is spelled in a given list of words?

Author Index

Subject Index